Lecture Notes in Computer Science 8676

Commenced Publication in 1973
Founding and Former Series Editors:
Gerhard Goos, Juris Hartmanis, and Jan van Leeuwen

More information about this series at http://www.springer.com/series/7412

Hiroyuki Yoshida · Janne J. Näppi
Sanjay Saini (Eds.)

Abdominal Imaging

Computational
and Clinical Applications

6th International Workshop, ABDI 2014
Held in Conjunction with MICCAI 2014
Cambridge, MA, USA, September 14, 2014

 Springer

Editors
Hiroyuki Yoshida
3D Imaging Research
Department of Radiology
Massachusetts General Hospital
Harvard Medical School
Boston, MA
USA

Janne J. Näppi
3D Imaging Research
Department of Radiology
Massachusetts General Hospital
Harvard Medical School
Boston, MA
USA

Sanjay Saini
Department of Radiology
Massachusetts General Hospital
Harvard Medical School
Boston, MA
USA

ISSN 0302-9743   ISSN 1611-3349   (electronic)
Lecture Notes in Computer Science
ISBN 978-3-319-13691-2   ISBN 978-3-319-13692-9   (eBook)
DOI 10.1007/978-3-319-13692-9

Library of Congress Control Number: 2014956526

LNCS Sublibrary: SL6 – Image Processing, Computer Vision, Pattern Recognition, and Graphics

Springer Cham Heidelberg New York Dordrecht London

Printed on acid-free paper

Springer International Publishing AG Switzerland is part of Springer Science+Business Media
(www.springer.com)

Preface

The Sixth International Workshop on Abdominal Imaging: Computational and Clinical Applications, was held in conjunction with the 17th International Conference on Medical Image Computing and Computer-Assisted Intervention (MICCAI) on September 14, 2014, at the Massachusetts Institute of Technology, Cambridge, USA.

In the abdomen, the appearances of organs and diseases are complex and subtle, and thus the development of computational models that are useful in clinical practice is highly challenging. Nevertheless, diagnosis often relies on the quantitative measurement of organs and lesions, because their volumes and shapes are strong indicators of disorders. Given the complexity and high variability of abdominal organs, the identification of distinct computational challenges for integrative models of organs and abnormalities is essential for understanding anatomy and disease, evaluating treatment, and planning intervention.

Leveraging the success of the previous workshops, the Sixth International Workshop on Abdominal Imaging aimed to provide a comprehensive forum for reviewing clinical opportunities in computational abdominal imaging and for sharing emerging state-of-the-art techniques for solving computationally challenging image analysis and visualization problems, by bringing together leading researchers and clinician-scientists from around the world.

In response to a call for papers, a total of 33 papers were initially submitted to the workshop from 10 countries. These papers underwent a two-tier review process. The first tier was a double-blinded scientific peer-review, in which each paper was reviewed by a minimum of two and in most cases by three expert reviewers from the Scientific Review Committee and the Workshop Committee. Based on the results of this initial review, 30 papers were moved forward to the second tier, in which these papers were revised by incorporating the reviewers' initial comments and were re-reviewed by the Workshop Committee for final acceptance. As a result, 28 papers were accepted to be published in the proceedings volume.

The Outstanding Paper Award was established for recognizing outstanding scientific work and clinical applications presented at the workshop. From the papers that earned an average score of 1–3 in the above first-tier review, the Award Committee, which consisted of at least three members from the Workshop Committee, selected an awarding paper from the candidate papers based on scientific merit and clinical innovation of the paper. As a result, the below paper was selected for receiving the award, and an award certificate was presented to the first author at the opening session of the workshop: Parameter Estimation for Personalization of Liver Tumor Radiofrequency Ablation by Chloé Audigier, Tommaso Mansi, Hervé Delingette, Saikiran Rapaka, Viorel Mihalef, Daniel Carnegie, Emad Boctor, Michael Choti, Ali Kamen, Dorin Comaniciu, and Nicholas Ayache.

To provide past and future perspectives of the research topics described in the accepted papers, three plenary lectures were presented at the workshop: (1) recent advances in liver ablation and needle biopsy by Dr. Aaron Fenster from Robarts Research Institute and University of Western Ontario; (2) the role of CT/MRI perfusion as imaging biomarkers for tumor response evaluation and prediction of survival by Dr. Dushyant Sahani from Massachusetts General Hospital and Harvard Medical School; and (3) MR enterography for severity assessment in Crohn's disease: imaging endpoints in clinical trials and inflammatory bowel disease practice by Dr. Joel G. Fletcher from Mayo Clinic.

As a result of all the above activities, the full-day workshop successfully provided a forum among participants for in-depth and interactive discussions of state-of-the-art research and technologies, exchange of emerging ideas, initiation of collaborations, and the exploration of new clinical applications for diagnostic and interventional procedures in abdominal imaging.

We would like to express our sincere appreciation to the authors whose contributions to this proceedings book have required considerable commitment of time and effort. We also thank the members of the Scientific Review Committee for their excellent work in reviewing the submitted manuscripts on a tight schedule, and the members of the Editorial Board for their outstanding job in compiling the papers in this proceedings volume.

October 2014

Hiroyuki Yoshida
Janne J. Näppi
Sanjay Saini

Workshop Organization

Organizing Committee

Hiroyuki Yoshida   Massachusetts General Hospital/Harvard Medical School, USA

Janne J. Näppi   Massachusetts General Hospital/Harvard Medical School, USA

Sanjay Saini   Massachusetts General Hospital/Harvard Medical School, USA

Nobuhiko Hata   Brigham and Women's Hospital/Harvard Medical School, USA

Program Chair

Janne J. Näppi   Massachusetts General Hospital/Harvard Medical · School, USA

Workshop Committee

Philippe C. Cattin	Medical Image Analysis Center/University of Basel, Switzerland
Jamshid Dehmeshki	Kingston University London, UK
Aaron Fenster	Robarts Research Institutes/ University of Western Ontario, Canada
Hiroshi Fujita	Gifu University, Japan
Stefaan Gryspeerdt	Stedelijk Ziekenhuis, Belgium
Lubomir Hadjiyski	University of Michigan, USA
Kenneth R. Hoffman	University at Buffalo, USA
Hideaki Haneishi	Chiba University, Japan
David Hawkes	University College London, UK
David R. Holmes	Mayo Clinic College of Medicine, USA
Weimin Huang	Institute for Infocomm Research, Singapore
Hongbing Lu	Fourth Military Medical University, China
Lakhmi C. Jain	University of South Australia, Australia
Hiroshi Kawahira	Chiba University, Japan
Se Hyung Kim	Seoul National University, South Korea
Jong Hyo Kim	Seoul National University, South Korea
Hongbing Lu	Fourth Military Medical University, China
Sandy Napel	Stanford University, USA
Peter Nöel	Technische Universität München, Germany
Kensaku Mori	Nagoya University, Japan

Yuichi Motai	Virginia Commonwealth University, USA
Sandy Napel	Stanford University, USA
Emanuele Neri	University of Pisa, Italy
Noboru Niki	Tokushima University, Japan
Daniele Regge	Institute for Cancer Research and Treatment, Italy
Akinobu Shimizu	Tokyo University of Agriculture and Technology, Japan
Yoshihisa Sinagawa	Siemens, USA
Yoshihisa Tsuji	Kyoto University Hospital, Japan
Frans Vos	Delft University of Technology/Academic Medical Center Amsterdam, The Netherlands
Simon Warfield	Boston Children's Hospital/Harvard Medical School, USA

Program Committee

Onur Afacan	Boston Children's Hospital/Harvard Medical School, USA
Alborz Amir-Khalili	University of British Columbia, Canada
Chloe Audigier	Inria Sophia Antipolis, France
Jordan Bano	IRCAD/ICube, France
Amalia Cifor	University of Oxford, UK
Moti Freiman	Boston Children's Hospital/Harvard Medical School, USA
Romane Gauriau	Institut Mines-Télécom/Philips Research MediSys, France
Benjamin Irving	University of Oxford, UK
June Goo Lee	University of Pittsburgh, USA
Sang Ho Lee	Massachusetts General Hospital/Harvard Medical School, USA
Jiang Liu	Institue for Infocomm Research, Singapore
Ahmed Maklad	Tokushima University, Japan
Masahiro Oda	Nagoya University, Japan
Danielle Pace	Massachusetts Institutes of Technology, USA
Frank Preiswerk	University of Basel, Switzerland
Holger Roth	National Institutes of Health, USA
Peter Schüffler	ETH Zurich, Switzerland
Christine Tanner	ETH Zurich, Switzerland
Sergio Vera	Universitat Autònoma de Barcelona, Spain
Huafeng Wang	Stony Brook University, USA/Beihang University, China
Amir Yavariabdi	Université d'Auvergne, France

Scientific Review Committee

Onur Afacan
Boston Children's Hospital/Harvard Medical School, USA

Alborz Amir-Khalili
University of British Columbia, Canada

Chloe Audigier
Inria Sophia Antipolis, France

Jordan Bano
IRCAD/ICube, France

Philippe C. Cattin
University of Basel, Switzerland

Yufei Chen
Tongji University, China

Amalia Cifor
University of Oxford, UK

Moti Freiman
Boston Children's Hospital/Harvard Medical School, USA

Hiroshi Fujita
Gifu University, Japan

Romane Gauriau
Institut Mines-Télécom/Philips Research MediSys, France

Lubomir Hadjiyski
University of Michigan, USA

Hideaki Haneishi
Chiba University, Japan

David Hawkes
University College London, UK

Kenneth R. Hoffman
University at Buffalo, USA

David R. Holmes
Mayo Clinic College of Medicine, USA

Weimin Huang
Institute for Infocomm Research, Singapore

Benjamin Irving
University of Oxford, UK

Hiroshi Kawahira
Chiba University, Japan

Jong Hyo Kim
Seoul National University, South Korea

June Goo Lee
University of Pittsburgh, USA

Sang Ho Lee
Massachusetts General Hospital/Harvard Medical School, USA

Jiang Liu
Institue for Infocomm Research, Singapore

Hongbing Lu
Fourth Military Medical University, Chiina

Ahmed Maklad
Tokushima University, Japan

Kensaku Mori
Nagoya University, Japan

Janne J. Näppi
Massachusetts General Hospital/Harvard Medical School, USA

Emanuele Neri
University of Pisa, Italy

Noboru Niki
Tokushima University, Japan

Peter Nöel
Technische Universität München, Germany

Masahiro Oda
Nagoya University, Japan

Danielle Pace
Massachusetts Institutes of Technology, USA

Frank Preiswerk
University of Basel, Switzerland

Daniele Regge
Institute for Cancer Research and Treatment, Italy

Holger Roth
National Institutes of Health, USA

Peter Schüffler
ETH Zurich, Switzerland

Akinobu Shimizu
Tokyo University of Agriculture and Technology, Japan

Yoshihisa Sinagawa
Siemens, USA

Contents

Gastrointestinal Tract - Crohn's Disease

Gastrointestinal Tract - Colonoscopy, Colonography

Abdominal Operation Planning - Registration, Segmentation

Special Topics

Liver and Pancreas - Ablation, Perfusion, and Segmentation

Parameter Estimation for Personalization of Liver Tumor Radiofrequency Ablation

Chloé Audigier[1,2]([⊠]), Tommaso Mansi[2], Hervé Delingette[1], Saikiran Rapaka[2],
Viorel Mihalef[2], Daniel Carnegie[4], Emad Boctor[3], Michael Choti[4],
Ali Kamen[2], Dorin Comaniciu[2], and Nicholas Ayache[1]

[1] Asclepios Research Group, INRIA Sophia-Antipolis, Sophia-Antipolis, France
chloe.audigier@inria.fr
[2] Imaging and Computer Vision, Siemens Corporate Technology, Princeton, NJ, USA
[3] Department of Radiology, Johns Hopkins Medical Institutions,
Baltimore, MD, USA
[4] Department of Surgery, Johns Hopkins Medical Institutions, Baltimore, MD, USA

Abstract. Mathematical modeling has the potential to assist radiofrequency ablation (RFA) of tumors as it enables prediction of the extent of ablation. However, the accuracy of the simulation is challenged by the material properties since they are patient-specific, temperature and space dependent. In this paper, we present a framework for patient-specific radiofrequency ablation modeling of multiple lesions in the case of metastatic diseases. The proposed forward model is based upon a computational model of heat diffusion, cellular necrosis and blood flow through vessels and liver which relies on patient images. We estimate the most sensitive material parameters, those need to be personalized from the available clinical imaging and data. The selected parameters are then estimated using inverse modeling such that the point-to-mesh distance between the computed necrotic area and observed lesions is minimized. Based on the personalized parameters, the ablation of the remaining lesions are predicted. The framework is applied to a dataset of seven lesions from three patients including pre- and post-operative CT images. In each case, the parameters were estimated on one tumor and RFA is simulated on the other tumor(s) using these personalized parameters, assuming the parameters to be spatially invariant within the same patient. Results showed significantly good correlation between predicted and actual ablation extent (average point-to-mesh errors of 4.03 mm).

Keywords: Radiofrequency ablation · Heat diffusion · Inverse modeling · Liver

1 Introduction

In radiofrequency ablation (RFA), a probe is placed within the malignant tissue with electrodes at its tip to create heat, thus causing coagulative necrosis at temperatures above $50\,°C$. In order to prevent recurrence, the procedure needs

© Springer International Publishing Switzerland 2014
H. Yoshida et al. (Eds.): ABDI 2014, LNCS 8676, pp. 3–12, 2014.
DOI: 10.1007/978-3-319-13692-9_1

to generate a necrosis that covers completely the tumor, which relies on optimal heat duration and probe placement. The results of RFA are significantly improved by the experience of the clinicians [1]: for the same physician, survival rate of treated patients increased twofolds over a four years period. This learning curve is partly due to the difficult assessment of the cooling effect of the large vessels, porous circulation and blood coagulation, which results in suboptimal ablation and local recurrences in up to 60 % of the cases [2]. To improve the planning of the procedure, computerized simulations have been devised to better predict the extent of the necrosis and eventually modify the probe position or the duration of heating for example. A patient-specific tool showing the extent of ablation given the probe position, the heat duration and patient images will potentially be beneficial in providing a personalized treatment planning and guidance, as it could improve the current clinical outcome. Studies [3–5] have investigated the finite element method (FEM) to simulate the heat transfer on generic human anatomies and eventually optimize the placement of the probes [6]. Simulations with animal-specific [7] or patient-specific anatomies were also recently considered [8] with the inclusion of cooling effects computed from simulated hepatic venous flow and hepatic parenchymal flow. However, nominal tissue parameters were employed in these studies with values often based on *ex vivo* experiments on animal tissue sometimes with a large varying range between published studies. Because tissue properties are patient-specific and can depend on the current state of the tissue, a proper estimation of those parameters is needed but has been often overlooked. In this paper, we present a computational model of heat transfer and cellular death during RFA which is based on patient-specific tissue parameters and anatomies estimated from CT (Sect. 2). Our framework is adapted to situation where no temperature map is available. We rely on the Lattice-Boltzmann Method (LBM) to compute not only heat diffusion, cellular necrosis as in [8] but also blood and parenchyma flow in the liver tissue. This latter method is based on a computational fluid Dynamics (CFD) solver which incorporates a porous part to deal with the liver parenchyma. This framework is particularly efficient for the personalization as it provides a fast solver and naturally accounts for the flow transition between veins and parenchyma. The model is then personalized based on the first ablation. This information is used to plan subsequent ablation(s) of the same or additional lesions to treat. This can be validated in case of the ablation of multiple tumors inside the liver, assuming that the parameters are spatially invariant within the same patient. In Sect. 3, heat conductivity and porosity were selected as the most sensitive parameters for predicting the necrosis extent. After their estimation on patient specific data, we demonstrate improved prediction accuracy. Sect. 4 concludes the paper.

2   Mathematical Model of RFA Simulation

The simulation of heat transfer inside the liver depends on the patient-specific anatomy (Sect. 2.1) and on the blood flow inside the main vessels and the parenchyma considered as a porous medium (Sect. 2.2). The different steps of our method are illustrated in Fig. 1.

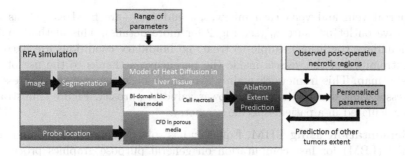

Fig. 1. Estimation of the personalized parameters and the forward model (blue: input, green: processes, purple: output) (Color figure online).

2.1 Patient-Specific Liver Anatomy

Volumetric binary images of the parenchyma, tumors, hepatic veins, vena cava, portal vein and the hepatic artery when visible are generated from a semi-automatic segmentation [9] of preoperative CT images. A multi-label mask image is created to identify the different structures of this detailed anatomical model of patient's liver and circulation tree. To define the computational domain, a level set representation of the liver, without tumor and vessels is computed. From the vessel masks, a porosity map is created to identify the porous parenchyma and the vessels. Because non-visible, the walls of the vessels are extrapolated using 26 connectivities dilatation of the vessels masks. The vessel extremities, which do not have walls are manually identified.

2.2 Hepatic Blood Flow Computation

Model Description. The blood in the main vessels and in the parenchyma are combined in the generalized 3D incompressible Navier-Stokes equation for fluid flow in porous media, thus considerably easing the definition of boundary conditions between vessels and parenchyma, improving on [8]. More precisely, writing **v** as the blood velocity and p the pressure inside the liver, we solve:

$$\frac{\partial \mathbf{v}}{\partial t} + \mathbf{v}.\nabla\mathbf{v} = -\frac{1}{\rho}\nabla p + \mu_e \nabla^2.\mathbf{v} + \mathbf{F} \qquad \mathbf{F} = -\frac{\mu(1-\epsilon)^2}{\alpha^2\epsilon^2}\mathbf{v} \qquad (1)$$

The added force **F** represents the total body force due to the presence of a porous medium [10]. **F** depends on the porosity coefficient ϵ (fraction of blood volume over the total volume) whose default values are 1 in the CT-visible vessels, 0.1 in the porous parenchyma [7], and 0.04 in the vessel walls to model an impermeable medium. Experiments have been performed to obtain a sufficiently small porosity (0.04) to avoid flowing through the vessel wall. At the border of the liver, no flux boundary conditions are used whereas Dirichlet boundary conditions are applied at the inlets of portal vein and vena cava and at the outlet of the vena cava:

the portal vein and vena cava inflow, φ_p and $\varphi_{vc_{in}}$ are fixed as well as the vena cava outlet pressure p_0 (see Fig. 2 for more details). This method makes the boundary conditions simple to treat: no boundary conditions are fixed on the extremities of the vessels inside the parenchyma thanks to the use of the porosity map. This framework mainly avoids the occurrence of shear stress on the vessel walls due to their much lower value of porosity. Figure 2 illustrates flows calculated in a patient-specific geometry.

Implementation using LBM. Equation 1 is solved using Lattice Boltzmann Method (LBM) for fast computation on general purpose graphics processing units (GPU). LBM has been developed for CFD and is now a well-established discretization method. In RFA, it has been validated in [8] through a comparison with an analytical solution, for a similar accuracy as FEM. An isotropic Cartesian grid with 19-connectivity topology and Neumann boundary conditions is employed. A Multiple-Relaxation-Time (MRT) model is used for increased stability [11]. At position $\mathbf{x}$ for the edge $\mathbf{e}_i$, the governing equation is: $\mathbf{f}(\mathbf{x} + \mathbf{e}_i \Delta x, t + \Delta t) = \mathbf{f}(\mathbf{x}, t) + \mathbf{A}[\mathbf{f}^{eq}(\mathbf{x}, t) - \mathbf{f}(\mathbf{x}, t)] + \Delta t \mathbf{g}(\mathbf{x}, t)$. In this equation, $\mathbf{f}(\mathbf{x}) = \{f_i(\mathbf{x})\}_{i=1..19}$ is the vector of distribution function with $f_i(\mathbf{x})$ being the probability of finding a particle travelling along the edge $\mathbf{e}_i$ of the node $\mathbf{x}$ at a given time; $c = \Delta x / \Delta t$; $c_s^2 = 1/4$; Δx is the spacing; $f_i^{eq}(\mathbf{x}, t) = \omega_i \rho [1 + \frac{\mathbf{e}_i \cdot \mathbf{v}}{c c_s^2}]$; $g_i(\mathbf{x}, t) = \omega_i \rho \frac{\mathbf{e}_i \cdot \mathbf{F}}{c_s^2}$, $\boldsymbol{\omega} = \{\omega_i\}_{i=1..19}$ is the vector of weighting factors and $\mathbf{A}$ the MRT matrix. The fluid mass density and velocity are computed from the LBM distributions as $\rho = \sum_{i=1}^{19} f_i(\mathbf{x}, t)$ and $\rho \mathbf{v} = \sum_{i=1}^{19} \mathbf{e}_i f_i(\mathbf{x}, t) + \frac{\Delta t}{2} \rho \mathbf{F}$ and are updated at every node of the grid for every timestep Δt.

2.3 Model of Heat Transfer and Cellular Necrosis in Liver Tissue

This model describes how the heat flows from the probe through the liver while accounting for the cooling effect of the main vessels and parenchyma. Its main

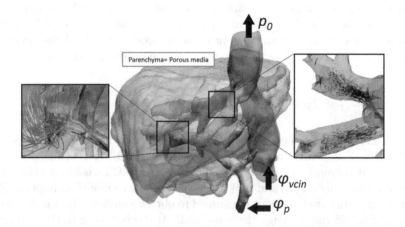

Fig. 2. Set-up and results of the hepatic blood flow computation with a zoom inside the vena cava on the right and at the extremities of the hepatic veins on the left.

parameters are then optimized to match the observed extent of the necrosis. Assuming blood vessels and surrounding tissue isolated from each other, the temperature is computed by solving the diffusion equation:

$$\rho_t c_t \frac{\partial T}{\partial t} = Q + \nabla \cdot (d_t \nabla T) \tag{2}$$

everywhere in the domain, to which we add either the cooling term $H(T_{b0} - T)/(1 - \epsilon)$ when a point belongs to a large vessel, where blood velocity is high, (Pennes model [12]) or $-\epsilon \rho_b c_b \mathbf{v} \cdot \nabla T/(1 - \epsilon)$ when it belongs to the parenchyma, where tissue is dominating (WK model [13]). T, Q, $\mathbf{v}$ and T_{b0} stand for temperature, source term, blood velocity and the mean temperature (assumed constant) of the blood in large vessels. A weakly coupling model is considered: the blood flow has an influence on the temperature distribution through the WK model but the temperature does not affect the blood flow (coagulation is not considered here), which allows us to speed up the calculations since the blood flow distribution is computed only once, at the beginning of the simulation. The discretization of the bioheat equation also relies on LBM using a no-flux boundary condition on the liver boundary defined as a level-set function. Tissue necrosis is computed using a 3-state model based on the simulated temperatures [14] using Eq. 3, where k_f, k_b are the damage and recovery rate respectively.

$$A \xrightarrow[k_b]{\xleftarrow{k_f(T)}} V \xrightarrow{k_f(T)} D \qquad k_f(T) = \bar{k_f} e^{T/T_k}(1 - A) \tag{3}$$

2.4 Parameter Estimation

As parameters in the heat transfer and cellular necrosis equation are customarily taken from the literature, we aim to personalize them given the observed extent of the necrotic region measured post-operatively as temperature maps are not readily available. Most of the parameters are defined as constant whereas the heat capacity c_t and conductivity $dt = \bar{dt} * (1 + 0.00161) * (T - 310) W (mK)^{-1}$ are temperature dependent and therefore spatially distributed [8]. Using DAKOTA[1], we first perform a sensitivity analysis to know which parameters mostly influence the volume and the point-to-mesh error [15] of the computed necrosis area. Then, we optimize the most sensitive ones: the heat conductivity and the porosity, as to minimize the average point-to-mesh error between computed and observed necrotic region. To this end, we use a gradient-free optimization method, the Constrained Optimization BY Linear Approximations (COBYLA), which required only a few numbers of forward simulations.

3 Experiments and Results

All experiments were executed on a Windows 7 desktop machine (Intel Xeon, 2.80 GHz, 45 GB RAM, 24 CPUs) with a Nvidia Quadro 6000 1.7 GB (448 CUDA cores).

---

[1] http://dakota.sandia.gov - multilevel framework for sensitivity analysis.

Table 1. Ranges of parameters values explored in the sensitivity analysis.

Notation	Parameter name	Min - Max
H	Convective transfer coefficient	24.4×10^4 48.8×10^4 W $(m^3 \text{ K})^{-1}$
$\bar{d}_t$	Heat conductivity	0.25 1.24 W$(m \text{ K})^{-1}$
$\bar{k}_f$	Damage rate coefficient	3.2×10^{-3} 3.4×10^{-3} s^{-1}
ϵ	Porosity	0.1 0.9

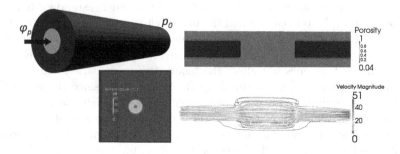

Fig. 3. Set-up of the synthetic case. *Top*: The cylinder with the porosity field used. The boundary conditions are the output pressure and the input flow. *Down*: The heat distribution initially applied and the velocity distribution used.

3.1 Sensitivity Analysis

We want to know the sensitivity of four uncertain parameters of our model: $\bar{d}_t$, H, $\bar{k}_f$, ϵ on the volume of the computed necrosis but also on the point-to-mesh error between the computed necrosis area and the one computed with the nominal parameters from the literature. To this end, a synthetic case has been setup to speed-up the process (Fig. 3). The range of parameters values used [3] are reported in Table 1. These parameters of interest were modelled with a uniformly distributed uncertainty, and the sensitivity analysis was performed using variance based decomposition to compute the global sensitivity indices (so-called Sobol indices). $\bar{d}_t$ has the largest total effect (0.58) as compared with $\bar{k}_f$, H and ϵ (0.16, 0.15, 0.43) on the volume of the lesion, whereas ϵ and $\bar{d}_t$ have the same larger total effect (0.37) as compared with $\bar{k}_f$ and H (0.16, 0.35) on the point-to-mesh error with respect to lesion obtained with nominal values. As it is not reasonable to try to estimate all of these four parameters at once, we decided to estimate only two of them: we chose $\bar{d}_t$ for its effect on the volume, as the nominal value of $\bar{k}_f$ [14] seemed accurate and ϵ. H was chosen large enough to maintain a constant temperature of 37 °C in the CT-visible vessels. We fixed the other parameters to nominal values for the personalization on patient data.

3.2   Verification of the Optimization Framework

In order to confirm the accuracy of the optimization framework, we considered a synthetic case on a regular cuboid domain where all the phenomena occurring during RFA were present (diffusion, reaction and advection) and with nominal parameters of tissue properties. First we simulated a necrotic area with generic parameters by emulating the clinical RFA protocol: during 7 min, we heated at 105 °C, the simulation continued for 3 more minutes without heating so that each cell reached a steady state. Then, the main parameters: $\bar{d}_t$ and ϵ are estimated by minimizing the mean of the point-to-mesh error between the computed necrotic region and the one created at the first step. We managed to obtain the estimated parameters with 6.1 % of error on $\bar{d}_t$ and 2.1 % on ϵ in 32 min after 36 iterations with a mean of the point-to-mesh error of 10^{-3} mm.

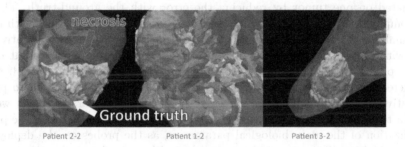

Fig. 4. Computed necrosis compared qualitatively well with the predicted lesion after personalization on the first tumor of each patient.

Table 2. Evaluation on patient data.

Patient	Tumor size	Probe diameter	Point-to-mesh error	DICE	Estimated parameters	
					$\bar{d}_t$	ϵ
1-1	5 cm	4 cm then 5 cm	4.06 ± 2.56 mm	72.0 %	0.250 W(m K)$^{-1}$	0.0997
1-2	3.5 cm	4 cm then 5 cm	4.65 ± 3.52 mm	74.9 %		
1-3	4.2 cm	4 cm then 5 cm	4.62 ± 3.32 mm	69.0 %		
2-1	1.5 cm	4 cm	2.57 ± 1.89 mm	77.2 %	0.275 W(m K)$^{-1}$	0.1028
2-2	1 cm	3.5 cm	5.66 ± 4.25 mm	60.9 %		
3-1	1 cm	3 cm	3.01 ± 2.05 mm	74.0 %	0.489 W(m K)$^{-1}$	0.1
3-2	1 cm	3 cm	3.64 ± 2.89 mm	74.1 %		

3.3 Evaluation on Patient Data

We evaluated our model on 3 patients, with 7 ablations (several tumors ablated for each patient) for whom pre- and post-operative CT images were available. Clinical RFA protocol was simulated: the probe was deployed within the tumor and cells in a diameter defined pre-operatively around the center of the tumor probe tip were heated at 105 °C during 7 min or 2 times 7 min. The diameter and heat duration were iteratively increased according to the size of the tumor. The simulation continued for 3 more minutes without any heat source so that each cell reached a steady state. The parameters were considered spatially invariant within the same patient. Nevertheless, the cell death model locally changes the properties of the tissue, and different parameters are related to different location inside the liver (H and ϵ are related to large vessels, and parenchyma respectively), but we consider that they have a constant value. The parameters are estimated on one tumor by reducing the error with the ground-truth. Then, we computed the cell death area of the other tumor(s) of this patient with the personalized parameters. The computed cell death area compared qualitatively well with the observed post-operative necrosis zone for tumor located at different place inside the liver, close to large vessels, on the border (Fig. 4, the predicted lesion was manually segmented by an expert and registered to pre-operative image). Quantitatively, average point-to-mesh errors (Table 2) were within tolerance in clinical routine for the four tumors estimated with the personalization of the main biological parameters, as the probes can be deployed in steps of 1 cm. The estimated heat conductivities were lower than the nominal value (0.512 W$(m\,K)^{-1}$), whereas the porosity was very close (0.1). Other experiments on patient 1 showed also a significant improvement of the correlation between predicted and actual ablation extent compared to the prediction using only nominal parameters (average point-to-mesh errors of 4.44 mm vs 4.98 mm, average Dice score of 72.0 % vs 68.5 %). Patient 2 presents a quite large Dice difference between the two cases. It might be due to segmentation or registration issues, and potentially to model limitations (assumptions, etc.), which will be further investigated in a pre-clinical setup. The main parameters are first considered with nominal values taken from the literature and then optimized to match the observed extent of the necrosis. Current errors can be explained by segmentation and registration processes but also by the limited number (2) of personalized parameters.

4 Discussion and Conclusion

The personalization of the sensitive tissue parameters allows to have a better estimation of the necrosis and to predict the outcome of RFA in case of multiple tumors inside the liver. As our framework totally rely on LBM, no advanced meshing techniques are required. All the computations are directly done from patient images: heat propagation and cell death modeling as well as the heat sink effect of blood vessels and porous circulation in the liver. The coupled computation of the porous and hepatic flow eliminates the difficulties in the setting of boundary conditions in the parenchyma, and the occurence of shear stress on the vessels wall is avoided as the Pennes Model is used in the big vessels where the flow is not accounted for. The current method needs several tumors for validation and is worth using only when no temperature maps are available, but it could be easily translated into clinical settings. Adaptation for RFA under image-guidance is considered: RFA procedure is usually done in several steps (increase in probe diameters for example). An intra-operative image is acquired at the end of the first step and used to personalize key parameters, providing a powerful guidance tool. No post-operative images are required. A necessary step before deploying this method in clinical settings is a pre-clinical validation with extensive data on larger populations to evaluate the computational model of RFA and to consider potential safety issue of the proposed application. Even if promising results are achieved with the use of patient-specific parameters, the impact of possible biases in the post- to the pre-operative image registration like the impact of the average simulation of the probe need to be investigated as well as the sensitivity of the results with respect to segmentation.

References

1. Hildebrand, P., Leibecke, T., Kleemann, M., Mirow, L., et al.: Influence of operator experience in radiofrequency ablation of malignant liver tumours on treatment outcome. Eur. J. Surg. Oncol. (EJSO) **32**, 430–434 (2006)
2. Kim, Y.S., Rhim, H., Cho, O.K., Koh, B.H., Kim, Y.: Intrahepatic recurrence after percutaneous radiofrequency ablation of hepatocellular carcinoma: analysis of the pattern and risk factors. Eur. J. Radiol. **59**, 432–441 (2006)
3. Altrogge, I., Preusser, T., Kroger, T., Haase, S., Patz, T., Kirby, R.M.: Sensitivity analysis for the optimization of radiofrequency ablation in the presence of material parameter uncertainty. Int. J. Uncertain. Quantification **2**(3), 295–321 (2012)
4. Chen, X., Saidel, G.M.: Mathematical modeling of thermal ablation in tissue surrounding a large vessel. J. Biomech. **131**, 011001 (2009)
5. Jiang, Y., Mulier, S., Chong, W., Diel Rambo, M., et al.: Formulation of 3D finite elements for hepatic radiofrequency ablation. IJMIC **9**, 225–235 (2010)
6. Kröger, T., Pätz, T., Altrogge, I., Schenk, A., et al.: Fast estimation of the vascular cooling in RFA based on numerical simulation. Open Biomed. Eng. J. **4**, 16–26 (2010)
7. Payne, S., Flanagan, R., Pollari, M., Alhonnoro, T., et al.: Image-based multi-scale modelling and validation of radio-frequency ablation in liver tumours. Philos. T. Roy. Soc. A **369**, 4233–4254 (2011)
8. Audigier, C., Mansi, T., Delingette, H., Rapaka, S., Mihalef, V., Sharma, P., Carnegie, D., Boctor, E., Choti, M., Kamen, A., Comaniciu, D., Ayache, N.: Lattice Boltzmann method for fast patient-specific simulation of liver tumor ablation from CT images. In: Mori, K., Sakuma, I., Sato, Y., Barillot, C., Navab, N. (eds.) MICCAI 2013, Part III. LNCS, vol. 8151, pp. 323–330. Springer, Heidelberg (2013)
9. Criminisi, A., Sharp, T., Blake, A.: GeoS: geodesic image segmentation. In: Forsyth, D., Torr, P., Zisserman, A. (eds.) ECCV 2008, Part I. LNCS, vol. 5302, pp. 99–112. Springer, Heidelberg (2008)
10. Guo, Z., Zhao, T.: Lattice-boltzmann model for incompressible flows through porous media. Phys. Rev. E **66**, 036304 (2002)

11. Pan, C., Luo, L.S., Miller, C.T.: An evaluation of lattice boltzmann schemes for porous medium flow simulation. Comput. Fluids **35**, 898–909 (2006)
12. Pennes, H.H.: Analysis of tissue and arterial blood temperatures in the resting human forearm. J. Appl. Physiol. **85**, 5–34 (1998)
13. Klinger, H.: Heat transfer in perfused biological tissue I: general theory. B. Math. Biol. **36**, 403–415 (1974)
14. O'Neill, D., Peng, T., Stiegler, P., Mayrhauser, U., et al.: A three-state mathematical model of hyperthermic cell death. Ann. Biomed. Eng. **39**, 570–579 (2011)
15. Zheng, Y., Barbu, A., Georgescu, B., Scheuering, M., Comaniciu, D.: Fast automatic heart chamber segmentation from 3d CT data using marginal space learning and steerable features. In: IEEE 11th International Conference on Computer Vision, 2007, ICCV 2007, pp. 1–8. IEEE (2007)

Automatic Identification and Localisation of Potential Malignancies in Contrast-Enhanced Ultrasound Liver Scans Using Spatio-Temporal Features

Spyridon Bakas[1]($\boxtimes$), Dimitrios Makris[1]($\boxtimes$), Paul S. Sidhu[2],
and Katerina Chatzimichail[3]

[1] Digital Imaging Research Centre, Faculty of Science, Engineering and Computing,
Kingston University, London, UK
{S.Bakas,D.Makris}@kingston.ac.uk
[2] Department of Radiology, King's College Hospital, Denmark Hill, London, UK
PaulSidhu@nhs.net
[3] Evgenidion Hospital, National and Kapodistrian University, Athens, Greece
Katerina@hcsl.com

Abstract. The identification and localisation of a focal liver lesion (FLL) in Contrast-Enhanced Ultrasound (CEUS) video sequences is crucial for liver cancer diagnosis, treatment planning and follow-up management. Currently, localisation and classification of FLLs between benign and malignant cases in CEUS are routinely performed manually by radiologists, in order to proceed with making a diagnosis, leading to subjective results, prone to misinterpretation and human error. This paper describes a methodology to assist clinicians who regularly perform these tasks, by discharging benign FLL cases and localise potential malignancies in a fully automatic manner by exploiting the perfusion dynamics of a CEUS video. The proposed framework uses local variations of intensity to distinguish between hyper- and hypo-enhancing regions and then analyse their spatial configuration to identify potentially malignant cases. Automatic localisation of the potential malignancy on the image plane is then addressed by clustering, using Expectation-Maximisation for Gaussian Mixture Models. A novel feature that combines description of local dynamic behaviour with spatial proximity is used in this process. Quantitative evaluation, on real clinical data from a retrospective multi-centre study, demonstrates the value of the proposed method.

Keywords: Localisation · Malignancy identification · Contrast-enhanced ultrasound · Focal liver lesion · Liver · Perfusion · Clustering

1 Introduction

Contrast-Enhanced Ultrasound (CEUS) is a modality widely accepted for the detection and characterisation of focal liver lesions (FLLs) [1]. In comparison with

© Springer International Publishing Switzerland 2014
H. Yoshida et al. (Eds.): ABDI 2014, LNCS 8676, pp. 13–22, 2014.
DOI: 10.1007/978-3-319-13692-9_2

conventional B-mode ultrasound (US), CEUS enhances the contrast between the liver and the FLL through the use of intravenously injected contrast agents [2]. CEUS has diagnostic accuracy higher than 95 % for the evaluation of malignant FLLs [3] and its sensitivity and specificity exceeds that of other modalities, such as contrast-enhanced computed tomography (CE-CT) and contrast-enhanced magnetic resonance imaging (CE-MRI) [4]. It is recognised as the most cost-efficient imaging solution for distinguishing between benign and malignant FLLs [1], after an inconclusive US scan. Also it is in the forefront of CEUS scope to help in reducing the radiation burden to population.

A CEUS liver scan is divided into three different phases over time, namely arterial, portal venous and late phase. These allow the observation of the flow of the intravenously injected contrast agent, by intensity changes in the captured plane. Recording these intensity changes for different tissues during a CEUS sequence leads to time-intensity curves (TICs). These curves describe the perfusion dynamics for different regions and lead to parameters, that allow for the differentiation of the nature of tissues [1]. Specifically, a tissue that shows increased perfusion (hyper-enhancing) in comparison with the rest healthy tissue (parenchyma), during the arterial phase, reveals the typical behaviour of a potentially malignant FLL. This FLL can only be confirmed as a malignancy if during the late phase its region is darker than the parenchyma [5].

Currently, radiologists routinely detect, localise and classify FLLs in CEUS data manually, through a time-consuming series of tasks, namely **(i)** identification of a reference frame for **(ii)** localising a region of interest (ROI), e.g. FLL, **(iii)** monitoring of the dynamic behaviour (i.e. brightness intensity changes) of different ROIs over time, and eventually classifying an FLL as benign or malignant. Each of these tasks requires a high-level of expertise, provides subjective results and is prone to misinterpretation and human error [1]. Processing of CEUS data poses a very challenging task due to intensity changes, acoustic shadows, low signal-to-noise ratio, the transducer movement, as well as the patient's irregular breathing patterns and the motion of the inner human organs that affect the ROIs' apparent 2D size and shapes.

While computer-aided solutions have been suggested for the aforementioned tasks of **(i)** [6] and **(iii)** [7–11] in CEUS data, no solution has ever been proposed for the automated localisation of the position and shape of an FLL in a CEUS recording (task **(ii)**). Considering the continuously increasing number of CEUS scans, automation of the localisation procedure is of much interest as it will assist the diagnostic procedure and the assessment of the repeatability and reproducibility of the examination on different patients or between different clinical centres, as it is expected to provide objective results.

Methods suggested thus far for the task of monitoring FLLs in CEUS (task **iii**) require the existence of prior manually initialised ROIs (e.g. FLL). A method is described in [10], which first compensates for rigid motion in CEUS video recordings and then displays TICs to assist radiologists to classify an FLL. Motion compensation is based on iterative maximisation of mutual information [12], which is dependent on an intensity constancy constraint. Another method described in [7], creates a non-rigid motion model by combining histogram information from a ROI with the detection of SIFT keypoints [13]. It then suggests an FLL classification decision based on obtained TICs. Both methods require the manual delineation of the ROI and the part of the image that needs re-alignment (e.g. the conical area of the ultrasonographic image, also named US mask) on a manually identified frame. Then another method, suggested in [8], proposes an affine transformation motion model, based entirely on SIFT keypoints [13], to monitor and classify an FLL based on its TIC. In addition, [8] introduces an automatic delimitation of the US mask based on an intensity change detection. A pixelwise analysis within a manually initialised FLL is performed in [11]. Specifically, after compensating for rigid motion similar to [10], micro-vasculature differences between benign and malignant FLLs are compared and the FLLs' spatial heterogeneity is quantified.

Furthermore, segmentation methods for the localisation of lesions have been applied in CT [14] and MRI [15,16] data. Specifically, these methods require some manually annotated areas in one slice by an operator, and then they either encode the pairwise similarity of intensity information between different pixels, or model the intensity relationship of each pixel to a set of global intensity clusters, across the 3rd dimension of the data (i.e. different depth slice). Even though the 3rd dimension in volumetric CT and MRI data can be considered relative to the temporal dimension of CEUS data, in CT and MRI the same tissues are represented with consistent brightness intensity across the 3rd dimension, making the localisation task much easier, especially if prior knowledge is included.

The aim of the present study is firstly to identify and categorise hyper- and hypo-enhancing FLLs in the first phase of a CEUS examination, and then to localise regions of potential malignancy within the liver region in CEUS video sequences, in a fully automatic manner and without considering any prior knowledge. This can be ultimately used as an objective initialisation of segmentation methods, as well as to attract the attention of radiologists in the suggested ROIs within the US mask that they might have missed.

2 Method

Specifically, this paper considers the problem of identifying and localising a potential malignancy by clustering together regions with the same dynamic behaviour (TIC) within the US mask, in a similar manner to the process performed conceptually by radiologists. After compensating for the motion included within the sequence of a patient's scan, the US mask is divided into smaller regions and their local TICs are obtained. Subsequently, dimensionality reduction is applied on the TICs for each individual patient, and the principal axes describing more than 90 % of the total variance are used in combination with location information to form the feature vector for each region. A framework based on the optimisation technique of Expectation-Maximisation (EM) with a set of Gaussian Mixture Models (GMM) is then used to segment the US mask into meaningful ROIs based on these feature vectors, and therefore localise the hyper-enhancing regions, i.e. potential malignancies. Figure 1 summarises the whole pipeline of the proposed method.

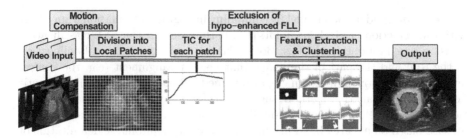

Fig. 1. Visual summary of the proposed method.

Initially, the US mask is automatically segmented on each patient's case by considering an intensity change detection, as described in [8], in order to remove all the irrelevant information - notably textual data provided for the CEUS operator. This US mask is then applied to every frame of the sequence, selecting only the relevant information, whilst removing the aforementioned artefacts. Then the optimal reference frame at time t_0 is automatically identified, as proposed in [6]. According to radiologists, this frame is expected to be the one with the maximum contrast between FLL and parenchyma.

Any present motion between the liver and the US transducer affects negatively the processing outcome and therefore the frames of each sequence need to be spatially realigned to compensate for any in-plane movements. Assuming there is only motion within –instead of across– the plane, and a simple translation is sufficient to describe the level of relative motion between the liver and the US transducer, the point-based registration technique of Compact And Real-time Descriptors (CARD) keypoints [17] is employed to automatically estimate the motion between all the frames and realign them according to the reference frame. This is done by first registering keypoints every two successive frames of the acquired sequence and then matching correspondent keypoints by using the Nearest Neighbour Distance Ratio in the descriptor space. The translation between every pair of successive frames is then estimated as the average displacement of the matched correspondences between them. The motion compensated video data can then be processed as a 3D volume, where the 3rd dimension depicts information from the temporal domain.

2.1   Local Time-Intensity Curves

Obtaining information from the brightness intensity of a single pixel (fine-grained resolution) is considered susceptible to speckle noise (i.e. very sensitive to "outliers" – excessively bright and dark pixels). Therefore, the spatial averaging through more coarse-grained resolutions was considered essential, by subdividing the US mask into B non-overlapping local neighbourhoods ("patches") of $n \times n$ pixels and avoid such an effect, where n is small compared with the overall size of the image. The pixel brightness intensity values are then averaged over each of these patches.

$$\bar{p}_b(t) = \frac{1}{n^2} \sum_{i_b=1}^{n^2} p_{i_b}(t). \tag{1}$$

where $p_{i_b}(t)$ is the intensity of the ith pixel within the bth block at time t.

The changes of the average brightness intensities of each patch ($\bar{p}_b$) over time (i.e. its dynamic behaviour) can lead to information similar to that used by radiologists. Such information are encompassed in the TICs of the local patches, by estimating the $\bar{p}_b$ for each frame in the sequence.

$$\mathbf{TIC_b} = [\bar{p}_b(1), \bar{p}_b(2), \ldots, \bar{p}_b(T)]. \tag{2}$$

where T refers to the number of frames of the CEUS video sequence.

2.2 Early Exclusion of Hypo-enhancement

A foreground mask is produced including only patches where potential malignancies may exist. Specifically, a patch is included in the mask if it is enhancing more than a certain proportion (ψ) of the maximum intensity value of the whole 3D volume. In addition, a morphological opening is used as noise removal, to exclude any patches that are not connected with any other neighbouring patches, or even if connected, the area that they cover is smaller than the size (ϕ) of the structuring element used for the morphological opening.

The resulting foreground mask for a hyper-enhancing case is expected to be solid, as the FLL would have enriched as much as the parenchyma until the end of the arterial phase. On the other hand, for a hypo-enhancing case, this mask is expected to have a 'hole' either in the middle or at the side of the mask, depending on where the FLL is located in relation to the parenchyma. This property is exploited to automatically discharge hypo-enhancing cases by separating them from hyper-enhancing cases after applying a specified threshold on the overlap metric of the Jaccard index between the foreground mask and its convex hull.

2.3 Feature Extraction and Clustering

Information of the dynamic behaviour of the foreground patches is essential to be considered in the clustering of the data. However, because T is large (see Sect. 3.1), the data included in each TIC is represented as a high-dimensional vector. Thus, principal component analysis (PCA) by eigenvalue decomposition is employed to reduce the dimensionality of the data and the computational complexity, as well as to create more meaningful feature vectors. The number of dimensions (d) is chosen such that the variance in the data accounted for by these d dimensions (v_d), exceeds a specified proportion, typically 90 %, of the total variance v_T ($v_d > 0.9 \cdot v_T$, for $1 \leq d \leq T$). The coordinates of the centre of each patch (x_{c_b}, y_{c_b}) are also included in each feature vector along with the PCA dimensions of the local TIC, such that each feature vector may represent both the spatial proximity and the dynamic behaviour of the local patch.

The optimisation technique of Expectation-Maximisation (EM) is used with a set of Gaussian Mixture Models (GMM) to perform the clustering of the feature vectors. This is done in an attempt to cluster together patches with similar dynamic behaviour. To find the optimal number of clusters for each case, an overestimated initial number of clusters is used to initialise a Bayesian Classifier with the functionality of a GMM Probability Distribution Function, based on the Figueiredo-Jain algorithm [18].

2.4   Region Selection

Radiologists extract various parameters from a TIC to describe different aspects of a ROI's perfusion and determine its functional features [1]. However, most of these parameters require a continuous sequence throughout the three phases of the exam. Due to the provided data comprising only a short sequence of the exam, including at most a small part of the portal venous phase, the only parameters possible to extract are: the peak intensity (PI), the time to reach the PI (TPI) and the regional blood flow (RBF), which is the area under the TIC from time zero until TPI. RBF is considered as the most useful parameter for the scope of this work as it implicitly includes information about the PI, the TPI and the slope of the TIC.

Sorting the identified clusters in descending order of their RBF is expected to reveal first the cluster with the most hyper-enhancing behaviour. In case of an actual hyper-enhancing FLL this cluster can provide sufficient information for the location, size, shape and nature of the FLL, whilst if it is an actual hypo-enhancing case, then the proposed method is expected to identify regions of the parenchyma that have a hyper-enhancing behaviour in relation to the rest of the image, if not a second FLL. For example, in Fig. 2, cluster depicted by (a) shows the largest RBF, which is typical of a malignant FLL. Furthermore, as the chosen cluster might include some irrelevant pixels (i.e. artefacts) on the image plane (Fig. 2), a proportion of the cluster's pixel population is used

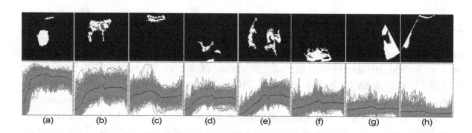

Fig. 2. Clusters obtained from a clinical case, during arterial phase, sorted in descending order of their regional blood flow. *The first row depicts the clusters visualised in the image space and the second row depicts the corresponding TICs, where the vertical and horizontal axes denote brightness intensity and time, respectively. Each of the curves depicts a different patch and the dark dotted curve in the middle of each of the 8 graphs is the average/centroid for each cluster.*

(e.g. the 1st quartile) to automatically provide the location of the potential malignancy on the image plane. This location can ultimately be used as an initialisation seed-point to an existing segmentation method.

3   Experiments and Results

3.1   Materials

The proposed method is evaluated through being applied to real clinical data of 63 case studies, of patients in different physical condition. These cases comprise 34 hyper- and 29 hypo-enhancing FLLs during the arterial phase of a CEUS scan and in most cases information from the portal venous phase was also included. Each case includes one sequence of duration between 3 and 82 s. The imaging plane was chosen such that most of the motion is within –instead of across– the plane, allowing for its compensation.

All data was acquired using Siemens ACUSON Ultrasound (US) systems (Mountainview CA). Specifically, 49 cases were captured at King's College Hospital in the UK, using an S2000 US system equipped with 4 (or) 6 MHz curvilinear transducer at spatial resolution 1024×768 pixels, and the remaining 14 cases were captured at Evgenidion Hospital in Greece, using a Sequoia C512 US system equipped with 6-2 MHz curvilinear transducer, at spatial resolution 768×576 pixels. In all examinations the second generation contrast medium SonoVue [19] (Bracco S.p.A., Italy) was used in a 2.4 ml bolus intravenous injection (into an arm vein). Specific acquisition parameters of the equipment, such as the transducer's field of view and gain, for each patient are unknown, as they were set by the radiologist individually at the start of each examination. The acquisition method of this data reflects true clinical practice and leads to increased variability. Examinations were performed by radiologists with 13–16 years of experience using CEUS. All data were obtained without prior knowledge of subsequent processing by a software tool and without any specific instructions being given to the radiologist beforehand, hence reflecting true clinical practice. Appropriate ethics and confidentiality procedures have been followed at all times.

3.2   Results

For evaluating the automatic identification of hyper-enhancing (i.e. potentially malignant) cases, the measures of true positive rate (sensitivity) and false positive rate (1-specificity) are used, in the range [0,1]. The positive and the negative samples refer to the hyper- and the hypo-enhancing cases, respectively. From the clinical point of view, the true positive (TP) rate should ideally be kept equal to 1, so no single potentially malignant case is missed. At the same time, the proposed method should discharge as many hypo-enhancing cases as possible, keeping the false positive (FP) rate low.

According to [1] the duration of the arterial phase is at least 10 s. This justifies our results, shown in Fig. 3(a), where the FP rate is as high as 0.8 (specificity = 0.2) when sequences with acquisition duration (AD) less than 10 s are considered. Then for sequences with AD more than 10 s, the FP rate drops to 0.46

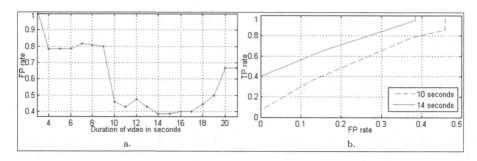

Fig. 3. Graph (a) denotes values of FP rate *(y axis)* for the acquisition duration of sequences being more than a certain number of seconds *(x axis)*, whilst TP rate is equal to 1. Graph (b) shows the ROC curves for cases with duration $\geq$ 10 & 14 s.

(specificity = 0.54). The best FP rate is equal to 0.38 (specificity = 0.62) and obtained when the AD is at least 14 s. Furthermore, two ROC curves are shown in Fig. 3(b) to assess the possible change of the FP rate in relation to the TP rate, for both AD above 10 and 14 s.

For evaluating the automatic localisation of the potential malignancies on the image plane, first the boundaries of the FLL have been manually annotated by a radiologist in the reference frame providing its ground truth (GT). The performance of the method is then assessed based on whether the location point provided by the proposed method (described in Sect. 2.4) is within the GT, or not. To measure this performance a correct localisation rate is used, over the number of hyper-enhancing cases with AD above 10 and 14 s, separately.

To provide some comparative results, a baseline approach is considered based on automatically thresholding the reference frame, using the Otsu's method [20]. This is expected to provide a foreground population of pixels that describe mostly the hyper-enhancing FLL. Then, similarly to the proposed method, a proportion of this population is used to obtain the location of the potential malignancy.

The best correct localisation rate achieved is 80 % and obtained for the 40 % of the chosen cluster's population (Table 1). On the other hand, the best result for the baseline method is 62.07 % after using 40 % of its mask's population.

Table 1. Correct localisation rate for a seed-point within the actual FLL.

Method	Population's proportion	Duration thr$\geq$10"	Duration thr$\geq$14"
Baseline	(25 %)	31.03 %	25 %
Baseline	(40 %)	62.07 %	55 %
Proposed method	(25 %)	51.72 %	**60 %**
Proposed method	(40 %)	**65.52 %**	80 %

4   Conclusions and Future Work

This paper demonstrates that the task of identifying and localising a potentially malignant FLL can be performed in a fully automatic manner. Specifically, the proposed framework firstly distinguishes between hyper- and hypo-enhancing cases by using only a video sequence of the arterial phase as input, and then automatically localises potential malignancies on the image plane. The first step is addressed by assessing local intensity variations and analysing their spatial configuration. Then, for the localisation step, a novel feature vector that encompasses the local dynamic behaviour and combines it with the spatial proximity is used in a clustering approach, using EM-GMM.

Experimental results show that the proposed method appears to perform adequately on identifying and localising FLLs with hyper-enhancing behaviour during the arterial phase. Such lesions are of significant importance to radiologists, as they may account for malignancies. FLLs of typical hypo-enhancing behaviour during the arterial phase are benign and therefore of less importance to radiologists.

Further improvements of the proposed framework should include the reduction of the FP rate, making the identification of potential malignancies more specific. Also coupling the proposed localisation approach with an iterative segmentation method might lead to a fully automated and precise approximation of the FLL boundaries, allowing the radiologists to use an automatic delineation of the FLL for its assessment.

References

1. Claudon, M., Dietrich, C.F., Choi, B.I., Cosgrove, D.O., Kudo, M., Nolsøe, C.P., et al.: Guidelines and good clinical practice recommendations for CEUS in the liver - update 2012: a WFUMB-EFSUMB initiative in cooperation with representatives of AFSUMB, AIUM, ASUM, FLAUS and ICUS. Ultrasound Med. Biol. **39**, 187–210 (2013)
2. Harvey, C.J., Blomley, M.J.K., Eckersley, R.J., Cosgrove, D.O.: Developments in ultrasound contrast media. Eur. Radiol. **11**, 675–689 (2001)
3. Strobel, D., Seitz, K., Blank, W., Schuler, A., Dietrich, C.F., von Herbay, A., et al.: Tumor-specific vascularization pattern of liver metastasis, hepatocellular carcinoma, hemangioma and focal nodular hyperplasia in the differential diagnosis of 1349 liver lesions in contrast-enhanced ultrasound (CEUS). Ultraschall Med. **30**, 376–382 (2009)
4. Westwood, M.E., Joore, M.A., Grutters, J.P.C., Redekop, W.K., Armstrong, N., Lee, K., et al.: Contrast-enhanced ultrasound using sonovue®(sulphur hexafluoride microbubbles) compared with contrast-enhanced computed tomography and contrast-enhanced magnetic resonance imaging for the characterisation of focal liver lesions and detection of liver metastases: a systematic review and cost-effectiveness analysis. Health Technol. Assess. **17**, 1–243 (2013)
5. Wilson, S.R., Burns, P.N.: Microbubble-enhanced US in body imaging: what role? Radiology **257**, 24–39 (2010)

6. Bakas, S., Hunter, G., Thiebaud, C., Makris, D.: Spot the best frame: towards intelligent automated selection of the optimal frame for initialisation of focal liver lesion candidates in contrast-enhanced ultrasound video sequences. In: 9th International Conference on Intelligent Environments, pp. 196–203. IEEE Press (2013)

7. Bakas, S., Chatzimichail, K., Hoppe, A., Galariotis, V., Hunter, G., Makris, D.: Histogram-based motion segmentation and characterisation of focal liver lesions in CEUS. Ann. BMVA **2012**, 1–14 (2012)

8. Bakas, S., Hoppe, A., Chatzimichail, K., Galariotis, V., Hunter, G., Makris, D.: Focal liver lesion tracking in CEUS for characterisation based on dynamic behaviour. In: Bebis, G., et al. (eds.) ISVC 2012, Part I. LNCS, vol. 7431, pp. 32–41. Springer, Heidelberg (2012)

9. Bakas, S., Sidhu, P.S., Sellars, M.E., Hunter, G.J.A., Makris, D., Chatzimichail, K.: Non-invasive offline characterisation of contrast-enhanced ultrasound evaluations of focal liver lesions: dynamic assessment using a new tracking method. In: 20th European Congress of Radiology (2014)

10. Rognin, N., Campos, R., Thiran, J.P., Messager, T., Broillet, A., Frinking, P., et al.: A new approach for automatic motion compensation for improved estimation of perfusion quantification parameters in ultrasound imaging. In: 8th French Conference on Acoustics, pp. 61–65 (2006)

11. Ta, C.N., Kono, Y., Barback, C.V., Mattrey, R.F., Kummel, A.C.: Automating tumor classification with pixel-by-pixel contrast-enhanced ultrasound perfusion kinetics. J. Vac. Sci. Technol. B Nanotechnol. Microelectron. **30**, 02C103 (2012)

12. Shekhar, R., Zagrodsky, V.: Mutual information-based rigid and nonrigid registration of ultrasound volumes. IEEE Trans. Med. Imaging **21**, 9–22 (2002)

13. Lowe, D.G.: Distinctive image features from scale-invariant keypoints. Int. J. Comput. Vis. **60**, 91–110 (2004)

14. Zhou, J., Huang, W., Xiong, W., Chen, W., Venkatesh, S.K., Tian, Q.: Delineation of liver tumors from CT scans using spectral clustering with out-of-sample extension and multi-windowing. In: Yoshida, H., Hawkes, D., Vannier, M.W. (eds.) Abdominal Imaging 2012. LNCS, vol. 7601, pp. 246–254. Springer, Heidelberg (2012)

15. Crum, W.R.: Spectral clustering and label fusion for 3D tissue classification: sensitivity and consistency analysis. Ann. BMVA **2009**, 1–12 (2009)

16. Song, Z., Tustison, N., Avants, B., Gee, J.: Adaptive graph cuts with tissue priors for brain MRI segmentation. In: 3rd International Symposium on Biomedical Imaging: Nano to Macro, pp. 762–765. IEEE Press (2006)

17. Ambai, M., Yoshida, Y.: CARD: compact and real-time descriptors. In: IEEE International Conference on Computer Vision, pp. 97–104 (2011)

18. Figueiredo, M.A.T., Jain, A.K.: Unsupervised learning on finite mixture models. IEEE Trans. Pattern Anal. Mach. Intell. **24**, 381–396 (2002)

19. Schneider, M.: Characteristics of sonovue. Echocardiography **16**, 743–746 (1999)

20. Otsu, N.: A threshold selection method from gray-level histograms. IEEE Trans. Syst. Man Cybern. **9**, 62–66 (1979)

A Semi-automated Toolkit for Analysis of Liver Cancer Treatment Response Using Perfusion CT

Elina Naydenova[1]([✉]), Amalia Cifor[1], Esme Hill[2], Jamie Franklin[3],
Ricky A. Sharma[2], and Julia A. Schnabel[1]

[1] Department of Engineering Science, Institute of Biomedical Engineering,
University of Oxford, Old Road Campus Research Building, Headington,
Oxford OX3 7DQ, UK
elina.naydenova@eng.ox.ac.uk
[2] Department of Oncology, University of Oxford, Old Road Campus Research
Building, Headington, Oxford OX3 7DQ, UK
[3] Department of Radiology, Churchill Hospital, Old Road, Oxford OX3 7LE, UK

Abstract. Delineation of hepatic tumours is challenging in CT due
to limited inherent tissue contrast, leading to significant intra-/inter-
observer variability. Perfusion CT (pCT) allows quantitative assessment
of enhancement patterns in normal and abnormal liver. This study aims
to develop a semi-automated perfusion analysis toolkit that classifies
hepatic tissue based on perfusion-derived parameters. pCT data from
patients with hepatic metastases were used in this study. Tumour motion
was minimized through image registration; perfusion parameters were
derived and then employed in the training of a machine learning algorithm used to classify hepatic tissue. This method was found to deliver
promising results for 10 data sets, with recorded sensitivity and specificity of the tissue classification in the ranges of 0.92–0.99 and 0.98–
0.99 respectively. This semi-automated method could be used to analyze
response over the treatment course, as it is not based on intensity values.

Keywords: Perfusion CT · Hepatic tumor · Registration · Motion ·
Tissue classification

1 Introduction

The global burden of cancer is continuously amassing with reported 14 million
new cases in 2012 [1]. Medical imaging has become an irreplaceable tool for
cancer diagnosis, no longer just visualizing anatomical structures but also providing functional information on tissue metabolism and functioning. Magnetic
Resonance Imaging (MRI) and Positron Emission Tomography (PET) have been
fundamental enablers of the latter development. However, both of these imaging modalities bear a high cost and are nowhere near as accessible as computed
tomography (CT). Adjusting the conventional imaging protocol to acquire perfusion computed tomography (pCT) data has been shown to benefit diagnosis, staging and therapy monitoring [2–4]. For example, pCT has been used to

© Springer International Publishing Switzerland 2014
H. Yoshida et al. (Eds.): ABDI 2014, LNCS 8676, pp. 23–32, 2014.
DOI: 10.1007/978-3-319-13692-9_3

detect perfusion changes in tumours undergoing chemotherapy [5,6], radiotherapy [7,8], and radio-frequency ablation [9]. In current clinical practice, pCT scans are typically analyzed using software which requires manual delineation - a time-consuming practice associated with significant inter- and intra-observer variation in derived parameters. Therefore, there is substantial clinical benefit in designing automated, reliable and accurate tools for CT data interpretation that require minimal clinical input and deliver reproducible results.

Liver cancer is the second most common cause of cancer deaths globally. Both early diagnosis and quantification of patients' response to treatment could hugely improve outcomes. However, several challenges remain unresolved - adverse effects of respiratory motion on analysis, a multitude of analytical models but no consensus on 'best practice', as well as the lack of a reproducible, structured and automated method for characterizing treatment response.

There are a limited number of studies that assess the reproducibility of pCT on human subjects [10,11], especially in anatomical regions most affected by motion, such as the liver. Ng et al. [12] reported high within-patient variability for perfusion parameters, derived for both tumour and normal hepatic tissue - 31 %–45 %. Chandler et al. [13] investigated the performance of standard rigid and non-rigid registration, based on intensity values, reporting a superior performance of the latter. Romain et al. [14] applied a rigid registration in conjunction with a block-matching approach. However, to satisfy the assumptions of rigidity, the authors employ manual identification of a box around the tumour region, requiring the input of a qualified radiologist.

Multiple perfusion analysis techniques have been proposed for pCT, some adopted from DCE-MRI. Modelling challenges stem from the dual blood supply of the liver and the resulting biphasic pattern of enhancement [6]. A gradient characterization method has been proposed to calculate hepatic arterial perfusion (HAP), hepatic portal perfusion (HPP) and hepatic perfusion index (HPI) [6]. Additionally, the use of two different models for the characterization of normal and tumour hepatic tissue has been applied to MRI data [15]. The dynamics of normal hepatic tissue are said to be best approximated by a single compartment supplied by two blood sources, the aorta and the portal vein [16]. The Extended Kety model, two compartments with bidirectional exchange and a single blood source, is a better approximation to perfusion in tumour hepatic tissue due to the predominantly arterial blood supply and the slower passage of contrast agent in tissue [17].

In this study we propose a combination of registration and perfusion analysis tools, applied to pCT data, to characterize normal and tumour hepatic tissue and detect changes in liver metastases over the course of treatment (Fig. 1). The methodology of this analysis is described first (Sect. 2), following the identified pipeline structure: registration, perfusion analysis, tissue classification. Next, Sect. 3 presents the outcomes of the perfusion analysis and quantifies the performance of the derived classification of hepatic tissue, whilst evaluating the effects of registration on both these steps. The contribution of this research is twofold: (1) propose a structured method for analyzing perfusion changes in the liver

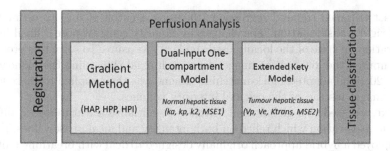

Fig. 1. Analysis pipeline: the pCT images are first registered; perfusion parameters are extracted from three pharmacokinetic models; machine learning applied to the perfusion parameters is used to classify liver tissue.

based on pCT data; (2) develop a multistage tool for automatic classification of hepatic tissue that requires minimal clinical input and delivers reproducible results.

2 Method

2.1 Data Acquisition Protocol

pCT liver scans for 5 patients with colorectal liver metastases (receiving systematic chemotherapy), obtained at baseline and 2–8 weeks after commencement of therapy were analyzed (10 volumes). At each scanning session, a dynamic CT sequence was performed, with a temporal sampling of one image per second for 45 s after injection of iodinated contrast at 5 ml/s via a pump injector. This results in a 4D data set comprised of 45 3D CT volumes. Each volume in this 4D data set, contains 8 slices (voxel size (mm) = [0.7012 0.7012 5], slice size (voxels) = [512 512 8]). The patient was instructed to hold their breath throughout and breath in a shallow fashion, if necessary. However, substantial motion was observed in some data sets, necessitating appropriate registration.

2.2 Registration

We propose a twofold registration framework which consists of an initial rigid step, followed by a diffeomorphic one. For each 4D patient dataset, we chose one volume in time, the middle volume of the time sequence, as a reference and registered the remaining 44 3D volumes in time to it.

In the first step, we adapted the classic block-matching technique [18]. Due to the limited anatomical information in the z-axis and the thickness of the slices, we chose to detect the correspondences in the two input volumes using 2D axial blocks rather than 3D ones. The search was performed in the 3D space in the usual way, using the normalized cross-correlation as similarity measure between 2D blocks. The obtained 3D displacement field was regularized with the least trimmed squared regression [19] using a cutoff of 0.75 to estimate a global rigid transformation. The changes in intensity contrast pose difficulties to registration, in spite of the locally used similarity measure. To solve this problem we computed the local phase images from each axial slice using the monogenic signal [20]. The adapted block-matching scheme was then applied to those local phase images instead of the original intensity volumes.

Next, we used this global rigid estimate to initialize a feature-based diffeomorphic registration which relied on both intensity and local phase values. Here, we employed a hybrid approach originally designed to deal with breathing motion in sequences of 2D US images of the liver [21]. The registration was driven by two types of forces estimated from the intensity and local phase values: Demons forces and block-matching correspondences. The smoothed updates yielded by each force were combined into a final deformation field. As above, the block-matching was performed in 3D using 2D blocks. However, the Demons forces were estimated using the entire 3D information.

2.3   Perfusion Analysis

Following registration of the data, three models were implemented to extract a family of perfusion variables - the gradient method [6] and the selective model fitting approach of two pharmacokinetic models, the Extended Kety model [17] and the Dual-input one-compartment model [16]. These models required identifying regions of interest (ROIs) in the aorta, portal vein and the spleen, which was performed by a radiologist. Additionally, the radiologist delineated the whole liver to reduce computation time and only limit analysis to relevant areas.

The procedure first described by Miles et al. [6] was followed to calculate HAP, HPP and HPI on a per voxel basis. Maps of the liver, for each one of these three perfusion parameters, were created.

The Extended Kety model (Fig. 2(a)) and the Dual-input one-compartment model (Fig. 2(b)) were implemented as described by [17] and [16] respectively. For the first model, three parameters (Ve, Vp, Ktrans) were optimized to fit the curve of each liver voxel. For the second model, three parameters (ka, kp, k2) were optimized. Mean square values (MSE) were calculated to evaluate the goodness of fit for both models.

2.4   Tissue Classification

Support Vector Machine (SVM) was used to classify hepatic tissue as either normal or tumourous based on perfusion features: HAP, HPP, HPI, ka, kp, k2, Ve, Vp, Ktrans, MSE_1, MSE_2; where MSE_1, MSE_2 are the mean square error values for the Dual-input one-compartment model and the Extended Kety model respectively. Additionally, x and y coordinates of each voxel within a slice were included as separate features in the classification to reflect spatial information. SVM was implemented using the '$svm - lib$' toolbox [22]. Normal and tumour tissue regions were delineated by a radiologist; this information was used to extract a training set and later assess classification performance.

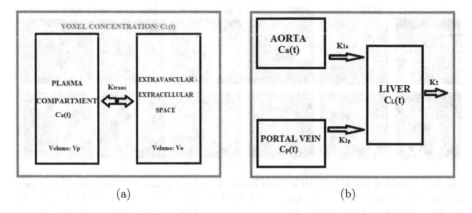

Fig. 2. (a) Extended Kety model: C_L - liver voxel concentration, C_a - arterial input, Vp - volume of the plasma compartment and Ve - volume of the extravascular - extracellular space. (b) Dual-input one-compartment model for hepatic perfusion: C_p denotes the tracer concentrations in portal vein respectively; k_{1a}, k_{1p} and k_2 denote the constants for arterial inflow, portal venous inflow and liver outflow.

Three key variables were varied to explore the performance of classification: size of training set, content of training set and number of perfusion features included into the SVM. The size of the training set was varied between 10 %– 60 % of the radiologist's delineation of normal and tumour hepatic tissue, in order to determine the minimum clinical input required to achieve satisfactory classification results for the rest of the liver. The contents of the training set were varied randomly to evaluate reproducibility of classification outcome (10-fold cross validation). The perfusion features in each training set were ranked according to their correlation with outcome; the number of features included in the SVM was varied following the order of ranking. The overlap between the automated classification and the radiologist's delineation was assessed by calculating the respective sensitivity, specificity and Jaccard index values; the dependence of these four metrics on size of training set, content of training set and number of perfusion features included into the SVM was also recorded.

3 Results

3.1 Perfusion Analysis Maps

The perfusion parameters derived were used to construct perfusion maps and some illustrative examples are included in Fig. 3. It was observed that certain parameters are clear indicators of the perfusion differences between normal and tumour tissue. However, for different patients, a different set of parameters would contain that information, with MSE2, HPP, Ka, Kp and Vp being the most common ones. Tumours were seen to have decreased HPP values compared to normal tissue; the HAP values were observed to be increased on the edge of

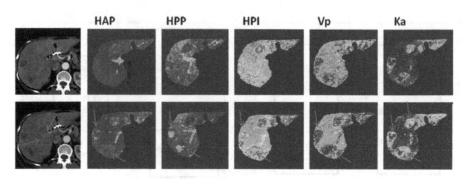

Fig. 3. Perfusion maps created on the basis of various perfusion parameters - upper row non-registered, lower row registered. Red arrows are included in the images to highlight regions where registration has a visible effect on perfusion outcomes (Color figure online).

most tumours but unchanged/decreased in its core, consistent with a necrotic core hypothesis.

The registration was seen to improve the outcomes for most perfusion parameters. We use one resolution level in the estimation of the global rigid transformation and two levels in the deformable step. The size of the blocks is $[9 \times 9]$ and the neighbourhood is $[17 \times 17 \times 8]$. Figure 3 (first column from left to right) shows an example of the average overlap of one slice across the temporal dimension before (top) and after (bottom) registration. We can clearly see that big blood vessels are better defined and the boundaries of tumours are sharper. The definition of the portal vein is crucial to perfusion analysis, as it is used as an input for the models employed.

3.2   Liver Tissue Classification

Tissue classification was performed for each data set, based on varying training set size and contents, as well as a varying number of perfusion features used to train the classification algorithm. Binary maps of normal and tumour hepatic tissue were created and these were compared to the manual radiologist's delineations for validations. Figure 4 visualizes the results for a particular data set: the amount of false negative values decreases with registration, improving the sensitivity of the classification (from 0.90 to 0.96). Including spatial information in the classification was observed to improve results - for the example in Fig. 4, sensitivity of 0.82 and specificity of 0.77 were recorded with no spatial information and 0.96 and 0.98 respectively, with spatial information. The number of features and the amount of data employed in training the algorithm were observed to affect the outcomes of the classification. Results for all patients are summarized in Fig. 5, including a comparison before and after registration. The reproducibility of results was assessed by calculating the standard deviation (as a percentage of the mean) for all metrics across all 10-fold cross validation

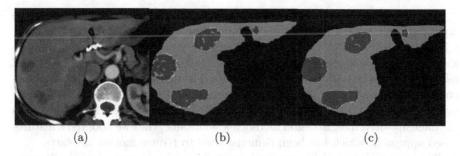

(a)   (b)   (c)

Fig. 4. Classification of hepatic tissue based on 20 % training set and two spatial features plus three perfusion features (HPP, ka and kp) for non-registered (b) and registered (c) data. True negative values - blue, true positive values - red, false negatives - orange, false positives - green. The registered pCT image is included for comparison (a) (Color figure online).

	1a	1a_reg	1b	1b_reg	2a	2a_reg	2b	2b_reg	3a	3a_reg	3b	3b_reg	4a	4a_reg	4b	4b_reg	5a	5a_reg	5b	5b_reg
Training features	MSE2, K2	MSE2, HPP	MSE2, Vp	MSE2, HPP	Vp, Kp	Ka, Kp	Vp, MSE2	HPP, Vp	MSE2, Vp	Vp, MSE2	Vp, MSE2	Ka, Kp	HPP, Ka	HPP, Kp	Ka, MSE2	MSE2, K2	Vp, K2	Vp, HPP	Vp, MSE2	Vp, K_trans
Sensitivity	0.952	0.953	0.939	0.953	0.929	0.931	0.991	0.990	0.990	0.990	0.920	0.931	0.965	0.954	0.986	0.986	0.968	0.964	0.948	0.961
Std Sensitivity*	1.17%	0.76%	1.23%	0.90%	2.52%	1.76%	0.13%	0.15%	0.12%	0.09%	1.92%	3.46%	0.38%	0.89%	0.19%	0.19%	0.62%	0.40%	1.19%	0.73%
Specificity	0.994	0.994	0.996	0.996	0.998	0.998	0.983	0.988	0.987	0.988	0.998	0.998	0.983	0.982	0.987	0.985	0.984	0.983	0.991	0.991
Std Specificity*	0.06%	0.10%	0.07%	0.06%	0.04%	0.03%	0.17%	0.19%	0.16%	0.20%	0.03%	0.04%	0.14%	0.18%	0.16%	0.11%	0.20%	0.18%	0.11%	0.16%
Jaccard index	0.917	0.931	0.916	0.918	0.876	0.873	0.981	0.985	0.984	0.980	0.860	0.872	0.954	0.942	0.988	0.974	0.928	0.922	0.919	0.928
Std Jaccard*	0.46%	0.40%	0.46%	0.40%	0.95%	0.92%	0.32%	0.25%	0.56%	0.22%	1.50%	1.29%	0.13%	0.26%	0.16%	0.04%	0.32%	0.25%	0.36%	0.22%
Displacement field (voxels)	2.178		2.252		2.344		2.614		2.654		2.955		3.132		3.638		3.893		5.134	

Fig. 5. Changes in sensitivity, specificity and Jaccard index across different patient sets, before and after registration. For each metric, standard deviation values (*) across 10-fold cross validation iterations are reported as a percentage of the respective mean values. Results are reported for training sets that are 20 % of the hepatic tissue delineated by the radiologist and classification based on two spatial variables plus the first two perfusion features that have been selected to be most relevant based on the training set, as described before. The patient data sets are denoted by number and a subscript letter, where 'a' refers to data at treatment start and 'b' to data acquired 2–8 weeks after that.

iterations (Fig. 5); all standard deviation values were observed to be below 4 %. Registration was observed to improve all four metrics across most data sets, especially for the data set with biggest deformation field. Sensitivity was observed to be in the range of 0.92–0.99, specificity in the range 0.98–0.99, and Jaccard index in the range 0.86–0.98, where all these values were calculated as averages across the 10-fold cross validation iterations. Additionally, specificity was seen to be maximized when less features were used (e.g. two features); whereas sensitivity was maximized when more features were included.

4   Conclusions

We have presented a structured quantitative method of analyzing liver perfusion changes on the basis of pCT data. This approach has three essential elements - registration, perfusion analysis and tissue characterization.

The registration method presented handles two issues which stem from the input data. First, pCT volumes are highly anisotropic (voxel size is [0.703 mm X 0.703 mm X 5 mm]) and consist of only 8 axial slices which offers limited anatomical content. Consequently, our registration needs to be robust enough without relying on much data down-sampling required in multi-resolution schemes. Second, the alignment of volumes across the temporal dimension resembles a multimodal registration problem, due to the injected perfusion contrast. This makes the intensity-driven registration methods less suitable; thus we adopted a feature-based approach, which has been demonstrated to reduce motion artefacts.

Three perfusion models were implemented in order to extract clinically valuable information. Perfusion parameters, derived from pharmacokinetic models, have the advantage of being intensity invariant. This would be of particular importance if this technique were used to analyze treatment response and a patient were scanned repeatedly. The characterization of hepatic tissue based on perfusion parameters delivered promising outcome for training sets as little as 20 % of the liver data. Moreover, the 10-fold cross validation, employing different randomly selected voxels for training, delivered little differences in sensitivity and specificity ($\pm 4\%$), which provides confidence in the reproducibility of the classification method. This analysis indicates that it is feasible to obtain clinically valuable functional imaging information from pCT data; moreover, this information could be used to characterize hepatic tissue in a semi-automated manner.

A potential clinical application could be a semi-automated characterization of metastases from pCT images: a clinician looks at a pCT image and identifies two small regions that they can classify with certainty - one tumourous and one normal; the classifier is trained on those initial inputs and the algorithm is then used to classify the rest of the liver. The above application would deliver personalized analysis of pCT data. The structured quantitative analysis of pCT data proposed could characterize the development of metastases, in terms of disease progression and response to treatment. To further improve and validate these suggestions, a study with a bigger population set, as well as 'ground truth' delineations from multiple radiologists, should be conducted.

Acknowledgments. This research has been supported by the Cancer Research UK and EPSRC Cancer Imaging Centre at Oxford. A.C would like to acknowledge the Oxford EPSRC IAA funding. E.H. is grateful to Oxfordshire Health Services Research Committee and CRUK/ESPRC Imaging Centre for her clinical research fellowship. E.N. also wishes to acknowledge the support of the RCUK Digital Economy Programme (Oxford Centre for Doctoral Training in Healthcare Innovation).

References

1. GLOBOCAN2012: International agency for research on cancer. http://globocan. iarc.fr/Pages/fact_sheets_cancer.aspx. Accessed June 2014
2. Miles, K.A., Griffiths, M.R.: Perfusion CT: a worthwhile enhancement? Br. J. Radiol. **76**, 220–231 (2003)

3. Beers, B.E.V., Leconte, I., Materne, R., Smith, A.M., Jamart, J., Horsmans, Y.: Hepatic perfusion parameters in chronic liver disease: dynamic CT measurements correlated with disease severity. Am. J. Roent. **176**, 667–673 (2001)
4. Tsushima, Y., Blomley, M.J.K., Kusano, S., Endo, K.: The portal component of hepatic perfusion measured by dynamic CT: an indicator of hepatic parenchymal damage. Dig. Dis. Sci. **44**, 1632–1638 (1999)
5. Dugdale, P.E., Miles, K.A., Bunce, I., Kelley, B.B., Leggett, D.A.C.: CT measurement of perfusion and permeability within lymphoma masses and its ability to assess grade, activity, and chemotherapeutic response. J. Comp. Assis. Tom. **23**, 540–547 (1999)
6. Miles, K.A., Hayball, M.P., Dixon, A.K.: Functional images of hepatic perfusion obtained with dynamic CT. Radiology **188**, 405–411 (1993)
7. Harvey, C.J., Blomley, M.J.K., Dawson, P., Morgan, J.A., et al.: Functional CT imaging of the acute hyperemic response to radiation therapy of the prostate gland: early experience. J. Comp. Assis. Tom. **25**, 43–49 (2001)
8. Harvey, C., Dooher, A., Morgan, J., Blomley, M., Dawson, P.: Imaging of tumour therapy responses by dynamic CT. Eur. J. Rad. **30**, 221–226 (1999)
9. Meijerink, M.R., van Waesberghe, J.H.T.M., van der Weide, L., van den Tol, P., et al.: Early detection of local RFA site recurrence using total liver volume perfusion CT. initial experience. Acad. Radiol. **16**, 1215–1222 (2009)
10. Gillard, J., Antoun, N., Pickard, N.B.J.: Reproducibility of quantitative CT perfusion imaging. Br. J. Radiol. **74**(882), 552–555 (2001)
11. Gandhi, D., Chepeha, D.B., Miller, T.: Correlation between initial and early follow-up ct perfusion parameters with endoscopic tumour response in patients with advanced squamous cell carcinomas of the oropharynx treated with organ-preservation therapy. AJNR Am. J. Neuroradiol. (2006)
12. Ng, C.S., Chandler, A.G., Herron, W.W.D., Anderson, E.F., Kurzrock, R., Charn-sangavej, C.: Reproducibility of CT perfusion parameters in liver tumours and normal liver. Radiology **260**, 762–770 (2011)
13. Chandler, A., Wei, W., Anderson, E.F., Herron, D.H., Ye, Z., Ng, C.S.: Validation of motion correction techniques for liver CT perfusion studies. Br. J. Radiol. **85**, e514–e522 (2012)
14. Romain, B., Lucidarme, O., Dauguet, J., Mul, S., et al.: Registration and functional analysis of ct dynamic image sequences for the follow-up of patients with hepatic tumors undergoing antiangiogenic therapy. IRBM **31**, 263–270 (2010)
15. Banerji, A., Naish, J.H., Watson, Y., Jayson, G.C., Buonaccorsi, G.A., Parker, G.J.: DCE-MRI model selection for investigating disruption of microvascular function in livers with metastatic disease. J. Magn. Res. Im. **35**, 196–203 (2012)
16. Materne, R., Beers, B.V., Smith, A., Leconte, I., et al.: Non-invasive quantification of liver perfusion with dynamic computed tomography and a dual-input one-compartmental model. Clin. Scien. **99**, 517–525 (2000)
17. Tofts, P.S.: Modeling tracer kinetics in dynamic Gd-DTPA MR imaging. J. Magn. Reson. Imaging **7**, 91–101 (1997)
18. Ourselin, S., Roche, A., Subsol, G., Pennec, X., Ayache, N.: Reconstructing a 3D structure from serial histological sections. Image Vis. Comput. **19**, 25–31 (2001)
19. Rousseeuw, P.: Least median of squares regression. J. Am. Stat. Assoc. **79**, 871–880 (1984)
20. Felsberg, M., Sommer, G.: The monogenic signal. IEEE Trans. Sig. Process **49**, 3136–3144 (2001)

21. Cifor, A., Risser, L., Heinrich, M.P., Chung, D., Schnabel, J.A.: Hybrid feature-based diffeomorphic registration for tumour tracking in 2-D liver ultrasound images. IEEE Trans. Med. Imaging **32**, 1647–1656 (2013)
22. Chang, C.C., Lin, C.J.: Libsvm. http://www.csie.ntu.edu.tw/cjlin/libsvm/. Accessed June 2014

Parameter Comparison Between Fast-Water-Exchange-Limit-Constrained Standard and Water-Exchange-Modified Dual-Input Tracer Kinetic Models for DCE-MRI in Advanced Hepatocellular Carcinoma

Sang Ho Lee[1(✉)], Koichi Hayano[2], Dushyant V. Sahani[2], Andrew X. Zhu[3], and Hiroyuki Yoshida[1]

[1] 3D Imaging Research, Department of Radiology, Massachusetts General Hospital and Harvard Medical School, 25 New Chardon St., Suite 400C, Boston, MA 02114, USA
{lee.sangho,yoshida.hiro}@mgh.harvard.edu

[2] Division of Abdominal Imaging and Intervention, Department of Radiology, Massachusetts General Hospital, 55 Fruit St., Boston, MA, USA
{khayano,dsahani}@partners.org

[3] Division of Hematology and Oncology, Department of Medicine, Massachusetts General Hospital Cancer Center, Harvard Medical School, and Dana-Farber/Partners Cancer Care, 55 Fruit St., Boston, MA 02114, USA
azhu@partners.org

Abstract. Dynamic contrast-enhanced MRI (DCE-MRI) data have often been analyzed using classic standard tracer kinetic models that assume a fast-exchange limit (FXL) of water. Recently, it has been demonstrated that deviations from the FXL model occurs when contrast agent arrives at the target tissue. However, no systematic analysis has been reported for the liver tumor with dual blood supply. In this study, we compared kinetic parameter estimates from DCE-MRI in advanced hepatocellular carcinoma that have the same physiological meaning between five different FXL standard dual-input tracer kinetic models and their corresponding water-exchange-modified (WX) versions. Kinetic parameters were estimated by fitting data to analytic solutions of five different FXL models and their WX versions based on a full two-site-exchange model for transcyto-lemmal water exchange or a full three-site-two-exchange model for transendo-thelial and transcytolemmal water exchange. Results suggest that parameter values differ substantially between the FXL standard and WX tracer kinetic models, indicating that DCE-MRI data are water-exchange-sensitive.

Keywords: Hepatocellular carcinoma · Dual-input tracer kinetic analysis · Water exchange · Dynamic contrast-enhanced MRI

© Springer International Publishing Switzerland 2014
H. Yoshida et al. (Eds.): ABDI 2014, LNCS 8676, pp. 33–47, 2014.
DOI: 10.1007/978-3-319-13692-9_4

1   Introduction

Dynamic contrast-enhanced MRI (DCE-MRI) enables quantification of the vascular characteristics of tissue and tumor [1], and has a potential role in monitoring hepatocellular carcinoma (HCC) response to systemic therapy [2]. Assessment of hemodynamic changes in the liver is especially challenging because of the dual blood supply to this organ [3]. The ability to accurately quantify the proportions of blood supply to HCC from the hepatic arterial system and from the portal venous system in vivo, as well as the microvascular density of the tumor tissue, may be of clinical value for diagnosis and treatment. Indeed, dual-input tracer kinetic models of DCE-MRI have become increasingly important for quantitative analysis of hepatic perfusion [4, 5].

Accurate estimation of kinetic parameters from DCE-MRI data still remains a challenging issue, especially when additional model parameters, such as intercompartmental water exchange rates, are included [6]. A tissue voxel typically consists of four water-containing compartments, two cellular compartments (red blood cells (RBC), and parenchyma cells) and two extracellular compartments (plasma space and interstitial space). It is widely accepted that water exchange between RBC and plasma is extremely rapid because of the high water permeability of the RBC membrane [7], and thus plasma and RBC can be considered a single water compartment with a single T1. The most commonly used models of tracer kinetics do not take into account the water exchange, which effectively assume that water exchange is in the fast exchange limit (FXL) [8]. This assumption enables the model to use a simple linear relationship between the relaxation rate of the tissue and the contrast agent (CA) concentration in the tissue. However, using this assumption may lead to underestimates of tissue CA concentration and inaccurate estimates of kinetic parameters [9] because the dependence of the relaxation rate on CA can be changed from the linear relationship to nonlinear dependences in tissue when the compartmental distributions of CA and water molecules are different [10]. Nevertheless, the importance of vascular-interstitial (transendothelial) and cellular-interstitial (transcytolemmal) water exchange in the analysis of DCE-MRI data is still debatable [11].

Water exchange would have a quantifiable effect on clinical T1-weighted DCE-MRI parameter estimates particularly when DCE-MRI data are acquired using a low flip angle [12]. Several variations of the tracer kinetic model have been proposed to evaluate the effect of water exchange on estimates of kinetic parameters including the two-site-exchange (2SX) and three-site-two-exchange (3S2X) models [6]. To date, there is no study that systematically compares DCE-MRI perfusion measurements between FXL standard dual-input tracer kinetic models and their corresponding water exchange-modified (WX) versions with different physiologic scenarios in the capillary-tissue system for the liver. The aim of this study was to compare kinetic parameter estimates and address the question of whether they are different or similar between the FXL standard model and its WX version, with use of five different dual-input tracer kinetic models, in the analysis of DCE-MRI data in advanced HCC.

2 Methods

2.1 Dual-Input Function

The liver receives blood from the hepatic artery and the portal vein, so the net input function $C_{in}(t)$ is modeled as a weighted sum of the two input functions: $C_{in}(t) = \gamma C_A(t) + (1 - \gamma)C_{PV}(t)$, where γ, $C_A(t)$, and $C_{PV}(t)$ are the arterial flow fraction, arterial blood concentration (in g/ml), and portal blood concentration (in g/ml), respectively. Each of $C_A(t)$ and $C_{PV}(t)$ was modeled as the superposition of a bolus shape (first-pass) and its shape after modification by the body transfer function (recirculation), describing a sums-of-exponentials function [13]. By each imposing the time lags of the first-pass bolus arrival to the hepatic artery and the portal vein ($t_{Lag,A1}$ and $t_{Lag,PV1}$), and those from the first-pass to the recirculation onset ($t_{Lag,A2}$ and $t_{Lag,PV2}$), $C_A(t)$ and $C_{PV}(t)$ become

$$
\begin{aligned}
C_A(t) = {}& a_{B,A}\left(t - t_{Lag,A1}\right)e^{-\mu_{B,A}\left(t-t_{Lag,A1}\right)}u\left(t - t_{Lag,A1}\right) \\
& - \frac{a_{B,A}a_{G,A}}{\mu_{B,A} - \mu_{G,A}}\left\{ \left(t-t_{Lag,A1} - t_{Lag,A2}\right)e^{-\mu_{B,A}\left(t-t_{Lag,A1}-t_{Lag,A2}\right)} \right. \\
& \left. - \frac{1}{\mu_{B,A} - \mu_{G,A}}\left(e^{-\mu_{G,A}\left(t-t_{Lag,A1}-t_{Lag,A2}\right)} - e^{-\mu_{B,A}\left(t-t_{Lag,A1}-t_{Lag,A2}\right)}\right)\right\} \\
& \times u\left(t - t_{Lag,A1} - t_{Lag,A2}\right),
\end{aligned}
\tag{1}
$$

$$
\begin{aligned}
C_{PV}(t) = {}& a_{B,PV}\left(t - t_{Lag,PV1}\right)e^{-\mu_{B,PV}\left(t-t_{Lag,PV1}\right)} \cdot u\left(t - t_{Lag,PV1}\right) \\
& - \frac{a_{B,PV}a_{G,PV}}{\mu_{B,PV} - \mu_{G,PV}}\left\{ \left(t - t_{Lag,PV1} - t_{Lag,PV2}\right)e^{-\mu_{B,PV}\left(t-t_{Lag,PV1}-t_{Lag,PV2}\right)} \right. \\
& \left. - \frac{1}{\mu_{B,PV} - \mu_{G,PV}}\left(e^{-\mu_{G,PV}\left(t-t_{Lag,PV1}-t_{Lag,PV2}\right)} - e^{-\mu_{B,PV}\left(t-t_{Lag,PV1}-t_{Lag,PV2}\right)}\right)\right\} \\
& \times u\left(t - t_{Lag,PV1} - t_{Lag,PV2}\right),
\end{aligned}
\tag{2}
$$

where $u(t)$ is the unit step function.

2.2 Tracer Kinetic Modeling

We consider dual-input sources of the plasma flow F to the liver: arterial plasma flow F_A, and portal plasma flow F_{PV}. Assuming that $C_A(t)$ and $C_{PV}(t)$ can be sampled from DCE-MR images, the concentration in tissue, $C_T(t)$, can be expressed as follows:

$$
C_T(t) = \left\{ v_P Q_P\left(t - t_{Lag,T}\right) + v_I Q_I\left(t - t_{Lag,T}\right)\right\} \otimes \frac{C_{in}(t)}{1 - H_{LV}} = v_P \bar{C}_P(t) + v_I \bar{C}_I(t),
\tag{3}
$$

where H_{LV} is the hematocrit of blood in large vessels ($\cong 0.45$) [14], v_P is the fractional plasma volume, v_I is the fractional interstitial volume, $Q_P(t)$ is the impulse response function of the plasma compartment (in ml/min/ml), $Q_I(t)$ is the impulse response function of the interstitial compartment (in ml/min/ml), $t_{\text{Lag,T}}$ is the time lag (delay) (in min) to account for the difference in bolus arrival time between $C_{\text{in}}(t)$ and $C_T(t)$, $\bar{C}_P(t)$ is the spatially averaged CA concentration of the plasma compartment, $\bar{C}_I(t)$ is the spatially averaged CA concentration of the interstitial compartment, and $\otimes$ is the convolution operator, respectively. We analyzed the DCE-MRI data with use of five different kinetic models: the Tofts-Kety (TK) model [15], extended TK (ETK) model [16], two-compartment exchange (2CX) model [17], adiabatic approximation to the tissue homogeneity (AATH) model [18], and distributed parameter (DP) model [19]. The $Q_P(t)$ and $Q_I(t)$ for the five models are given by

$$Q_{I,\text{TK}}(t) = \frac{v_P}{v_I}\frac{EF}{V_P}e^{-\frac{v_P EF}{v_I V_P}t},\tag{4}$$

$$Q_{P,\text{ETK}}(t) = \delta(t) \text{ and } Q_{I,\text{ETK}}(t) = \frac{v_P}{v_I}\frac{EF}{V_P}e^{-\frac{v_P EF}{v_I V_P}t},\tag{5}$$

$$Q_{P,2\text{CX}}(t) = \frac{F}{V_P}\left\{Be^{\alpha t} + (1-B)e^{\beta t}\right\}$$

$$\text{and } Q_{I,2\text{CX}}(t) = \frac{v_P}{v_I}\frac{F}{V_P}(A-B)\left(e^{\alpha t} - e^{\beta t}\right)$$

$$\text{with } A = \frac{\alpha + \left(1+\frac{v_P}{v_I}\right)\frac{PS}{V_P}}{\alpha - \beta} \text{ and } B = A - \frac{\frac{PS}{V_P}}{\alpha - \beta},$$

$$\text{where } \binom{\alpha}{\beta} = \frac{1}{2}\left[-\left\{\frac{F}{V_P} + \left(1+\frac{v_P}{v_I}\right)\frac{PS}{V_P}\right\} \pm \sqrt{\left\{\frac{F}{V_P} + \left(1+\frac{v_P}{v_I}\right)\frac{PS}{V_P}\right\}^2 - 4\frac{v_P}{v_I}\frac{F}{V_P}\frac{PS}{V_P}}\right],\tag{6}$$

$$Q_{P,\text{AATH}}(t) = \frac{F}{V_P}\left\{u(t) - u\left(t - \frac{V_P}{F}\right)\right\}$$

$$\text{and } Q_{I,\text{AATH}}(t) = \frac{v_P}{v_I}\frac{EF}{V_P}u\left(t - \frac{V_P}{F}\right)e^{-\frac{v_P EF}{v_I V_P}\left(t-\frac{V_P}{F}\right)},\tag{7}$$

$$Q_{P,\text{DP}}(t) = \frac{F}{V_P}\left\{u(t) - u\left(t - \frac{V_P}{F}\right)\right\}$$

$$\text{and } Q_{I,\text{DP}}(t) \cong \frac{v_P}{v_I}\frac{F}{V_P}\left[1 - e^{-\frac{PS}{F}}\left\{1 + \frac{v_P}{v_I}\frac{PS}{V_P}\frac{PS}{F}\left(t - \frac{V_P}{F}\right)\right\}\right]u\left(t - \frac{V_P}{F}\right),\tag{8}$$

where $Q_{P,\text{ETK}}(t)$, $Q_{P,2\text{CX}}(t)$, $Q_{P,\text{AATH}}(t)$, and $Q_{P,\text{DP}}(t)$ represent $Q_P(t)$ for the ETK, 2CX, AATH, and DP models, and $Q_{I,\text{TK}}(t)$, $Q_{I,\text{ETK}}(t)$, $Q_{I,2\text{CX}}(t)$, $Q_{I,\text{AATH}}(t)$, and $Q_{I,\text{DP}}(t)$ represent $Q_I(t)$ for the TK, ETK, 2CX, AATH, and DP models, respectively. Note that $Q_P(t)$ and $\bar{C}_P$ for the TK model do not apply because of the assumption that $v_P \ll v_I$ in the TK model [16], and that $Q_{I,\text{DP}}(t)$ is approximated using the first two terms of the Taylor series solution for the parenchyma phase [19]. Here, $\delta(t)$, V_P, PS, and $E = 1 - e^{-PS/F}$ denote the Dirac delta function, plasma volume (in ml), capillary wall permeability-surface area product (in ml/min), and extraction fraction, respectively. $\overline{C}_P(t)$, $\overline{C}_I(t)$, and $C_T(t)$ for each model can be derived as fully continuous-time functional forms by incorporating the dual-input functions, $C_A(t)$ and $C_{PV}(t)$ in Eqs. (1) and (2).

2.3   Water Exchange Modeling and MR Signal Intensity

To incorporate water exchange with each kinetic model, an intracellular pool is added as a third compartment, where the transcytolemmal water exchange is described by the mean intracellular water molecule lifetime τ_C (in sec). The effect of water exchange on the estimation of kinetic parameters is assessed based on a full 2SX model for the WX-TK model or a full 3S2X model for the WX-ETK, WX-2CX, WX-AATH, WX-DP models. Because the transendothelial water exchange is related to PS or extraction-flow product EF (in ml/min) depending on a kinetic model used, use of a fixed or predetermined water exchange rate constant would be to assume a limited value for PS (or EF) [11]. As an alternative, we assume that the transendothelial water exchange behavior is much like the tracer exchange behavior between the plasma and interstitial compartment. Therefore, the dependence of the transendothelial water exchange on PS (or EF) and that of the transcytolemmal water exchange on τ_C are specified mathematically, then they are constrained during fitting each kinetic model.

The decay of longitudinal magnetization M_q in the whole blood, interstitial space, and parenchyma cells (with q = B, I, and C, respectively) can be described by the following coupled Bloch-McConnell equations [20]:

$$\frac{d\mathbf{M}}{dt} = \mathbf{X}\mathbf{M} + \mathbf{C}, \tag{9}$$

where $\mathbf{M} = [M_B(t), M_I(t), M_C(t)]^T$, $\mathbf{C} = [R_{10B}M_{0B}, R_{10I}M_{0I}, R_{10C}M_{0C}]^T$, and

$$\mathbf{X} = \begin{bmatrix} -(R_{10B} + K_{BI}) & K_{IB} & 0 \\ K_{BI} & -(R_{10I} + K_{IB} + K_{IC}) & K_{CI} \\ 0 & K_{IC} & -(R_{10C} + K_{CI}) \end{bmatrix}, \tag{10}$$

where $\mathbf{X}$ is the exchange matrix of the 3S2X model, and K_{qr} denotes the rate of transfer of magnetization from compartment q to compartment r. The M_{0q} is the equilibrium magnetization in compartment q, and R_{10q} ($= 1/T_{10q}$) denotes the native longitudinal relaxation rate. Here it is assumed that the direct exchange of water between blood and parenchyma cells is negligible. The 3S2X of water between compartment q and r requires that $K_{qr}M_{0q} = K_{rq}M_{0r}$ [20]. The K_{qr} can be also expressed in terms of water mean lifetimes (τ_B, τ_I, and τ_C (in sec)) and volume fractions of the three compartments by keeping mass balance $K_{BI} = 1/\tau_B$, $K_{IC} = 1/\tau_I - (v_B/v_I)/\tau_B$, $K_{IB} = 1/\tau_I - (v_C/v_I)/\tau_C$, and $K_{CI} = 1/\tau_C$, where $v_B = v_P/(1 - H_{SV})$ is the fractional blood volume, and H_{SV} is the fractional blood volume, and H_{SV} is the hematocrit in small vessels ($\cong 0.25$) [14]. The three mean lifetimes are related by $v_I/\tau_I = v_B/\tau_B + v_C/\tau_C$ [6]. Here we assume that the water fraction in each compartment is 1 for simplicity [21, 22]. The longitudinal magnetization evolving from a 3S2X model can be expressed as a linear sum of the three compartmental longitudinal magnetizations (i.e., $M(t) = M_B(t) + M_I(t) + M_C(t)$). The transcytolemmal water exchange rate is related to τ_C, which is the ratio of the intracellular volume V_C (in ml) to the cell membrane permeability-surface area product PS_C (in ml/min). The cell to interstitium water transfer rate, K_{CI}, is given by [9]

$$K_{CI} = \frac{1}{\tau_C} = 60\frac{PS_C}{V_C} = 60\frac{PS_C}{v_C V_T}, \tag{11}$$

where $V_B/V_T + V_I/V_T + V_C/V_T = v_B + v_I + v_C = 1$, V_T is the tissue volume (in ml), V_B is the blood volume (in ml), V_I is the interstitial volume (in ml), and v_C is the fractional intracellular volume, respectively. The constant 60 is used to convert the time-scale from minutes to seconds. On the other hand, the transendothelial water exchange rate is related to PS (or EF). According to the physiologic assumption of each kinetic model, the CA is exchanged between the plasma and interstitial compartments by EF in the ETK and AATH models, whereas it is exchanged by PS in the 2CX and DP models. Thus, the blood to interstitium water transfer rate, K_{BI}, is constrained with the parameters to take into account the transendothelial tracer exchange for the 3S2X model:

$$K_{BI} = \frac{1}{\tau_B} = \begin{cases} 60\frac{PS}{V_B} & \text{for WX - 2CX and WX - DP models} \\ 60\frac{EF}{V_B} & \text{for WX - ETK and WX - AATH models} \end{cases}, \tag{12}$$

Note that K_{BI} (or K_{IB}) does not apply to the WX-TK model because it assumes that $v_P \ll v_I$ in the estimate of $C_T(t)$ [23]. Like the formalism presented in Eqs. (11) and (12), the interstitium to cell water transfer K_{IC} and the interstitium to blood water transfer K_{IB} can be given by

$$K_{IC} = \frac{1}{\tau_I} - \frac{v_B}{v_I}\frac{1}{\tau_B} = 60\frac{PS_C}{V_I} = 60\frac{PS_C}{v_I V_T}, \tag{13}$$

$$K_{IB} = \frac{1}{\tau_I} - \frac{v_C}{v_I}\frac{1}{\tau_C} = \begin{cases} 60\frac{PS}{V_I} & \text{for WX - 2CX and WX - DP models} \\ 60\frac{EF}{V_I} & \text{for WX - ETK and WX - AATH models} \end{cases}. \tag{14}$$

In the absence of CA, it is assumed that the water exchange system is in the FXL [23]. The FXL condition is also maintained to estimate the postcontrast relaxation rate $R_1(t)$ only in the dual feeding vessels during CA passage because they both consist of a single blood pool. After administration of CA, T1 can be replaced under the FXL condition by: $R_1(t) = 1/T_1(t) = R_{10} + r_1 C_T(t) = 1/T_{10} + r_1 C_T(t)$, where r_1 is the spin-lattice relaxivity, $R_1(t)$ and R_{10} are the post- and precontrast relaxation rates (in sec^{-1}), and $T_1(t)$ and T_{10} are the post- and precontrast T1 values (in sec), respectively. The relaxivities in tissue are assumed to be equal to those in aqueous solution ($r_1 = 4.5$ s^{-1} mM^{-1}, $r_2 = 5.5$ s^{-1} mM^{-1} at 21 °C and 1.5 T, where r_2 is the spin-spin relaxivity) [24]. The signal intensity obtained from a spoiled gradient echo sequence in the FXL as given by the Ernst-Anderson equation is [24]

$$S_T(t) = g \cdot PD \cdot e^{-TE\left\{\frac{1}{T_{20}^*}+r_2 C_T(t)\right\}} \sin(\theta) \frac{1 - e^{-TR \cdot R_1(t)}}{1 - \cos(\theta)e^{-TR \cdot R_1(t)}}, \tag{15}$$

where g is the machine gain, PD is the proton density, T_{20}^* is the precontrast effective T2 value, θ is the flip angle, and $S_T(t)$ is the MR signal intensity in the tissue. In the FXL, the entire tissue relaxes with a single effective $R_1(t)$ representing the weighted average of the three compartmental R_1 s, i.e., $R_1(t) = v_B R_{1B}(t) + v_I R_{1I}(t) + v_C R_{10C}$, where $R_{1B}(t)$ and $R_{1I}(t)$ denote the postcontrast longitudinal relaxation rates within the blood and interstitial spaces, respectively.

Similarly, in the absence of CA, R_{10C} for the water exchange model is calculated by: $R_{10C} = (R_{10} - v_I R_{10I})/v_C$ for the 2SX model [23], and $R_{10C} = (R_{10} - v_B R_{10B} - v_I R_{10I})/v_C$ for the 3S2X model [25], where R_{10B} and R_{10I} are assumed to be 0.74 and 0.5 s^{-1}, respectively [21, 25]. The effect of CA in the blood and interstitial spaces can be incorporated into the exchange matrix $\mathbf{X}$ by replacing R_{10B} and R_{10I} in Eq. (10) with $R_{1B}(t) = r_{1B}(1 - H_{SV})\overline{C}_P(t) + R_{10B}$ and $R_{1I}(t) = r_{1I}\overline{C}_I(t) + R_{10I}$, where r_{1B} and r_{1I} are the respective relaxivities which are held constant as $r_{1B} = r_{1I} = r_1$. For a spoiled gradient echo acquisition, the Ernst-Anderson equation using $\mathbf{X}$ from Eq. (10) is applied to find the signal in each compartment [6, 25]:

$$\mathbf{S} = g \cdot PD \cdot e^{-TE\left\{\frac{1}{T_{20}^*}+r_2 C_T(t)\right\}} \sin(\theta)\left[\mathbf{I} - \cos(\theta)e^{TR \cdot \mathbf{X}}\right]^{-1}\left(\mathbf{I} - e^{TR \cdot \mathbf{X}}\right)\mathbf{V}, \tag{16}$$

where $\mathbf{S} = [S_B(t), S_I(t), S_C(t)]^T$, $\mathbf{V} = [v_B, v_I, v_C]^T$, $\mathbf{I}$ is the 3×3 identity matrix, and $e^{TR \cdot \mathbf{X}}$ is a matrix exponential, which can be calculated based on a scaling and squaring algorithm with a Pade approximation method [26]. The transverse relaxation rate, $R_2^*(t) = 1/T_{20}^* + r_2 C_T(t)$, is assumed to be under the FXL condition for simplicity because the T1 effects are of primary concern in this study. For no dependence on T_{20}^*, the relative signal enhancement in the tissue, $E_T(t)$, can be used as an objective function for curve-fitting of DCE-MRI data, i.e., $E_T(t) = S_T(t)/S_T(0) - 1$, where $S_T(t) = S_B(t) + S_I(t) + S_C(t)$. Therefore, $E_T(t)$ is fitted using Eq. (16) with $\overline{C}_P(t)$, $\overline{C}_I(t)$, and $C_T(t)$ for the 3S2X model (i.e., WX-ETK, WX-2CX, WX-AATH, and WX-DP models).

When CA extravasation is high, the 3S2X model can be simplified to ignore a distinct blood volume contribution, and thus the 2SX model can be used. This system can be described using a two-pool exchange formalism [27]. The solution has a bi-exponential form with the T1 relaxation of the system described by two rate constants, R_{1S} and R_{1L}, where R_{1S} and R_{1L} are the rate constants for the component with the smaller and larger T1 s, and their respective fractional apparent populations, a_L and a_S, where $a_S + a_L = 1$. For the 2SX model, a closed-form expression of MR signal intensity is given by [23]

$$S_T(t) = g \cdot PD \cdot e^{-TE\left\{\frac{1}{T_{20}^*}+r_2 C_T(t)\right\}} \sin(\theta)\left\{a_S\left(\frac{1 - e^{-TR \cdot R_{1S}(t)}}{1 - \cos(\theta)e^{-TR \cdot R_{1S}(t)}}\right)\right.$$

$$\left. + a_L\left(\frac{1 - e^{-TR \cdot R_{1L}(t)}}{1 - \cos(\theta)e^{-TR \cdot R_{1L}(t)}}\right)\right\} \text{ with } (R_{1S}(t), R_{1L}(t)) = \frac{1}{2}\left\{2R_{10C} + r_{1I}\bar{C}_I(t)\right.$$

$$\left. + \frac{R_{10} - R_{10C} + K_{CI}}{v_I} \pm \sqrt{\left(2K_{CI} - r_{1I}\bar{C}_I(t) - \frac{R_{10} - R_{10C} + K_{CI}}{v_I}\right)^2 + 4K_{CI}K_{IC}}\right\}$$

$$\text{and } a_S(t) = \frac{1}{2} - \frac{1}{2}\left\{\frac{\left(\frac{R_{10C} - R_{10}}{v_I} - r_{1I}\bar{C}_I(t)\right)(v_I - v_C) + \frac{K_{CI}}{v_I}}{\sqrt{\left(2K_{CI} - r_{1I}\bar{C}_I(t) - \frac{R_{10} - R_{10C} + K_{CI}}{v_I}\right)^2 + 4K_{CI}K_{IC}}}\right\}.$$

$$(17)$$

The $E_T(t)$ for the FXL standard models and the 2SX model is given by $E_T(t) = S_T(t)/S_T(0) - 1$. Therefore, $E_T(t)$ is fitted using Eq. (15) with $C_T(t)$ for the FXL standard model, and using Eq. (17) with $\bar{C}_I(t)$ and $C_T(t)$ for the WX-TK model. An example of fitting the five different dual-input FXL standard models and their corresponding WX models to a voxel-level tissue enhancement curve in HCC is provided in Fig. 1.

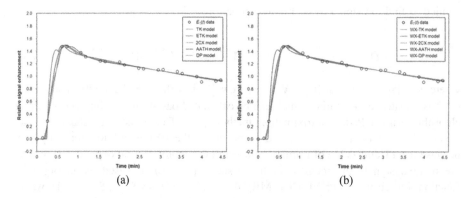

Fig. 1. Graphs illustrating examples of fitting (a) five different FXL standard dual-input tracer kinetic models and (b) their corresponding WX models to a voxel-level tissue enhancement curve which was sampled from the HCC in DCE-MRI data.

2.4 Kinetic Parameter Calculation

The parameters that can be directly estimated by parametric fitting are $\{F/V_P, \gamma, PS/V_P, v_P, v_I, t_{Lag,T}\}$ for the FXL standard models, and $\{F/V_P, \gamma, PS/V_P, v_P, v_I, \tau_C, t_{Lag,T}\}$ for the WX models. Thus, the total hepatic blood flow (BF), arterial blood flow (BF_A), portal blood flow (BF_{PV}), blood volume (BV), mean transit time (MTT) and PS

can further be computed for the FXL standard and WX models according to: $BV = 100 \cdot V_P / \{(1 - H_{SV}) \cdot m\} = 100 \cdot v_P / \{(1 - H_{SV}) \cdot \rho_T\}$ (in ml/100 g), where $m = \rho_T V_T$ is the mass of the tissue with density ρ_T (= 1.04 g/cm^3 in the case of soft tissues), $BF = BV \cdot F / V_P$ (in ml/min/100 g), $BF_A = \gamma BF$ (in ml/min/100 g), $BF_{PV} = (1 - \gamma)BF$ (in ml/min/100 g), $MTT = (V_P + V_I)/F$ (in min) ($MTT = V_I/F$ for the TK and WX-TK models), $PS = (1 - H_{SV}) \cdot BV \cdot PS/V_P$ (in ml/min/100 g). For the WX models, PS_C can additionally be calculated according to $PS_C = (100/\rho_T) \cdot \{(v_C/\tau_C)/60\}$ (in ml/min/100 g).

2.5 Patients and DCE-MRI Protocol

A total of 20 patients (gender, 18 men and 2 women; age range, 30–79 years; mean age, 59.55 years) with advanced HCC were included in this study. DCE-MRI of the liver was performed using a phased array body coil on a 1.5-T MRI system (Avanto; Siemens, New York, NY). First, three-dimensional (3D) volume interpolated excitation coronal T1-weighted sequence of varying flip angles of 10, 15, 30, 60, and 90 degrees were obtained in a breath hold before CA injection. Second, through the 20-gauge peripheral intravenous line in the arm, 0.1 mmol/kg bodyweight of Gd-DTPA contrast was power injected at 2 ml/s. Third, a series of coronal T1-weighted DCE-MR images were obtained using a 15-degree flip angle after 5-second delay after the initiation of CA injection, and the scanning continued for up to 4 min and 30 s. The acquisition parameters included: TR = 5 ms, TE = 1.58 ms, 5-mm slice thickness, 0-mm interslice gap, 20 slices, 352 × 384 matrix, and field of view of 366.37 × 400 mm. Two consecutive 7-second acquisitions forming two different time points were repeated 10 times with a delay of 21 s between them. The scanning time in every acquisition was 14 s with a break of 21 s, and the patients were asked to hold their breath during acquisition.

2.6 Image and Statistical Analysis

Image registration was performed initially before further kinetic analysis. To reduce movement-induced artifacts, we coregistered each set of dynamic series relative to the first precontrast image as a template by using the Insight Segmentation and Registration Toolkit (ITK) [28], which was conducted based on the serial procedures of 3D rigid, affine, and B-spline deformable registration methods. The native T1 of each voxel was estimated by using the precontrast images acquired with the five flip angles (10°, 15°, 30°, 60°, and 90°) [29]. The four sets of preconstrast images with flip angles, 10°, 30°, 60°, and 90°, were also coregistered to the first set of DCE-MR images (i.e., the precontrast image acquired with the flip angle 15°), respectively. Region of interest (ROI) analysis was performed by an experienced gastrointestinal surgeon to derive arterial and portal-venous input curves and to delineate the tumor. To calculate kinetic parameters, the same dual-input curves were used among the models for each patient by placing ROIs within the abdominal aorta (size: 5.2 mm^2) and the major portal vein branch (size: 5.2 mm^2). The target lesions were outlined in the central partitions of the imaging volume. The tissue enhancement curve corresponding to each voxel within tumor ROIs was separately fitted using the five FXL standard models and the five WX models. Statistical analysis was performed using SPSS version 20.0 (IBM SPSS statistics, version 20.0 for Windows; SPSS, Inc., Chicago, IL, USA, an IBM Company). Paired comparison of kinetic parameters (BF, γ, BF_A, BF_{PV}, BV, MTT, PS, ν_I, and E) that have the same physiological meaning between the FXL standard and WX models was evaluated using Wilcoxon signed-rank test for each parameter and for each model pair.

3 Results

The mean and standard deviation (SD) values for the different parameters for the different models, and the Wilcoxon signed-rank test results for each parameter for each model pair are summarized in Table 1.

The BF was higher with the FXL standard TK, ETK, 2CX, and DP models than with their corresponding WX models, whereas it was lower with the FXL standard AATH model. The BF_{PV}, PS, and ν_I were all higher with all FXL standard models than their corresponding WX models, whereas γ was lower with all FXL standard models. The BF_A was higher with the FXL standard TK, 2CX, and DP models than with their corresponding WX models, whereas it was lower with the FXL standard ETK and AATH models. The MTT was higher with the FXL standard TK and AATH models than with their corresponding WX models, whereas it was lower with the FXL standard ETK, 2CX, and DP models. The E was higher with the FXL standard TK and 2CX models than with their corresponding WX models, whereas it was lower with the FXL standard ETK, AATH, and DP models.

All parameters except the TK-model-derived E, the ETK-model-derived BF_A, MTT and E, the 2CX-model-derived γ and E, the AATH-model-derived BF, γ, BV, MTT, PS and E, and the DP-model-derived γ were statistically significantly different for the pairwise comparison between the FXL standard and WX models. In other words, BF (TK vs. WX-TK: $P < 0.001$, ETK vs. WX-ETK: $P = 0.002$, 2CX vs. WX-2CX: $P = 0.001$, and DP vs. WX-DP: $P < 0.001$), BF_{PV} (TK vs. WX-TK: $P = 0.001$, ETK vs. WX-ETK: $P < 0.001$, 2CX vs. WX-2CX: $P = 0.004$, and DP vs. WX-DP: $P = 0.028$), BV (TK vs. WX-TK: $P < 0.001$, ETK vs. WX-ETK: $P < 0.001$, 2CX vs. WX-2CX: $P < 0.001$, and DP vs. WX-DP: $P < 0.001$), and PS (TK vs. WX-TK: $P < 0.001$, ETK vs. WX-ETK: : $P = 0.021$, 2CX vs. WX-2CX: $P < 0.001$, and DP vs. WX-DP: $P = 0.012$) were statistically significantly different in the pairwise comparison with all models except the AATH model, γ (TK vs. WX-TK:$P = 0.022$ and ETK vs. WX-ETK: $P = 0.004$) with the TK and ETK models, BF_A (TK vs. WX-TK: $P = 0.001$, 2CX vs. WX-2CX: $P = 0.002$, AATH vs. WX-AATH: $P = 0.007$, and DP vs. WX-DP: $P = 0.001$) with all models except the ETK model, MTT (TK vs. WX-TK: $P = 0.014$, 2CX vs. WX-2CX: $P = 0.044$, and DP vs. WX-DP: $P = 0.028$) with the TK, 2CX and DP models, ν_I (TK vs. WX-TK: $P < 0.001$, ETK vs. WX-ETK: $P < 0.001$, 2CX vs. WX-2CX: $P = 0.011$, AATH vs. WX-AATH: $P = 0.001$, and DP vs. WX-DP: $P < 0.001$) with all models, and E (DP vs. WX-DP: $P = 0.021$) with only the DP model, respectively. An example of parametric maps in HCC for several selected parameters that were statistically significantly different for each model pair is provided in Fig. 2.

Table 1. Statistics (mean ± SD) for ROI analysis of each parameter in HCC, and the Wilcoxon signed-rank test results to compare each model pair (FXL vs. WX) for each parameter.

Parameter	Model	Mean ± SD		P-value
		FXL	WX	
BF (ml/min/100 g)	TK	156.6 ± 96.40	133.4 ± 86.17	**<0.001**
	ETK	39.97 ± 21.13	36.74 ± 21.78	**0.002**
	2CX	66.86 ± 34.43	49.94 ± 26.89	**0.001**
	AATH	45.41 ± 21.59	49.20 ± 24.17	0.057
	DP	59.52 ± 27.17	53.47 ± 28.13	**<0.001**
γ	TK	0.655 ± 0.280	0.702 ± 0.255	**0.022**
	ETK	0.381 ± 0.217	0.459 ± 0.220	**0.004**
	2CX	0.713 ± 0.304	0.730 ± 0.256	0.627
	AATH	0.574 ± 0.263	0.637 ± 0.284	0.052
	DP	0.512 ± 0.287	0.517 ± 0.263	0.852
BF_A (ml/min/100 g)	TK	105.7 ± 89.75	95.36 ± 81.05	**0.001**
	ETK	16.59 ± 14.20	17.56 ± 17.90	0.550
	2CX	50.68 ± 36.74	38.71 ± 27.23	**0.002**
	AATH	26.09 ± 18.45	33.50 ± 22.58	**0.007**
	DP	31.85 ± 24.19	29.44 ± 22.88	**0.001**
BF_{PV} (ml/min/100 g)	TK	50.87 ± 49.16	38.09 ± 39.04	**0.001**
	ETK	23.38 ± 13.27	19.18 ± 13.51	**<0.001**
	2CX	16.18 ± 19.39	11.23 ± 14.95	**0.004**
	AATH	19.32 ± 16.03	15.70 ± 15.34	0.478
	DP	27.66 ± 19.23	24.03 ± 18.35	**0.028**
BV (ml/100 g)	TK	54.15 ± 30.82	46.10 ± 27.61	**<0.001**
	ETK	20.83 ± 10.26	18.45 ± 9.339	**<0.001**
	2CX	24.69 ± 11.10	17.89 ± 8.733	**<0.001**
	AATH	16.83 ± 7.968	18.97 ± 8.092	0.079
	DP	24.19 ± 10.51	21.01 ± 10.35	**<0.001**
MTT (min)	TK	1.461 ± 2.404	1.315 ± 2.066	**0.014**
	ETK	4.442 ± 1.964	4.605 ± 2.739	0.823
	2CX	1.917 ± 2.147	2.212 ± 1.916	**0.044**
	AATH	2.008 ± 2.237	1.817 ± 1.583	0.502
	DP	2.061 ± 2.400	2.398 ± 2.768	**0.028**
PS (ml/min/100 g)	TK	116.4 ± 73.39	98.42 ± 66.30	**<0.001**
	ETK	34.06 ± 24.52	31.63 ± 22.40	**0.021**
	2CX	42.48 ± 29.32	16.22 ± 10.58	**<0.001**
	AATH	21.54 ± 17.29	20.03 ± 12.42	0.502
	DP	6.495 ± 4.756	5.452 ± 3.649	**0.012**
v_I	TK	0.274 ± 0.082	0.257 ± 0.091	**<0.001**
	ETK	0.201 ± 0.082	0.171 ± 0.076	**<0.001**
	2CX	0.231 ± 0.141	0.181 ± 0.108	**0.011**
	AATH	0.273 ± 0.197	0.163 ± 0.073	**0.001**
	DP	0.280 ± 0.076	0.220 ± 0.088	**<0.001**
E	TK	0.617 ± 0.074	0.606 ± 0.057	0.108
	ETK	0.649 ± 0.124	0.651 ± 0.104	0.296
	2CX	0.391 ± 0.134	0.346 ± 0.136	0.263
	AATH	0.376 ± 0.179	0.407 ± 0.119	0.852
	DP	0.147 ± 0.108	0.197 ± 0.183	**0.021**

Note—Bold numbers indicate statistical significance in the Wilcoxon signed-rank test (two-tailed $P < 0.05$).

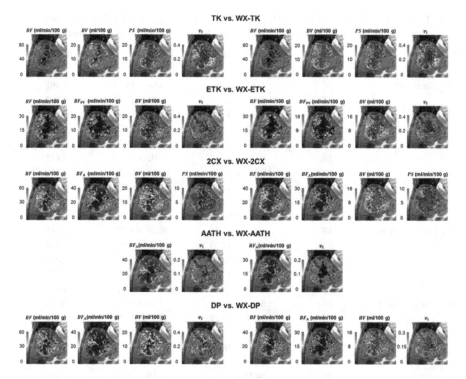

Fig. 2. Parametric maps obtained with five FXL standard models (TK, ETK, 2CX, AATH, and DP) and their corresponding WX versions (WX-TK, WX-ETK, WX-2CX, WX-AATH, and WX-DP) in HCC. Each model pair except for the pair of the AATH and WX-AATH models displays four kinetic parameters that were most significantly different between the FXL standard and WX models. Note that only two kinetic parameters were statistically significantly different between the AATH vs. WX-AATH models (see Table 1).

4 Discussion

On the whole, the AATH model was relatively less influenced by intercompartmental water exchange as compared to other models, although the AATH-model-derived BF_A and v_I were significantly different between the FXL standard and WX models. Of the kinetic parameters investigated, E was relatively consistent between the FXL standard and WX models; only the DP-model-derived E was different between them. However, no parameters were consistent over all pairs between the FXL standard and WX models.

In the present study, although we focused on the comparison of kinetic parameters that have the same physiological meaning between the FXL standard and WX models, we could obtain additional parameters such as τ_C, PS_C and v_C by using the WX models as shown in Fig. 3, which may provide valuable information relating to tumor cell characteristics in addition to tumor microvascular characteristics. Therefore, further investigations are warranted to prove whether it is useful for the prediction of clinical outcome.

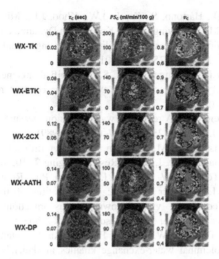

Fig. 3. Additional parametric maps of mean intracellular water molecule lifetime (τ_C) (left), cell membrane permeability-surface area product (PS_C) (middle), and fractional intracellular volume (v_C) (right) obtained with five different WX models.

5 Conclusion

We developed novel WX dual-input tracer kinetic models for liver DCE-MRI with various physiologic scenarios in the capillary-tissue system based on a full 3S2X model as well as a full 2SX model for intercompartmental water exchange. Results suggest that parameter values differ substantially and they are not interchangeable between the FXL standard and WX tracer kinetic models, indicating that DCE-MRI data are potentially water-exchange-sensitive in the clinically relevant DCE-MRI protocol. Consequently, the WX model may influence the predictability of clinical outcome differently from the FXL standard model.

References

1. Padhani, A.R.: Dynamic contrast-enhanced MRI in clinical oncology: current status and future directions. J. Magn. Reason. Imaging **16**, 407–422 (2002)
2. Sahani, D.V., Jiang, T., Hayano, K., Duda, D.G., Catalano, O.A., Ancukiewicz, M., Jain, R.K., Zhu, A.X.: Magnetic resonance imaging biomarkers in hepatocellular carcinoma: association with response and circulating biomarkers after sunitinib therapy. J. Hematol. Oncol. **6**, 51 (2013). doi:10.1186/1756-8722-6-51
3. Chiandussi, L., Greco, F., Sardi, G., Vaccarino, A., Ferraris, C.M., Curti, B.: Estimation of hepatic arterial and portal venous blood flow by direct catheterization of the vena porta through the umbilical cord in man. Preliminary results. Acta Hepatosplenol. **15**, 166–171 (1968)
4. Materne, R., Smith, A.M., Peeters, F., Dehoux, J.P., Keyeux, A., Horsmans, Y., Van Beers, B.E.: Assessment of hepatic perfusion parameters with dynamic MRI. Magn. Reson. Med. **47**, 135–142 (2002)

5. Koh, T.S., Thng, C.H., Hartono, S., Kwek, J.W., Khoo, J.B., Miyazaki, K., Collins, D.J., Orton, M.R., Leach, M.O., Lewington, V., Koh, D.M.: Dynamic contrast-enhanced MRI of neuroendocrine hepatic metastases: a feasibility study using a dual-input two-compartment model. Magn. Reson. Med. **65**, 250–260 (2011)

6. Li, X., Rooney, W.D., Springer Jr., C.S.: A unified magnetic resonance imaging pharmacokinetic theory: intravascular and extracellular contrast reagents. Magn. Reson. Med. **54**, 1351–1359 (2005)

7. Herbst, M.D., Goldstein, J.H.: A review of water diffusion measurement by NMR in human red blood cells. Am. J. Physiol. **256**, C1097–C1104 (1989)

8. Donahue, K.M., Weisskoff, R.M., Burstein, D.: Water diffusion and exchange as they influence contrast enhancement. J. Magn. Reson. Imaging **7**, 102–110 (1997)

9. Landis, C.S., Li, X., Telang, F.W., Coderre, J.A., Micca, P.L., Rooney, W.D., Latour, L.L., Vetek, G., Palyka, I., Springer Jr., C.S.: Determination of the MRI contrast agent concentration time course in vivo following bolus injection: effect of equilibrium transcytolemmal water exchange. Magn. Reson. Med. **44**, 563–574 (2000)

10. Landis, C.S., Li, X., Telang, F.W., Molina, P.E., Palyka, I., Vetek, G., Springer Jr., C.S.: Equilibrium transcytolemmal water-exchange kinetics in skeletal muscle in vivo. Magn. Reson. Med. **42**, 467–478 (1999)

11. Koh, T.S., Bisdas, S., Koh, D.M., Thng, C.H.: Fundamentals of tracer kinetics for dynamic contrast-enhanced MRI. J. Magn. Reson. Imaging **34**, 1262–1276 (2011)

12. Donahue, K.M., Weisskoff, R.M., Chesler, D.A., Kwong, K.K., Bogdanov Jr., A.A., Mandeville, J.B., Rosen, B.R.: Improving MR quantification of regional blood volume with intravascular T1 contrast agents: accuracy, precision, and water exchange. Magn. Reson. Med. **36**, 858–867 (1996)

13. Orton, M.R., d'Arcy, J.A., Walker-Samuel, S., Hawkes, D.J., Atkinson, D., Collins, D.J., Leach, M.O.: Computationally efficient vascular input function models for quantitative kinetic modelling using DCE-MRI. Phys. Med. Biol. **53**, 1225–1239 (2008)

14. Brix, G., Griebel, J., Kiessling, F., Wenz, F.: Tracer kinetic modelling of tumour angiogenesis based on dynamic contrast-enhanced CT and MRI measurements. Eur. J. Nucl. Med. Mol. Imaging **37**(Suppl 1), S30–S51 (2010)

15. Tofts, P.S., Brix, G., Buckley, D.L., Evelhoch, J.L., Henderson, E., Knopp, M.V., Larsson, H.B., Lee, T.Y., Mayr, N.A., Parker, G.J., Port, R.E., Taylor, J., Weisskoff, R.M.: Estimating kinetic parameters from dynamic contrast-enhanced T(1)-weighted MRI of a diffusable tracer: standardized quantities and symbols. J. Magn. Reson. Imaging **10**, 223–232 (1999)

16. Sourbron, S.P., Buckley, D.L.: On the scope and interpretation of the tofts models for DCE-MRI. Magn. Reson. Med. **66**, 735–745 (2011)

17. Brix, G., Bahner, M.L., Hoffmann, U., Horvath, A., Schreiber, W.: Regional blood flow, capillary permeability, and compartmental volumes: measurement with dynamic CT–initial experience. Radiology **210**, 269–276 (1999)

18. St. Lawrence, K.S., Lee, T.Y.: An adiabatic approximation to the tissue homogeneity model for water exchange in the brain: I. Theoretical derivation. J. Cereb. Blood Flow Metab. **18**, 1365–1377 (1998)

19. Koh, T.S.: On the a priori identifiability of the two-compartment distributed parameter model from residual tracer data acquired by dynamic contrast-enhanced imaging. IEEE Trans. Biomed. Eng. **55**, 340–344 (2008)

20. Spencer, R.G., Fishbein, K.W.: Measurement of spin-lattice relaxation times and concentrations in systems with chemical exchange using the one-pulse sequence: breakdown of the Ernst model for partial saturation in nuclear magnetic resonance spectroscopy. J. Magn. Reson. **142**, 120–135 (2000)

21. Paudyal, R., Poptani, H., Cai, K., Zhou, R., Glickson, J.D.: Impact of transvascular and cellular-interstitial water exchange on dynamic contrast-enhanced magnetic resonance imaging estimates of blood to tissue transfer constant and blood plasma volume. J. Magn. Reson. Imaging 37, 435–444 (2013)

22. Zhang, J., Kim, S.: Uncertainty in MR tracer kinetic parameters and water exchange rates estimated from T -weighted dynamic contrast enhanced MRI. Magn. Reson. Med. (2013)

23. Yankeelov, T.E., Rooney, W.D., Li, X., Springer Jr., C.S.: Variation of the relaxographic "shutter-speed" for transcytolemmal water exchange affects the CR bolus-tracking curve shape. Magn. Reson. Med. 50, 1151–1169 (2003)

24. Tofts, P.S., Berkowitz, B., Schnall, M.D.: Quantitative analysis of dynamic Gd-DTPA enhancement in breast tumors using a permeability model. Magn. Reson. Med. 33, 564–568 (1995)

25. Bains, L.J., McGrath, D.M., Naish, J.H., Cheung, S., Watson, Y., Taylor, M.B., Logue, J.P., Parker, G.J., Waterton, J.C., Buckley, D.L.: Tracer kinetic analysis of dynamic contrast-enhanced MRI and CT bladder cancer data: a preliminary comparison to assess the magnitude of water exchange effects. Magn. Reson. Med. 64, 595–603 (2010)

26. Higham, N.J.: The scaling and squaring method for the matrix exponential revisited. SIAM J. Matrix Anal. Appl. 26, 1179–1193 (2005)

27. Buckley, D.L., Kershaw, L.E., Stanisz, G.J.: Cellular-interstitial water exchange and its effect on the determination of contrast agent concentration in vivo: dynamic contrast-enhanced MRI of human internal obturator muscle. Magn. Reson. Med. 60, 1011–1019 (2008)

28. Ibanez, L., Schroeder, W., Ng, L., Cates, J.: The ITK Software Guide. Kitware, Inc., Clifton Park (2005)

29. Fram, E.K., Herfkens, R.J., Johnson, G.A., Glover, G.H., Karis, J.P., Shimakawa, A., Perkins, T.G., Pelc, N.J.: Rapid calculation of T1 using variable flip angle gradient refocused imaging. Magn. Reson. Imaging 5, 201–208 (1987)

Kinetic Textural Biomarker for Predicting Survival of Patients with Advanced Hepatocellular Carcinoma After Antiangiogenic Therapy by Use of Baseline First-Pass Perfusion CT

Sang Ho Lee[1](✉), Koichi Hayano[2], Dushyant V. Sahani[2],
Andrew X. Zhu[3], and Hiroyuki Yoshida[1]

[1] 3D Imaging Research, Department of Radiology,
Massachusetts General Hospital and Harvard Medical School,
25 New Chardon St., Suite 400C, Boston, MA 02114, USA
{lee.sangho,yoshida.hiro}@mgh.harvard.edu
[2] Division of Abdominal Imaging and Intervention,
Department of Radiology, Massachusetts General Hospital,
55 Fruit St., Boston, MA 02114, USA
{khayano,dsahani}@partners.org
[3] Division of Hematology and Oncology, Department of Medicine,
Massachusetts General Hospital Cancer Center,
Harvard Medical School, and Dana-Farber/Partners Cancer Care,
55 Fruit St., Boston, MA 02114, USA
azhu@partners.org

Abstract. Previous texture analysis studies of liver CT images have shown the potential to achieve hepatic malignancy or predict overall survival (OS). However, to date, most studies have mainly focused on assessing texture features of the non-contrast CT or portal-phase image in the dynamic contrast-enhanced CT sequence. The aim of this study was to quantify texture features of physiologically-based kinetic parametric images, and to develop prognostic kinetic textural biomarkers for 1-year survival (1YS) and OS in patients with advanced hepatocellular carcinoma (HCC) following antiangiogenic therapy in comparison among five different tracer kinetic models. Mean, standard deviation, coefficient of variation, skewness, and kurtosis of the pixel distribution histogram within HCC were derived from baseline first-pass perfusion CT parameters. Results suggest that texture analysis of kinetic parametric images can provide better chances of finding effective prognostic biomarkers for the prediction of survival than a mean value analysis alone.

Keywords: Hepatocellular carcinoma · Antiangiogenic treatment · Kinetic texture · Perfusion CT

1 Introduction

Perfusion CT (PCT) has been increasingly used for quantifying tumor vascularity and monitoring the response of hepatocellular carcinoma (HCC) and various other solid

© Springer International Publishing Switzerland 2014
H. Yoshida et al. (Eds.): ABDI 2014, LNCS 8676, pp. 48–61, 2014.
DOI: 10.1007/978-3-319-13692-9_5

tumors to antiangiogenic therapy [1, 2, 3]. Because of the rapid scanning speed and high spatial and temporal resolution, PCT imaging has attracted interest as a potential means to quantify hemodynamic parameters by modeling of tracer kinetics [4].

Spatial heterogeneity in the tumor is a well-known feature of malignancy that reflects areas of high cell density, necrosis, hemorrhage, and myxoid change [5]. However, visual analysis of diagnostic images largely depends on assessing morphologic information such as size and shape, and thus the human visual system has difficulties in discriminating textural information such as coarseness and regularity that result from local spatial variations in image intensity [6]. Furthermore, PCT imaging provides detailed anatomical information on dynamic absorption of contrast agent (CA), which yields 4D data (3D plus time). Thus, human interpretation of PCT data is a challenging task because of the high amount of data with limited visualization options, and can be subjective. Previous studies for liver CT texture analysis have mainly focused on assessing texture features of the non-contrast CT or portal-phase image in the dynamic contrast-enhanced CT sequence [7, 8, 9], and a few studies have reported that texture features derived from the portal-phase image were associated with survival of patients with colorectal cancer [10, 11, 12]. Altough those studies showed the potentials of texture features that predicted favorable clinical outcomes, we note that such texture features can only reflect the spatial association attributes of pixel intensity distribution at a single temporal phase that does not contain information on the washin-washout behavior of CA. In comparison, none of these issues has as yet been addressed for the texture analysis of physiologically-based kinetic parametric images in HCC.

Texture features derived from kinetic parameter maps can reflect spatiotemporal enhancement patterns for comprehensive characterization of tumor vascular heterogeneity [13] because the distribution of kinetic parameter values can represent spatial variation in temporal enhancement based on the full-time-points measurements. To date, no studies have been performed to assess the kinetic textural features of HCC, and to determine whether kinetic texture is related to overall survival (OS). The aim of this study was to compare the predictive capability of the kinetic textural features derived from five different tracer kinetic models in the analysis of baseline first-pass PCT data to find an optimal prognostic kinetic textural biomarker with respect to 1-year survival (1YS) as well as association with OS in patients with advanced HCC treated with a combination of antiangiogenic treatment and chemotherapy.

2   Methods

2.1   Tracer Kinetic Modeling and Parameter Calculation

We consider a single-input source of the plasma flow F (in ml/min) to the liver [14]. Assuming that the feeding arterial blood concentration $C_A(t)$ (in g/ml) can be sampled from PCT images, the CA concentration in the liver tissue, $C_T(t)$ (in g/ml), during the first pass can be expressed as follows [15]:

$$C_T(t) = \frac{F}{V_T} R_T(t - t_{\text{Lag,T}}) \otimes \frac{C_A(t)}{1 - H_{\text{LV}}},$$

(1)

where H_{LV} is the hematocrit of blood in large vessels ($\cong 0.45$) to the input CA concentration in blood plasma [15], V_T is the tissue volume (in ml), F/V_T is the hepatic perfusion (in ml/min/ml), $R_T(t)$ is the tissue residue function, $t_{Lag,T}$ is the time lag (delay) (in min) to account for the difference in bolus arrival times between $C_A(t)$ and $C_T(t)$, and $\otimes$ is the convolution operator, respectively. We analyzed the first-pass PCT data with use of five different kinetic models: the Tofts-Kety (TK) model [16], extended TK (ETK) model [17], two-compartment exchange (2CX) model [18], adiabatic approximation to the tissue homogeneity (AATH) model [19], and distributed parameter (DP) model [20]. The tissue residue functions $R_T(t)$ for the five models are given by

$$R_{T,TK}(t) = E e^{-\frac{v_P}{v_I} \frac{EF}{V_P} t}, \tag{2}$$

$$R_{T,ETK}(t) = \frac{V_P}{F} \delta(t) + E e^{-\frac{v_P}{v_I} \frac{EF}{V_P} t}, \tag{3}$$

$R_{T,2CX}(t) = A e^{\alpha t} + (1-A) e^{\beta t}$ with

$$\binom{\alpha}{\beta} = \frac{1}{2}\left[-\left\{ \frac{F}{V_P} + \left(1 + \frac{v_P}{v_I}\right)\frac{PS}{V_P}\right\} \pm \sqrt{\left\{\frac{F}{V_P} + \left(1 + \frac{v_P}{v_I}\right)\frac{PS}{V_P}\right\}^2 - 4\frac{v_P}{v_I}\frac{F}{V_P}\frac{PS}{V_P}}\right]$$

and $A = \dfrac{\alpha + \left(1 + \frac{v_P}{v_I}\right)\frac{PS}{V_P}}{\alpha - \beta}$

$$\tag{4}$$

$$R_{T,AATH}(t) = u(t) + \left(E e^{-\frac{v_P}{v_I}\frac{EF}{V_P}\left(t - \frac{V_P}{F}\right)} - 1\right) u\left(t - \frac{V_P}{F}\right), \tag{5}$$

$$R_{T,DP}(t) = u(t) - e^{-\frac{PS}{F}}\left[1 + \frac{PS}{V_P}\int_0^{t - \frac{V_P}{F}} e^{-\frac{v_P}{v_I}\frac{PS}{V_P}\tau}\sqrt{\frac{v_P}{v_I}\frac{V_P}{F}\frac{1}{\tau}}I_1\left(2\frac{PS}{V_P}\sqrt{\frac{v_P}{v_I}\frac{V_P}{F}}\tau\right)d\tau\right]$$

$$u\left(t - \frac{V_P}{F}\right) \cong u(t) - e^{-\frac{PS}{F}}\left[1 + \frac{v_P}{v_I}\frac{PS}{V_P}\frac{PS}{F}\left(t - \frac{V_P}{F}\right)\right]u\left(t - \frac{V_P}{F}\right) \tag{6}$$

where $R_{T,TK}(t)$, $R_{T,ETK}(t)$, $R_{T,2CX}(t)$, $R_{T,AATH}(t)$ and $R_{T,DP}(t)$ represent the $R_T(t)$ of the TK, ETK, 2CX, AATH, and DP models, respectively. Note that $R_{T,DP}(t)$ is approximated using the first two terms of the Taylor series solution for the parenchyma phase [20]. The $u(t)$ is the unit step function, $\delta(t)$ is the Dirac delta function, $I_1(t)$ is the modified Bessel function of the first kind, v_P is the plasma volume fraction, v_I is the interstitial volume fraction, V_P is the plasma volume (in ml), PS is the permeability-surface area product (in ml/min), and $E = 1 - e^{-PS/F}$ is the extraction fraction, respectively. For a PCT dataset consisting of N images obtained with a time interval $\Delta t = t_{k+1} - t_k$ for $k = 0, \ldots, N-1$, a trapezoidal convolution operation to approximate $C_T(t)$ for each model is given by

$$C_T[k] \cong \frac{F}{V_T} \frac{\Delta t}{2(1 - H_{LV})} \sum_{i=0}^{k-1} [R_T(i\Delta t - t_{Lag,T})C_A[k - i]$$

$$+ R_T((i + 1)\Delta t - t_{Lag,T})C_A[k - (i + 1)]], \tag{7}$$

where $R_T(t) = 0$ if $t \leq t_{Lag,T}$. The parameters that can be directly estimated by parametric fitting in Eq. (7) are F/V_P, PS/V_P, v_P, v_I, and $t_{Lag,T}$ [18]. Therefore, the blood flow (BF), blood volume (BV), mean transit time (MTT), and PS parameters can be calculated by: $BV = 100 \cdot V_P/\{(1 - H_{SV}) \cdot m\} = 100 \cdot v_P/\{(1 - H_{SV}) \cdot \rho_T\}$ (in ml/100 g), where H_{SV} is the hematocrit in small vessels ($\cong 0.25$), and $m = \rho_T V_T$ is the mass of the tissue with density ρ_T (=1.04 g/cm^3 in the case of soft tissues), $BF = BV \cdot F/V_P$ (in ml/min/ 100 g), $MTT = (V_P + V_I)/F$ (in min) ($MTT = V_I/F$ for the TK model), and $PS = (1 - H_{SV}) \cdot BV \cdot PS/V_P$ (in ml/min/100 g). In this study, the following six parameters were used for the analysis of each model: BF, BV, MTT, PS, v_I, and E.

2.2 Kinetic Textural Features

We considered it as essential to extract informative kinetic textural features related to spatiotemporal association of intratumoral enhancement patterns for obtaining effective prognostic biomarkers for survival. In this study, five spatial features were calculated for the volumetric images of the pixelwise kinetic features. The mean, standard deviation (SD), coefficient of variation (CV), skewness, and kurtosis of the pixel distribution histogram within HCC were obtained from each image map of the six kinetic parameters (i.e., BF, BV, MTT, PS, v_I, and E), and thus a total of 5×6 kinetic textural feature components were created for each kinetic model. Note that we regarded the mean as a part of texture features that is referred to as the first moment, although in practice it was used for comparison with other higher order moments. Let X be a kinetic parameter, and x_i be individual parameter values for pixel locations $i = 1, \cdots, M$, where M is the total number of pixels within HCC. The equations for the five spatial features are given by

$$Mean(X) = \frac{1}{M} \sum_{i=1}^{M} x_i, \tag{8}$$

$$SD(X) = \sqrt{\frac{1}{M - 1} \sum_{i=1}^{M} (x_i - Mean(X))^2}, \tag{9}$$

$$CV(X) = \frac{SD(X)}{Mean(X)}, \tag{10}$$

$$Skew(X) = \frac{M}{(M - 1)(M - 2)} \sum_{i=1}^{M} \left(\frac{x_i - Mean(X)}{SD(X)}\right)^3, \tag{11}$$

$$Kurt(X) = \left\{ \frac{M(M+1)}{(M-1)(M-2)(M-3)} \sum_{i=1}^{M} \left(\frac{x_i - Mean(X)}{SD(X)} \right)^4 \right\} \\ - \frac{3(M-1)^2}{(M-2)(M-3)}, \tag{12}$$

where $Mean(X)$, $SD(X)$, $CV(X)$, $Skew(X)$, and $Kurt(X)$ denote the mean, corrected sample SD, CV, skewness, and kurtosis of X within HCC, respectively [21]. Each kinetic textural feature was denoted by substituting X with its corresponding kinetic parameter.

2.3   Patients and Perfusion CT Protocol

A total of 22 patients (gender, 15 men and 7 women; age range, 28–79 years; mean age, 61.18 years) with advanced HCC were included in this study. PCT was performed with a 16-section mutidetector row CT scanner (LightSpeed; GE Medical Systems, Milwaukee, WI). For initial localization of the tumor, a CT scan of the liver was obtained without CA during a breath hold at the end of expiration. After tumor localization, a 2-cm tumor region was selected independently for PCT imaging in the maximal diameter of the tumor. A dynamic study of the selected area was performed in a single breath hold of 35 s at the end of expiration at a static table position. The duration of dynamic scanning was chosen based on patient maximum breath-hold capacity and to minimize radiation dose and respiratory artifacts from longer scan duration. A total of 70 ml of nonionic iodinated CA (Isovue; Bracco, Princeton, NJ) (300 mgI/ml) was injected at a rate of 7 ml/s through an 18-gauge intravenous cannula. The following CT parameters were used to acquire dynamic data; rotation time, 0.5 s; cine acquisition at every 0.6 s; 100 kVp; 200 to 240 mA; 4 sections per gantry rotation; 5-mm section thickness; field of view, 36 cm; and matrix, 512×512 pixels. Scanning was initiated after a 5-second delay from the start of injection, and images were acquired for a total duration of 35 s.

2.4   Image Processing and Analysis

To enhance contrast-to-noise ratios, PCT images were denoised based on multiple observations Gaussian process regression [22]. To reduce movement-induced artifacts, each set of PCT images was aligned to the first precontrast image as a template by use of a 3D rigid, affine, and B-spline deformable registration in the Insight Segmentation and Registration Toolkit [23] (Fig. 1). Region of interest (ROI) analysis was performed by an experienced gastrointestinal surgeon to derive an arterial input curve and delineate the tumor. The same arterial input curve was used across all of the models within each patient by placing an ROI in the aorta (size: 4 mm²) on one of the four axial images, from which a first-pass atrial input function (AIF) was fitted by a gamma-variate function [14]. The tissue concentration-time curve corresponding to each voxel within the tumor ROIs was separately fitted using the five kinetic models.

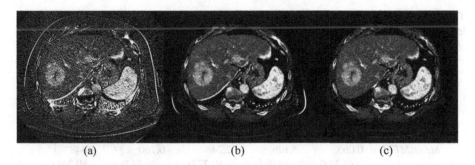

(a)   (b)   (c)

Fig. 1. Example of subtraction between pre- and postcontrast images with (a) original PCT data sets, (b) denoised PCT data sets, and (c) denoised and registered PCT data sets.

2.5 Treatment and Follow-up

All 22 patients underwent antiangiogenic therapy. The eligibility, treatment schedule, and the dose modification schema have been detailed previously [24]. Briefly, patients were treated with bevacizumab at a dose of 10 mg/kg i.v. on day 1 of cycle 1 (14 days). For the subsequent 28-day cycle, patients were treated with bevacizumab at 10 mg/kg on days 1 and 15, gemcitabine at 1000 mg/m^2 i.v. at a dose rate infusion of 10 mg/m^2/min on days 2 and 16, and oxaliplatin at 85 mg/m^2 at a 2-hour i.v. infusion on days 2 and 16 of every cycle. The dose of bevacizumab was fixed at 10 mg/kg. Treatment was continued until onset of disease progression, unacceptable toxicity, or withdrawal of consent. All patients were followed up until death, although one patient was still alive and interval-censored. In the patient cohort, median survival time was 11.62 months.

2.6 Statistical Analysis

The primary clinical endpoint of the analysis was OS, which was defined as the time between baseline PCT imaging and death. Survival risk prediction was estimated for 1 year. For each kinetic textural feature, optimal cut-off (threshold) values for predicting 1YS were derived from receiver operating characteristic (ROC) analysis by using the point closest to the top-left corner of the ROC plot as the optimal threshold. The cut-off point selection was performed based on a leave-one-out cross-validation (LOOCV). In the process of LOOCV, ROC analysis was carried out for estimating the cut-off value using the training data, and then the validation data were assigned to either the "low-risk" or the "high-risk" group based on the cut-off value. An optimized cut-off value was defined for each feature, as the value that was most frequently selected in the LOOCV procedure. Kinetic textural features derived from the different kinetic models were compared in terms of 1YS discrimination using cross-validated Kaplan-Meier analysis, and association with OS using a univariate Cox proportional hazard model regarding the continuous feature values. The significance of separation between the cross-validated Kaplan-Meier curves was assessed using the log rank test and its permutation distribution. Hazard ratio was considered the ratio of hazards for a two-fold change in the feature values. For each feature, 1000 random permutations were performed, and associated permutation-based P values were provided.

Table 1. Optimal cut-off values of kinetic textural features and their log-rank test results from leave-one-out cross-validated Kaplan-Meier analysis with respect to 1-year survival prediction.

Parameter	Cut-off value (P-value)				
	TK	ETK	2CX	AATH	DP
Mean(BF)	236.2 (0.999)	52.37 (0.783)	50.43 (0.348)	54.89 (**0.032**)	55.41 (0.756)
Mean(BV)	33.63 (0.998)	5.531 (0.285)	19.20 (0.424)	17.97 (**0.047**)	17.85 (0.185)
Mean(MTT)	0.065 (0.248)	3.126 (0.907)	2.248 (0.277)	0.760 (0.832)	1.348 (0.244)
Mean(PS)	153.4 (0.781)	34.60 (0.818)	84.67 (0.424)	30.24 (0.766)	24.54 (0.284)
Mean(v_I)	0.051 (0.790)	0.569 (0.505)	0.597 (0.539)	0.263 (0.446)	0.260 (0.202)
Mean(E)	0.528 (**0.046**)	0.636 (0.329)	0.612 (0.527)	0.437 (**0.012**)	0.440 (0.142)
SD(BF)	195.4 (0.300)	27.80 (0.750)	12.16 (0.198)	16.46 (0.051)	18.38 (0.339)
SD(BV)	18.08 (0.298)	3.396 (0.438)	15.45 (0.424)	5.247 (0.164)	5.232 (0.281)
SD(MTT)	0.127 (0.134)	4.854 (0.119)	1.227 (0.317)	1.177 (0.387)	1.641 (0.100)
SD(PS)	138.6 (0.300)	15.56 (0.581)	129.7 (0.424)	17.17 (**0.014**)	17.91 (0.137)
SD(v_I)	0.034 (0.618)	0.457 (0.430)	0.346 (0.248)	0.138 (0.507)	0.152 (0.636)
SD(E)	0.133 (0.156)	0.189 (0.472)	0.179 (0.218)	0.230 (**0.014**)	0.226 (0.561)
CV(BF)	0.820 (0.829)	0.765 (0.318)	0.259 (0.281)	0.518 (**0.011**)	0.268 (0.865)
CV(BV)	0.488 (0.348)	0.623 (0.236)	0.953 (0.235)	0.204 (0.307)	0.204 (0.474)
CV(MTT)	3.176 (0.281)	1.340 (0.097)	0.813 (0.075)	1.823 (**0.017**)	1.805 (0.091)
CV(PS)	1.045 (0.880)	0.567 (0.459)	1.661 (0.634)	0.663 (**0.017**)	0.685 (0.498)
CV(v_I)	0.586 (0.059)	0.669 (0.733)	0.604 (0.650)	0.739 (0.949)	0.434 (0.782)
CV(E)	0.260 (0.156)	0.271 (0.262)	0.256 (0.198)	0.416 (**0.005**)	0.456 (0.561)
Skew(BF)	1.692 (0.743)	2.726 (0.294)	1.809 (**0.012**)	1.402 (0.215)	0.903 (0.907)
Skew(BV)					

(Continued)

Table 1. (*Continued*)

Parameter	Cut-off value (*P*-value)				
	TK	ETK	2CX	AATH	DP
	2.222	2.289	6.725	2.145	2.172
	(0.786)	(0.499)	(0.243)	(0.076)	(0.413)
Skew(*MTT*)	28.55	7.018	1.852	7.225	28.15
	(0.045)	(0.763)	**(0.011)**	**(0.013)**	**(0.016)**
Skew(*PS*)	2.713	2.429	6.463	2.164	1.624
	(0.861)	(0.132)	(0.243)	(0.893)	(0.214)
Skew(v_I)	10.54	-0.231	-0.408	0.874	1.025
	(0.787)	(0.343)	(0.118)	(0.901)	(0.239)
Skew(*E*)	0.542	-0.973	0.371	-1.318	-0.299
	(0.065)	(0.912)	(0.099)	**(0.009)**	(0.349)
Kurt(*BF*)	4.097	23.85	9.160	12.49	11.81
	(0.358)	(0.200)	(0.126)	(0.470)	(0.270)
Kurt(*BV*)	6.186	22.91	44.38	23.42	27.17
	(0.786)	(0.122)	(0.424)	(0.708)	(0.153)
Kurt(*MTT*)	1142	98.69	3.880	55.07	719.1
	(0.045)	(0.522)	**(0.028)**	**(0.013)**	**(0.016)**
Kurt(*PS*)	10.27	26.56	41.50	9.489	8.941
	(0.953)	(0.146)	(0.243)	(0.059)	(0.919)
Kurt(v_I)	123.1	-1.586	0.864	11.88	6.742
	(0.880)	(0.665)	(0.313)	(0.585)	(0.451)
Kurt(*E*)	5.875	6.960	0.749	2.633	-0.307
	(0.156)	(0.645)	(0.070)	**(<0.001)**	(0.893)

Note.—Bold numbers indicate statistical significance at two-sided $P < 0.05$ for the permutation-based test.

3 Results

Table 1 shows the optimized cut-off values of the kinetic textural features determined by means of ROC analysis with LOOCV for each model along with their log-rank permutation test P values. With the ETK model, the cross-validated Kaplan-Meier curves were not significantly different between the two groups ($P > 0.05$). The TK-model-derived *Mean*(*E*), *Skew*(*MTT*) and *Kurt*(*MTT*) were predictive of 1YS with cut-off values of 0.528 ($P = 0.046$), 28.55 ($P = 0.045$) and 1142 ($P = 0.045$), respectively. The 2CX-model-derived *Skew*(*BF*), *Skew*(*MTT*) and *Kurt*(*MTT*) were predictive of 1YS with cut-off values of 1.809 ($P = 0.012$), 1.852 ($P = 0.011$) and 3.880 ($P = 0.028$), respectively. The AATH-model-derived *Mean*(*BF*), *Mean*(*BV*), *Mean*(*E*), *SD*(*PS*), *SD*(*E*), *CV*(*BF*), *CV*(*MTT*), *CV*(*PS*), *CV*(*E*), *Skew*(*MTT*), *Skew*(*E*), *Kurt*(*MTT*) and *Kurt*(*E*) were predictive of 1YS with cut-off values of 54.89 ml/min/100 g ($P = 0.032$), 17.97 ml/100 g ($P = 0.047$), 0.437 ($P = 0.012$), 17.17 ml/min/100 g ($P = 0.014$), 0.230 ($P = 0.014$), 0.518 ($P = 0.011$), 1.823 ($P = 0.017$), 0.663 ($P = 0.017$), 0.416 ($P = 0.005$), 7.225 ($P = 0.013$), −1.318 ($P = 0.009$), 55.07 ($P = 0.013$), 2.633 ($P < 0.001$),

Table 2. Results from univariate Cox's proportional hazards regression analysis of kinetic textural features with respect to overall survival.

Parameter	Hazard ratio (P-value)				
	TK	ETK	2CX	AATH	DP
Mean(BF)	0.696 (0.358)	1.045 (0.931)	3.092 (0.465)	1.580 (0.283)	1.512 (0.353)
Mean(BV)	0.470 (0.340)	0.989 (0.983)	0.654 (0.538)	3.818 (0.115)	3.746 (0.147)
Mean(MTT)	1.122 (0.596)	1.206 (0.675)	1.097 (0.847)	1.030 (0.920)	1.178 (0.510)
Mean(PS)	0.709 (0.372)	0.895 (0.844)	0.890 (0.673)	1.451 (0.597)	1.258 (0.705)
Mean(v_I)	0.949 (0.930)	0.335 (0.163)	0.992 (0.980)	1.111 (0.645)	1.042 (0.866)
Mean(E)	46.45 (0.238)	0.053 (0.277)	1.462 (0.802)	0.030 (**0.005**)	0.482 (0.397)
SD(BF)	0.791 (0.711)	1.180 (0.522)	1.271 (0.469)	1.385 (**0.031**)	1.237 (0.219)
SD(BV)	0.871 (0.826)	1.169 (0.626)	0.965 (0.835)	1.597 (0.076)	1.394 (0.144)
SD(MTT)	1.057 (0.595)	1.546 (0.106)	0.898 (0.706)	1.127 (0.402)	1.241 (0.134)
SD(PS)	0.747 (0.586)	1.106 (0.704)	0.990 (0.938)	2.621 (**0.003**)	2.624 (0.058)
SD(v_I)	1.137 (0.644)	1.876 (0.409)	1.855 (0.247)	0.993 (0.955)	1.027 (0.850)
SD(E)	1.159 (0.720)	0.934 (0.857)	1.444 (0.325)	4.574 (**0.015**)	1.035 (0.943)
CV(BF)	1.992 (0.276)	1.105 (0.646)	1.243 (0.529)	1.347 (0.086)	1.205 (0.314)
CV(BV)	2.092 (0.423)	1.122 (0.658)	0.983 (0.939)	1.359 (0.223)	1.285 (0.237)
CV(MTT)	1.097 (0.643)	1.832 (0.078)	0.899 (0.639)	1.329 (0.224)	1.694 (0.086)
CV(PS)	1.815 (0.398)	1.079 (0.714)	1.064 (0.782)	3.404 (**0.002**)	1.733 (0.213)
CV(v_I)	1.164 (0.593)	1.644 (0.259)	1.193 (0.456)	0.969 (0.782)	1.009 (0.936)
CV(E)	1.103 (0.803)	1.002 (0.995)	1.357 (0.362)	7.044 (**<0.001**)	1.214 (0.633)
Skew(BF)	1.460 (0.166)	0.998 (0.988)	0.820 (0.361)	1.116 (0.318)	0.895 (0.394)
Skew(BV)	1.597 (0.188)	1.022 (0.895)	1.128 (0.534)	1.646 (0.089)	0.989 (0.964)

(*Continued*)

Table 2. (*Continued*)

Parameter	Hazard ratio (*P*-value)				
	TK	ETK	2CX	AATH	DP
Skew(*MTT*)	1.305 (0.265)	1.366 (0.211)	0.779 (0.130)	1.348 (**0.048**)	1.341 (0.058)
Skew(*PS*)	1.481 (0.192)	0.977 (0.789)	1.171 (0.326)	0.859 (0.327)	1.883 (0.140)
Skew(v_I)	1.283 (0.178)	0.002 (0.740)	0.849 (0.610)	1.000 (0.998)	1.032 (0.889)
Skew(*E*)	0.844 (0.437)	628.2 (0.636)	0.690 (**0.030**)	0.587 (0.459)	0.256 (0.057)
Kurt(*BF*)	1.193 (0.240)	1.074 (0.363)	0.879 (0.337)	1.004 (0.972)	0.998 (0.990)
Kurt(*BV*)	1.207 (0.339)	1.106 (0.307)	1.049 (0.584)	1.041 (0.808)	0.848 (0.298)
Kurt(*MTT*)	1.161 (0.230)	1.207 (0.184)	0.813 (**0.036**)	1.555 (0.107)	1.089 (0.310)
Kurt(*PS*)	1.178 (0.270)	1.071 (0.333)	1.062 (0.477)	0.838 (0.175)	0.991 (0.947)
Kurt(v_I)	1.013 (0.903)	4.427 (0.923)	0.811 (0.215)	0.989 (0.901)	1.005 (0.961)
Kurt(*E*)	0.904 (0.509)	1.068 (0.676)	0.880 (0.318)	0.688 (**0.019**)	1.022 (0.930)

Note.—Bold numbers indicate statistical significance at two-sided permutation $P < 0.05$.

respectively. The DP-model-derived *Skew*(*MTT*) and *Kurt*(*MTT*) were predictive of 1YS with cut-off values of 28.15 ($P = 0.016$) and 719.1 ($P = 0.016$), respectively.

Table 2 shows the hazard ratios and the corresponding *P* values for the parameters determined by the univariate Cox proportional hazard model for each kinetic model. In these results, only the 2CX and AATH models were statistically significantly associated with OS. The 2CX-model-derived *Skew*(*E*) and *Kurt*(*MTT*) were associated with OS with hazard ratios of 0.690 ($P = 0.030$) and 0.813 ($P = 0.036$), respectively. The AATH-model-derived *Mean*(*E*), *SD*(*BF*), *SD*(*PS*), *SD*(*E*), *CV*(*PS*), *CV*(*E*), *Skew*(*MTT*) and *Kurt*(*E*) were associated with OS with hazard ratios of 0.030 ($P = 0.005$), 1.385 ($P = 0.031$), 2.621 ($P = 0.003$), 4.574 ($P = 0.015$), 3.404 ($P = 0.002$), 7.044 ($P < 0.001$), 1.348 ($P = 0.048$) and 0.688 ($P = 0.019$), respectively.

In these analyses, only the AATH-model-derived *Mean*(*E*), *SD*(*PS*), *SD*(*E*), *CV*(*PS*), *CV*(*E*), *Skew*(*MTT*) and *Kurt*(*E*), and the 2CX-model-derived *Kurt*(*MTT*) remained consistently significant for both the prediction of 1YS and association with OS. Therefore, among the kinetic parameters investigated, *MTT*, *PS* and *E* led to the favorable predictability of survival with their texture attributes. As a result, we could find additional seven significant features as prognostic biomarkers for survival by using higher-order histogram moments for kinetic textural description in HCC, while only a

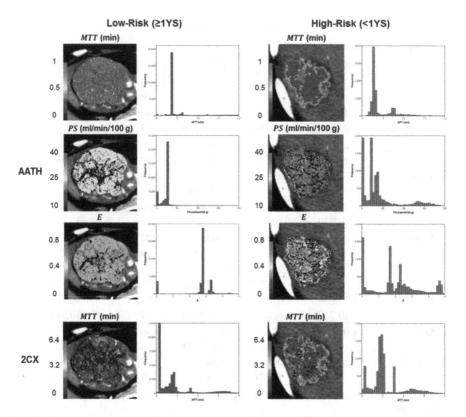

Fig. 2. Parameter maps and histograms of the volumetric HCC ROIs for the AATH-model-derived *MTT*, *PS* and *E*, and the 2CX-model-derived *MTT* in a low-risk woman aged 57 years who survived for 25.53 months (left), and a high-risk man aged 53 years who survived for 6.47 months (right). For the AATH model, $Skew(MTT) = 6.556$, $SD(PS) = 13.96$, $CV(PS) = 0.620$, $Mean(E) = 0.518$, $SD(E) = 0.195$, $CV(E) = 0.376$, and $Kurt(E) = 2.814$ in the low-risk patient, while $Skew(MTT) = 39.46$, $SD(PS) = 43.14$, $CV(PS) = 1.120$, $Mean(E) = 0.400$, $SD(E) = 0.286$, $CV(E) = 0.715$, and $Kurt(E) = -0.650$ in the high-risk patient. For the 2CX model, $Kurt(MTT) = 16.41$ in the low-risk patient, while $Kurt(MTT) = 1.662$ in the high-risk patient.

single significant feature by using a mean value analysis alone. Two examples of cases from each risk group are shown in Fig. 2, with cross-sectional parameter maps and histograms of the volumetric HCC ROIs for the AATH-model-derived *MTT*, *PS* and *E*, and the 2CX-model-derived *MTT*. The cross-validated Kaplan-Meier plots for the eight significant features are shown in Fig. 3.

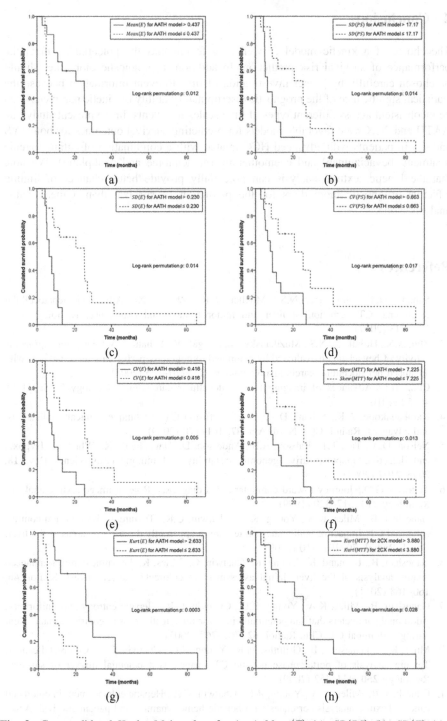

Fig. 3. Cross-validated Kaplan-Meier plots for (a–g) *Mean(E)* (a), *SD(PS)* (b), *SD(E)* (c), *CV(PS)* (d), *CV(E)* (e), *Skew(MTT)* (f), and *Kurt(E)* (g) derived with the AATH model, and (h) *Kurt(MTT)* derived with the 2CX model.

4   Conclusion

The choice of a kinetic model as well as a feature has the potential to affect the performance of survival risk prediction. In addition, a prognostic biomarker should be chosen carefully by proper investigation of time-to-event information because the statistical significance of the prognostic discriminatory ability of kinetic parameters can be inconsistent across different types of time scales for events. In the present study, the AATH and 2CX were favorable models for predicting survival outcomes for both 1YS and OS in patients with advanced HCC treated with a combination of antiangiogenic treatment (bevacizumab) and chemotherapy (gemcitabine and oxaliplatin). We note that the kinetic textural analysis can potentially provide better chances of finding effective prognostic biomarkers for the prediction of survival than a mean value analysis alone.

References

1. Sahani, D.V., Holalkere, N.S., Mueller, P.R., Zhu, A.X.: Advanced hepatocellular carcinoma: CT perfusion of liver and tumor tissue-initial experience. Radiology **243**, 736–743 (2007)
2. Zhu, A.X., Holalkere, N.S., Muzikansky, A., Horgan, K., Sahani, D.V.: Early antiangiogenic activity of bevacizumab evaluated by computed tomography perfusion scan in patients with advanced hepatocellular carcinoma. Oncologist **13**, 120–125 (2008)
3. Choi, B.I.: Advances of imaging for hepatocellular carcinoma. Oncology **78**(Suppl 1), 46–52 (2010)
4. Kambadakone, A.R., Sahani, D.V.: Body perfusion CT: Technique, clinical applications, and advances. Radiol. Clin. North Am. **47**, 161–178 (2009)
5. Nelson, D.A., Tan, T.T., Rabson, A.B., Anderson, D., Degenhardt, K., White, E.: Hypoxia and defective apoptosis drive genomic instability and tumorigenesis. Genes Dev. **18**, 2095–2107 (2004)
6. Tourassi, G.D.: Journey toward computer-aided diagnosis: Role of image texture analysis. Radiology **213**, 317–320 (1999)
7. Ganeshan, B., Miles, K.A., Young, R.C., Chatwin, C.R.: Texture analysis in non-contrast enhanced CT: Impact of malignancy on texture in apparently disease-free areas of the liver. Eur. J. Radiol. **70**, 101–110 (2009)
8. Ganeshan, B., Burnand, K., Young, R., Chatwin, C., Miles, K.: Dynamic contrast-enhanced texture analysis of the liver: Initial assessment in colorectal cancer. Invest. Radiol. **46**, 160–168 (2011)
9. Ganeshan, B., Miles, K.A., Young, R.C., Chatwin, C.R.: Hepatic entropy and uniformity: Additional parameters that can potentially increase the effectiveness of contrast enhancement during abdominal CT. Clin. Radiol. **62**, 761–768 (2007)
10. Miles, K.A., Ganeshan, B., Griffiths, M.R., Young, R.C., Chatwin, C.R.: Colorectal cancer: Texture analysis of portal phase hepatic CT images as a potential marker of survival. Radiology **250**, 444–452 (2009)
11. Ganeshan, B., Miles, K.A., Young, R.C., Chatwin, C.R.: Hepatic enhancement in colorectal cancer: Texture analysis correlates with hepatic hemodynamics and patient survival. Acad. Radiol. **14**, 1520–1530 (2007)

12. Ng, F., Ganeshan, B., Kozarski, R., Miles, K.A., Goh, V.: Assessment of primary colorectal cancer heterogeneity by using whole-tumor texture analysis: Contrast-enhanced CT texture as a biomarker of 5-Year survival. Radiology **266**, 177–184 (2013)

13. Lee, S.H., Kim, J.H., Cho, N., Park, J.S., Yang, Z., Jung, Y.S., Moon, W.K.: Multilevel analysis of spatiotemporal association features for differentiation of tumor enhancement patterns in breast DCE-MRI. Med. Phys. **37**, 3940–3956 (2010)

14. Lee, S.H., Hayano, K., Sahani, D., Yoshida, H.: Use of tracer kinetic model-driven biomarkers for monitoring antiangiogenic therapy of hepatocellular carcinoma in first-pass perfusion CT. In: Yoshida, H., Warfield, S., Vannier, M.W. (eds.) Abdominal Imaging 2013. LNCS, vol. 8198, pp. 270–279. Springer, Heidelberg (2013)

15. Brix, G., Griebel, J., Kiessling, F., Wenz, F.: Tracer kinetic modelling of tumour angiogenesis based on dynamic contrast-enhanced CT and MRI measurements. Eur. J. Nucl. Med. Mol. Imag. **37**(Suppl 1), S30–S51 (2010)

16. Tofts, P.S., Brix, G., Buckley, D.L., Evelhoch, J.L., Henderson, E., Knopp, M.V., Larsson, H.B., Lee, T.Y., Mayr, N.A., Parker, G.J., Port, R.E., Taylor, J., Weisskoff, R.M.: Estimating kinetic parameters from dynamic contrast-enhanced T(1)-weighted MRI of a Diffusable tracer: Standardized quantities and symbols. J. Magn. Reson. Imag. **10**, 223–232 (1999)

17. Sourbron, S.P., Buckley, D.L.: On the scope and interpretation of the tofts models for DCE-MRI. Magn. Reson. Med. **66**, 735–745 (2011)

18. Brix, G., Bahner, M.L., Hoffmann, U., Horvath, A., Schreiber, W.: Regional blood flow, capillary permeability, and compartmental volumes: measurement with dynamic CT–initial experience. Radiology **210**, 269–276 (1999)

19. St. Lawrence, K.S., Lee, T.Y.: An adiabatic approximation to the tissue homogeneity model for water exchange in the brain: I. Theoretical derivation. J. Cereb. Blood Flow Metab. **18**, 1365–1377 (1998)

20. Koh, T.S.: On the a priori identifiability of the two-compartment distributed parameter model from residual tracer data acquired by dynamic contrast-enhanced imaging. IEEE Trans. Biomed. Eng. **55**, 340–344 (2008)

21. Microsoft [Computer software]: Excel. Microsoft Corporation, Redmond, WA (1996)

22. Zhu, F., Carpenter, T., Rodriguez Gonzalez, D., Atkinson, M., Wardlaw, J.: Computed tomography perfusion imaging denoising using gaussian process regression. Phys. Med. Biol. **57**, N183–N198 (2012)

23. Ibanez, L., Schroeder, W., Ng, L., Cates, J.: The ITK Software Guide. Kitware, Inc., Clifton Park (2005)

24. Zhu, A.X., Blaszkowsky, L.S., Ryan, D.P., Clark, J.W., Muzikansky, A., Horgan, K., Sheehan, S., Hale, K.E., Enzinger, P.C., Bhargava, P., Stuart, K.: Phase II study of gemcitabine and oxaliplatin in combination with bevacizumab in patients with advanced hepatocellular carcinoma. J. Clin. Oncol. **24**, 1898–1903 (2006)

Feasibility of Single-Input Tracer Kinetic Modeling with Continuous-Time Formalism in Liver 4-Phase Dynamic Contrast-Enhanced CT

Sang Ho Lee[1(✉)], Yasuji Ryu[3], Koichi Hayano[2], and Hiroyuki Yoshida[1]

[1] 3D Imaging Research, Department of Radiology, Massachusetts General Hospital and Harvard Medical School, 25 New Chardon St., Suite 400C, Boston, MA 02114, USA
{lee.sangho,yoshida.hiro}@mgh.harvard.edu
[2] Division of Abdominal Imaging and Intervention, Department of Radiology, Massachusetts General Hospital, 55 Fruit St., Boston, MA 02114, USA
khayano@partners.org
[3] Department of Radiology, Graduate School of Medical Science, Kanazawa University, 13-1 Takara-Machi, Kanazawa, Ishikawa 920-8641, Japan
yryu-kanazawa@umin.ac.jp

Abstract. The modeling of tracer kinetics with use of low-temporal-resolution data is of central importance for patient dose reduction in dynamic contrast-enhanced CT (DCE-CT) study. Tracer kinetic models of the liver vary according to the physiologic assumptions imposed on the model, and they can substantially differ in the ways how the input for blood supply and tissue compartments are modeled. In this study, single-input flow-limited (FL), Tofts-Kety (TK), extended TK (ETK), Hayton-Brady (HB), two compartment exchange (2CX), and adiabatic approximation to the tissue homogeneity (AATH) models were applied to the analysis of liver 4-phase DCE-CT data with fully continuous-time parameter formulation, including the bolus arrival time. The bolus arrival time for the 2CX and AATH models was described by modifying the vascular transport operator theory. Initial results indicate that single-input tracer kinetic modeling is feasible for distinguishing between hepatocellular carcinoma and normal liver parenchyma.

Keywords: Continuous-time tracer kinetic modeling · Bolus arrival time · Vascular transport operator · Four-phase dynamic contrast-enhanced CT

1 Introduction

Dynamic contrast-enhanced CT (DCE-CT) that involves intravenous administration of iodinated contrast agent (CA) can measure the vascular physiology of tumors through an analysis of the temporal changes of CT attenuation during sequential imaging. The fitting of a predefined compartmental model involves estimation of the values of kinetic parameters that provide a best fit to an observed concentration-time curve [1, 2].

© Springer International Publishing Switzerland 2014
H. Yoshida et al. (Eds.): ABDI 2014, LNCS 8676, pp. 62–73, 2014.
DOI: 10.1007/978-3-319-13692-9_6

A mathematical model is applied to the arterial and the tissue tracer concentration to estimate the physiologic parameters of interest.

Assessment of hemodynamic changes is particularly challenging for the liver due to its dual blood supply [3]. A dual-input model has potential to provide the physiologic proportions of blood supply to the liver tissue from the hepatic arterial system and from the portal venous system in vivo [4]. However, practical application of a dual-input model has various limitations. First, the hepatic artery may be difficult to locate, because it is thin and hardly visible on images. Therefore, the hepatic arterial input is generally approximated by sampling of the concentration-time curve at the abdominal aorta [4, 5, 6], which is a global input that supplies blood to the abdominal cavity. Thus, because the delay and dispersion of the CA to the aorta-hepatic artery pathway are prone to errors in the estimation of the flow [7], most of the currently developed dual-input liver models might not generate a precise physiological reality, although they would be physiologically more accurate than single-input models. Second, the low temporal resolution of 4-phase DCE-CT data may hamper the use of dual-input models with different physiologic scenarios because of high uncertainty in the intervals of data points that might contain mixed hepatic arterial and portal flow information. Furthermore, an additional parameter, such as arterial flow fraction in the dual-input models, can cause the total number of unknown parameters to exceed the effective degrees of freedom in measured data. Therefore, it may be necessary to make simplifying assumptions in order to reduce the number of parameters down to a manageable number, while providing a reasonable goodness-of-fit as well as enabling the study of different tracer kinetic models with varying degrees of complexity in the capillary-tissue system. Ultimately, there is a trade-off between computational cost and potential benefits of a precise model.

Tumor angiogenesis in the liver develops generally from the arterial blood supply rather than from the portal circulation, because the portal blood supply decreases with advancement of the tumor and eventually the tumor is fed mainly by arterial flow [8]. Thus, hepatic tumor circulation differs from the overall circulation pattern [9].

We performed a pilot study to evaluate six different single-input tracer kinetic models with the fundamental biophysical concepts and tracer kinetic principles of dynamic contrast-enhanced imaging: the flow-limited (FL) model [1], Tofts-Kety (TK) model [10], extended TK (ETK) model [11], Hayton-Brady (HB) model [12], two compartment exchange (2CX) model [13], and adiabatic approximation to the tissue homogeneity (AATH) model [14]. For parametric fitting of 4-phase DCE-CT data, the six models were extended to a fully continuous-time parameter formulation, including the bolus arrival time. Thus, the aim of this study was to investigate the discriminatory ability of each model between hepatocellular carcinoma (HCC) and normal liver parenchyma, and to demonstrate the potential of single-input tracer kinetic modeling in liver 4-phase DCE-CT.

2 Methods

2.1 Arterial Input Function

To derive the continuous formulation of each kinetic model in the time domain, first an arterial input function (AIF) needs to be modeled as a continuous-time functional form.

The AIF was acquired on the abdominal aorta with use of a sums-of-exponentials model from individual patients [15]. By imposing the bolus arrival time $(t_{\mathrm{Lag,A}})$ in the artery [16], a functional form for the AIF model can be given by $C_A(t) = \{A_B(t - t_{\mathrm{Lag,A}})e^{-\mu_B(t - t_{\mathrm{Lag,A}})} + A_G\left(e^{-\mu_G(t - t_{\mathrm{Lag,A}})} - e^{-\mu_B(t - t_{\mathrm{Lag,A}})}\right)\}u(t - t_{\mathrm{Lag,A}})$, where $C_A(t)$ is the arterial blood concentration of CA (in g/ml), and $u(t)$ is the unit step function. The $A_B = a_B - a_B a_G/(\mu_B - \mu_G)$, $A_G = a_B a_G/(\mu_B - \mu_G)^2$, μ_B and μ_G are scaling constants that govern the height and shape of the AIF.

2.2   Continuous-Time Formulation of Tracer Kinetic Models

Once the AIF is modeled as a continuous-time functional form, an analytic solution for each kinetic model can be derived by incorporating the scaling constants of the AIF. Adopting the approach of a linear time-invariant system, the concentration of CA for the liver tissue, $C_T(t)$, can be described as a convolution integral between the impulse response function, $Q_T(t)$, and $C_A(t)$,

$$C_T(t) = Q_T(t) \otimes \frac{C_A(t)}{1 - H_{\mathrm{LV}}},\tag{1}$$

where H_{LV} is the hematocrit of blood in large vessels ($\cong 0.45$) [1], and $\otimes$ denotes the convolution operator. All models considered here basically fall under this assumption. The impulse response functions $Q_T(t)$, for the six different models are given by

$$Q_{T,\mathrm{FL}}(t) = v_P \frac{F}{V_P} e^{-\frac{v_P\,F}{v_D\,V_P}t},\tag{2}$$

$$Q_{T,\mathrm{TK}}(t) = v_P \frac{EF}{V_P} e^{-\frac{v_P EF}{v_I V_P}t},\tag{3}$$

$$Q_{T,\mathrm{ETK}}(t) = v_P \delta(t) + v_P \frac{EF}{V_P} e^{-\frac{v_P EF}{v_I V_P}t},\tag{4}$$

$$Q_{T,\mathrm{HB}}(t) = \frac{A_{\mathrm{HB}}}{a - b}\left(e^{-bt} - e^{-at}\right),\tag{5}$$

$$Q_{T,\mathrm{2CX}}(t) = v_P \frac{F}{V_P}\left\{Ae^{\alpha t} + (1 - A)e^{\beta t}\right\}\tag{6}$$

$$\text{with } \binom{\alpha}{\beta} = \frac{1}{2}\left[-\left\{\frac{F}{V_P} + \left(1 + \frac{v_P}{v_I}\right)\frac{PS}{V_P}\right\} \pm \sqrt{\left\{\frac{F}{V_P} + \left(1 + \frac{v_P}{v_I}\right)\frac{PS}{V_P}\right\}^2 - 4\frac{v_P}{v_I}\frac{F}{V_P}\frac{PS}{V_P}}\right]$$

$$\text{and } A = \frac{\alpha + \left(1 + \frac{v_P}{v_I}\right)\frac{PS}{V_P}}{\alpha - \beta},$$

$$Q_{\text{T,AATH}}(t) = v_P \frac{F}{V_P} \left\{ u(t) + \left(E e^{-\frac{v_P EF}{v_I V_P}\left(t - \frac{V_P}{F}\right)} - 1 \right) u\left(t - \frac{V_P}{F}\right) \right\}, \tag{7}$$

where $Q_{\text{T,FT}}(t)$, $Q_{\text{T,TK}}(t)$, $Q_{\text{T,ETK}}(t)$, $Q_{\text{T,HB}}(t)$, $Q_{\text{T,2CX}}(t)$ and $Q_{\text{T,AATH}}(t)$ represent the $Q_T(t)$, for the FL, TK, ETK, HB, 2CX, and AATH models, respectively. Note that $\delta(t)$ is the Dirac delta function, v_P is the plasma volume fraction, v_I is the interstitial volume fraction, $v_D = v_P + v_I$ is the relative distribution volume, V_P is the plasma volume (in ml), F is the plasma flow (in ml/min), PS is the permeability-surface area product (in ml/min), and $E = 1 - e^{-PS/F}$ is the extraction fraction, respectively. The A_{HB}, a and b are reparametrization of the compartmental variables [12]. To account for the difference in bolus arrival times between $C_A(t)$, and $C_T(t)$, a time lag (delay) to the liver tissue, $t_{\text{Lag,T}}$, can be imposed on either $C_A(t)$, or $Q_T(t)$ to calculate $C_T(t)$. For the AIF described above, the analytic forms of $C_T(t)$, are given explicitly for the six different models by

$$C_{\text{T,FL}}(t) = Q_{\text{T,FL}}\left(t - t_{\text{Lag,T}}\right) \otimes \frac{C_A(t)}{1 - H_{\text{LV}}}$$

$$= \frac{v_P}{1 - H_{\text{LV}}} \frac{F}{V_P} \left[\frac{a_B}{\left(\mu_B - \frac{v_P}{v_D}\frac{F}{V_P}\right)^2} \left(1 + \frac{a_G}{\mu_G - \frac{v_P}{v_D}\frac{F}{V_P}}\right) e^{-\frac{v_P}{v_D}\frac{F}{V_P}(t - t_{\text{BAT}})} \right.$$

$$+ \frac{1}{\mu_B - \frac{v_P}{v_D}\frac{F}{V_P}} \left\{ A_G - \frac{a_B - A_G(\mu_B - \mu_G)}{\mu_B - \frac{v_P}{v_D}\frac{F}{V_P}} \right\} e^{-\mu_B(t - t_{\text{BAT}})}$$

$$\left. - \frac{A_G}{\mu_G - \frac{v_P}{v_D}\frac{F}{V_P}} e^{-\mu_G(t - t_{\text{BAT}})} - \frac{A_B}{\mu_B - \frac{v_P}{v_D}\frac{F}{V_P}} (t - t_{\text{BAT}}) e^{-\mu_B(t - t_{\text{BAT}})} \right] u(t - t_{\text{BAT}}), \tag{8}$$

$$C_{\text{T,TK}}(t) = Q_{\text{T,TK}}\left(t - t_{\text{Lag,T}}\right) \otimes \frac{C_A(t)}{1 - H_{\text{LV}}}$$

$$= \frac{v_P}{1 - H_{\text{LV}}} \frac{EF}{V_P} \left[\frac{a_B}{\left(\mu_B - \frac{v_P}{v_I}\frac{EF}{V_P}\right)^2} \left(1 + \frac{a_G}{\mu_G - \frac{v_P}{v_I}\frac{EF}{V_P}}\right) e^{-\frac{v_P}{v_I}\frac{EF}{V_P}(t - t_{\text{BAT}})} \right.$$

$$+ \frac{1}{\mu_B - \frac{v_P}{v_I}\frac{EF}{V_P}} \left\{ A_G - \frac{a_B - A_G(\mu_B - \mu_G)}{\mu_B - \frac{v_P}{v_I}\frac{EF}{V_P}} \right\} e^{-\mu_B(t - t_{\text{BAT}})}$$

$$\left. - \frac{A_G}{\mu_G - \frac{v_P}{v_I}\frac{EF}{V_P}} e^{-\mu_G(t - t_{\text{BAT}})} - \frac{A_B}{\mu_B - \frac{v_P}{v_I}\frac{EF}{V_P}} (t - t_{\text{BAT}}) e^{-\mu_B(t - t_{\text{BAT}})} \right] u(t - t_{\text{BAT}}), \tag{9}$$

$$C_{T,ETK}(t) = Q_{T,ETK}(t - t_{Lag,T}) \otimes \frac{C_A(t)}{1 - H_{LV}} = v_P \frac{C_A(t - t_{Lag,T})}{1 - H_{LV}} + C_{T,TK}(t) \qquad (10)$$

$$C_{T,HB}(t) = Q_{T,HB}(t - t_{Lag,T}) \otimes \frac{C_A(t)}{1 - H_{LV}}$$

$$= \frac{A_{HB}}{1 - H_{LV}} \left[\frac{a_B}{(\mu_B - b)^2(a - b)} \left(1 + \frac{a_G}{\mu_G - b}\right) e^{-b(t - t_{BAT})} \right.$$

$$- \frac{a_B}{(\mu_B - a)^2(a - b)} \left(1 + \frac{a_G}{\mu_G - a}\right) e^{-a(t - t_{BAT})}$$

$$+ \frac{1}{(\mu_B - a)(\mu_B - b)} \left\{ A_B \left(\frac{1}{\mu_B - a} + \frac{1}{\mu_B - b}\right) - A_G \right\} e^{-\mu_B(t - t_{BAT})}$$

$$+ \frac{A_G}{(\mu_B - a)(\mu_B - b)} e^{-\mu_G(t - t_{BAT})}$$

$$\left. + \frac{A_B}{(\mu_B - a)(\mu_B - b)} (t - t_{BAT}) e^{-\mu_B(t - t_{BAT})} \right] u(t - t_{BAT}),$$

$$(11)$$

$$C_{T,2CX}(t) = Q_{T,2CX}(t - t_{Lag,T}) \otimes \frac{C_A(t)}{1 - H_{LV}}$$

$$= \frac{v_P}{1 - H_{LV}} \frac{F}{V_P} \left[\frac{a_B A}{(\mu_B + \alpha)^2} \left(1 + \frac{a_G}{\mu_G + \alpha}\right) e^{\alpha(t - t_{BAT})} \right.$$

$$+ \frac{a_B(1 - A)}{(\mu_B + \beta)^2} \left(1 + \frac{a_G}{\mu_G + \beta}\right) e^{\beta(t - t_{BAT})}$$

$$- \frac{1}{(\mu_B + \alpha)(\mu_B + \beta)}$$

$$\times \left[A_B \left\{ 1 - \frac{A(\alpha - \beta)}{\mu_B + \alpha} + \frac{(1 - A)(\alpha - \beta)}{\mu_B + \beta} + \frac{\mu_B + (1 - A)\alpha + A\beta}{\mu_B - \mu_G} \right\} \right.$$

$$\left. - \frac{a_B}{\mu_B - \mu_G} \{\mu_B + \alpha - A(\alpha - \beta)\} \right] e^{-\mu_B(t - t_{BAT})}$$

$$- \frac{A_G}{\mu_G + \beta} \left\{ 1 - \frac{A(\alpha - \beta)}{\mu_G + \alpha} \right\} e^{-\mu_G(t - t_{BAT})}$$

$$\left. - \frac{A_B}{\mu_B + \beta} \left\{ 1 - \frac{A(\alpha - \beta)}{\mu_B + \alpha} \right\} (t - t_{BAT}) e^{-\mu_B(t - t_{BAT})} \right] u(t - t_{BAT}),$$

$$(12)$$

$$C_{T,AATH}(t) = Q_{T,AATH}(t - t_{Lag,T}) \otimes \frac{C_A(t)}{1 - H_{LV}}$$

$$= \frac{v_P}{1 - H_{LV}} \frac{F}{V_P} \left[\left\{ \frac{a_B}{\mu_B^2} \left(1 + \frac{a_G}{\mu_G} \right) - \frac{1}{\mu_B} \left(\frac{A_B}{\mu_B} - A_G \right) e^{-\mu_B(t - t_{BAT})} \right. \right.$$

$$\left. - \frac{A_G}{\mu_G} e^{-\mu_G(t - t_{BAT})} - \frac{A_B}{\mu_B}(t - t_{BAT}) e^{-\mu_B(t - t_{BAT})} \right\} u(t - t_{BAT})$$

$$- \left[\frac{a_B}{\mu_B^2} \left(1 + \frac{a_G}{\mu_G} \right) - \frac{a_B E}{\left(\mu_B - \frac{v_P EF}{v_I V_P} \right)^2} \left(1 + \frac{a_G}{\mu_G - \frac{v_P EF}{v_I V_P}} \right) e^{-\frac{v_P EF}{v_I V_P}\left(t - \frac{V_P}{F} - t_{BAT}\right)} \right.$$

$$- \frac{1}{\left(\mu_B - \frac{v_P EF}{v_I V_P} \right)^2} \left[\left(1 - \frac{\frac{v_P EF}{v_I V_P}}{\mu_B} \right)^2 \{a_B - A_G(2\mu_B - \mu_G)\} \right.$$

$$\left. - E\left\{ a_B - A_G\left(2\mu_B - \mu_G - \frac{v_P EF}{v_I V_P} \right) \right\} \right] e^{-\mu_B\left(t - \frac{V_P}{F} - t_{BAT}\right)}$$

$$- A_G \left(\frac{1}{\mu_G} - \frac{E}{\mu_G - \frac{v_P EF}{v_I V_P}} \right) e^{-\mu_G\left(t - \frac{V_P}{F} - t_{BAT}\right)}$$

$$\left. - A_B \left(\frac{1}{\mu_B} - \frac{E}{\mu_B - \frac{v_P EF}{v_I V_P}} \right) \left(t - \frac{V_P}{F} - t_{BAT} \right) \right] e^{-\mu_B\left(t - \frac{V_P}{F} - t_{BAT}\right)} u\left(t - \frac{V_P}{F} - t_{BAT} \right) \right],$$

$$(13)$$

where $C_{T,FL}(t)$, $C_{T,TK}(t)$, $C_{T,ETK}(t)$, $C_{T,HB}(t)$, $C_{T,2CX}(t)$ and $C_{T,AATH}(t)$ represent $C_T(t)$ for the FL, TK, ETK, HB, 2CX, and AATH models, respectively. The $t_{BAT} = t_{Lag,A} + t_{Lag,T}$ is the bolus arrival time from the injection site of CA to the target tissue.

2.3   Kinetic Parameter Calculation

Model fitting was performed with a constrained nonlinear optimization algorithm based on MINPACK-1 [17], which yields the sum of squared errors as a measure of the goodness-of-fit [18]. The number of curve-fitting parameters was limited to at most four to avoid over-fitting to the data. The parameters that can be directly estimated by parametric fitting for each model are as follows: $\{F/V_P, v_P, v_I, t_{Lag,T}\}$ for the FL model, $\{EF/V_P, v_P, v_I, t_{Lag,T}\}$ for the TK and ETK models, $\{A_{HB}, a, b, t_{Lag,T}\}$ for the HB model, and $\{F/V_P, PS/V_P v_P, v_I\}$ for the 2CX and AATH models. With these parameterizations, blood flow (BF) for the FL, 2CX, and AATH models, blood volume (BV) for all models except the HB model, mean transit time (MTT) for the FL, 2CX, and AATH models, permeability-surface area product (PS) for the 2CX and AATH models, extraction-flow product (EF) for all models except the HB model, and efflux rate constants (EF/V_I for the TK, ETK, and AATH models, and PS/V_I for the 2CX model, where V_I is the interstitial volume (in ml)) can be computed according to: $BV = 100 \cdot V_P / \{(1 - H_{SV}) \cdot m\}$ (in ml/100 g), where H_{SV} is the hematocrit in small vessels ($\cong 0.25$) [1], and $m = \rho_T V_P / v_P$ is the mass of the tissue with density ρ_T ($= 1.04$ g/cm^3 in the case of soft tissue), $BF = BV \cdot F/V_P$ (in ml/min/100 g),

$MTT = v_D V_P/(v_P F)$ (in min), $PS = (1 - H_{SV}) \cdot BV \cdot PS/V_P$ (in ml/min/100 g), $EF = (1 - H_{SV}) \cdot E \cdot BF$ (in ml/min/100 g), $EF/V_I = (v_P/v_I) \cdot EF/V_P$ (min^{-1}), and $PS/V_I = (v_P/v_I) \cdot PS/V_P$ (min^{-1}).

The $t_{Lag,T}$ for the 2CX and AATH models was modeled by modifying the vascular transport operator (VTO) theory [19], so that it could directly be estimated during the fitting procedure. Originally, the VTO theory was designed to estimate a pure delay of concentration-time curves at inflow and outflow on intravascular transport along a single path. The VTO consists of two components in series, a pure delay and a fourth-order linear differential operator that gives a dispersive delay. The parameters of the VTO are MTT and relative dispersion (RD), which is the standard deviation (SD) of the impulse response divided by MTT. To calculate SD at the target tissue, we used the tissue reside function, $R_T(t) = Q_T(t) \cdot V_P/(v_P F)$ instead of the impulse outflow response, $h_T(t) = -dR_T(t)/dt$ in [19], and then multiplied v_D into the SD to calculate the RD for each of the 2CX and AATH models. The RD and its corresponding $t_{Lag,T}$ for the 2CX and AATH models can be given by

$$RD_{2CX} = v_D \sqrt{\int_0^\infty (\tau - MTT)^2 R_{T,2CX}(\tau)d\tau}$$

$$= v_D \sqrt{-\frac{A}{\alpha^3}(2 + \alpha MTT(2 + \alpha MTT)) - \frac{1 - A}{\beta^3}(2 + \beta MTT(2 + \beta MTT))},$$

$$(14)$$

$$RD_{AATH} = v_D \sqrt{\int_0^\infty (\tau - MTT)^2 R_{T,AATH}(\tau)d\tau}$$

$$= v_D \sqrt{\frac{V_P}{F}\left[\begin{array}{l}\frac{1}{3}\left(\frac{V_P}{F}\right)^2 + MTT\left(MTT - \frac{V_P}{F}\right) \\ + \frac{v_I}{v_P}\left(\frac{V_P}{EF}\right)^2\left[2\left(\frac{v_I}{v_P}\right)^2 + E\left(1 - \frac{F}{V_P}MTT\right)\left\{E\left(1 - \frac{F}{V_P}MTT\right) + 2\frac{v_I}{v_P}\right\}\right]\end{array}\right]},$$

$$(15)$$

$$t_{Lag,T} = MTT\left(1 - \frac{RD}{0.48}\right), \qquad (16)$$

where RD_{2CX}, RD_{AATH}, $R_{T,2CX}(t)$ and $R_{T,AATH}(t)$ are the RD and $R_T(t)$ for the 2CX and AATH models, respectively. The constant 0.48 is a maximum RD for the dispersiveness of the operator [19]. In case that $t_{Lag,T}$ was a negative value or a value greater than a stipulated threshold, it was assigned a value of 0 in the curve-fitting process so that it could converge into a new value.

2.4 Patients and DCE-CT Imaging

We investigated nine patient HCC cases to demonstrate clinical applicability of the six different single-input tracer kinetic models with the proposed continuous-time parameter formalism in 4-phase liver DCE-CT. The patients were scanned with a 64 multidetector CT scanner (LightSpeed VCT or Discovery CT750 HD; GE Medical Systems, Milwaukee, WI). A total of 1.7 ml/kg (80 to 135 ml) of nonionic iodinated CA (Iomeron; Eisai, Tokyo, 350 mg/ml) was injected with 30 s injection duration time at the rate of 3–5 ml/s and a volume as per 550–600 mgI/kg weight. The arterial-phase timing was determined with bolus tracking technology (Smart Prep; GE Healthcare), and scan was initiated 17 s after the preselected threshold of 200 HU was attained, with a region of interest (ROI) placed in the aorta above the celiac axis branching, where the $t_{Lag,A}$ was determined by observation of a snapshot to show the onset time of temporal enhancement in the aorta. The portal-venous phase and delayed phase initiated at 70 s and 150 s, respectively, after the preselected threshold of 200 HU was attained. In the patient cohort, $t_{Lag,A}$ ranged from 10 to 16 s, and the time when the preselected threshold of 200 HU was attained ranged from 14 to 24 s. The following CT parameters were used for obtaining volume data: 120 kVp, Auto mA, 16×0.625 mm detector collimation, 2.5 mm slice thickness, 95 to 120 slices, and a pitch of 1.

2.5 Image Processing and Analysis

To enhance contrast-to-noise ratios, DCE-CT images were denoised by use of multiple observations Gaussian process regression [20]. To reduce movement-induced artifacts, we coregistered each set of dynamic images with the portal-phase image as a template by using the Insight Segmentation and Registration Toolkit [21]. The registration was performed based on serial applications of 3D rigid, affine, and symmetric force Demons deformable registration methods with use of a multiresolution scheme [16]. For curve-fitting of the 4-phase DCE-CT data, 2D spatial filtering with a 5×5 pixel median kernel was applied on each DCE-CT sequence before extracting a voxel-level tissue concentration-time curve for fitting. ROIs were manually drawn by an experienced radiologist over a primary HCC and its adjacent normal tissue for each patient. Mean values in the ROIs (in total, 9 HCC and 9 normal tissue ROIs) were recorded for each parameter for each model for each patient. An example of fitting the voxel-level 4-phase DCE-CT data in HCC and normal tissue with the six different kinetic models is shown in Fig. 1.

2.6 Statistical Analysis

The predictable value of each parameter was evaluated by measuring the area under the receiver operating characteristic curve (A_Z). The Mann-Whitney (MW) test was used to test for differences in the mean values of each parameter between normal liver parenchyma and HCC ROIs. To assess the independent impact of each parameter on differentiation between HCC and normal liver parenchyma, binary logistic regression (BLR) analysis was performed with bootstrapping with 1000 replications. A P value <0.05 indicated a significant difference.

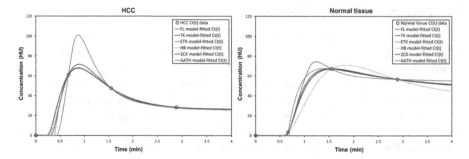

Fig. 1. Graphs illustrating examples of fitting the voxel-level 4-phase DCE-CT data with the FL, TK, ETK, HB, 2CX, and AATH models in the HCC (left) and normal liver tissue (right).

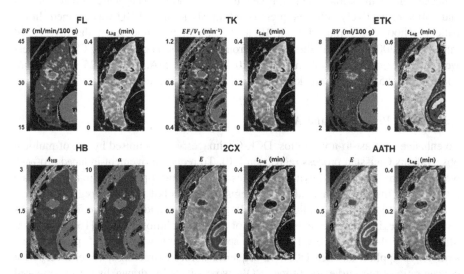

Fig. 2. Parametric maps obtained with six different tracer kinetic models for a patient with HCC. Each model displays two most significant parameters that yielded relatively higher discriminatory ability between HCC and normal liver tissue.

3 Results

Results of ROI analysis and comparison of the various hepatic microcirculatory parameters for the different models are shown in Table 1. In all of the applicable models, the ROIs of HCC showed increased BF and BV, earlier bolus arrival time $t_{Lag,T}$, shorter MTT, and smaller E than those of the normal liver tissue. The three parameters (i.e., A_{HB}, a, and b) for the HB model were all higher in the HCCs than in the normal liver tissue. The EF and EF/V_I were higher in the HCC with the TK, ETK, and AATH models, whereas the EF and PS/V_I were lower with the 2CX model. The v_I was lower in the HCC with the FL, TK, ETK, and AATH models, whereas it was higher with the 2CX model. The PS was higher in the HCC with the AATH model,

Table 1. Statistics (mean ± SD) for ROI analysis of each parameter in the HCC and background liver tissue, and the corresponding results of MW and BLR tests.

Parameter	Model	Mean ± SD		A_Z	P-value	
		HCC	Normal		MW	BLR
BF (ml/min/100 g)	FL	100.2 ± 84.53	40.52 ± 15.32	0.840	**0.014**	**0.027**
	2CX	93.49 ± 51.31	44.14 ± 13.09	0.938	**0.001**	**0.011**
	AATH	75.95 ± 40.71	41.19 ± 12.82	0.840	**0.014**	**0.018**
BV (ml/100 g)	FL	11.74 ± 7.681	6.958 ± 2.378	0.790	**0.040**	0.253
	TK	36.41 ± 22.86	20.44 ± 8.038	0.802	**0.031**	0.137
	ETK	11.70 ± 6.870	4.935 ± 1.053	0.975	**<0.001**	**0.009**
	2CX	24.97 ± 7.750	20.30 ± 4.343	0.654	0.297	0.056
	AATH	18.88 ± 6.872	14.78 ± 2.977	0.679	0.222	**0.048**
MTT (min)	FL	0.560 ± 0.338	1.366 ± 1.097	0.765	0.063	0.080
	2CX	0.658 ± 0.332	1.125 ± 0.783	0.679	0.222	0.060
	AATH	0.791 ± 0.421	1.316 ± 0.983	0.691	0.190	0.066
PS (ml/min/100 g)	2CX	29.01 ± 21.60	56.44 ± 45.14	0.765	0.063	0.113
	AATH	23.91 ± 16.41	18.46 ± 4.744	0.556	0.730	0.224
EF (ml/min/100 g)	TK	119.4 ± 156.1	29.70 ± 12.51	0.802	**0.031**	**0.042**
	ETK	38.27 ± 39.50	23.88 ± 8.052	0.519	0.931	0.154
	2CX	13.46 ± 11.68	19.11 ± 6.205	0.716	0.136	0.315
	AATH	16.85 ± 9.953	13.08 ± 2.833	0.593	0.546	0.209
EF/V_I or PS/V_I (min^{-1})	TK	4.947 ± 5.314	1.243 ± 0.708	0.827	**0.019**	**0.024**
	ETK	85.22 ± 159.9	1.197 ± 0.647	0.654	0.297	0.360
	2CX	181.7 ± 224.1	235.2 ± 321.8	0.531	0.963	0.675
	AATH	29.61 ± 62.90	0.985 ± 0.539	0.580	0.605	0.313
v_I	FL	0.173 ± 0.119	0.238 ± 0.081	0.753	0.077	0.345
	TK	0.265 ± 0.110	0.287 ± 0.071	0.605	0.489	0.665
	ETK	0.211 ± 0.146	0.262 ± 0.097	0.753	0.077	0.518
	2CX	0.179 ± 0.168	0.152 ± 0.132	0.556	0.730	0.695
	AATH	0.199 ± 0.154	0.209 ± 0.132	0.531	0.863	0.895
E	2CX	0.224 ± 0.108	0.605 ± 0.192	0.963	**<0.001**	**0.002**
	AATH	0.304 ± 0.093	0.438 ± 0.084	0.877	**0.006**	**0.004**
A_{HB}	HB	16.49 ± 11.19	3.119 ± 2.459	0.975	**<0.001**	**0.004**
a		14.63 ± 3.312	7.470 ± 5.046	0.877	**0.006**	**0.004**
b		5.690 ± 2.530	2.648 ± 1.320	0.864	**0.008**	**0.006**
$t_{Lag,T}$ (min)	FL	0.028 ± 0.026	0.141 ± 0.087	0.926	**0.001**	**0.004**
	TK	0.034 ± 0.034	0.142 ± 0.087	0.877	**0.006**	**0.004**
	ETK	0.089 ± 0.049	0.271 ± 0.092	0.963	**<0.001**	**0.021**
	HB	0.021 ± 0.026	0.026 ± 0.043	0.531	0.863	0.778
	2CX	0.020 ± 0.024	0.156 ± 0.084	0.988	**<0.001**	**0.002**
	AATH	0.057 ± 0.036	0.181 ± 0.072	0.963	**<0.001**	**0.002**

Note—MW = Mann-Whitney, and BLR = binary logistic regression. Bold numbers indicate statistical significance ($P < 0.05$).

while it was lower with the 2CX model. Considering parameters with $A_Z > 0.95$ as well as statistical significance in both the MW and BLR tests, the ETK-model-derived BV ($A_Z = 0.975$, MW: $P < 0.001$, and BLR: $P = 0.009$) and $t_{Lag,T}$ ($A_Z = 0.963$, MW: $P < 0.001$, and BLR: $P = 0.021$), the HB-model-derived A_{HB} ($A_Z = 0.975$, MW: $P < 0.001$ BLR: $P = 0.004$), and the 2CX-model-derived E ($A_Z = 0.963$, MW: $P < 0.001$, and BLR: $P = 0.002$) and $t_{Lag,T}$ ($A_Z = 0.988$, MW: $P < 0.001$, and BLR: $P = 0.002$), and the AATH model-derived $t_{Lag,T}$ ($A_Z = 0.963$, MW: $P < 0.001$, and BLR: $P = 0.002$) led to a favorable outcome in this study. However, we note that all of the six different single-input models showed statistical significance in terms of discrimination between HCC and normal liver tissue. Parametric maps for two most significant parameters for each model that yielded relatively higher discriminatory ability between HCC and normal liver tissue are shown in Fig. 2.

4 Conclusion

We developed six different tracer kinetic models for 4-phase DCE-CT data analysis with fully continuous-time parameter formulation based on the linear time-invariant system, including the bolus arrival time. In particular, we enabled 4-phase data fitting with full two-compartment models such as the 2CX and AATH models by introducing the VTO theory. Because kinetic parameter values differ substantially among different models, the selection of a tracer kinetic model influences its discriminatory ability. The preliminary results indicate that single-input tracer kinetic modeling of the liver is feasible although the portal venous contribution to tumor perfusion is still an open question. Further work is encouraged to establish the clinical usefulness of the proposed approach in the imaging diagnosis and prognosis of HCC.

Acknowledgments. This study was supported in part by grant CA187877 from the National Cancer Institute at the National Institutes of Health.

References

1. Brix, G., Griebel, J., Kiessling, F., Wenz, F.: Tracer kinetic modelling of tumour angiogenesis based on dynamic contrast-enhanced CT and MRI measurements. Eur. J. Nucl. Med. Mol. Imaging 37(Suppl 1), S30–S51 (2010)
2. Sourbron, S.P., Buckley, D.L.: Tracer kinetic modelling in MRI: Estimating perfusion and capillary permeability. Phys. Med. Biol. 57, R1–R33 (2012)
3. Schenk Jr., W.G., McDonald, J.C., McDonald, K., Drapanas, T.: Direct measurement of hepatic blood flow in surgical patients: with related observations on hepatic flow dynamics in experimental animals. Ann. Surg. 156, 463–471 (1962)
4. Koh, T.S., Thng, C.H., Lee, P.S., Hartono, S., Rumpel, H., Goh, B.C., Bisdas, S.: Hepatic metastases: In vivo assessment of perfusion parameters at dynamic contrast-enhanced MR imaging with dual-input two-compartment tracer kinetics model. Radiology 249, 307–320 (2008)

5. Koh, T.S., Thng, C.H., Hartono, S., Kwek, J.W., Khoo, J.B., Miyazaki, K., Collins, D.J., Orton, M.R., Leach, M.O., Lewington, V., Koh, D.M.: Dynamic contrast-enhanced MRI of neuroendocrine hepatic metastases: A feasibility study using a dual-input two-compartment model. Magn. Reson. Med. **65**, 250–260 (2011)

6. Materne, R., Smith, A.M., Peeters, F., Dehoux, J.P., Keyeux, A., Horsmans, Y., Van Beers, B.E.: Assessment of hepatic perfusion parameters with dynamic MRI. Magn. Reson. Med. **47**, 135–142 (2002)

7. Calamante, F., Willats, L., Gadian, D.G., Connelly, A.: Bolus delay and dispersion in perfusion MRI: Implications for tissue predictor models in stroke. Magn. Reson. Med. **55**, 1180–1185 (2006)

8. Matsui, O.: Detection and characterization of hepatocellular carcinoma by imaging. Clin. Gastroenterol. Hepatol. **3**, S136–S140 (2005)

9. Miles, K.A.: Functional computed tomography in oncology. Eur. J. Cancer **38**, 2079–2084 (2002)

10. Tofts, P.S., Brix, G., Buckley, D.L., Evelhoch, J.L., Henderson, E., Knopp, M.V., Larsson, H.B., Lee, T.Y., Mayr, N.A., Parker, G.J., Port, R.E., Taylor, J., Weisskoff, R.M.: Estimating kinetic parameters from dynamic contrast-enhanced T(1)-weighted MRI of a diffusable tracer: Standardized quantities and symbols. J. Magn. Reson. Imag. **10**, 223–232 (1999)

11. Sourbron, S.P., Buckley, D.L.: On the scope and interpretation of the Tofts models for DCE-MRI. Magn. Reson. Med. **66**, 735–745 (2011)

12. Hayton, P., Brady, M., Tarassenko, L., Moore, N.: Analysis of dynamic MR breast images using a model of contrast enhancement. Med. Image Anal. **1**, 207–224 (1997)

13. Brix, G., Bahner, M.L., Hoffmann, U., Horvath, A., Schreiber, W.: Regional blood flow, capillary permeability, and compartmental volumes: Measurement with dynamic CT–initial experience. Radiology **210**, 269–276 (1999)

14. St Lawrence, K.S., Lee, T.Y.: An adiabatic approximation to the tissue homogeneity model for water exchange in the brain: I. Theoretical derivation. J. Cereb. Blood Flow Metab. **18**, 1365–1377 (1998)

15. Orton, M.R., d'Arcy, J.A., Walker-Samuel, S., Hawkes, D.J., Atkinson, D., Collins, D.J., Leach, M.O.: Computationally efficient vascular input function models for quantitative kinetic modelling using DCE-MRI. Phys. Med. Biol. **53**, 1225–1239 (2008)

16. Lee, S.H., Ryu, Y., Hayano, K., Yoshida, H.: Continuous-time flow-limited modeling by convolution area property and differentiation product rule in 4-Phase liver dynamic contrast-enhanced CT. In: Yoshida, H., Warfield, S., Vannier, M.W. (eds.) Abdominal Imaging 2013. LNCS, vol. 8198, pp. 259–269. Springer, Heidelberg (2013)

17. Moré, J.J., Garbow, B.S., Hillstrom, K.E.: User Guide for MINPACK-1 (1980)

18. Markwardt, C.B.: Non-linear least squares fitting in IDL with MPFIT. In: Proceedings of Astronomical Data Analysis Software and Systems XVIII, Quebec, Canada, ASP Conference Series, vol. 411, p. 251 (2009)

19. King, R.B., Deussen, A., Raymond, G.M., Bassingthwaighte, J.B.: A vascular transport operator. Am. J. Physiol. **265**, H2196–H2208 (1993)

20. Zhu, F., Carpenter, T., Rodriguez Gonzalez, D., Atkinson, M., Wardlaw, J.: Computed tomography perfusion imaging denoising using gaussian process regression. Phys. Med. Biol. **57**, N183–N198 (2012)

21. Ibanez, L., Schroeder, W., Ng, L., Cates, J.: The ITK Software Guide. Kitware, Inc., Clifton Park (2005)

Metastatic Liver Tumor Segmentation Using Texture-Based Omni-Directional Deformable Surface Models

Eugene Vorontsov[1], Nadine Abi-Jaoudeh[2], and Samuel Kadoury[1(✉)]

[1] MEDICAL, École Polytechnique de Montréal, Montréal, Canada
{eugene.vorontsov, samuel.kadoury}@polymtl.ca
[2] Radiology and Imaging Sciences, National Institutes of Health,
Bethesda, MD, USA
abijaoudehn@cc.nih.gov

Abstract. The delineation of tumor boundaries is an essential task for the diagnosis and follow-up of liver cancer. However accurate segmentation remains challenging due to tissue inhomogeneity and high variability in tumor appearance. In this paper, we propose a semi-automatic liver tumor segmentation method that combines a deformable model with a machine learning mechanism. More precisely, segmentation is performed by an MRF-based omni-directional deformable surface model that uses image information together with a two-class (tumor, non-tumor) voxel classification map. The classification map is produced by a kernel SVM classifier trained on texture features, as well as intensity mean and variance. The segmentation method is validated on a metastatic tumor dataset consisting of 27 tumors across a set of abdominal CT images, using leave-one-out validation. Compared to pure voxel and gradient approaches, our method achieves better performance in terms of mean distance and Dice scores on the group of 27 liver tumors and can deal with highly pathological cases.

Keywords: Segmentation · Deformable model · GLCM · SVM · Tumor · Liver · CT image

1 Introduction

The segmentation of metastatic liver tumors from abdominal CT images is required for the diagnosis of liver cancer, intra-operative navigation, pre-procedural planning and targeted clinical therapies such as radiotherapy. While manual segmentation by an expert tends to be accurate, the process is very time consuming and requires expert knowledge of the imaged tissue and imaging modality. Instead, the largest two diameters in the transverse plane are typically used to estimate tumor size, greatly sacrificing accuracy for time [1]. As the amount of medical image data continues to increase, the development of automated computer-driven segmentation methods is becoming increasingly feasible. Automating the segmentation process continues to be an area of active research in fields such as radiology and liver oncology.

© Springer International Publishing Switzerland 2014
H. Yoshida et al. (Eds.): ABDI 2014, LNCS 8676, pp. 74–83, 2014.
DOI: 10.1007/978-3-319-13692-9_7

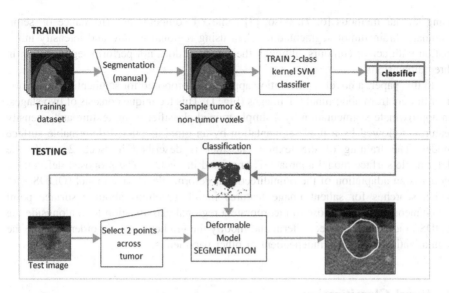

Fig. 1. Flow chart illustrating the training process and the testing process for unseen cases.

Automatic segmentation of tumors is particularly challenging due to their highly variable size, shape, intensity and texture. This is especially the case with liver tumors. Due to the high blood perfusion of the liver and epithelial fenestration in the blood vessels, the liver is often invaded by other metastasizing cancers [2]. In fact, metastatic tumors are even more common in the liver than primary tumors such as hepatocellular carcinomas. Furthermore, both metastatic tumors and primary liver tumors can present different morphologies: diffuse tumors with unclear boundaries that marble liver tissue; focal tumors which are typically smooth singular masses; and multi-focal tumors that appear as multiple, typically smaller, focal tumors spread through the liver. The liver itself can also appear variable due to natural inter-patient differences, cirrhosis of the liver tissue, and prior surgical lesioning of the liver.

Automatic liver tumor segmentation methods must be able to deal with these important challenges. Early methods used simple models of pixel intensity information such as region growing from a seed point [3]. Unfortunately, such methods do not produce reliable tumor segmentations, require very specific stopping criteria, and tend to suffer from leakage of the segmentation volume into unrelated image sections. Recent tumor segmentation models typically use machine learning to train a pixel classifier. In [4], image segments are projected onto a lower-dimensional discriminant manifold and their classification is regularized by a conditional random field.

To regularize the segmentation process, deformable models offer the advantage of direct control over the optimization of the tumor surface, by enforcing the existence of only one surface, and can control surface uniformity. However, deformable model approaches have not been extensively investigated for tumor segmentation. A deformable model was used in [5] to regularize an initial liver tumor segmentation attained by thresholding and a trained fuzzy clustering model with reasonable but low performance. However, promising results were attained with brain tumor segmentation using similar methods [6, 7]. Also, [8] achieved competitive performance on semi-automatic brain tumor segmentation when using regional texture and intensity information with active contours, although their method does not perform segmentation in three dimensions.

In this paper, a novel segmentation approach is proposed for segmenting metastatic liver tumors from abdominal CT images (Fig. 1). This technique consists of two stages: an approximate segmentation by a simple trained classifier using texture and intensity features, followed by a final segmentation by an omnidirectional deformable surface model. The training of the texture classifier is described in Sect. 2, while the deformable surface model approach is presented in Sect. 3. The proposed deformable model is an adaptation of the omnidirectional deformable surface model (ODDS) [9], which searches for salient image features in all directions about a surface point simultaneously. We propose to incorporate a regional classification term alongside the ODDS gradient edge-detector term and modify the gradient term, in order to make the regularization parameter independent of other parameters.

2 Voxel Classification

The first stage in the segmentation process is the classification of voxels as *tumor* or *non-tumor* from an input CT image. This classification is performed by a kernel SVM classifier trained on texture features from reference CT images. The resulting binary classification is then used as one of the inputs to the deformable surface model in the second stage of the segmentation.

2.1 Feature Extraction from CT Images

Given an input CT image, an approximate segmentation is generated without regularization by classifying individual voxels as tumor or non-tumor, in order to automatically identify tumor regions within the liver. A feature vector is associated with each voxel, composed of local texture information and first order local image statistics.

Texture information, representing second order image statistics, is derived using a gray-level co-occurrence matrix (GLCM). For each voxel, the GLCM is computed over a $3 \times 3 \times 3$ cubic volume centered on the voxel of interest. Since the GLCM is directional, in order to make the texture computation orientation-invariant, features were taken as the average texture values across all 26 adjacency directions in the cube (voxels are considered adjacent if their faces, edges, or corners touch).

Various parameterizations were tested for texture feature retrieval. Feature values are computed from the GLCM about each voxel for the following eight textures: energy, entropy, correlation, cluster prominence, cluster shade, Haralick's correlation, inertia, and inverse difference moment. In order to capture texture patterns that do not fit into the cubic volume, the same texture evaluation was repeated on the images at multiple resolutions. Images were downscaled by a factor of two by Gaussian blurring and sub-sampling. Finally, feature evaluation was performed at seven different quantization levels of the CT image.

The combination of these eight features, at two scales and seven quantization levels, produced 112 texture features. In addition, mean and variance over the cubic volume were included as two first order statistics features, producing 114 dimensional feature vectors. Since the feature vector may include redundant features, only the most salient features were chosen before training a classifier.

The importance of each feature was analyzed by first performing principal component analysis (PCA) dimensionality reduction on the data. Each feature vector was mean centered and normalized by its variance and the dataset was then dimensionally reduced via PCA, retaining 99.9 % of the variance in the data. This reduced the feature dimensionality from 114 to 11. As a first step to identifying features which were most sampled by PCA, each element in each of the eleven 114-dimensional eigenvectors was normalized by the mean magnitude of its corresponding feature across the mean-centered, normalized dataset. This was done in order to reduce the dependence of the element size on its corresponding feature size in the dataset. Each eigenvector was then normalized to range from 0 to 1, the magnitudes of each element were averaged together across the eigenvectors and the resulting vector was again normalized. This allowed the salience of the features corresponding with each element to be estimated. The final feature vectors used for training were assembled from only salient image features and then whitened with PCA without dimensionality reduction.

2.2 Training the Texture Classifier

Training was performed using a kernel support vector machine (kernel SVM), as implemented in the scikit-learn Python toolkit [10], with a radial basis function (RBF) kernel for optimal classification. For each set of training data, the SVM soft margin parameter C and the RBF parameter γ were chosen via grid search on a validation subset of the training data.

A two-class classification was learned from a balanced training set containing an equal amount of data points in each class: *tumor* and *non-tumor*. The *tumor* data points were sampled from manually segmented tumors validated by a radiologist; the *non-tumor* data points were densely sampled from around the periphery of the tumor edges in order to obtain an optimal discrimination between the two classes at their true boundaries in the images (Fig. 1). A randomly sampled subset of the training data was used during training, limiting training time and the resulting number of support vectors in the classifier to practical levels.

3 Deformable Surface Model Segmentation

After training a voxel classifier for the tumor and non-tumor datasets, unseen tumors are segmented from CT liver images using a deformable surface model with the voxel classification as an input to the model. The proposed model is adapted from ODDS, which initially considers the image gradient at each voxel [9]. It deforms an initial closed surface (represented by a triangle mesh) by displacing mesh vertices towards salient image features derived from image gradients and voxel classification. Displacements for each vertex are considered omnidirectionally as points arranged in a close-packed cubic lattice throughout a spherical volume centered on the vertex. All vertices share the same set of displacement vectors so that translating the whole mesh would require assigning the same displacement vector to each vertex.

The model is optimized by minimizing an energy function, set up as a Markov random field (MRF), using the fast primal dual algorithm (FastPD) [11]:

$$E = \sum_{v \in V} U_{unary}(v, d_v) + \alpha \sum_{(v,w) \in E} U_{binary}(d_v, d_w). \tag{1}$$

Here unary and binary potentials U, are evaluated over the set of all vertices V and the set of all edges E. Unary potentials consider image features at a displacement d_v from a vertex v. Binary potentials regularize mesh deformation by penalizing dissimilar displacements (d_v, d_w) for each pair of vertices (v, w) sharing an edge. The scalar α controls the degree of regularization.

The unary potential considers both edge features and texture-based voxel classification (texture features), weighted by an empirically set weight τ:

$$U_{unary}(v, d_v) = \left[F_{grad}(v, d_v) + \tau F_{tex}(v, d_v) \right]^{-1}. \tag{2}$$

In the edge detection term, the salience of an edge at some point x is determined by the magnitude of the image gradient projected onto the mesh surface normal at that point:

$$F_{grad}(x) = \| n \cdot \nabla [G_\sigma * I(x)] \| \frac{g_{max}[g_{max} + \| \nabla [G_\sigma * I(x)] \|]}{g_{max}^2 + \| n \cdot \nabla [G_\sigma * I(x)] \|^2}. \tag{3}$$

Unlike traditional ODDS, the image I is smoothed by a Gaussian kernel G_σ to smooth gradient changes between voxels due to their grid-like positioning and to locally spread gradient information in case of sub-sampling the image from the search space. The influence of overly strong gradients on surface deformation is attenuated by g_{max} which acts as an approximate upper bound on the gradient magnitude.

The texture term considers voxel classification in a small volume about a position x. The goal is to assign a high score when *tumor* voxels in that volume are likely to be within the mesh and *non-tumor* voxels are likely to be outside of the mesh. Voxel class information is taken from a classification map with *tumor* voxels set to a value of 0 and *non-tumor* voxels set to a value of 1. The texture term is evaluated for a volume of N voxels by summing voxels c_i from the map on one half of the volume and subtracting on the other:

$$F_{tex}(x) = \tau \left(max \left\{ 0, \sum_i^N c_i(x) \cdot (I[n \cdot p_i(x) > 0] - I[n \cdot p_i(x) < 0]) \right\} \right)^2. \tag{4}$$

In Eq. 4, p_i is the position of the voxel with respect to the sample volume origin and n is the initial surface normal, considered to point outward from the closed surface. The term $I(\cdot)$ returns 1 or 0 depending on whether its argument is true or false, respectively and is used to determine the side of the normal that the point falls on.

Finally, the binary potential penalizes differences in pairwise vertex displacements.

$$U_{pairwise}(d_v, d_w) = \left\| \frac{d_w - d_v}{r} \right\|^3 . \tag{5}$$

In order to make this term independent of α, it was normalized by the cube of the search space radius.

4   Experimental Results and Discussion

The proposed segmentation method was tested on hypovascular metastatic liver tumors in CT images. A dataset of 27 manually segmented tumors was assembled from 8 abdominal CT images with hepatic venous phase enhancement. In-plane resolutions ranged from 0.63 mm to 0.88 mm and slice thickness ranged from 0.4 mm to 1.25 mm. In order to maximize the amount of information provided to the SVM voxel classifier during training, the segmentation method was tested in a leave-one-out manner over the images.

4.1   Voxel Classification

During initial testing, it was observed that from the initial set of texture features used for classification, many were highly redundant; applying PCA dimensionality reduction while retaining 99.9 % of the variance, the feature vector size was reduced from 114 to 11. By analyzing the contribution of each feature in the PCA projection as described in Sect. 2.1, it was found to be negligible for all features except those corresponding to the following six types: mean, variance, energy, cluster prominence; and in the downscaled images, correlation and Haralick's correlation. Four of these are texture features. The SVM classifier was trained with 26-dimensional feature vectors composed of the four texture feature types at six quantization levels together with the mean and variance features.

Example classification maps computed in our experiments are shown in Fig. 2. Classification performance was evaluated by evaluating the sensitivity and specificity of tumor voxel classification. Non-tumor voxels were considered only around the perimeter of each tumor. The average sensitivity and specificity, respectively, were found to be 0.83 ± 0.19 and 0.78 ± 0.14 when averaged over all tumors or 0.81 ± 0.13 and 0.72 ± 0.22 when averaged over all images. It was found that classification accuracy was slightly improved by whitening the data, making the accuracy between the two classes more equal in some cases. This is consistent with the behaviour described by [12] where the maximum margin can be poorly established due to a large variance in some directions of non-whitened data.

4.2   Liver Tumor Segmentation

Tumors were segmented with the omni-directional deformable surface model using image gradient information and a voxel classification map described in Sect. 3.

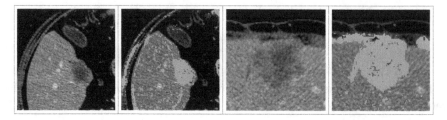

Fig. 2. Sample classification results using the SVM classifier (leave-one-out tests). Classification overlayed on CT image slice in light green (uniform light gray) in frames 2, 4.

The deformable model was initialized semi-automatically for each test. To segment a tumor, a spherical mesh was initialized on the tumor, spanning two points selected by the operator. The parameters α (Eq. 1), τ (Eq. 2), and g_{max} (Eq. 3) were determined experimentally and then reused across all leave-one-out tests. Other parameters were set automatically. The search space radius was set to 90 % of the radius of the initial spherical mesh. The point spacing in the search spaces was set to some integer multiple of the smallest image voxel spacing so that the search space radius was no larger than 15 voxels (to maintain reasonable computational performance). In cases where the integer multiple was 2 or higher, the class map was blurred to accommodate its sub-sampling.

Tumor segmentation was evaluated using the Dice score and quantitative metrics, related to the distance between the surface of the ground truth segmentation and the surface produced by the tested method: mean absolute distance (MAD), root mean squared distance (RMSD), and maximum absolute distance (Max AD). The proposed segmentation method was compared to two other approaches: voxel-based segmentation by simple region growing on the classification map and segmentation by using the deformable model with only gradient features. The proposed method produced superior results, listed in Table 1. Deformable model parameters τ, and g_{max} were experimentally chosen as 10000 and 20, respectively, in both the proposed method when using only gradient features; α was set to 10 in the the proposed method and 1 in the latter. Examples of segmentation results are shown in Fig. 3.

Region growing was performed directly on the classification map. The map was blurred to reduce leakage, reduce the number of holes in the segmented regions, and improve tumor boundary smoothness. To further reduce leakage and improve boundary smoothness, each voxel was only added to the growing region if it had at least 8 neighbours (in any of the 26 directions) that were already in the region. Surface meshes were created about the segmented regions using the marching cubes algorithm and only the outer closed surface was retained for each region. In 8 of the 27 cases, the segmentation leaked far into other tumors and regions. The remaining cases were successfully segmented; however, even considering only the successfully segmented tumors, this method scored significantly lower results than the proposed method in the MAD ($p \leq 0.05$), RMSD ($p \leq 0.05$), and Dice scores ($p \leq 0.01$).

Segmentation using just a gradient-based deformable model without voxel class information failed for most tumors. The proposed method scored significantly higher

Table 1. Average liver tumor segmentation results for the described methods. "# tum." is the number of tumors in the test set. Results that are "excl. failed" are excluding results for lesions with failed segmentations. "MAD": mean absolute distance (mm) between segmented surface and ground truth surface. "RMSD": root mean squared distance (mm^2). "Max AD": maximum absolute distance.

	# tum.	Dice score	MAD	RMSD	Max AD
Proposed method	27	**0.81 ± 0.06**	**1.3 ± 0.6**	**1.6 ± 0.9**	**5.2 ± 3.3**
Classifier + region growing	27	0.57 ± 0.22	7.9 ± 13.3	9.5 ± 9.8	20.3 ± 28.7
Classifier + region growing (excl. failed)	19	0.64 ± 0.18	1.9 ± 0.6	2.2 ± 0.4	6.0 ± 2.6
Deformable model (gradient only)	27	0.49 ± 0.12	3.9 ± 2.1	4.8 ± 2.5	10.4 ± 5.1

($p \leq 0.01$) in all metrics. As this naive segmentation method relied only on image gradient information, the mesh tended to migrate away from the tumor toward irrelevant edges with high gradient magnitude. In the proposed method, the classification map supports tumor boundary detection and keeps the mesh localized on the tumor.

One particular challenge with the proposed deformable model in our method lies in the regularization term. Currently, regularization is performed over mesh vertex displacements, smoothing the displacement field. However, this promotes global translation of the surface mesh and in a few cases has caused the mesh vertices to migrate to one end of the tumor, resulting in under-segmentation of the opposite end. Directly regularizing surface smoothness could allow more reliable and more accurate segmentations. However, directly controlling surface smoothness cannot be done with the currently used FastPD optimization approach or with alpha expansion. Such a model

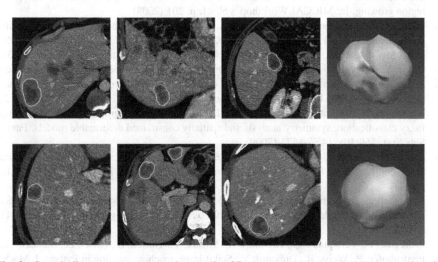

Fig. 3. Sample liver tumor segmentation results. 2D contours are green (gray) – ground truth; white – proposed method. Rightmost: 3D models of sample segmentation results.

would thus lose the benefit of a guaranteed sub-optimality bound offered by these approaches but would also likely gain the advantage of being able to segment more complex tumor shapes (for example, multiple tumors pressed together).

5 Conclusion

In this paper, a new semi-automatic 3D tumor segmentation method was proposed and tested on 27 metastatic liver tumors in abdominal CT scans. The proposed method uses an omni-directional deformable surface model for segmentation that exploits image gradient features and regional voxel class information produced by a 2-class kernel SVM based on mean, variance, and GLCM features. Only four of the eight tested GLCM texture features were found to be significant for training the classifier (two at each of the two tested image scales), suggesting a high degree of redundancy among these features. Segmentation results are promising and warrant further investigation of deformable model approaches to tumor segmentation. Further work will focus on improving the deformable model, as well as applying the method to other lesions than liver tumors and to other modalities than CT, such as MRI or ultrasound images.

References

1. Eisenhauer, E.A., Therasse, P., Bogaerts, J., Schwartz, L.H., Sargent, D., Ford, R., Dancey, J., Arbuck, S., Gwyther, S., Mooney, M.: New response evaluation criteria in solid tumours: revised RECIST guideline (version 1.1). Eur. J. Cancer **45**(2), 228–247 (2009)
2. Ananthakrishnan, A., Gogineni, V., Saeian, K.: Epidemiology of primary and secondary liver cancers. Semin. Interv. Radiol. **23**(1), 47–63 (2006)
3. Qi, Y., Xiong, W., Leow, W.K., Tian, Q., Zhou, J., Liu, J., Han, T., Venkatesh, S.K., Wang, S.: Semi-automatic segmentation of liver tumors from CT scans using Bayesian rule-based 3D region growing. In: MICCAI Workshop, vol. 41, p. 201 (2008)
4. Kadoury, S., Abi-Jaoudeh, N., Valdes, P.A.: Higher-order CRF tumor segmentation with discriminant manifold potentials. In: Mori, K., Sakuma, I., Sato, Y., Barillot, C., Navab, N. (eds.) MICCAI 2013, Part I. LNCS, vol. 8149, pp. 719–726. Springer, Heidelberg (2013)
5. Hame, Y.: Liver tumor segmentation using implicit surface evolution. Midas J. 1–10. (2008)
6. Rajendran, A., Dhanasekaran, R.: Fuzzy clustering and deformable model for tumor segmentation on MRI brain image: a combined approach. Procedia Eng. **30**, 327–333 (2012)
7. Khotanlou, H., Colliot, O., Atif, J., Bloch, I.: 3D brain tumor segmentation in MRI using fuzzy classification, symmetry analysis and spatially constrained deformable models. Fuzzy Sets Syst. **160**(10), 1457–1473 (2009)
8. Sachdeva, J., Kumar, V., Gupta, I., Khandelwal, N., Ahuja, C.K.: A novel content-based active contour model for brain tumor segmentation. Magn. Reson. Imaging **30**(5), 694–715 (2012)
9. Kainmueller, D., Lamecker, H., Heller, M.O., Weber, B., Hege, H.-C., Zachow, S.: Omnidirectional displacements for deformable surfaces. Med. Image Anal. **17**(4), 429–441 (2013)
10. Pedregosa, F., Varoquaux, G., Gramfort, A., Michel, V., Thirion, B., Grisel, O., Blondel, M., Prettenhofer, P., Weiss, R., Dubourg, V.: Scikit-learn: machine learning in Python. J. Mach. Learn. Res. **12**, 2825–2830 (2011)

11. Komodakis, N., Tziritas, G., Paragios, N.: Performance vs computational efficiency for optimizing single and dynamic mrfs: setting the state of the art with primal-dual strategies. Comput. Vis. Image Underst. **112**(1), 14–29 (2008)
12. Shivaswamy, P.K., Jebara, T.: Maximum relative margin and data-dependent regularization. J. Mach. Learn. Res. **11**, 747–788 (2010)

Automated Navigator Tracker Placement
for MRI Liver Scans

Takao Goto[1,2(✉)] and Satoshi Ito[2]

[1] MR Engineering, GE Healthcare Japan,
Hino, Tokyo, Japan
Takao.Goto@ge.com
[2] Department of Information Sciences, Faculty of Engineering,
Utsunomiya University, Tochigi, Japan

Abstract. We present a new method for automated placement of a navigator tracker for MRI liver scans. The tracker is used for the navigator echo sequence. It localizes the region acquiring the MR signal to monitor respiratory motion. Accurate placement of the tracker at the boundary between the lung and liver while observing scout images is a complicated task for operators, adversely affecting their workflow. Our proposed method uses ensemble-based classifiers to detect pixels and a right landmark on the upper edge of the liver, following identification of the area containing the edge pixels in the superior/inferior direction. The navigator tracker location is computed from the peak location of the upward convex shape formed by the edge pixels after fitting to a quadratic function. Our method placed the navigator tracker with a mean error of 6.79 mm for the desired location in 126 volunteers. A computational time was approximately 3 s.

Keywords: Adaboost · Navigator echo · Random forests · Operator workflow

1 Introduction

In magnetic resonance imaging (MRI) liver scans, a variety of motion compensation techniques have been proposed to eliminate the effects from the motion of respiration and heartbeats [1–4]. The navigator echo sequence is one such technique [5–7]. It acquires the magnetic resonance (MR) signal (the navigator echo) synchronized with the motion while monitoring the movement at either the head or tail of the original pulse sequence, for instance, which produces the contrast images T1 and T2. Figure 1 shows an example of how the navigator sequence functions in the time series. The navigator tracker is typically placed on the boundary between the lung and liver so as not to overlap the right edge of the body and the heart. The MR system is then able to selectively excite the cylindrical region of the navigator tracker to generate the navigator echo, as shown in Fig. 2. A one-dimensional Fourier transform of the navigator echo yields a projection (the navigator profile) reflecting the liver movement. The steepest point in the navigator profile indicates the boundary between the lung and liver. It is normally identified by the threshold method in general signal processing. In the navigator tracker, the diameter is 10–20 mm and the length is 10–20 cm, although the dimensions change depending on the size of the liver and lung.

© Springer International Publishing Switzerland 2014
H. Yoshida et al. (Eds.): ABDI 2014, LNCS 8676, pp. 84–93, 2014.
DOI: 10.1007/978-3-319-13692-9_8

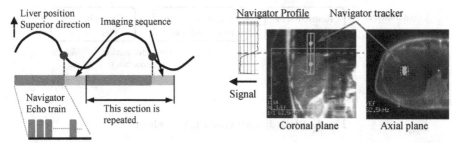

Fig. 1. Navigator echo sequence in MRI.   **Fig. 2.** Navigator tracker monitoring respiratory motion.

The operator must place the tracker carefully at an appropriate position by considering the coronal, axial, and sagittal planes of the scout images. The navigator signal may be contaminated by the effects of the heartbeat, large lung vessels, and fat components owing to inappropriate placement of the tracker. This results in degradation of image quality caused by miss-triggering of the navigator. Accordingly, the placement of the navigator tracker is a troublesome process and worsens the workflow.

Therefore, automating adjustment of the navigator tracker would simplify the operator's workflow. One approach that segments the surface of diaphragm [8] has been proposed and may be suitable for our purpose. However, no techniques have yet been proposed for automatically adjusting the navigator tracker other than our previously developed approach [9]. In our previous method, the initial measurement of the liver dome (the dome portion of the liver located directly under the diaphragm) in the superior/inferior (S/I) direction highly depends on the projection plot along the S/I direction, followed by the binarization of the coronal image. This binarization step sometimes fails owing to inappropriate noise values detected in the axial images. It is also easily affected by wraparound artifacts and inhomogeneities in the intensity of the receiver coils. In our new approach, we use the output confidence value of the ensemble classifier, without using any noise values. Furthermore, we employ another ensemble classifier to detect a right landmark corresponding to the right edge of the liver dome, since this right edge is sometimes lost as a result of faulty edge recognition. Similar to the previous method, we analyzed the axial and coronal images obtained by a typical scout scan to compute the location of the tracker, with no additional time consumed in the total examination time.

2 Methods

2.1 Algorithm for Automated Navigator Tracker Placement

To determine the location of the navigator tracker, we must know the shape of the liver dome. One approach is to segment the lung and then extract the shape of the lower edge of the lung. This may appear to be an easy and direct method, yet lung segmentation in MR scout images is a difficult task due to inhomogeneities in the intensity, the existence of thick lung vessels, and the disappearance of the heart wall as a result of a

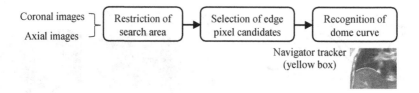

Fig. 3. Block diagram (Color figure online).

heartbeat. All these problems disrupt the segmentation approach and thus make segmentation more difficult. Therefore, we utilized the local characteristics of the patch-basis and classified whether the pixel at the center of the patch close to the liver dome is on the true edge pixels on the liver dome or not. This approach is robust against the inhomogeneities in intensity and the ensemble-based classifier helps to distinguish between the various vessels and the heart wall.

Figure 3 depicts a block diagram of the algorithm for automated navigator tracker placement. There are 3 steps in the processing pipeline for analyzing the coronal and axial images of the scout scan: restriction of the search area, selection of edge pixel candidates, and recognition of the curve of the liver dome. We used the single-shot fast spin echo (SSFSE) sequence because it is robust with respect to inhomogeneities in the magnetic field and is generally used as a scout scan. The scan parameters were: TR/TE = 1100/80 ms, slice thickness 8 mm, slice spacing 5 mm, and field of view of 480 mm × 480 mm. The scan time was a total of 20 s for the case of acquisition of one sagittal, seven coronal, and five axial slices. No intensity correction and non-breath holding were applied. A 512 × 512 reconstruction matrix was converted via linear interpolation to 256 × 256 axial and coronal images.

Restriction of search area: The first step is to restrict the search area for edge pixels on the curve of the liver dome. Five axial images are used to extract the maximum lengths of the right/left (R/L) and anterior/posterior (A/P) directions of the body through the morphology process. After the axial images are converted into binary images by setting the image noise as a threshold value [10], erosion and dilation using a 5 × 5 structuring element are applied. Three coronal slices with an A/P location close to the center of the body on the axial slices were selected. Typically, the coronal slice in the middle location is used to place a tracker. The other two slices are for backup purposes when the number of detected edge pixels in the middle is insufficient to recognize the dome curve. In the next step, to identify the average location of the liver dome in the S/I direction, we first selected the edge pixels that satisfy the prior information of the edge pixels on the liver dome in the limited R/L search range, which was set in only the R/L direction and started at 60 % of the right half of the area and ended at the R/L center of the body as shown in the inside area of both yellow lines of Fig. 4(a). The 60 % range was selected to decrease the number of faulty edge pixels on the right side, following testing from 40 % to 70 % in steps of 10 %. In terms of the prior information, we utilized the characteristics that the intensity of a liver pixel is brighter than that of a lung pixel. To avoid the noise effect, a 9 × 9 and 10 × 9 patch area is placed above and below the edge pixel and the median value in the each patch is

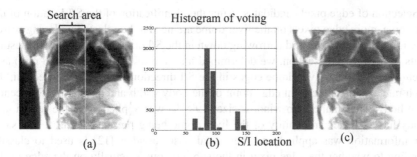

Search area   Histogram of voting

(a)   (b)   S/I location   (c)

Fig. 4. S/I location by voting (a) detected liver dome edges (cross mark) (b) histogram of voting along S/I (c) detected S/I location (horizontal line).

compared. The orientation of the liver dome is within a 60° to 120° span since the dome curve has a convex shape. This span was empirically determined from the training datasets. The orientation θ is computed by: $\theta = \arctan((\partial I(i,j)/\partial y)/(\partial I(i,j)/\partial x))$, where $I(i,j)$ denotes the discrete signal of the coronal image, i and j are the location of the R/L and S/I directions, respectively. The prior information is not sufficient to select the true edge pixels of the liver dome. Therefore, we applied the random forests (RF) classifier [11] to classify whether the edge pixels were true edges of the liver dome or not. A random forest is a powerful ensemble machine learning technique that uses stochastically trained trees. It produces accurate results and fast computation times for the learning step. Our RF classifier consists of 50 trees which number decided by a comparison of 10–100 trees every 10 steps. Patch areas of 10 × 13 and 25 × 13 pixels are placed above and below the edge pixel. We call both patches "area sub-window". The feature vector formed by alignment of the pixel intensity inside the sub-window following normalization by the variance, forms the input of the classifier. In the learning step, the sub-window was manually extracted from the training images and a training matrix was created following normalization by the variance in the sub-window. The sums of votes of the RF classifier along the same S/I location are used to form a histogram. The bin with the maximum number of votes indicates the most plausible location of the liver dome (Fig. 4(b) and (c)).

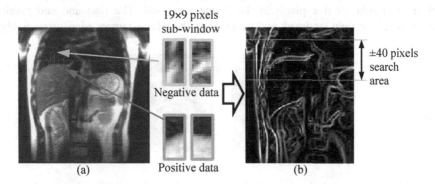

19×9 pixels
sub-window

Negative data

Positive data

±40 pixels
search
area

(a)   (b)

Fig. 5. Classification of the dome edge of a liver: (a) sub-window data, (b) classification results: true edge pixel (green), false edge pixel (yellow) (Color figure online).

Selection of edge pixel candidates: After the identification of the S/I location of the liver dome, more edge pixels on the liver dome are need to be selected widening search range in the R/L direction and narrowing down in the S/I direction. Based on the testing results of the previous section, we determined a region of ± 40 pixels (± 75 mm) as a searching area for the liver dome edges in the S/I direction. For the R/L direction, the search range starts at the right edge point of the body width and ends at the R/L center of the body. The smaller sub-window size (19 × 9) was applied since the search area already has a greater probability of the liver dome being present within it. The same prior information was applied and then AdaBoost classifier [12] is used to classify according to whether the edge pixel in the sub-window is actually on the edge of the liver dome or not. This search step is the same as our previous method [9]. Figure 5 shows an example of the sub-window and true (positive green color) and false (negative yellow color) datasets. Similarly, the right landmark of the liver dome was classified from the candidates of the true edge in the same search area. The RF classifier was used, as well as S/I location classifier. Fifty trees, the normalized feature vector, and a 19 × 19 sub-window size were applied and the number of trees was decided by the same comparison as the S/I location classifier. If multiple right landmarks are detected, then a weighted average of the location is adopted as a true right landmark and the weight is computed from the votes of each right landmark classified as true. As for a left landmark, it was difficult to detect since heartbeat often make the image blurring or shading on the upper left edge of the liver. The minimum covariance determinant (MCD) estimation method [13] was used to remove the remaining faulty edge pixels as outliers, using the location of the edges from the coronal images as the input vector. MCD estimation is a robust method to obtain a true covariance matrix of datasets excluding outliers.

Recognition of dome curve: Occasionally, some of the true edge pixels are classified as false. In particular, cysts, hepatocellular carcinomas, and other changes in tissue contrast due to liver disease occur on the liver dome. We connected these pixels using dynamic programming to find a minimum cost path that consist of the true edge pixels on the liver dome, not to connect the liver vessels or fat tissue, where the cost is computed from the inverse of the derivative coronal image. Furthermore, to add a neighboring area of the detected edge pixels to the cost, the density map of a Gaussian kernel with a center point corresponding to the location of the detected edge pixel and with a bandwidth of five pixels in the image was used. The start and end pixels correspond to the right landmark and the pixel on the leftmost upper edge, respectively

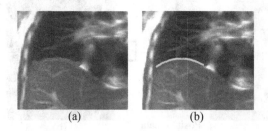

(a)   (b)

Fig. 6. Identification of tracker location via (a) start and end points (red circles) via dynamic programming and (b) the regression curve and tracker (rectangular box) (Color figure online).

(Fig. 6(a), red circles). If the right landmark is not detected, then the rightmost edge pixel is used instead. Following this edge pixel retrieval step, those pixels are fitted to a quadratic function using the least squares method. Accordingly, the peak point of the liver dome is determined approximately from the coefficients of the quadratic term (Fig. 6(b)). Finally, the detected edge pixels on the upper edge of the liver are recognized as a curve by fitting them to a quadratic function. The center of the navigator tracker is placed on the peak location of the curve. As we allowed a non-breath holding scan in the scout scan, the dome peak sometimes disappeared when data acquisition was performed during the inspiration period. In such a case, we placed the navigator tracker on the middle point of the curve in the R/L direction. Meanwhile, in the A/P direction, the navigator tracker was placed on the center of the body height, since the anterior side may introduce a fat signal near the body surface, which has a high intensity and contaminates the navigator profile. In the posterior side, the liver movement is greatest [14], resulting in degradation of the image quality.

2.2 Evaluation Method

We obtained informed consent from every volunteer after receiving institutional review and approval. We collected datasets from a total of 126 healthy volunteers. The error was calculated from the difference between the location of the navigator tracker determined by the algorithm and the manually identified center location, which was determined by common consent between one application specialist in MRI and one scientist in the field of image processing.

3 Results

Table 1 shows the number of samples, volunteers, and success rates in the S/I location of the liver dome and the right landmark detection. The sample represents the extracted sub-window data for the training and classification (testing) steps and the success rate was calculated from the number of samples successfully classified according to the labeled data of the sample. Table 2 shows the mean and the maximum of the absolute

Table 1. Number of samples, volunteers and success rate in sub-window datasets.

		Identification of right landmark	Superior/Inferior location of liver
Training set	Positive sample	555	2154
	Negative sample	1000	1796
	Number of volunteers	47	30
Classification set	Positive sample	614	3500
	Negative sample	619	3500
	Number of volunteers	8	35
	Success rate [%]	93	92

Table 2. Error in navigator tracker placement.

		Previous method	Proposed method
R/L	Absolute mean	5.79	5.62
	Absolute maximum	29.06	23.44
S/I	Absolute mean	3.75	2.01
	Absolute maximum	102.2	16.88
A/P	Absolute mean	1.26	1.44
	Absolute maximum	13.12	15.0
E. D.	Mean distance	9.26	6.79
	Maximum distance	102.19	25.24

E. D. = Euclidian Distance
Unit [mm]

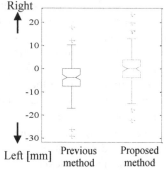

Fig. 7. Box-plot of R/L error.

value of the error in the navigator tracker placement in the comparison of the previous method and the proposed method. The Euclidian distance error is a distance in three-dimensional space calculated from the error in the three directions. Figure 7 shows box-plots of the errors in the R/L direction. In the previous method, the R/L error was a 3–4 mm shift from 0 mm in the left direction. On the other hand, the proposed method did not show such a shift. In the A/P direction, the error was unchanged between both methods. The absolute maximum error in the R/L and A/P directions was almost the same for both methods. As well as the mean error, the maximum error in the S/I direction was significantly lower.

Figure 8 shows the results of automated navigator tracker placement for three volunteers. Our algorithm worked successfully not only for a normal volunteer (Fig. 8 (a)), but also for an obese volunteer (Fig. 8(b)). The navigator tracker was placed at the peak of the liver dome in the coronal image and in the middle of the A/P direction in the axial image. Figure 8(c) is the case of a large error in the previous method. The identification of the average location in the S/I direction failed due to a wrong noise value in the binarization. The tracker position shifted in the inferior direction in the coronal image. The yellow dashed lines in the axial images indicate the slices of the coronal images in the scout scan.

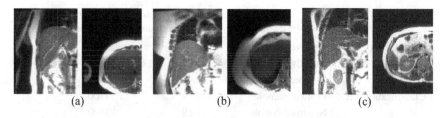

Fig. 8. Results of navigator tracker placement (a) normal volunteer, error: R0.94, S0.94, A1.88 (b) obese volunteer, error: R2.3, S0, A0 (c) tracker position with a large error in the previous method, error: R15.94, I79.69, A0.94. The first character of each error denotes the error directions of R/L, S/I and A/P. The unit of the error is millimeter.

We developed the program using MATLAB R2012a. The computation time using a laptop of 2.7 GHz Core i5 was ~ 3 s.

4 Discussion and Conclusion

The error in the tracker placement in the R/L direction was larger than in the other directions. The reason for this is that the shape of the curve of the liver dome was much more varied since we did not use the breath-holding technique in acquiring the scout images. Thus, the curve shape tends to have an upward convex peak when the navigator echo was acquired in the expiration period. In contrast, the curve shape tends to appear flat when the navigator echo was acquired in the inspiration period. It may be difficult to account for such variations in the current algorithm. It is thus necessary to investigate how the curve shape changes in actual patients. In the previous method, the distribution of the R/L error was shifted to the left side more than in the proposed method. In our observation, the location of the dome peak is likely to be close to the heart, particularly when the scout images were acquired in the inspiration period. Furthermore, the base part of the right ventricle disappeared as an effect of motion, so that the edge pixels were also detected just below the heart. This observation explains why the dome peak tends to be shifted to the left side. On the other hand, the right landmark was sufficient to recover this shift. The center of the R/L error distribution in the proposed method shifted closer to the 0 mm error as shown in Fig. 7. The maximum absolute error of 23.44 mm in the R/L (Table 2) was shifted to the right direction. This was acceptable because the tracker position is not yet closed to the fat on the right side of the body. Fat portion generates a strong signal and contaminates the navigator signal, resulting in a miss-triggering of the navigator. In the left direction, the maximum error was 22.34 mm. This location is close to the heart, in which case it has the potential to affect the navigator signal due to the heartbeat. We need to investigate whether a proximity to the heart does not contaminate the navigator echo profile and does not cause miss-triggering in the navigator sequence. Our previous method for identifying the S/I location of the liver dome mistakenly determined the location of the shoulder as the liver dome in two cases. This was because the previous method searches the steepest step in the projection profile of the S/I direction by a template matching and the boundary of the shoulder had the steepest step in physically small volunteers. The new method correctly detected the average location of the liver dome for such a dataset and the case of Fig. 8(c). The random forests classifiers find the true boundary of the liver and the lung by the learned features in the sub-window. As the length of the navigator tracker is typically 10–20 cm in the liver scans, the mean distance error of 2.01 mm and the absolute maximum of 16.88 mm in the S/I direction don't affect the navigator performance. In the A/P direction, the detection method is the same as in the previous so that the error was similar. Furthermore, the absolute maximum error of 15 mm from the body center is acceptable since the position of the tracker is far from the fat area on the surface of the body. In the Euclidian distance, the proposed method effectively reduced the S/I error that dominated the maximum error in the previous method. We believe that it is important to specify the values of the allowable range in the all directions by checking that the actual navigator profile and the navigator sequence works correctly at the detected tracker position. This depends on the navigator sequence types, patient's diseases and the size of body. In terms of the sub-window, we did not compare the error by changing the size and types of the feature vector of the sub-window. These may potentially improve the accuracy of tracker placement.

From the standpoint of the workflow, the standard scout scan is available without any modification in our proposed method and the only limitation is the need to obtain three coronal slices scanned around the middle of the body height (in the A/P direction). Interviews with three technologists, each with more than five years experience in MRI system operation at different facilities, indicated that it takes around 15–90 s to place the tracker depending on the situation of the patients, even for a skilled operator. Since the computational time was sufficiently fast, the time saved in the workflow would be around 15–90 s in most cases.

We demonstrated the ability of our algorithm to determine the appropriate location of the navigator tracker. In particular, the new method for measuring the S/I location of the liver dome did not produce the large error in the S/I direction comparing to the previous method. Furthermore, the right landmark identification greatly helped to recover the error in the R/L direction effectively. The computation time was acceptable for practical clinical use and did not affect the current workflow. For practical use in clinical environments, further studies regarding the applicability and robustness of the proposed technique in large numbers of patients with liver disease will be necessary. Automated adjustment of the tracker size is the next topic to be addressed. Both automated placement and size adjustment will help the operator and decrease the total study time required for MRI liver scans.

References

1. Ehman, R.L., Felmlee, J.P.: Adaptive techniques for high resolution MR imaging of moving structures navigator echoes. Radiology 173(4), 255–263 (2006)
2. Dold, C., Zaitsev, M., Speck, O., Firle, E.A., Hennig, J., Sakas, G.: Advantages and limitations of prospective head motion compensation for MRI using an optical motion tracking device. Acad. Radiol. 13(9), 1093–1103 (2006)
3. Haacke, E.M., Lenz, G.W.: Improving MR image quality in the presence of motion by using rephasing gradients. AJR Am. J. Roentgenol. 148(6), 1251–1258 (1987)
4. Deng, J., Omary, R.A., Larson, A.C.: Multishot diffusion-weighted SPLICE PROPELLER MRI of the abdomen. Magn. Reson. Med. 59(5), 947–953 (2008)
5. Klessen, C., Asbach, P., Kroencke, T.J., Fischer, T., Warmuth, C., Stemmer, A., Hamm, B., Taupitz, M.: Magnetic resonance imaging of the upper abdomen using a free-breathing T2-weighted turbo spin echo sequence with navigator triggered prospective acquisition correction. J. Magn. Reson. Imaging 21(5), 576–582 (2005)
6. Wang, Y., Rossman, P.J., Grimm, R.C., Riederer, S.J., Ehman, R.L.: Navigatorecho-based real-time respiratory gating and triggering for reduction of respiration effects in three-dimensional coronary MR angiography. Radiology 198(1), 55–60 (1996)

7. Inoue, Y., Hata, H., Nakajima, A., Iwadate, Y., Ogasawara, G., Matsunaga, K.: Optimal techniques for magnetic resonance imaging of the liver using a respiratory navigator-gated three-dimensional spoiled gradient-recalled echo sequence. J. Magn. Reson. Imaging (2014). doi:10.1016/j.mri.2014.05.013

8. Yalamachili, R., Chittajallu, D., Balanca, P., Tamarappoo, B., Berman, D., Dey, D., Kakadiaris, I.: Automatic segmentation of the diaphragm in non-contrast CT images. In: ISBI 2010 7th International Symposium on Biomedical Imaging: From Nano to Macro, Rotterdam, Netherlands, pp. 900–903 (2010)

9. Goto, T., Kabasawa, H.: Robust automated navigator tracker positioning for MRI liver scans. In: Proceedings of 22nd Annual Meeting ISMRM, Milan, Italy 1614 (2014)

10. Gudbjartsson, H., Pats, S.: The Rician distribution of noisy MRI data. Magn. Reson. Med. **36**(2), 910–914 (1996)

11. Breiman, L.: Random forests. Mach. Learn. **45**(1), 5–32 (2001)

12. Freund, Y., Schapire, R.E.: A decision-theoretic generalization of on-line learning and an application to boosting. J. Comput. Syst. Sci. **55**, 119–139 (1997)

13. Rousseeuw, P.J., Van Drissen, K.: A fast algorithm for the minimum covariance determinant estimator. Technometrics **41**(3), 212–223 (1999)

14. Gierada, D.S., Curtin, J.J., Erickson, S.J., Prost, R.W., Strandt, J.A., Goodman, L.R.: Diaphragmatic motion: fast gradient-recalled-echo MR imaging in healthy subjects. Radiology **194**(3), 879–884 (1995)

Pancreatic Blood Flow Measurements in the Pig Pancreatitis Model Using Perfusion CT with Deconvolution Method

Yoshihisa Tsuji[1(✉)], Kazutaka Yamada[2], Miori Kisimoto[2],
Shujiro Yazumi[3], Hiroyoshi Isoda[4], and Tsutomu Chiba[1]

[1] Department of Gastroenterology and Hepatology,
Kyoto University Hospital, Kyoto, Japan
ytsuji@kuhp.kyoto-u.ac.jp
[2] Department of Radiology,
Obihiro University of Agriculture and Veterinary Medicine, Hokkaido, Japan
[3] Digestive Disease Center, Kitano Hospital, Osaka, Japan
[4] Department of Radiology, Kyoto University Hospital, Kyoto, Japan

Abstract. Introduction: We compared pancreatic blood flow (PBF) measured by perfusion CT with deconvolution method and Laser Doppler Flow (LDF) to determine whether uncollected contrast material from the pancreas affects measurement of perfusion CT, using porcine pancreatitis model (n = 7). Materials and Methods: The pancreas was divided into head and tail. We arranged that PBF of tail was circulated by single input/output vessel. Ischemic pancreatitis was induced to tail, shutting off input/output vessel for 30 min. PBF was measured both by perfusion CT with deconvolution method and LDF, during the overall course. We calculated uncollected ratio of contrast material, assuming area-under-curve differences between the input and output vessels correspond to uncollected. Results: tail PBF measured by perfusion CT with deconvolution was significantly correlated with LDF, despite of pancreatitis (P < 0.05). The uncollected ratio was 19 %. Discussion: Although the uncollected ratio was not few, result of perfusion CT was significantly related with LDF.

Keywords: Severe acute pancreatitis · Pancreatic ischmiea · Perfusion · Pancreatic blood flow · Deconvolution · Perfusion CT

1 Introduction

Perfusion CT is one kind of dynamic enhanced CT, which can measure target tissue blood flow by analyzing the time density curve of contrast material of input and/or output vessels [1, 2]. Recently, deconvolution method, algorithm for analyzing tissue perfusion, is used to evaluate tissue perfusion in pancreatic diseases. As previous papers reported, perfusion CT is useful to predict development of pancreatic necrosis [3, 4]. Importantly, deconvolution method provides a more robust analysis without high injection rates. The estimated perfusion values are theoretically independent of cardiac output or potential bolus delays. Therefore, perfusion CT with deconvolution method could be desirable to perform for unstable condition patients.

© Springer International Publishing Switzerland 2014
H. Yoshida et al. (Eds.): ABDI 2014, LNCS 8676, pp. 94–102, 2014.
DOI: 10.1007/978-3-319-13692-9_9

The deconvolution operation is only the inversion process of the convolution operation. There are three kinds of deconvolution methods: model-free deconvolution, parametric deconvolution, and model-based deconvolution. Model-free deconvolution methods do not impose any constraints on the form of the tissue residue function or the structure of the tissue, where a tracer exchange parameter such as capillary permeability cannot be measured, and instead blood flow, blood volume and mean transit time can be calculated from the tissue residue function. Parametric methods do not make any explicit physiologic assumptions, but they do assume that the tissue residue function has a known analytical form. The model-based deconvolution methods can be incorporated with any compartment tracer kinetic models, which provide a well-defined relation between a parametric representation of the tissue residue function and physiologic parameters.

To use deconvolution method for pancreatic disease, major question is still remaining. Deconvolution method with box-modified transfer function (box-MTF) [5], one of model-based deconvolution methods, is used to evaluate pancreatic blood flow and assumes that contrast material is non-diffusible. According to a previous paper, a complex input blood flow of targeted tissue can be regarded as a series of scaled and time shifted perfect boluses. The system's response can be represented as the sum of a correspondingly scaled and time shifted series of responses functions. Mathematically, this is known as a convolution. However, in previous text book [6], microvasculature of pancreatic tissue is disturbed in early stage of acute pancreatitis. Thereby, bleeding is often seen in the microscopic findings of the pancreas [7]. From this reason, in pancreatic tissue with inflammation, contrast material is diffusible and amount of the leakage can increase. Therefore, deconvolution method with box MTF may be potentially unsuitable for pancreatic perfusion CT analyses.

In this study, we compared pancreatic blood flow (PBF) measured by perfusion CT with deconvolution method and Laser Doppler Flow (LDF) [8] to determine whether uncollected contrast material from the pancreas affects measurements results of perfusion CT, using animal pancreatitis model.

2 Materials and Methods

2.1 Acute Pancreatitis in Porcine Model

Seven female pigs weighing 15–20 kg were used as pancreatitis models. All treatment and measurements were performed on a CT table (Asteon 4, Toshiba, Tochigi, Japan). Following the administration of a general anesthetic, the abdomen was opened for the duration of the experiment to enable LDF measurements (Omegawave Inc., Tokyo, Japan). All procedures were performed at the Obihiro University of Agriculture and Veterinary Medicine following approval by that institution's Animal Care Committee.

We removed the peritoneum enveloping the pancreas and divided the pancreas into head and tail sections (Fig. 1(a)). Pancreatic tail was isolated, and then, we arranged that PBF was circulated only by single input (splenic artery) and single output vessel (splenic vein). Then, pancreatitis was induced by ischemic procedure to pancreatic tail, shutting off both input and output vessel for 30 min [9]. PBFs in the head and tail were

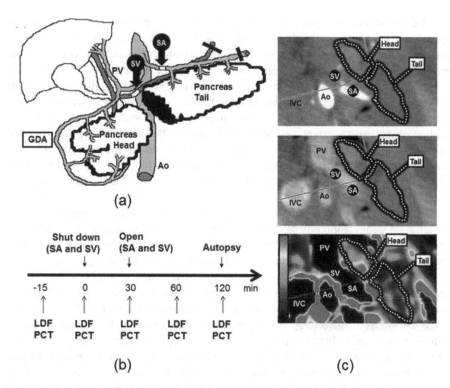

Fig. 1. Schema and pancreatic perfusion image. (a) SA; Splenic Artery, SV; Splenic Vein, GDA; gastro-duodenal artery, Ao: Abdominal aorta, PV, portal vein, IVC; inferior venous cava, LDF; measurement by Laser Doppler flow; PCT; measurement by perfusion CT; min; minutes. SA and SV were indicated by black arrows. (b) Study protocol. (c) Dynamic CT image of pancreas at arterial phase (upper), at portal phase (middle), and color map of PBF based on PCT (bottom) are shown. PBF is displayed on the left-sided scale bar. The area surrounded by the dotted line represents the pig pancreas.

measured both by perfusion CT with deconvolution method and LDF, at the timing of 15 min before (−15 min), the same timing of the start (0 min), and after the ischemic procedure (30, 60 and 120 mins) (Fig. 1(b)). We then extracted the pancreas at 120 min after inducing ischemia and evaluated damage assigning the pathology score, which was obtained by microscopic evaluation of degrees of edema, acinar necrosis, inflammation, and hemorrhage in pancreas [10]. Since elevation of amylase is one of important findings of pancreatitis, we also collected blood sample and then measured it at each time point, using amylase measurement kit (Wako, Osaka, Japan).

2.2 Perfusion CT with Deconvolution Method

Contrast material was injected from a central vein for 10 s at a speed of 4 ml/s. At the same timing, CT scan (80 Kvp and 60 mA, CTDIvol 70–100 mGy) was performed for 48 s at the same location. Dynamic CT data was transferred to commercial workstation

(Ziostation2, Ziosoft, inc., Tokyo, Japan) and analyzed using packaged software in the workstation. Then, pancreatic perfusion was showed as color map on the workstation. Also, the time-density curve (TDC) in each pixel was obtained to analyzing perfusion.

For any input function, we can predict the pattern of contrast material concentrations in the pancreas (considered to be the output) as the convolution of the input function by the pancreas transfer function R(t):

$$(Output) = (input) \otimes R(t) \tag{1}$$

where the transfer function R(t) is the TDC of the tissue due to an idealized instantaneous injection of one unit of tracer. The pancreas or the pattern of the contrast material concentration, Ct(t) has one input Ca(t). Based on functions (1), we obtain the following function for the deconvolution method for pancreatic perfusion analysis:

$$Ct(t) = Ca(t) \otimes R(t) = \int Ca(t-s)R(s)ds. \tag{2}$$

$$PBF = R(0)$$

PBF can be obtained from the plateau height of the PBF* R(t) curve, since R(t) at t = 0 has unit height as it is defined as arising from a unit volume bolus [5, 11]. Based on function (2) and referring to previous paper [12], PBF values was calculated at each pixel, and showed them as color map (Fig. 1(c)). To measure PBF on color map, we established three ROIs of 3–5 mm diameter, drawn over the central portion of the pancreas, in each of the head and tail sections of the pancreas. The PBF of the head and tail are defined to be the averaged PBFs from the three ROIs. The same leveled ROI is selected for both deconvolution method and LDF, using the marker. The ROIs exclude vessel branches distributed to the pancreas.

Assuming area-under-the-curve of Ct(t) differences between the input and output vessel correspond to uncollected contrast matter, we calculated uncollected ratio of contrast matter from the pancreas.

2.3   LDF Blood Flow Measurements

LDF, an established non-invasive technique for continuous monitoring of microcirculation in vivo [8], was also used to evaluate changing of PBF in our study. LDF measures blood flow rates emitting a laser beam from the tip of a probe and passing the beam through the body. The beam is reflected and/or scattered by the moving erythrocytes undergoing a change of the wave length (Doppler shift), dependent on the number and velocities of the cells in the investigated sample volume but not on the direction of their movement. Therefore, measurements correlate with the changing wavelength of the beam. LDF measurement was performed inserting a probe in abdominal cavity and touching surface of pancreatic head and tail.

Three regions of interest (ROIs) of LDF measurements were set over the center of each section of the pancreas. The ROIs positions of measurement of PBF by LDF were set on the place as consisted with those of perfusion CT.

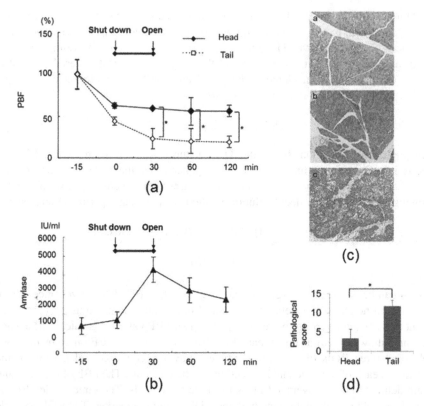

Fig. 2. PBF decline and pancreatitis. (a) PBF values after ischemic-reperfusion procedure are shown as % in comparison with those before. PBF in pancreatic tail at 30, 60 and 120 mins are significantly slower compared to those in head. (b) Changes in serum amylase values over time. (c) The pancreata are extracted and stained with H.E. The top image shows a healthy pig pancreas, the middle image shows a pig pancreas (head section) after 120 min of treatment, and the bottom image shows a pig pancreas (tail section) after 120 min of treatment. (d) Pathological scores indicate significant inflammation for the pancreatic tail (*$p < 0.05$).

2.4   Statistical Analysis

We used Spearman's coefficient for the validity of correlating LDF and perfusion CT measurement values for PBF. Differences between groups were analyzed by the Mann-Whitney U-test. P values below 0.05 were considered statistically significant. Each value is displayed as an average value ± standard deviation. All statistical analyses were performed using SPSS 11 (SPSS Inc., Chicago, IL).

3   Results

3.1   Ischemic Pancreatitis in Tail Sections

The results of LDF indicated that PBF of the head section of the pig pancreas decreased mildly. Comparing to PBF of head, PBF of tail declined significantly at the time points of 30, 60 and 120 mins ($P < 0.05$) (Fig. 2(a)). Ischemic procedure was accompanied by a rise in amylase over time (Fig. 2(b)). Pathological evaluation was performed at 120 min after the start of the experiment, and showed that pancreatitis was not confirmed in the pancreatic head section (Fig. 2(c), where PBF had declined somewhat, while the tail section, where PBF had been reduced, was marked by significant damage and pancreatitis (Fig. 2(c). The pathological damage scores of tail were significantly worse than those of head (11.8 ± 1.5 vs 3.4 ± 2.4, $P < 0.05$) (Fig. 2(d)).

3.2   Correlation Between LDF and Perfusion CT in Pancreatic Blood Flow Measurements

Measurement results were summarized in Table 1. Before ischemia, head PBF measured by perfusion CT and LDF were 28.2 ± 7.2 and 26.3 ± 4.1 ml/100 g/min, respectively. After ischemia (0–120 min), both of average head PBF measured by perfusion CT and LDF were mildly reduced (15.5 ± 8.3 and 14.1 ± 7.9 ml/100 g/min, respectively) (Fig. 3(a)). During the overall course, the results of head PBF measured by perfusion CT and LDF showed significant correlations ($P < 0.05$, correlation coefficient = 0.52) (Fig. 3(b)).

Table 1. Pig pancreas blood flow. PBF: Pancreatic Blood Flow, PCT: Perfusion CT with deconvolution method, LDF: Laser Doppler Flow.

	Pancreas head		Pancreas tail	
	PCT	LDF	PCT	LDF
PBF before ischemia (−15 min) (ml/100 g/min)	28.2 ± 7.2	26.3 ± 4.1	22.3 ± 5.6	28.1 ± 7.2
Average PBF after ischemia (0–120 min) (ml/100 g/min)	15.5 ± 8.3	14.1 ± 7.9	6.7 ± 2.1	5.8 ± 1.7

On the other hand, PBF of the tail section changed dramatically, before and after ischemic procedure (Table 1). Before ischemia, PBF measured by perfusion CT and LDF were 22.3 ± 5.6 ml/100 g/min and 28.1 ± 7.2 ml/100 g/min, respectively. After ischemia (0–120 min), average PBF of tail measured by perfusion CT and LDF were 6.7 ± 2.1 ml/100 g/min and 5.8 ± 1.7 ml/100 g/min, respectively (Fig. 3(c)). These results from perfusion CT and LDF were significantly correlated ($P < 0.01$, correlation coefficient = 0.77) (Fig. 3(d)).

3.3   Uncollected Ratio of Contrast Matter

At timing of 120 min, average AUC values of splenic artery and vein were 2258 ± 499 and 1829 ± 213, respectively. The difference between the two was 429. The uncollected ratio was 19.0 %.

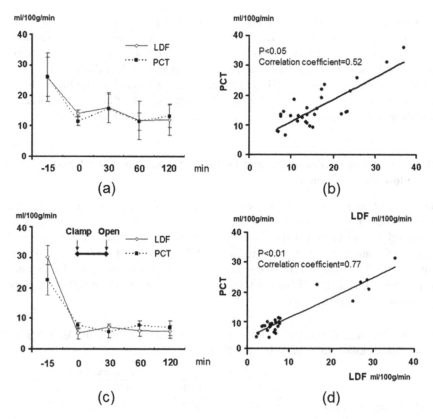

Fig. 3. Comparisons of pig PBF measured by PCT and LDF. Changes and relationship of PBF measured by LDF and PCT in the pig pancreas head section were shown in (a) and (b), respectively. Also changes and relationship of PBF by LDF and PCT in tail were shown in (c) and (d), respectively.

4 Discussion

As we showed in this presented study, uncollected ratio of contrast material in inflammatory tissue was not few. In brain perfusion CT with deconvolution method, such leakage can affect to the accuracy of measurement. However, PBF measured by perfusion CT with deconvolution method was significantly correlated with LDF. One of the reasons may be the followings. Although a maximum CT value of brain artery is almost same as that of pancreatic artery, transfer of contrast material from feeding artery to cerebral tissue is more limited due to blood brain barrier, comparing to that to pancreas. Then cerebral CT value can be much less comparing to pancreas. In actual in dynamic CT, pancreatic CT values rise to more than 100 HU given the large AUC value. Meanwhile, cerebral CT values in dynamic CT rise by no more than 6–8 HU. Thereby, AUC of TDC of brain tissue is much smaller than that of pancreas. Comparing to other algorithm (e.g. maximum slope method), AUC of TDC is more important in deconvolution with box-MTF. Thus, by leakage of contrast material, TDC and perfusion analysis of deconvolution with box-MTF in pancreas may be less affected than those in brain.

We obtained dynamic CT data for 48 s to perform deconvolution analysis. The 48 s may be not enough to observe circulation of contrast material in pancreatic tissue. For example, compartment model, which is algorithm to measure tissue permeability, is required to obtain dynamic CT data based on much longer observing time, e.g. 300 s. In this presented study, uncollected contrast material may be passing through slowly, not leakage. From this regards, we can improve scan protocol for pancreatic perfusion CT, since there is no evidence that 48 s is best observing time for deconvolution analysis. To evaluate this possibility, additional study is required.

To induce enough inflammation to cause pancreatitis by shutting off input and output vessels, reperfusion is important. Damage associated molecular patterns (DAMPs) (e.g. free-radical oxidant, NO, recognized system of particle of damaged cells, cytokines and chemokines) prevail in blood and organ by reperfusion. Inflammatory pathway of acinar cell and macrophage was activated by DAMPs resulting in producing more damage in pancreas. In this model, we shut off these vessels for 30 min. The reason why shut off for 30 min, not longer time (e.g. 1 h), was selected was not to destroy all micro-vasculature of pancreas referring previous study, and to maintain blood flow after the splenic artery and vein were opened.

In conclusion, PBF measured by perfusion CT with deconvolution method was significantly correlated with direct measurement based on other device, LDF. However, it was expected that the certain amount of uncollected contrast material existed in the pancreatic tail which had inflammation. Thereby, accuracy of the pancreatic perfusion CT with deconvolution method may be limited, and we can evaluate pancreatic circulation semi-quantitatively using perfusion CT with the deconvolution method, especially in the case with pancreatitis.

References

1. Miles, K.A., Griffiths, M.R.: Perfusion CT: a worthwhile enhancement? Br. J. Radiol. **76**, 220–231 (2003)
2. Tsuji, Y., Takahashi, N., Tsutomu, C.: Pancreatic perfusion CT in early stage of severe acute pancreatitis. Int J Inflam. **2012**, 497386 (2012)
3. Tsuji, Y., Yamamoto, H., Yazumi, S., Watanabe, Y., Matsueda, K., Yamamoto, H., Chiba, T.: Perfusion computerized tomography can predict pancreatic necrosis in early stages of severe acute pancreatitis. Clin Gastroenterol Hepatol. **5**, 1484–1492 (2007)
4. Sahani, D.V., Holalkere, N.S., Kambadakone, A., Matthes, K., Mino-Kenudson, M., Brugge, W.R.: Role of computed tomography perfusion in the evaluation of pancreatic necrosis and pancreatitis after endoscopic ultrasound-guided ablation of the pancreas in a porcine model. Pancreas **38**, 775–781 (2009)
5. Axel, L.: Tissue mean transit time from dynamic computed tomography by a simple deconvolution technique. Invest. Radiol. **18**, 94–99 (1983)
6. Beger, H.G., Warshaw, A.L., Büchler, M.W., Kozarek, R.A., Lerch, M.M., Neoptolemos, J. P., Shiratori, K., Whitcomb, D.C., Rau, B.M.: The Pancreas: An Integrated Textbook of Basic Science, Medicine, and Surgery, 2nd edn. Blackwell Publishing, Oxford (2009)

102   Y. Tsuji et al.

7. Bradley, E.L., 3rd.: A clinically based classification system for acute pancreatitis. In: Summary of the International Symposium on Acute Pancreatitis, Atlanta, Ga, September 11 through 13, 1992 (Arch Surg. vol. 128, pp. 586–590) (1993)
8. Krejci, V., Hiltebrand, L., Banic, A., Erni, D., Wheatley, A.M., Sigurdsson, G.H.: Continuous measurements of microcirculatory blood flow in gastrointestinal organs during acute haemorrhage. Br. J. Anaesth. 84, 468–475 (2000)
9. Witzigmann, H., Ludwig, S., Armann, B., Gäbel, G., Teupser, D., Kratzsch, J., Pietsch, U. C., Tannapfel, A., Geissler, F., Hauss, J., Uhlmann, D.: Endothelin(A) receptor blockade reduces ischemia/reperfusion injury in pig pancreas transplantation. Ann. Surg. 238, 264–274 (2003)
10. Schmidt, J., Rattner, D.W., Lewandrowski, K., Compton, C.C., Mandavilli, U., Knoefel, W. T., Warshaw, A.L.: A better model of acute pancreatitis for evaluating therapy. Ann. Surg. 215, 44–56 (1992)
11. Eastwood, J.D., Lev, M.H., Azhari, T., Lee, T.Y., Barboriak, D.P., Delong, D.M., Fitzek, C., Herzau, M., Wintermark, M., Meuli, R., Brazier, D., Provenzale, J.M.: CT perfusion scanning with deconvolution analysis: pilot study in patients with acute middle cerebral artery stroke. Radiology 222, 227–236 (2002)
12. Kishimoto, M., Tsuji, Y., Katabami, N., Shimizu, J., Lee, K.J., Iwasaki, T., Miyake, Y., Yazumi, S., Chiba, T., Yamada, K.: Measurement of canine pancreatic perfusion using dynamic computed tomography: influence of input-output vessels on deconvolution and maximum slope methods. Eur. J. Radiol. 77, 175–181 (2011)

A Bottom-Up Approach for Automatic Pancreas Segmentation in Abdominal CT Scans

Amal Farag[✉], Le Lu, Evrim Turkbey, Jiamin Liu,
and Ronald M. Summers

Imaging Biomarkers and CAD Laboratory,
Department of Radiology and Imaging Sciences,
National Institutes of Health Clinical Center,
Bld. 10. Rm. 1C224D, Bethesda, MD, USA
`amal.alyl@gmail.com`

Abstract. Organ segmentation is a prerequisite for a computer-aided diagnosis (CAD) system to detect pathologies and perform quantitative analysis. For anatomically high-variability abdominal organs such as the pancreas, previous segmentation works report low accuracies when comparing to organs like the heart or liver. In this paper, a fully-automated bottom-up method is presented for pancreas segmentation, using abdominal computed tomography (CT) scans. The method is based on a hierarchical two-tiered information propagation by classifying image patches. It labels superpixels as pancreas or not via pooling patch-level confidences on 2D CT slices over-segmented by the Simple Linear Iterative Clustering approach. A supervised random forest (RF) classifier is trained on the patch level and a two-level cascade of RFs is applied at the superpixel level, coupled with multi-channel feature extraction, respectively. On six-fold cross-validation using 80 patient CT volumes, we achieved 68.8 % Dice coefficient and 57.2 % Jaccard Index, comparable to or slightly better than published state-of-the-art methods.

Keywords: Pancreas · Random forest · CT · Hierarchical two-tiered information propagation

1 Introduction

Segmentation of the pancreas is an important step in the development of computer aided diagnosis (CAD) systems that can provide quantitative analysis for diabetic patients and a necessary input for subsequent methodologies for pancreatic cancer detection. The literature is rich for automatic segmentation of numerous organs in CT scans with high sensitivity (>90 %), such as the liver, heart and kidneys. Yet, for segmentation of the pancreas, high accuracy in automatic segmentation remains a challenge. The pancreas shows high anatomical variations in shape, size and location

© Springer International Publishing Switzerland 2014
H. Yoshida et al. (Eds.): ABDI 2014, LNCS 8676, pp. 103–113, 2014.
DOI: 10.1007/978-3-319-13692-9_10

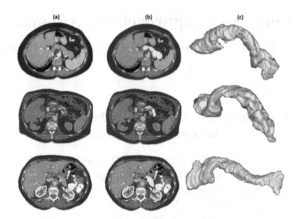

Fig. 1. Three color-coded masks in column (b) show the ground-truth pancreas segmentations for the slices in (a) of different patients. The corresponding 3D views are in (c) (Colour figure online).

that change from patient to patient. The amount of visceral fat tissue in the proximity can drastically vary the boundary contrast as well. All these factors make pancreas organ segmentation very challenging. Figure 1 shows different slices from three different patient cases and the ground-truth 3D segmented volumes of the pancreas to better visualize some of the variations and challenges mentioned.

Previous literature for pancreas segmentation in abdominal CT images are mostly top-down approaches that rely on atlas based approaches or statistical shape modeling or both [1–3]. In [1], Okada et al. perform multi-organ segmentation by combining inter-organ spatial interrelations with probabilistic atlases, which incorporates various a priori knowledge into the model, and a shape model to obtain results for seven organs. Shimizu et al. [2] utilize three-phase contrast-enhanced CT data which are first registered together for a particular patient and then registered to a reference patient by landmark-based deformable registration. A patient-specific probabilistic atlas guided segmentation is conducted, followed by an intensity-based classification and post-processing. Validation of the approach in [2] was conducted on 20 multi-phase datasets with an obtained Jaccard

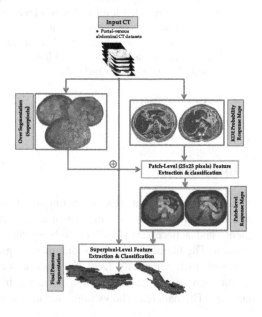

Fig. 2. Overall segmentation framework.

of 57.9 %. The state-of-the-art result thus far for single-phase datasets is obtained by Wolz et al. [3]. A hierarchical weighted subject-specific atlas-based registration approach was implemented, with a Dice overlap using leave-one-out of 69.6 % on 150 patients and 58.2 % on a sub-population of 50 patients.

In this paper, a new bottom-up approach for pancreas segmentation is proposed with single phase CT patient data volumes. Our method is motivated to improve segmentation accuracy of highly deformable organs, such as the pancreas, by leveraging middle-level representation of image segments. Over segmentation of all 2D slices of a patient abdominal CT scan is first obtained as a semi-structured representation referred to as superpixels. The superpixel labeling maps are projected back to the 3D volumetric space. Random forest classifiers are trained once on the patch-level and in a two-level cascade fashion on the superpixel level, with multi-phase feature extraction processes, respectively.

Leave-one-patient-out criterion is used as default in [1, 3], for up to 150 patients. Here we would argue that leave-one-out based dense volume registration and label fusion process may be computationally impractical in clinical practice. More importantly, it does not scale up easily when large scale datasets are present. Thus, we employ 6-fold cross validation which exploits less data for training but more scans for testing. Classification models are compactly encoded by random forest classifiers through training, instead of label masks of $(n - 1)$ scans in leave-one-out of n patients. Our bottom-up approach is much more efficient than [1, 3] in both memory and computation speed. In the literature a similar framework that utilizes superpixel methods and performs feature extraction and classification can be found for pathological region detection and segmentation within an organ [4]. MRI data is used and the overall feature extraction, classification and implementation details are significantly different from the proposed approach in this paper.

2 Methods

The overall bottom-up pancreas segmentation framework is illustrated in Fig. 2. This section describes how to generate superpixels and each classification layer of our two-tiered approach in details.

2.1 Boundary-Preserving Over Segmentation

There are two main broad categories of superpixel methods: gradient ascent and graph-based methods. Thorough examination and analysis of one gradient ascent and three graph-based superpixel algorithms are conducted, i.e., watershed [6], SLIC [5, 10], efficient graph-based [7] and Entropy rate [8]. Evaluation is executed to find the most suitable set of parameters to obtain high boundary recalls (critical to the segmentation accuracy for the pancreas), in a range of distances of (1, 2, ..., 6) pixels from the semantic pancreas ground-truth boundary annotation.

Quantitative and qualitative results can be found in Figs. 3 and 4. Based on Fig. 3, the SLIC approach provides the best boundary recall of >90 %, under the distance of

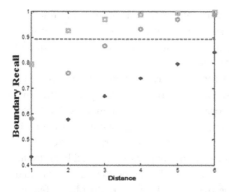

Fig. 3. Superpixels boundary recall results evaluated on 41 patient scans. The SLIC [5] results are represented in cyan, the watershed [6] in red, while the entropy rate [8] and efficient graph [7] based methods are depicted in green and blue, respectively. The red line represents the 90 % marker (Colour figure online).

2 pixels. The extension of superpixels to supervoxels is possible but we prefer 2D superpixel representation in this study, due to the potential boundary leakage problem of supervoxels deteriorating the pancreas segmentation more severely in multiple CT slices.

2.2 Patch-Level Feature Extraction and Labeling

This step consisted of two main components: feature extraction and classification. In the feature extraction stage, 14 different image features were computed and concatenated with additional dense D-SIFT [10], to capture fine-grained gradient or texture features, which results in 46 total features.

Figure 6 shows the three sets of data information used for computations. The goal is to generate pancreas class-conditional response maps, as seen in Fig. 6 (d, h).

The Scale Invariant Feature Transform [9] is a texture feature extractor and descriptor. In this paper, we adopt the Dense Scale Invariant Feature Transform (dSIFT) [10] which is based on SIFT [9] with several different extensions. Publically

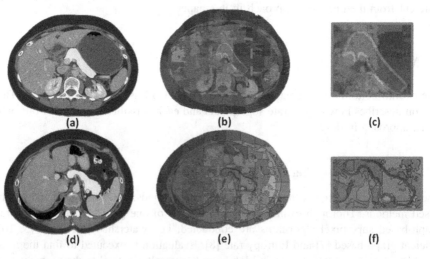

Fig. 4. Sample superpixels results from the SLIC method. First column are different slices from different patient scans with the ground-truth pancreas segmentation in yellow (a & d). The second column depicts the over segmentation results with the pancreas contours superimposed on the image (b & e). Finally, (c) and (f) show zoomed-in areas of the pancreas superpixels results from (b) and (e) (Colour figure online).

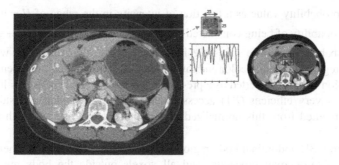

Fig. 5. Sample slice with center positions superimposed as green dots. The 25 × 25 image patch and corresponding D-SIFT descriptors are shown on the right-hand side (Colour figure online).

available VLFeat implementation is employed. In Fig. 5, a sample image slice depicts the dSIFT process, where the descriptors are densely and uniformly extracted from image grids with inter-distances of 3 pixels. The green points on the image represent the patch center positions. Once the center positions are known, dSIFT is computed with bin size of 6 pixels and geometry of [2 × 2] bins, which results in 32 dimensional descriptors, for each image patch. For implementation and spatial bin configuration details, refer to [10]. The image patch size is chosen to be 25 × 25, a trade-off between the description power and computational efficiency. We empirically evaluated the size range from 15 to 35 pixels using small sub-sampled datasets for classification, as described later. Stable performance statistics are observed and we report quantitative experimental results using the default patch size of 25 × 25 pixels.

From the CT intensity modality, the mean, median and standard deviation (std) statistics over the full 25 × 25 pixel range per patch, $\mathcal{P}$, are extracted. The same intensity statistics within the intersected sub-region, $\mathcal{P}'$ of $\mathcal{P}$, and the underlying superpixel supporting mask (the superpixel where the patch center resides), obtained from Sect. 2.1, and the original patch are also extracted. The idea is that an image patch, $\mathcal{P}$, may be divided into more than one superpixel. The second set of statistics is calculated with respect to the most representative superpixel. In this manner, object boundary-preserving intensity features are obtained [12].

We also built similar features in the class-conditional probability density function (PDF) space. The ground-truth pancreas voxel intensities from 26 randomly selected patient CT scans were used as positive class samples and all remaining voxels were considered as negatives. These distributions were used to create kernel density estimators (KDE) that represent the CT intensity distributions of the positive $\{X^+\}$ and negative class $\{X^-\}$ of pancreas and non-pancreas voxels' CT image information. Let $X^+ = (h_1^+, h_2^+, ..., h_n^+)$ and $X^- = (h_1^-, h_2^-, ..., h_m^-)$ where h_n^+ and h_m^- represent the intensity values for the positive and negative pixel samples for all 7 patient CT scans over the entire abdominal CT Hounsfield range. The kernel density estimators $f^+(X^+) = \frac{1}{n}\sum_{i=1}^{n} K(X^+ - X_i^+)$ and $f^-(X^-) = \frac{1}{m}\sum_{j=1}^{m} K(X^- - X_j^-)$ were computed where $K(\cdot)$ is assumed to be a Gaussian kernel. The normalized likelihood ratio was computed which becomes a probability value as a function of intensity in the range of $H = [0:1:4095]$. Thus, the probability of being considered pancreas is formulated as: $y^+ = \frac{f^+(X^+)}{f^+(X^+)+f^-(X^-)}$. Sample probability response maps are illustrated in Fig. 5 (c) and (g), where high probability regions are red in color and low probabilities in blue. In implementation, the above function can be converted as a pre-computed look-up table over $H = [0:1:4095]$, which allows very efficient $O(1)$ access time. The mean, median and std statistics are then computed from this normalized probability channel as well, with respect to $\mathcal{P}$ and $\mathcal{P}'$.

The overall 3D abdominal body region per patient can be reliably segmented using a standard table-removal procedure and all voxels outside the body are removed. We then compute the normalized relative x-axis and y-axis positions $\in [0, 1]$ at each of the image patch centroids, against the segmented body region. This provides the final two features extracted at the patch level for each axial slice in the patient volumes.

The total 46 patch level features were used to train the random forest (RF) classifier C_1. The classifier training was carried-out using six-fold cross validation. Figure 6 (d) and (h) show the computed response maps for the patch-level classification of two illustrative slices from different patients. The red color shows areas of high probability corresponding to the pancreas. From the response maps, the relative x and y positions as features are clearly important in separating positive and negative classes. The trained RF classifier is able to recognize the negative class patches residing in the background, such as liver, vertebrae and muscle using spatial location cues. For example, note the implicit vertical and horizontal decision boundary lines in Fig. 6 (d, h). Comparing Fig. 6 (d) and (h) versus (c) and (g) respectively, it demonstrates the superior descriptive and discriminative power of the feature descriptor on image patches ($\mathcal{P}$ and $\mathcal{P}'$) than single pixel intensities. Organs with similar CT values are significantly depressed in the patch-level response maps.

In summary, SIFT and its variations, e.g., D-SIFT have shown to be informative, especially through spatial polling or packing [13]. Our defined 14 features also capture a wide range of visual information and pixel-level correlations per image patch. Both good classification recall and specificity have been obtained in cross-validation using Random Forest implementation of 50 trees and minimum leaf of 150 (i.e., the tree-bagger() function in Matlab). In future work, we plan to exploit the deep convolutional neural network based approach for dense patch labeling [16], without pre-defined features.

2.3   Superpixel-Level Feature Extraction and Classification

In this stage, the 2D superpixel supporting maps (recording the spatial partitioning using SLIC), the original CT image slices and the probability response maps from the patch classification are used for feature extraction on a superpixel level. Treating the collection of CT voxels and the per-voxel/patch response values (from C_1) within any superpixel as two empirical unordered distributions, higher 1–4 order statistics such as mean, std, skewness, kurtosis [14] and 7 percentiles (20, 30, 40, ..., 90 %) were computed. This results in 24 features for each instance that are used to train a cascade of two random forest classifiers. A cascade of random forests was employed here, due to the highly unbalanced quantities between foreground (pancreas) superpixels and background (the rest of CT volume) superpixels, which is general for rare event detection [15]. The superpixel labels are inferred from the overlapping ratio r of the superpixel label map and the ground-truth object level pancreas mask. If $r \geq 0.5$, the superpixel is labeled as positive; if $r \leq 0.2$, negative. For a small portion of superpixels with $0.5 > r > 0.2$, they are ambiguous to assign labels and thus not used for training. A two-level cascaded random forest classification hierarchy was found to be sufficient and implemented to obtain C_2 and C_3. Figure 7 shows the receiver operating curves (ROC) for 6-fold cross validation. From the AUC values, C_3 is harder to train since it employs the hard negatives as negative samples but classified positively by C_2. RF with 50–200 trees are evaluated, with similar empirical performances.

The binary 3D pancreas volumetric mask is simply obtained by stacking the binary superpixel classification/labeling outcomes from 2D axial slices. No further post-processing is employed since the major focus of this paper is to investigate the performance effects of using superpixels as a middle-level representation on organ segmentation. Post-processing could improve the segmentation accuracy, such as 3D morphological operators, connected component analysis, surface-based level-set or graph-cut based MRF/CRF optimization. This is left for future work.

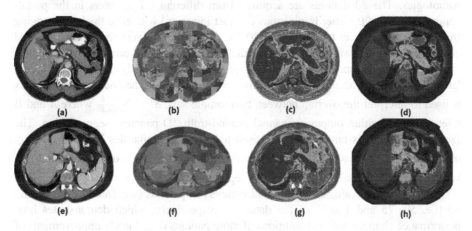

Fig. 6. Two sample slices from different patients are shown in (a) and (e). The corresponding superpixels segmentation (b, f), probability response maps (c, g) and patch-level probability response maps (d, h) are shown. In (c, g) and (d, h), red represents highest probabilities. In (d, h) the purple color represents areas where probabilities are so small and can be deemed insignificant areas of interest (Color figure online).

3   Experimental Results and Validation

Data & Metrics: We use 80 single-phase annotated abdominal CT patient scans to assess the accuracy and robustness measures for pancreas segmentation using the proposed method. 17 of the subjects are from a kidney donor transplant list of healthy patients that have abdominal CT scans prior to kidney extraction. The remaining 63

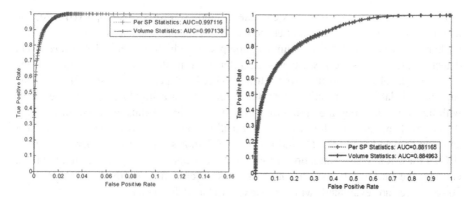

Fig. 7. ROC curves to analyze the superpixel classification results, in a two layer cascade of RF classifiers: (a) the first layer classifier, C_2 and (b) the second layer classifier, C_3. Red plots are using each superpixel as a count to calculate sensitivity and specificity. In blue plots, superpixels are weighted by their size (e.g., numbers of pixels) for calculation (Color figure online).

patients are selected by a radiologist from the Picture Archiving and Communications System (PACS) that had neither pancreatic cancer lesions nor major abdominal pathologies. The 80 datasets are acquired from different CT scanners in the portal-venous phase (~ 70 s after intravenous contrast injection) with slice thickness ranging from 1.5–2.5 mm with tube voltage 120 kV and varying image resolutions. Manual ground-truth segmentations of the pancreas for all 80 cases are provided by a medical student and verified/modified by a radiologist. Several similarity metrics were calculated to validate the accuracy and robustness of our method. The Dice similarity index is used to interpret the overlap between two sample sets, $SI = 2 \frac{|A \cap B|}{|A| + |B|}$ where A and B refer to the algorithm output or manual ground-truth 3D pancreas segmentation. The Jaccard index (JI) is another statistic used to compute similarities between the segmentation result against the reference standard, $JI = \frac{|A \cap B|}{|A \cup B|}$. The volumetric recall (i.e. sensitivity) and precision values are also reported.

Our results are evaluated on different numbers of patients (see Table 1): 41, 60 and 80 (i.e. 50, 75 and 100 % of the datasets), respectively, which demonstrates how performance changes with the additions of more patients data. Steady improvements of ~ 4 % in the Dice coefficient and ~ 5 % for the Jaccard index are observed, from 41 to 60, and 60 to 80. Our best segmentation result (Dice of 68.8 % at 80 patients in 6-fold cross validation) is closely approaching the highest accuracy level of [3] (Dice of 69.6 % at 150 patients in leave-one-out), with less than 1 % difference. At 41 patients, our result is 2.2 % better than [3] with 50 patients (Dice coefficients of 60.4 % versus 58.2 %). Leave-one-out validation translates to performing computationally demanding 3D dense non-rigid registration and label fusion of numerous volumes to the target case, in order to obtain the segmentation of one patient. However, larger standard deviations in performance measurements are observed for our method. In summary, our bottom-up segmentation approach is a more computationally efficient (2–3 min versus 30 min) method that demonstrates comparable results against the state-of-the-art [3], using 6-fold cross validation instead of leave-one-out [3].

Table 1. Comparison with state-of-the-art segmentation methods. Average Dice overlap (Similarity Index, SI), Jaccard Index (JI) and Recall/Precision

Reference	N Patients	Dice (Similarity Index)	Jaccard Index	Precision	Recall
Wolz et al. [3]	50	58.2 % ± 20.0 [0 81.2]	43.5 % ± 17.8 [0 68.6]		
Wolz et al.	150	69.6 % ± 16.7 [6.9 90.9]	55.5 % ± 17.1 [3.6 83.3]	67.9 % ± 18.2 [6.0 91.8]	74.1 % ± 17.1 [8.0 93.4]
Proposed	41	60.4 % ± 22.3 [2.0 96.4]	46.7 % ± 22.8 [0 93.0]	55.6 % ± 29.8 [1.2 100]	80.8 % ± 21.2 [4.8 99.8]
Proposed	60	64.9 % ± 22.6 [0 94.2]	51.7 % ± 22.6 [0 89.1]	70.3 % ± 29.0 [0 100]	69.1 % ± 25.7 [0 98.9]
Proposed	80	68.8 % ± 25.6 [0 96.6]	57.2 % ± 25.4 [0 93.5]	71.5 % ± 30.0 [0 100]	72.5 % ± 27.2 [0 100]

Discussion: Our protocol is arguably harder than the leave-one-out criterion in [1, 3] since less patient datasets are exploited in training and more separate patient scans for testing. In fact, [3] does demonstrate a notable performance drop from using 149 patients in training versus 49 patients, i.e., mean Dice coefficients decreased from 69.6

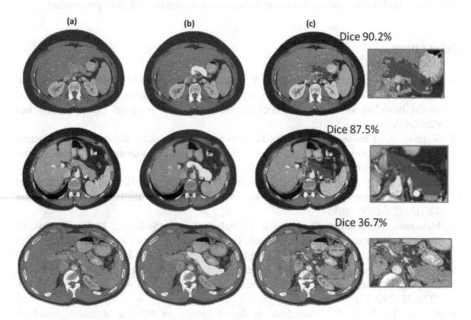

Fig. 8. Segmentation results with computed good, fair and poor Dice coefficients for the pancreas. Sample original slices for three patients are shown in (a) and the corresponding groundtruth manual segmentations in (b) are in yellow. Final segmentations are shown in red in (c) with Dice coefficients for the volume above each slice. The zoomed-in areas of the slice segmentations in the orange boxes are shown to the right of the image (Colour figure online).

to 58.2 %. This indicates that the multi-atlas fusion approaches [1, 3] may actually achieve lower segmentation accuracies than reported, if under six-fold cross validation.

Figure 8 shows samples of final pancreas segmentation results for three different patients, where good result refers to computed Dice coefficient above 90 % (15 patients), fair result as $50\% \leq Dice \leq 90\%$ (49 patients) and poor for $Dice < 50\%$ (16 patients).

4   Conclusions

In this paper a hierarchical two-tiered method was proposed based on a bottom-up information propagation from image patches to segments. The SLIC superpixel generation algorithm [5] provided the best overall pancreas organ-level boundary recall by partitioning each 2D CT axial slice into over-segmentation label maps of all patients. Their final binary labeling masks can be straightforwardly stacked and projected back into the 3D CT scan space, to form the pancreas segmentation mask. Random forest classifier and cascade of RF classifiers were trained at the image patch- and superpixel-level respectively, via extracting multi-channel features. Based on a six-fold cross validation of the 80 CT datasets, our results are comparable and slightly better than the state-of-the art work [1, 3]. A Dice coefficient of 68.8 % and Jaccard index of 57.2 % was obtained, versus 69.6 % and 55.5 % in [3] and JI of 46.6 % [1]. Further analysis of the approach will be conducted on employing additional datasets and exploiting superpixel based 2D/3D random field models, i.e., taking superpixels as nodes to form intra- and inter-slice graph connections, for more structurally sophisticated post-processing.

References

1. Okada, T., Linguraru, M.G., Yoshida, Y., Hor, M., Summers, R.M., Chen, Y., Tomiyama, N., Sato, Y.: Abdominal multi-organ segmentation of CT images based on hierarchical spatial modeling of organ interrelations. In: Abdominal Imaging. Computational and Clinical Applications (2012)
2. Shimizu, A., Kimoto, T., Kobatake, H., Nawano, S., Shinozaki, K.: Automated pancreas segmentation from three-dimensional contrast-enhanced computed tomography. Int. J. Comput. Assist. Radiol. Surg. 5, 85–98 (2010)
3. Wolz, R., Chu, C., Misawa, K., Fujiwara, M., Mori, K., Rueckert, D.: Automated abdominal multi-organ segmentation with subject-specific atlas generation. IEEE Trans. Med. Imaging 32(7), 1723–1730 (2013)
4. Mahapatra, D., Schuffler, P., Tielbeek, J., Makanyanga, J., Stoker, J., Taylor, S., Vos, F., Buhmann, J.: Automatic detection and segmentation of Crohn's disease tissues from abdominal MRI. IEEE Trans. Med. Imaging 32, 2332–2348 (2013)
5. Achanta, R., Shaji, A., Smith, K., Lucchi, A., Fua, P., Susstrunk, S.: SLIC superpixels compared to state-of-the-art superpixel methods. IEEE Trans. Pat. Ana. Mach. Intel. 34(11), 2274–2282 (2012)
6. Vincent, L., Soille, P.: Watersheds in digital spaces: an Efficient algorithm based on immersion simulations. IEEE Trans. Pat. Ana. Mach. Intel. 13, 83–598 (1991)
7. Felzenszwalb, P., Huttenlocher, D.: Efficient graph-based image segmentation. Int. J. Comput. Vis. 59(2), 167–181 (2004)

8. Liu, M., Tuzel, O., Ramalingam, S., Chellappa, R.: Entropy rate superpixel segmentation. In: IEEE Conference on CVPR, pp. 2099–2104, (2011)

9. Lowe, D.G.: Distinctive image features from scale-invariant keypoints. Int. J. Comput. Vis. **60**(2), 91–110 (2004)

10. VLFEAT toolbox. http://www.vlfeat.org/overview/dsift.html

11. Breiman, L.: Random forests. Mach. Learn. **45**(1), 5–32 (2001)

12. Kim, J., Grauman, K.: Boundary preserving dense local regions. In: IEEE Conference on CVPR, pp. 1553–1560 (2011)

13. Gilinsky, A., Zelnik-Manor, I.: SIFTpack: a compact representation for efficient SIFT matching. In: IEEE Conference on ICCV, (2013)

14. Groeneveld, R., Meeden, G.: Measuring skewness and kurtosis. Statistician **33**, 391–399 (1984)

15. Viola, P., Jones, M.J.: Robust real-time face detection. Int. J. Comput. Vis. **57**(2), 137–154 (2004)

16. Roth, H., Lu, L., Seff, A., Chery, K., Liu, J., Hoffman, J., Wang, S., Turkbey, E., Summers, R.M.: A New 2.5D representation for lymph node detection using random sets of deep convolutional neural network observations. http://arxiv-web3.library.cornell.edu/pdf/1406.2639v1.pdf (2014)

Gastrointestinal Tract - Crohn's Disease

Spatially-Constrained Probability Distribution Model of Incoherent Motion (SPIM) in Diffusion Weighted MRI Signals of Crohn's Disease

Sila Kurugol[1,2]($\boxtimes$), Moti Freiman[1,2], Onur Afacan[1,2],
Jeannette M. Perez-Rossello[1], Michael J. Callahan[1], and Simon K. Warfield[1,2]

[1] Computational Radiology Laboratory, Harvard Medical School,
Boston Children's Hospital, 300 Longwood Avenue, Boston, MA 02115, USA
{Sila.Kurugol,Moti.Freiman,Onur.Afacan,Jeannette.Perez-Rossello,
Michael.Callahan,Simon.Warfield}@childrens.harvard.edu
[2] Department of Radiology, Harvard Medical School, Boston Children's Hospital,
300 Longwood Avenue, Boston, MA 02115, USA

Abstract. Diffusion Weighted imaging (DWI) of the body provides important information about the physiological and microstructural properties of tissues and has great potential for imaging inflammatory activity and improve diagnosis and follow up of Crohn's disease. The two main challenges for DWI are the lack of realistic signal decay models of heterogeneous diffusion and inherently low signal-to-noise ratio (SNR), which makes robust parameter estimation challenging. Increasing the SNR requires long scan times that are not clinically practical. In this work, to address both challenges, we propose a novel Spatially-constrained Probability distribution model of incoherent Motion (SPIM) of water molecules. This model is composed of a probability model of diffusion that we propose to account for the heterogeneity of incoherent motion within multiple compartment tissue microenvironments in each voxel and a spatial homogeneity prior proposed by Freiman et al. for robust parameter estimation. We evaluated the performance of proposed SPIM model in both simulated and in-vivo DWI data from 5 healthy and 24 Crohn's disease subjects. SPIM model substantially reduced parameter estimation errors, with a reduction of 35 % for perfusion and 7 % for perfusion fraction and 4 % for diffusion parameters. Coefficient of variation of estimated parameters decreased using SPIM compared to simple bi-exponential signal decay model, which indicates an increase in robustness. Parameters estimated using SPIM model better discriminated enhancing and non-enhancing stages of Crohn's disease.

Keywords: Diffusion-weighted imaging · Crohn's disease · Spatial homogeneity prior · Probability distribution model of incoherent motion

1 Introduction

Crohn's disease is a chronic inflammatory bowel disease, which has relapsing, and remitting clinical course and is increasing in incidence. Long-standing

© Springer International Publishing Switzerland 2014
H. Yoshida et al. (Eds.): ABDI 2014, LNCS 8676, pp. 117–127, 2014.
DOI: 10.1007/978-3-319-13692-9_11

inflammation can result in bowel obstruction, stricture, fistula, abscess and an increased risk for small and large bowel malignancy. Identifying disease stage is crucial for determining the correct treatment options [1]. Diffusion-weighted imaging (DWI) is a noninvasive body imaging technique and has potential to improve diagnosis, characterization and follow up of lesions and inflammatory activity in bowel.

DWI enables characterization of tissue micro-environment through measurement of variations in mobility of water molecules. These variations can be due to various factors including the compartment in which water molecules are located (intravascular, extracellular, or intracellular spaces), cellularity, cell membrane integrity and hindrances such as presence of large molecules [2].

DWI signal decays as a function of the amount of incoherent motion of water molecules present in the tissue and the diffusion weighting parameter called "b-value" (Fig. 1(a)). There are two approaches currently used in practice to model this signal and quantitatively characterize the diffusivity of the tissue from DWI. One is mono-exponential signal decay model, with the apparent diffusion coefficient (ADC) as the decay rate parameter [3], and the other is bi-exponential signal decay model that represents a slow diffusion component associated with the Brownian motion of water molecules and a fast diffusion component associated with bulk motion of intravascular molecules in the micro-capillaries [4,5]. This second approach, called Intra-voxel incoherent motion (IVIM) model, has two decay rate parameters, one for fast and one for slow diffusion component.

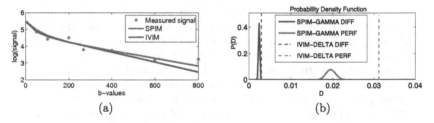

Fig. 1. (a) Diffusion signal at different b-values and fitted models using SPIM and IVIM, (b) Comparison of probability density functions (pdfs) modeling fast (PERF) and slow diffusion (DIFF) components. IVIM uses Dirac Delta pdfs, proposed SPIM model uses a mixture of Gamma pdfs.

The reduction in microvascular volume that is a feature of the inflammatory process in Crohn's disease [6] may induce changes in the fast diffusion decay component in DWI which cannot be identified independently using the mono-exponential ADC model analysis. IVIM was previously used to identify this component [7]. However, IVIM has limitations because size of each voxel in DWI images is on the order of $10\,\mathrm{mm}^3$ and the measured signal is a combination of signal arising from a heterogeneous micro-environment within each voxel. IVIM model is too simplistic to capture the heterogeneity of diffusion components within a voxel.

Another reason why current models fail to provide robust quantitative measures of disease activity in clinical settings is inherent low signal-to-noise ratio (SNR) in DWI signals. Increasing the SNR requires long scan times that are not practical in clinical settings.

In this work, we first propose a novel model that accounts for the heterogeneity of diffusion (DIFF) and perfusion (PERF) components. As opposed to the two Dirac delta functions modeling diffusion and perfusion distributions in IVIM, our model uses a Probability distribution model of Incoherent Motion (PIM). PIM is a mixture model of two probability density functions (pdfs), one representing the slow diffusion and the other representing the fast diffusion component (perfusion). The variations of these pdfs around the means represent the heterogeneities of the micro-environment within a voxel (see Fig. 1(b)).

To account for the problem of low SNR in DWI signal, Freiman et al. recently introduced a spatially constrained model which produces estimates of signal decay parameters for all voxels simultaneously, rather than solving for each voxel independently [8,9]. We integrate this spatially constrained model with our probability distributions model of diffusion for each voxel and introduce a novel Spatially-constrained Probability distribution model of incoherent Motion (SPIM) of water molecules. As a result, the robustness of parameter estimates from the DWI data is increased without acquiring additional data, while utilizing a more realistic model of heterogeneous diffusion components.

We evaluated the performance of proposed SPIM approach on both simulated and in-vivo DWI data. Our experiments on simulated data compared the proposed SPIM model with IVIM model in term of the parameter estimation errors in low SNR images. We computed the coefficient of variation of estimated parameter within ROIs in liver, spleen and kidneys of five healthy volunteers as a measure of robustness of SPIM model compared to IVIM. We also assessed the clinical impact in a study cohort of 24 pediatric Crohn's disease patients from two disease stage groups, one with non-enhancing and the other with enhancing ileum regions in their bowel.

2   Methods

2.1   Probability Distribution Model of Incoherent Motion (PIM)

We model the heterogeneous diffusion of water molecules in a multiple compartment tissue micro-environment within a voxel using a probability distribution model of diffusion random variable D.

Probability distribution of diffusion in ADC model corresponds to a single Dirac Delta function ($p(D) = \delta(D - ADC)$). In IVIM model, it corresponds to a mixture of two Dirac Delta functions. However, these models do not represent the heterogeneity in diffusion and perfusion components within a voxel. Therefore we model the probability distribution of diffusion with a two component mixture model $p(D)$, one for fast diffusion (perfusion) and the other for slow diffusion. Variance of each pdf represents the heterogeneity in diffusion and perfusion components.

A Gamma distribution instead of normal distribution is used to model each component because of its positive support $(D > 0)$. Each Gamma probability density function $(p_{k_i,\theta_i}(D))$ given by

$$p_{k_i,\theta_i}(D) = \frac{D^{k_i-1}}{\Gamma(k_i)\theta_i^{k_i}} \exp(-D/\theta_i) \tag{1}$$

has two parameters, one shape parameter k_i and one scale parameter θ_i. $\Gamma(k_i)$ is the Gamma function.

Two component mixture model of diffusion is then given by

$$p_v(D) = f_v p_{k_{1,v},\theta_{1,v}}(D) + (1 - f_v)p_{k_{2,v},\theta_{2,v}}(D) \tag{2}$$

where the weights $f_v \in [0,1]$ and $1 - f_v$ represent the volume fraction of perfusion and diffusion in voxel v respectively.

The exponentially decaying signal $(S_{v,i})$ for each voxel v measures at b-value i can be formulated using the pdf $p(D)$ of diffusion within a voxel as follows:

$$S_{v,i} = So_v \int p_v(D) \exp(-b_i D) \mathrm{d}D. \tag{3}$$

The integral in this equation is the Laplace transform of $p_v(D)$. Using the analytical expression of the Laplace transform of Gamma distribution for each Gamma in $p_v(D)$, we obtain

$$S_{v,i} = So_v(f_v \exp(-k_{1,v}\log(1 + b_i\theta_{1,v})) + (1 - f_v)(\exp(-k_{2,v}\log(1 + b_i\theta_{2,v})))). \tag{4}$$

The parameters $(\alpha_v = \{So, f, \theta_1, k_1, \theta_2, k_2\})$ of the model at each voxel v can be estimated by solving a maximum likelihood estimation problem given by

$$\hat{\alpha}_v = \arg\max_{\alpha_v} p(S_v|\alpha_v) = \prod_{i=1}^{N} p(S_{v,i}|\alpha_v). \tag{5}$$

The measured signal in DWI $(M_{v,i})$ is a sum of the signal component $(S_{v,i})$ and the noise component. To model this noise component, we use a Gaussian approximation for the non-central χ-distributed parallel imaging acquisition noise [10]. Taking the negative log of the maximum likelihood estimator; we obtain the following least-squares minimization problem:

$$\hat{\alpha}_v = \arg\min_{\alpha_v} \sum_{i=1}^{N} (M_{v,i} - S_{v,i})^2 \tag{6}$$

where $S_{v,i}$ is given by Eq. 4. The model parameters can be estimated by solving a non-linear least squares minimization problem for each voxel. However, the special structure of our cost function allows us to use an improved optimization strategy which separates the optimization problem into linear and nonlinear parts. Rearranging of $S_{v,i}$ in the form of

$$S_{v,i} = c_{v,j} \sum_{j=1}^{2} \Phi_j(\theta_j, k_j) \tag{7}$$

we obtain the least squares problem of the form $\sum_{i=1}^{N} \left(M_{v,i} - c_{v,j} \sum_{i=1}^{2} \Phi(\theta_j, k_j) \right)^2$ where $c_{v,1} = So_v f_v$, $c_{v,2} = So_v(1 - f_v)$ are the linear parameters and θ_j, k_j are the nonlinear parameters. We solve this separable problem using variable projection optimization algorithm [11] which leads to an improved parameter estimation.

2.2 Spatially-Constrained Probability Distribution Model of Incoherent Motion (SPIM)

Due to low SNR of the measured DWI signals, instead of solving the least squares optimization for each voxel independently, we integrate the spatial homogeneity prior model proposed in [8] into our formulation. The parameter estimation is then performed by maximizing the posterior distribution given by the product of likelihood and prior terms as follows:

$$\hat{\alpha} = \arg \max_{\alpha} p(\alpha|S) \propto p(S|\alpha)p(\alpha) \tag{8}$$

The spatial homogeneity prior can be decomposed into a product form using a continuous-valued Markov Random Fields formulation given by

$$p(S|\alpha)p(\alpha) \propto \prod_v p(S_v|\alpha_v) \prod_{v_p \sim v_q} p(\alpha_{v_p}, \alpha_{v_q}) \tag{9}$$

where each spatial prior term $p(\alpha_{v,p}, \alpha_{v,q})$ is defined over a neighborhood ($v_p \sim v_q$). Taking the negative log of Eq. 9, we obtain

$$\hat{\alpha} = \arg \min_{\alpha} \sum_v \phi(S_v; \alpha_v) + \sum_{v_p \sim v_q} \psi(\alpha_{v_p}, \alpha_{v_q}) \tag{10}$$

where $\phi(S_v; \alpha_v) = -\log p(S_v|\alpha_v)$ is the negative data likelihood term explained in the previous section and $\psi(\alpha_{v_p}, \alpha_{v_q}) = -\log p(\alpha_{v_p}, \alpha_{v_q})$ is the spatial homogeneity term defined using the L1 norm as follows:

$$\psi(\Theta_{v_p}, \Theta_{v_q}) = \alpha W |\Theta_{v_p} - \Theta_{v_q}| \tag{11}$$

Here $\alpha \geq 0$ is the weight that determines the amount of spatial homogeneity, and W is a diagonal weighting matrix that accounts for the different scales of the parameters in α_v.

The continuous MRF formulation of the energy minimization problem for estimation of the parameters is difficult to solve due to its high dimensionality. To efficiently estimate the model parameters, we use the "fusion bootstrap moves" solver proposed in [8]. This algorithm works as follows: At each iteration, a model based bootstrap algorithm [12] first generates a proposal signal for each voxel using the residuals between measured signal and current signal model from the previous iteration. The parameters of the proposal signal are then estimated independently for each voxel by solving the Eq. 7 as described in Sect. 2.1. Finally a binary graph cut solver [13] that minimizes the energy function in Eq. 10 is used to fuse the current parameter estimates with the new proposed parameter estimates into a new estimate of parameters that better fit the observed DWI signal while imposing the spatial homogeneity constraints.

3   Experimental Results

3.1   Simulated Data Experiments

For our simulated data experiments, we generated 3D images of reference parametric maps, of size $100 \times 100 \times 5$ voxels, sampled from a mixture of Gamma distributions with parameters $\alpha = \{S_o, f_v, \theta_1, k_1, \theta_2, k_2\} = \{200, 0.15, 100, 0.01, 100, 0.1\}$ for innermost region, $\{200, 0.25, 900, 1/3 \times 0.01, 400, 0.05\}$ for middle region, and $\{200, 0.35, 400, 0.005, 900, 1/3 \times 0.1\}$ for outermost region in units of $10^3 \, \mu m^2/ms$. We then computed simulated DWI images from these parametric maps using Eq. 3. We finally added noise to the data. The noise is sampled from a Rician distribution with σ values ranged from $2 - 8$, which implies an SNR of $100 - 25$ for the chosen signal value of $S_o = 200$ at b-value = 0.

We estimated the model parameters from the simulated DWI data using the proposed SPIM approach that integrates the probabilistic model of diffusion with spatial homogeneity constraints. We compared the results with the IVIM approach that fits a bi-exponential decay function to estimate slow and fast diffusion (perfusion) parameters for each voxel independently. For comparing parameters of mixture of Gamma distributions model with IVIM, we computed the means of the Gamma distributions, which we compare with the perfusion and diffusion parameters of IVIM model. We also compared the perfusion fraction coefficient parameter(f_v) that exist in both models. The true values of mean and variance parameters for diffusion and perfusion $\{D, \sigma_D^2, D^*, \sigma_{D*}^2\}$ were $\{1, 0.01, 10, 1\}$ for innermost region, $\{3, 0.01, 20, 1\}$ for middle and $\{2, 0.01, 30, 1\}$ for innermost region in units of $10^3 \, \mu m^2/ms$.

Figure 2 shows the reference parametric maps compared to the parametric maps estimated from the proposed SPIM approach. The computed mean and standard deviation of the absolute error percentage between the reference and estimated parameters for each noise level are shown in Fig. 3. Our SPIM model improved the mean error of parameters by 35 % for perfusion and 7 % for perfusion fraction and 4 % for diffusion.

3.2   In-vivo DWI Experiments on Healthy Subjects

We acquired abdominal DWI images from 5 healthy subjects using a 1.5-T MRI scanner (Magnetom Avanto, Siemens Medical Solutions, Erlangen, Germany) with a body-matrix coil and a spine array coil for signal reception.

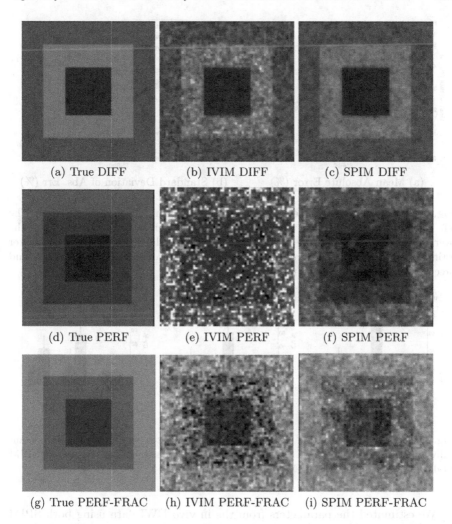

(a) True DIFF   (b) IVIM DIFF   (c) SPIM DIFF

(d) True PERF   (e) IVIM PERF   (f) SPIM PERF

(g) True PERF-FRAC   (h) IVIM PERF-FRAC   (i) SPIM PERF-FRAC

Fig. 2. Results of simulated data. The first column depicts the reference parametric maps (DIFF, PERF, and PERF-FRAC). The second and third columns show parametric maps calculated using IVIM model and proposed SPIM model respectively. The proposed SPIM model better estimates the parameters compared to the IVIM model.

Free-breathing single-shot echo-planar imaging was performed using the following parameters: repetition time/echo time (TR/TE) = 6800/59 ms; SPAIR fat suppression; matrix size = 192×156; field of view = 300×260 mm; number of excitations = 1; slice thickness/gap = 5 mm/0.5 mm; 40 axial slices; 8 b-values = 5, 50, 100, 200, 270, 400, 600, 800 s/mm^2. A tetrahedral gradient scheme, first proposed in Conturo et al. [14], was used to acquire 4 successive images at each b-value with an overall scan acquisition time of 4 min. Diffusion trace-weighted images at each b-value were generated using geometric averages of the images acquired in each diffusion sensitization direction [15].

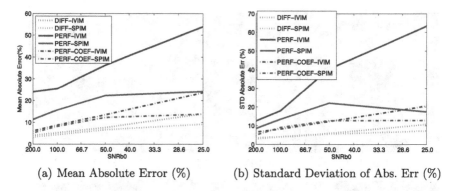

(a) Mean Absolute Error (%)   (b) Standard Deviation of Abs. Err (%)

Fig. 3. Performance of incoherent motion parameter estimators on simulated data. The left and right plots depict accuracy and precision of each estimator by means of the overall mean and standard deviation of the absolute valued errors of the parameter estimates respectively. The proposed SPIM model improved both the accuracy and precision of the parameter estimates.

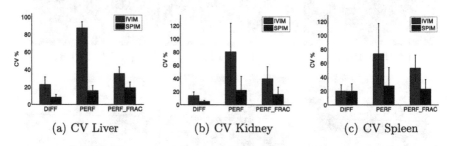

(a) CV Liver   (b) CV Kidney   (c) CV Spleen

Fig. 4. Coefficient of Variation (CV) of parameter estimates computed over ROIs manually annotated in liver, spleen and kidney regions of five subjects are compared. SPIM model results in reduction of CVs for all parameters.

We estimated the parameters from the in-vivo DWI data using both SPIM and IVIM approaches. To measure the precision of the parameter estimation, we calculated the Coefficient of Variation (CV) of parameter estimates over three region of interests (ROIs) manually annotated in liver, spleen and kidneys. We compared the results for SPIM and IVIM approaches in Fig. 4. CV decreased for all parameters using SPIM model, which indicates an increase in robustness.

We present the parametric maps obtained using IVIM and SPIM methods in Fig. 5. Improvements of parameter estimations can especially be observed in parametric images of perfusion and perfusion fraction.

3.3   In-vivo DWI Experiments on Crohn's Disease Patients

To demonstrate the clinical significance of improvements in parameter estimation, we analyzed DWI imaged from 24 subjects with Crohn's disease. We evaluated the performance of the estimated parameters to discriminate patients from

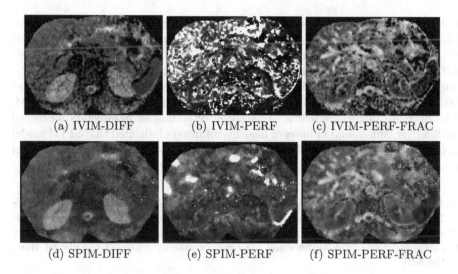

    (a) IVIM-DIFF   (b) IVIM-PERF   (c) IVIM-PERF-FRAC

    (d) SPIM-DIFF   (e) SPIM-PERF   (f) SPIM-PERF-FRAC

Fig. 5. The top and bottom rows show parameter maps estimated for a slice using IVIM and SPIM models respectively. Improvements of parameter estimations can especially be observed in parametric images of perfusion and perfusion fraction.

Table 1. Estimated parameters (mean ± std) of the IVIM and proposed SPIM method for two groups of Crohn's disease patients are reported in $\mu m^2/ms$. Statistical significance of the difference between non-enhancing (n1 = 11) and enhancing ileum groups (n2 = 13) was evaluated using two tailed two sample Student's t-test. Significant ones ($p < 0.01$) are in bold.

	IVIM			SPIM		
	Non-enhancing	Enhancing	p-value	Non-enhancing	Enhancing	p-value
Diffusion	1.99 ± 0.40	1.60 ± 0.47	0.0406	1.78 ± 0.42	1.19 ± 0.47	**0.0040**
Perfusion	33.40 ± 23.82	29.54 ± 13.58	0.6391	34.89 ± 16.75	28.58 ± 17.26	0.3748
Perf-frac	0.49 ± 0.21	0.21 ± 0.10	**0.0008**	0.62 ± 0.10	0.26 ± 0.13	**10^{-7}**

two groups with different stages of Crohn's disease, one with enhancing and the other with non-enhancing ileum regions in their bowel. The parameters estimated from two groups are compared in Table 1. SPIM method decreased the standard deviation of parameters estimated within each group and increased the discriminative power of parameter estimates. Perfusion fraction was the most effective to discriminate non-enhancing ileum regions from enhancing ilea.

4   Conclusions

Diffusion imaging has potential to provide clinically important quantitative imaging biomarkers for clinical applications including Crohn's disease. However, current techniques for estimating the parameters from DWI data do not provide reliable or specific enough parameter estimates. We have presented a new model that uses a more realistic probability distribution model of diffusion measured for each heterogeneous microenvironment in a voxel. Using this model together with the spatial homogeneity prior, we obtained the combined SPIM model for parametric DWI imaging. We showed that SPIM model improves the parameter estimation in both simulated and in-vivo experiments in comparison to IVIM. The decrease in the coefficient of variation of estimated parameters measured within liver, spleen and kidneys of healthy volunteers indicated that SPIM model is more robust compared to IVIM. The parameters estimated with SPIM model better discriminated enhancing and non-enhancing stages of Crohn's disease.

Acknowledgments. This work is supported by the National Institute of Diabetes & Digestive & Kidney Diseases of the NIH under award R01DK100404 and by the Translational Research Program at Boston Children's Hospital. The content is solely the responsibility of the authors and does not necessarily represent the official views of the NIH.

References

1. Kirk, G., Clements, W.: Crohn's disease and colorectal malignancy. Int. J. Clin. Pract. **53**, 314–315 (1999)
2. Chavhan, G.B., AlSabban, Z., Babyn, P.S.: Diffusion-weighted imaging in pediatric body MR imaging: principles, technique, and emerging applications. RadioGraphics **34**, E73–E88 (2014)
3. Stejskal, E., Tanner, J.: Spin diffusion measurements: spin-echo in the presence of a time dependent field gradient. J. Chem. Phys. **42**, 288–292 (1965)
4. Koh, D.M., Collins, D.J., Orton, M.R.: Intravoxel incoherent motion in body diffusion-weighted MRI: reality and challenges. AJR Am. J. Roentgenol. **196**, 1351–1361 (2011)
5. Bihan, D.L., Breton, E., Lallemand, D., Aubin, M.L., Vignaud, J., Laval-Jeantet, M.: Separation of diffusion and perfusion in intravoxel incoherent motion MR imaging. Radiology **168**, 497–505 (1988)
6. Thornton, M., Solomon, M.J.: Crohn's disease: in defense of a microvascular aetiology. Int. J. Colorectal Dis. **17**, 287–297 (2002)
7. Freiman, M., Perez-Rossello, J.M., Callahan, M.J., Bittman, M., et al.: Characterization of fast and slow diffusion from diffusion-weighted MRI of pediatric Crohn's disease. J. Magn. Reson. Imaging **37**, 156–163 (2013). http://dx.doi.org/10.1002/jmri.23781
8. Freiman, M., Perez-Rossello, J.M., Callahan, M.J., Voss, S.D., et al.: Reliable estimation of incoherent motion parametric maps from diffusion-weighted MRI using fusion bootstrap moves. Med. Image Anal. **17**, 325–336 (2013). http://dx.doi.org/10.1016/j.media.2012.12.001
9. Freiman, M., Afacan, O., Mulkern, R.V., Warfield, S.K.: Improved multi B-value diffusion-weighted MRI of the body by simultaneous model estimation and image reconstruction (SMEIR). In: Mori, K., Sakuma, I., Sato, Y., Barillot, C., Navab, N. (eds.) MICCAI 2013, Part III. LNCS, vol. 8151, pp. 1–8. Springer, Heidelberg (2013)

10. Dietrich, O., Raya, J.G., Reeder, S.B., Ingrisch, M., Reiser, M.F., Schoenberg, S.O.: Influence of multichannel combination, parallel imaging and other reconstruction techniques on MRI noise characteristics. Magn. Reson. Imaging **26**, 754–762 (2008)

11. O'Leary, D.P., Rust, B.W.: Variable projection for nonlinear least squares problems. Comput. Optim. Appl. **54**, 579–593 (2013)

12. Davidson, R., Flachaire, E.: The wild bootstrap, tamed at last. J. Econometrics **146**, 162–169 (2008)

13. Lempitsky, V., Rother, C., Roth, S., Blake, A.: Fusion moves for Markov random field optimization. IEEE Trans. Pattern Anal. Mach. Intell. **32**, 1392–1405 (2010)

14. Conturo, T.E., McKinstry, R.C., Akbudak, E., Robinson, B.H.: Encoding of anisotropic diffusion with tetrahedral gradients: a general mathematical diffusion formalism and experimental results. Magn. Reson. Med. **35**, 399–412 (1996)

15. Mulkern, R.V., Vajapeyam, S., Robertson, R.L., Caruso, P.A., Rivkin, M.J., Maier, S.E.: Biexponential apparent diffusion coefficient parametrization in adult vs newborn brain. Magn. Reson. Imaging **19**, 659–668 (2001)

Semi-automatic Crohn's Disease Severity Estimation on MR Imaging

Peter J. Schüffler[1(✉)], Dwarikanath Mahapatra[1], Robiel Naziroglu[2],
Zhang Li[2], Carl A.J. Puylaert[3], Rado Andriantsimiavona[4],
Franciscus M. Vos[2,3], Doug A. Pendsé[5], C. Yung Nio[3], Jaap Stoker[3],
Stuart A. Taylor[5,6], and Joachim M. Buhmann[1]

[1] Department of Computer Science, ETH Zurich, Universitätstrasse 6,
Zurich, Switzerland
peter.schueffler@inf.ethz.ch
[2] Quantitative Imaging Group, TU Delft, Lorentzweg 1, Delft, The Netherlands
[3] Department of Radiology, AMC, Meibergdreef 9,
Amsterdam, The Netherlands
[4] Biotronics3D Ltd, 205 Marsh Wall, London, UK
[5] Centre for Medical Imaging, UCL, 250 Euston Road, London, UK
[6] Department of Radiology, UCLH, 235 Euston Road, London, UK

Abstract. Crohn's disease (CD) is a chronic inflammatory bowel disease which can be visualized by magnetic resonance imaging (MRI). For CD grading, several non-invasive MRI based severity scores are known, most prominent the MaRIA and AIS. As these scores rely on manual MRI readings for individual bowel segments by trained radiologists, automated MRI assessment has been more and more focused in recent research. We show on a dataset of 27 CD patients that semi-automatically measured bowel wall thickness (ABWT) and dynamic contrast enhancement (DCE) completely outperform manual scorings: the segmental correlation to the Crohn's Disease Endoscopic Index of Severity (CDEIS) of ABWT and DCE is significantly higher ($r = .78$) than that of MaRIA ($r = .45$) or AIS ($r = .51$). Also on a per-patient basis, the models with ABWT and DCE show significantly higher correlation ($r = .69$) to global CDEIS than MaRIA ($r = .46$).

Keywords: Computer vision · Crohn's disease · Crohn's disease severity · MRI

1 Introduction

Crohn's disease (CD) belongs to the chronic inflammatory bowel diseases. The severity of acute CD is an important indicator for different therapeutic strategies and for the documentation of treatment response. One measure for CD severity is the Crohn's Disease Endoscopic Index of Severity (CDEIS) [1]: For that, the bowel is virtually partitioned into the five segments terminal ileum, right colon, transverse colon, left (and sigmoid) colon and rectum. Each segment is individually scored based on ulcerations and diseased surface identified in the segment. The patients' CDEIS is then the mean of the segmental scores plus additional scores for stenosis in the bowel.

© Springer International Publishing Switzerland 2014
H. Yoshida et al. (Eds.): ABDI 2014, LNCS 8676, pp. 128–138, 2014.
DOI: 10.1007/978-3-319-13692-9_12

Regular endoscopic examinations as they occur for CD patients come with several drawbacks. They are time consuming for the gastroenterologist and invasive for the patient with the risk of bowel perforation. Further, occurring stenosis can impede the continuation of the uncomfortable examination.

Magnetic resonance imaging (MRI) has therefore been identified as an alternative for CD severity assessment [2–5]. With MRI, the abdomen is non-invasively visualized in a 3D volume. The bowel wall and surface can be inspected regardless of potential stenosis. In 2009, Rimola et al. [2, 3] introduced the Magnetic Resonance Index of Activity (MaRIA) calculating a segmental CD severity score based on the following features scored in MRI: wall thickness (mm), relative contrast enhancement (RCE), presence of edema and ulcers. They showed a significant correlation of this score to the CDEIS (Spearman r = .80). In 2012, Steward et al. [4] presented an MRI score of the weighted sum of mural thickness and mural T2. Although this measure was developed to predict the histopathological Acute Inflammation Score (AIS, R squared = .52), it usually correlates to the CDEIS as well. Schüffler et al. [5] showed in 2013 that there might be a set of MRI models with even higher correlation to the CDEIS: Enhancement T1 and comb sign were able to improve the correlation of the two scores by 18 %.

However, all scores rely on the manual detailed inspection of MRI scans. This can be time consuming and quite subjective. E.g., the inter-observer variability of scored wall thickness in MRI has been shown to significantly change with the radiologists' experience: more experienced radiologists had a higher inter-observer agreement [6].

Vos et al. [7] and Tielbeek et al. [8] therefore had the vision of automatic MRI processing for CD severity assessment. They reviewed computerized techniques to be able to extract relevant MRI features such as wall thickness and contrast enhancement.

In this paper, we describe a novel computer-generated model for CD severity determination incorporating the semi-automatic features bowel wall thickness and dynamic contrast enhancement. On a dataset of 27 CD patients, we validate these features together with our best manual model derived by an exhaustive search and compare them to the MaRIA and AIS. We illustrate that the semi-automatic features alone are able to predict the CDEIS more accurately than comprehensively manually scored features. The high objectivity and reproducibility of the semi-automatic model is a further clear benefit compared to manual methods.

2 Methods

2.1 MRI Protocol

Twenty-seven CD patients underwent ileocolonoscopy with CDEIS determination and MRI examination at the Academic Medical Center (AMC) Amsterdam, The Netherlands, within one month. MRI was performed with a 3 Tesla scanner (Intera, Philips Healthcare), according to following protocol [9]: Patients fasted for four hours and drank 1,6 L of mannitol solution (2.5 %, Osmitrol, Baxter), one hour before the scan. Pre-contrast sequences comprising axial and coronal T2-weighted single-shot FSE sequences with and without fat saturation as well as coronal 3D T1-weighted spoiled gradient-echo sequence with fat saturation were acquired. Patients were then administered 20 mg of butylscopolamine bromide (Buscopan, Boehringer, Ingelheim) for bowel relaxation and 0.2 mL/kg bodyweight of gadobutrol (1.0 mmol/mL; Gadovist, Bayer Schering Pharma) as contrast agent. A dynamic contrast enhancement (DCE-)MRI was performed over 6 min. After a second dose of 20 mg of butylscopolamine, contrast-enhanced axial and coronal 3D T1-weighted spoiled gradient-echo sequences with fat saturation were acquired. All sequences except for the DCE-MRI were used for manual inspection at the 3DNETMEDICAL platform (www. biotronics3d.com). The DCE-MRI was used for automatic feature extraction (see Sect. 2.4).

2.2 Manual MRI Scoring

Four radiologists with 1–18 years of experience in abdominal MRI independently scored 12 CD related features on the five individual bowel segments of all 27 patients (terminal ileum, right colon, transverse colon, left (and sigmoid) colon and rectum). Binary features (absent/present) were abscess, comb sign, fistula and ulcers. Categorical features (normal, mild, moderate, marked) were T1 enhancement, length, mural T2 signal, pattern, perimural T2 signal. Numerical features were relative contrast enhancement (RCE) and wall thickness. A patient wide binary feature was the presence of enlarged lymph nodes.

Of the 27 * 5 = 135 bowel segments, 2 segments had been resected, 5 segments could not be judged by the radiologists due to bad bowel distention and 6 segments could not be assessed by colonoscopy due to stenosis. Therefore, the manual dataset comprises 122 segments * 4 observers = 488 samples with 12 features, each.

2.3 Automatic Bowel Wall Thickness Measurement (ABWT)

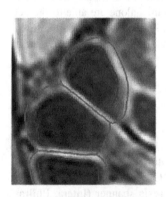

Fig. 1. Example of inner (blue) and outer (red) automatic bowel wall segmentation. The wall thickness is the mean distance between the inner and outer bowel wall (Colour figure online).

Bowel wall thickness has been found to correlate well to the CDEIS [2–4]. While normal wall thickness ranges from 2 to 3 mm, diseased wall can expand to over 15 mm due to inflammation or lesions. The semi-automatic measuring, as described in [10], starts from the manual indication of a center line in the lumen of a bowel segment (region of interest, ROI). The automatic steps are then [10]: (i) Starting from the center line, segment the inner bowel wall. (ii) Starting from the inner bowel wall, segment the outer bowel wall. (iii) Average the distance between inner and outer bowel wall over the ROI as Automatic Bowel Wall Thickness measure (ABWT). Although a ROI is needed to start the computational process, the indication of a (rough) centerline can be performed much faster than the accurate manual measuring of wall thickness throughout all three dimensions. Figure 1 illustrates the automatic inner and outer bowel wall segmentation of a typical example. Note that this is a three dimensional segmentation procedure.

2.4 Dynamic Contrast Enhancement (DCE)

DCE-MRI monitors the distribution and metabolism of the contrast agent in the bowel wall during 6 min after injection. The idea is to record a higher and faster contrast agent uptake in diseased regions than in normal regions. For this, 450 individual 3D scans are shot at a rate of 0.82 sec per scan (resolution $2.78 \times 2.78 \times 2.5$ mm at $227 \times 227 \times 14$ px). After DCE-MRI, contrast-enhanced coronal T1-weighted high resolution Isotropic Volume Examination (THRIVE) sequences were acquired at $1.02 \times 1.02 \times 2$ mm and $400 \times 400 \times 100$ px (see Fig. 2).

The DCE feature generation, as described in [11], starts from the manual indication of a diseased ROI. The automatic steps are then [11]: (i) Register the DCE-MRI to the post-contrast THRIVE sequences to remove breathing motion artifacts and to get pixel-wise image correspondence. A more detailed description of the 3D registration can be found in [11]. (ii) Extract the change of the signal intensity in the ROI over time as the time intensity curve (TIC). (iii) Fit a bi-exponential model $S(t)$ to the TIC:

$$S(t) = A_1 e^{-\lambda_1 t} - A_2 e^{-\lambda_2 t} \tag{1}$$

where A_1 is related to the steepness of the TIC and defines the final DCE feature.

An example of DCE-MRI and THRIVE is illustrated in Fig. 2. The top left image shows the THRIVE before contrast agent application and DCE-MRI. The top right THIRVE was shot after contrast agent application and DCE-MRI. The bottom row shows two DCE-MRI scans before and during contrast agent uptake. Note the different resolution of the two sequences. The DCE frames are registered to each other, but not yet to the THRIVE post contrast. The diseased ROI indicated by the red arrow has a slightly faster enhancement than normal regions.

Figure 3 plots two example TICs for a normal (green, lower curve) and a diseased ROI (red, upper curve). Each TIC is modeled by a bi-exponential model (black curves). The TIC is usually significantly steeper for diseased regions than for normal regions [11].

2.5 Model Development

To find the best linear regression model of manual MRI features, we followed an exhaustive search strategy [5]. All $2^{12} - 1 = 4095$ combinations of manual features were cross-validated on 27 CD patients. For cross-validation, the models were learned on the data of 18 randomly drawn patients and tested on the remaining nine patients. The Spearman rank correlation coefficient between the predicted segmental MRI scores of the test patients and the CDEIS was recorded. This procedure was repeated 50 times with different random patient subsets. The models were then ranked by their median cross-validated correlation to the CDEIS. The best model is subjected for further validation: ABWT and DCE were added to the model to measure the performance gain.

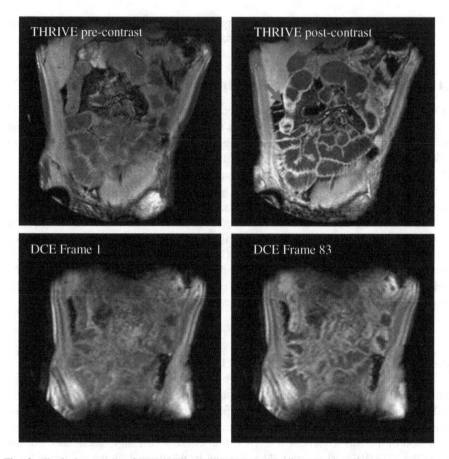

Fig. 2. Typical example of THRIVE and DCE-MRI. TOP LEFT: 2D slice of a pre-contrast THRIVE scan in our dataset. TOP RIGHT: Corresponding post-contrast THRIVE slice after DCE-MRI (during DCE-MRI, a contrast agent is applied to the patient). CD affected regions show a slightly enhanced signal, as indicated by the red arrow. BOTTOM: Two registered 2D slices of the DCE sequence of the same patient (time frames 1 and 83). 450 such frames are shot during six minutes. The spatial resolution of DCE-MRI is much smaller than of THRIVE.

Finally, ABWT and DCE were cross-validated as a single "automatic" model in the same procedure as described above.

Feature extraction was performed with MATLAB (2013b). Linear regression modeling and validation was performed with R Statistical language, version 3.0.0.

3   Results

3.1   ABWT Correlates to CDEIS

ABWT corresponds to the manual measured wall thickness, scored by four observers in our dataset. As shown in Fig. 4 (left), the correlation of wall thickness to the CDEIS is

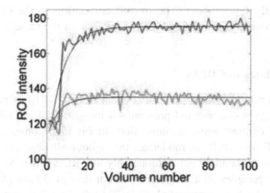

Fig. 3. TIC of a normal bowel segment (green, bottom) and a diseased segment (red, top). The mean MR signal intensity in a given ROI is measured in 100 consecutive DCE frames. At the beginning, the contrast agent is applied to the patient. Diseased regions typically show significantly enhanced drug uptake resulting in steeper curves. The black curves represent the fitted bi-exponential models S(t), whose coefficients A_1 serve as DCE feature (Colour figure online).

$r = .44 \pm .08$. Each observer is indicated by a specific color. Note the relative high number of segments with a normal CDEIS but thickened bowel wall and vice versa. The right plot displays ABWT versus CDEIS. Here, some samples with a high CDEIS could not be processed (e.g. due poor image quality). However, among the measured

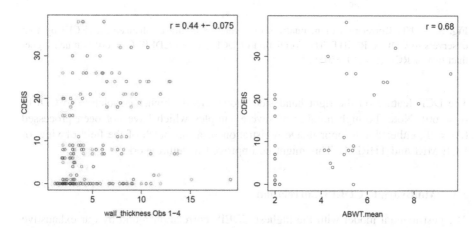

Fig. 4. LEFT: Correlation of manually scored wall thickness by four observers to CDEIS. Each observer is denoted by a color. RIGHT: The correlation of ABWT to CDEIS ($r = .68$) is much higher than that of wall_thickness ($r = .44 \pm .08$).

cases, there are only few outliers. The overall correlation to the CDEIS is r = .68 without standard deviation since the objective measure is the same for all observers.

3.2   DCE Correlates to CDEIS

DCE best corresponds to relative contrast enhancement (RCE), a ratio of the MRI signal in THRIVE post-contrast and pre-contrast images. DCE, in addition, accounts for the "speed" of contrast agent accumulation. In Fig. 5 becomes apparent that the correlation of RCE to CDEIS is moderate, throughout all observers r = .30 ± .05. Further, very severe cases might get a comparably low RCE value. Another problem is the difficulty of the complex RCE measuring: In our dataset, 39 samples have negative RCE and three samples have extremely high RCE (400–500). This nicely demonstrates the need of an automated method to facilitate relative contrast enhancement measuring.

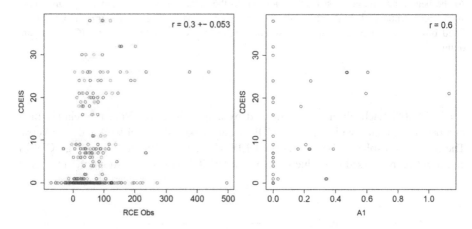

Fig. 5. LEFT: Correlation of manually scored relative contrast enhancement (RCE) by four observers to CDEIS. RIGHT: The correlation of DCE (A_1) to CDEIS (r = .60) is much higher than that of RCE (r = .30 ± .05).

The DCE feature on the right hand side shows clearly higher correlation to CDEIS (r = .60). Note the high number of severe samples which have not been processed (A_1 = 0), either due to poor image registration or a mismatch of the field of view of DCE-MRI and THRIVE. This might be improved in future work.

3.3   Multivariate CDEIS Correlation

The best manual model with the highest CDEIS correlation found by our exhaustive search consists of abscess, comb_sign, muralT2 and ulcers. Note that muralT2 and ulcers have already been identified by Rimola et al. [2, 3] and Steward et al. [4] as important severity predictors. The median Spearman correlation of this model to the CDEIS is r = .57 (Fig. 6, middle box "Best manual"). Indeed, the specific combination of these four features shows significantly higher correlation to CDEIS than the MaRIA ($r = .45$) or AIS ($r = .51$) (Fig. 6, second and third box). The addition of ABWT or DCE (A_1) to the manual model raises the correlation to the CDEIS significantly to $r = .67$ and $r = .69$, respectively (Fig. 6, fifth and sixth box). Interestingly, when ABWT and DCE are combined as a stand-alone MRI model, the correlation to CDEIS can even be increased to $r = .78$ (Fig. 6, right box); larger than their univariate CDEIS correlation.

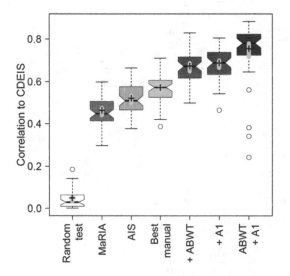

Fig. 6. Spearman correlation to CDEIS of different models. Each box is a 50-fold cross-validated model. Horizontal lines indicate median, cross and bar indicate mean and standard deviation of folds. Random test: The best manual model was cross-validated with randomly permuted CDEIS label. The information in the features is not random. MaRIA: The MaRIA on our dataset reaches a segmental correlation of $r = .45$. AIS: The MRI based AIS has a median correlation of $r = .51$. Our best manual model (middle, $r = .57$) can significantly be improved by the two automatic features ABWT ($r = .67$) or A1 ($r = 69$). However, the two automatic features alone, ABWT + A1, show a superior segmental CDEIS correlation ($r = .78$).

3.4   Global View

We tested our models with the semi-automatic features for global CDEIS prediction. A high segmental CDEIS correlation should propagate to a high correlation per patient. A patient's CDEIS is the mean of his or her segmental scores plus additional 3 points for non-ulcerated stenosis or ulcerated stenosis. Rimola et al. define the global MaRIA as the sum of the segmental scores [2, 3].

For testing, we followed a leave-one-patient-out cross-validation procedure: our manual model including ABWT and DCE and the model consisting solely of ABWT and DCE were trained on the data of 26 patients. The predicted segmental scores of the remaining patient were then averaged to the global MRI score. Figure 7(A) shows the cross-validated global MRI scores of all patients predicted by abscess, comb_sign, muralT2, ulcers, ABWT and DCE. Each patient is denoted by a number and each observer by a color. The overall correlation to global CDEIS is $r = .66$.

In Fig. 7(B), the cross-validation of the model consisting of ABWT and DCE is depicted. There is no inter-observer variance for these computer-generated features. The correlation to the CDEIS is $r = .69$, which is higher than combined with manual features.

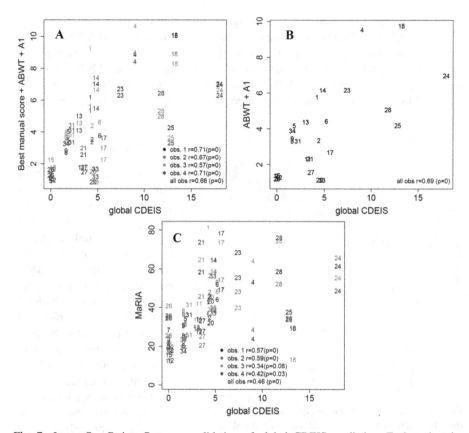

Fig. 7. Leave-One-Patient-Out cross-validation of global CDEIS prediction. Each patient is denoted by a number and each observer by a color. A: Our best manual features plus ABWT and DCE show a correlation of r = .66, B: Only ABWT and DCE (r = .69). The high segmental correlation of the automatic features to the CDEIS (Fig. 6) clearly propagates to the global view. The semi-automatic features are the same for all observers (no variance). C: MaRIA on the same patients (r = .46).

As comparison, we illustrate in Fig. 7(C) the relation of the global CDEIS and MaRIA. Again, there is an inter-observer variance due to manual features. The correlation of the two scores ranges from r = .34 (observer 3) to r = .59 (observer 2).

4 Discussion

We emphasize in this paper the potential benefit of computer-read MRI features for CD severity assessment. While most automatic MRI processing methods refer to organ detection and segmentation, the use of automatically extracted clinically relevant features such as bowel wall thickness or DCE for CD severity assessment is completely new.

Automated feature extraction might improve CD severity judgments in two ways. First, it may enable standardized and more objective scorings compared to manual scorings which clearly showed a considerably high inter-observer variance in our experiments. Second, the time of manual MRI processing by physicians can be reduced or replaced by cheaper computer processing time. Especially the measurements of RCE and wall thickness are time consuming – two features for which we propose computational analogs.

Surely, our semi-automatic features still need manual interaction (e.g. both rely on the indication of ROIs). The fully automatic processing of CD MRI will be a topic for future work (e.g. automatic CD detection). The calculation of DCE is especially complex and not successful on all bowel segments: DCE-MRI usually has a smaller field of view than THRIVE imaging. Interesting bowel segments could therefore be missed by DCE-MRI, which impedes the DCE feature extraction in these parts. Also, the registration process might fail in some cases due to the complex image structure.

While this might be improved in future work, we have already shown promising results in this paper with automatic features. The models with ABWT and DCE clearly demonstrate a superior correlation to the CDEIS than any manual model. On segment basis, the correlation is improved from 45 % (MaRIA) to 78 %. On per patient basis, there is an improvement from 46 % (MaRIA) to 69 %.

5   Conclusion

We demonstrated the clear improvement of MRI based CD severity assessment by the use of computer-aided feature extraction. Semi-automatically measured bowel wall thickness and dynamic contrast enhancement had a higher correlation to the CDEIS than any other manual model in our dataset, including the MaRIA and AIS. While the univariate correlation of the new features to the CDEIS was 60 and 68 %, the combination of these two in a linear regression model reaches a correlation of 78 %. We propose to validate these new features on further datasets in upcoming studies.

Semi-automatic MRI processing clearly reduces the inter-expert variability observed in conventional manual MRI features. Fully automatic MRI assessment, however, would require enhanced methods for disease detection, bowel segment detection and feature extraction. The research on automatic MRI processing will significantly facilitate and accelerate MRI inspection and improve our understanding of radiologic signs of Crohn's disease.

Acknowledgments. This study was partly funded from the European Community's Seventh Framework Program (FP7/2007-2013): the VIGOR ++ Project (grant agreement nr. 270379).

References

1. Mary, J.Y., Modigliani, R.: Development and validation of an endoscopic index of the severity for Crohn's disease: A Prospective multicentre study. Groupe d'Etudes Therapeutiques des Affections Inflammatoires du Tube Digestif (GETAID). Gut **30**, 983–989 (1989)

2. Rimola, J., Ordas, I., Rodriguez, S., Garcia-Bosch, O., Aceituno, M., Llach, J., Ayuso, C., Ricart, E., Panes, J.: Magnetic resonance imaging for evaluation of Crohn's disease: validation of parameters of severity and quantitative index of activity. Inflamm. Bowel Dis. **17**, 1759–1768 (2011)
3. Rimola, J., Rodriguez, S., Garcia-Bosch, O., Ordas, I., Ayala, E., Aceituno, M., Pellise, M., Ayuso, C., Ricart, E., Donoso, L., Panes, J.: Magnetic resonance for assessment of disease activity and severity in ileocolonic Crohn's disease. Gut **58**, 1113–1120 (2009)
4. Steward, M.J., Punwani, S., Proctor, I., Adjei-Gyamfi, Y., Chatterjee, F., Bloom, S., Novelli, M., Halligan, S., Rodriguez-Justo, M., Taylor, S.A.: Non-perforating small bowel Crohn's disease assessed by MRI enterography: derivation and histopathological validation of an MR-based activity index. Eur. J. Radiol. **81**, 2080–2088 (2012)
5. Schüffler, Peter J., Mahapatra, Dwarikanath, Tielbeek, Jeroen A.W., Vos, Franciscus M., Makanyanga, Jesica, Pendsé, Doug A., Nio, CYung, Stoker, Jaap, Taylor, Stuart A., Buhmann, Joachim M.: A model development pipeline for Crohn's disease severity assessment from magnetic resonance images. In: Yoshida, H., Warfield, S., Vannier, M.W. (eds.) Abdominal Imaging 2013. LNCS, vol. 8198, pp. 1–10. Springer, Heidelberg (2013)
6. Tielbeek, J.A.W., Makanyanga, J.C., Bipat, S., Pendse, D.A., Nio, C.Y., Vos, F.M., Taylor, S.A., Stoker, J.: Grading Crohn disease activity with MRI: interobserver variability of MRI features, MRI scoring of severity, and correlation with Crohn disease endoscopic index of severity. Am. J. Roentgenol. **201**, 1220–1228 (2013)
7. Vos, F.M., Tielbeek, J.A.W., Naziroglu, R.E., Li, Z., Schüffler, P.J., Mahapatra, D., Wiebel, A., Lavini, C., Buhmann, J.M., Hege, H., Stoker, J., van Vliet, L.J.: Computational modeling for assessment of IBD: To be or not to be? In: Engineering in Medicine and Biology Society (EMBC), 2012 Annual International Conference of the IEEE, pp. 3974–3977 (2012)
8. Tielbeek, J.A.W., Vos, F.M., Stoker, J.: A Computer-assisted model for detection of MRI signs of Crohn's disease activity: future or fiction? Abdom. Imaging **37**, 967–973 (2012)
9. Ziech, M.L., Lavini, C., Caan, M.W., Nio, C.Y., Stokkers, P.C., Bipat, S., Ponsioen, C.Y., Nederveen, A.J., Stoker, J.: Dynamic contrast-enhanced MRI in patients with luminal Crohn's disease. Eur. J. Radiol. **81**, 3019–3027 (2012)
10. Naziroglu, R.E., Van Vliet, L.J., Vos, F.M.: Measuring and quantifying bowel wall thickening for assessing Crohn's disease severity. In: VIGOR ++ Workshop 2014 (2014)
11. Li, Z., Tielbeek, J.A.W., Caan, M.W.A., Ziech, M.L.W., Nio, C.Y., Stoker, J., van Vliet, L. J., Vos, F.M.: Expiration phase template-based motion correction of free-breathing abdominal dynamic contrast enhanced MRI. in submission (2013)

Combining Multiple Expert Annotations Using Semi-supervised Learning and Graph Cuts for Crohn's Disease Segmentation

Dwarikanath Mahapatra[1]($\boxtimes$), Peter J. Schüffler[1], Jeroen A.W. Tielbeek[2],
Carl A.J. Puylaert[2], Jesica C. Makanyanga[3], Alex Menys[3],
Rado Andriantsimiavona[4], Jaap Stoker[2], Stuart A. Taylor[3,5],
Franciscus M. Vos[2,6], and Joachim M. Buhmann[1]

[1] Department of Computer Science, ETH Zurich, Zürich, Switzerland
dwarikanath.mahapatra@inf.ethz.ch
[2] Department of Radiology, Academic Medical Center, Amsterdam, The Netherlands
[3] Centre for Medical Imaging, University College London, London, UK
[4] Biotronics3D, London, UK
[5] University College London Hospitals, London, UK
[6] Quantitative Imaging Group, Delft University of Technology,
Delft, The Netherlands

Abstract. We propose a graph cut (GC) based approach for combining annotations from multiple experts and segmenting Crohns disease (CD) tissues in magnetic resonance (MR) images. Random forest (RF) based semi supervised learning (SSL) predicts missing expert labels while a novel self consistency (SC) score quantifies the reliability of each expert label and also serves as the penalty cost in a second order Markov random field (MRF) cost function. The final consensus label is obtained by GC optimization. Experimental results on synthetic images and real CD patient data show our final segmentation to be more accurate than those obtained by competing methods. It also highlights the effectiveness of SC score in quantifying expert reliability and accuracy of SSL in predicting missing labels.

Keywords: Graph cut · Crohn's disease · Magnetic resonance · Random forest · Markov random field

1 Introduction

Greater awareness about the seriousness of Crohn's disease (CD) within the medical imaging community has led to machine learning (ML) based analysis of magnetic resonance (MR) images to segment diseased regions [1–3] and predict disease severity [4]. Success of ML segmentation algorithms depend to a large extent on the accuracy of expert annotations. It is a common practice in medical image segmentation to obtain annotations from multiple experts, although combining them is not trivial since manual segmentations tend to be subjective,

© Springer International Publishing Switzerland 2014
H. Yoshida et al. (Eds.): ABDI 2014, LNCS 8676, pp. 139–147, 2014.
DOI: 10.1007/978-3-319-13692-9_13

prone to inter-observer and intra-observer variability, and of varying accuracy. We propose to combine multiple expert annotations using semi supervised learning (SSL) and graph cuts (GC). The consensus annotation is used to design a ML approach for segmenting regions with CD activity.

One of the first methods to combine multiple annotations was STAPLE [5] which employed Expectation-maximization (EM) to find sensitivity and specificity values that maximize the data likelihood. MAP-STAPLE [6], used MRFs to incorporate spatial constraints in STAPLE and generate a spatially consistent estimation of the ground truth. Commowick et al. in [7] adapt the STAPLE algorithm to determine spatially varying performance levels using sliding windows. The above algorithms fuse multiple labels independently from the original images, and hence do not assess their visual consistency. Raykar et al. [8] incorporate visual consistency of labels by simultaneous estimation of performance and learning. Chatelain et al. in [9] use Random forests (RF) to determine most coherent expert decisions based on the consistency of decisions with respect to the image features but do not account for missing annotations.

The following factors are important to obtain a consensus annotation of multiple experts: (1) predict missing annotations; (2) fuse annotations according to the reliability or consistency of experts; and (3) ensure spatial consistency of the final annotation. To achieve the above objectives we predict missing labels using SSL, quantify the reliability of each expert using a novel self-consistency (SC) score, and use Markov random fields (MRF) to impose spatial smoothness. SC is also used to define MRF penalty costs in the absence of true label information. The final (ground truth) annotation is obtained using GC optimization and is used to design a ML method to segment CD regions from unseen patient data.

Our work has two novelties: (1) a novel SC score to quantify the consistency and accuracy of each expert. It is calculated for each voxel from spatial feature distributions, and relates the annotations to image features. (2) missing expert labels are predicted using SSL that exploits the information from existing expert labels. Previous methods employed an iterative EM approach for this purpose while SSL predicts missing labels in one step. Graph cuts are used to determine the final labels because: (a) no iterative approach is employed as in EM based approaches of [6,7]; and (b) globally optimum labels can be obtained thus reducing chances of getting stuck in local minima. We describe our method in Sect. 2, present our results in Sect. 3 and conclude with Sect. 4.

2   Method

2.1   Predicting Missing Labels

Let us consider a multi-supervised learning scenario with a training set $S = \{(x_n, y_n^1, \cdots, y_n^r)\}_{r=1}^R$ of samples x_n, and the corresponding labels y_n^r provided by R experts. Missing labels are commonly encountered when multiple experts annotate data. In previous approaches [6,7] missing labels were predicted by combining Maximum A Posteriori (MAP) with iterative EM optimization to maximize the joint likelihood. We use semi-supervised RF classifiers (RF-SSL) to predict the missing labels by using knowledge from the given labels and image features. Unlike previous methods [10], a 'single shot' RF method for SSL without the need for iterative retraining was introduced in [11]. We use this SSL classifier as it is shown to outperform other approaches.

For labeled samples the information gain over data splits at each node of the RF is maximised and encourages separation of the labeled data [11,12]. However for SSL the objective function encourages separation of the labeled training data and simultaneously separates different high density regions. It is achieved via the following mixed information gain:

$$I_j = I_j^U + \alpha I_j^S \tag{1}$$

where $I_j^S = H(S_j) - \sum_{i \in \{L,R\}} \frac{|S_j^i|}{|S_j|} H(S_j^i)$ is the information gain from the labeled data; H is the entropy of training points, and S_j^L and S_j^R the subsets going to the left and right children of node j. I_j^U depends on both labeled and unlabeled data, and is defined using differential entropies over continuous parameters as

$$I_j^U = \log|\Lambda(S_j)| - \sum_{i \in \{L,R\}} \frac{|S_j^i|}{|S_j|} \log|\Lambda(S_j)| \tag{2}$$

Λ is the covariance matrix of the assumed multivariate distributions at each node. For further details we refer the reader to [11]. Thus the above cost function is able to combine the information gain from labeled and unlabeled data without the need for an iterative procedure.

To reduce computation time we select a region of interest (ROI) by taking the union of all expert annotations and determining its bounding box rectangle. The size of the rectangle is expanded by ± 20 pixels along rows and columns to give the final ROI. For each ROI pixel we calculate the mean and variance of intensity and 2D curvature values from a 15×15 neighborhood to give 4 features. Additionally, we extract spatial context features using the sampling template shown in Fig. 1(a). The circle center is the current voxel and at each point corresponding to a red 'X' we calculate the mean intensity, and curvature values from a 3×3 window. The 'X's are located at distances of 3, 6, 9, 12 pixels from the center, and the angle between consecutive rays is $45°$. 64 context features are obtained from the 32 points and the final vector has $(64 + 4 =)68$ values.

Each voxel has $r(\leq R)$ known labels and the unknown $R - r$ labels are predicted by SSL. The feature vectors of all samples (labeled and unlabeled) are inputted to the RF-SSL classifier which returns the missing labels. Note that although the same sample (hence feature vector) has multiple labels, RF-SSL treats it as another sample with similar feature values as other samples. The missing labels are predicted based on the split configuration (of decision trees in RFs) that leads to maximal global information gain. Hence the prediction of missing labels is not directly influenced by the other labels of the same sample but takes into account global label information [11].

2.2 Self Consistency of Experts

Self consistency of expert annotations is important to determine the reliability of each annotator. Region with similar labels are expected to have a consistent distribution of features. Figure 1(b) shows an example annotation in which the annotated diseased boundary is shown in red. For any given point i (indicated by the arrow) of the annotated region (labeled diseased or normal) we calculate the distribution of intensity values (normalized to be in $[0, 1]$) over a 15×15 neighborhood (yellow square). Then we compare the corresponding distributions of all similarly labeled points (diseased or normal) within a 35×35 neighborhood (points within the larger green square). The difference between two feature distributions is given by the χ^2 distance,

$$S(p,q) = \frac{1}{2} \sum_{k=1}^{K} \frac{[h_p(k) - h_q(k)]^2}{h_p(k) + h_q(k)}, \tag{3}$$

where p, q are two points under consideration, h_p, h_q are the respective normalized histograms and k denotes the kth bin of the K-bin normalized histograms. $S \in [0, 1]$ is used as it gives a normalized distance measure with 0 indicating identical distributions. The self-consistency score for a point i (SC_i) is derived from the average S with respect to all similarly labeled points within the larger green square. It is defined as

$$SC_i = 1 - \frac{1}{N_l} \sum_{n_l=1}^{N_l} S(i, n_l) \tag{4}$$

$S(i, n_l)$ denotes the χ^2 distance between i and all similarly labeled points n_l within the green square. N_l is the set of points within the 35×35 window with the same label as i.

An expert with high consistency will assign similar labels to regions having similar features. Thus by comparing the intensity distribution of a point i with other points of the same label, we get an estimate of its consistency. Boundary pixels of high consistency annotations have similar histograms, giving high SC. Non-boundary foreground pixels in the 35×35 window that are far from the boundary have different distributions and are fewer compared to foreground pixels on or near the boundary. Thus for boundary points neighboring pixels within the 35×35 window have similar features and give a reliable SC score. A point with high consistency has low value of S. Since we assign higher score for higher segmentation consistency the formulation as given in Eq. 4 is used.

We average $S(i, n_l)$ over points within a 35×35 neighborhood only, as feature consistency is higher in the local neighborhood. If we consider all the labeled points in the annotation, S would be biased towards the predominant label. It also reduces the computation time. Note that here we define the consistency score of each voxel i which is required for obtaining the ground truth segmentation. An overall consistency score for each annotation can be obtained by averaging the SC_i over all constituent pixels.

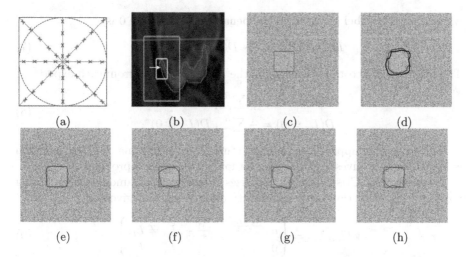

Fig. 1. (a) template for context feature extraction; (b) calculation of self consistency score; (c) synthetic image with ground truth segmentation in red; (d) synthetic image with simulated expert annotations; final segmentation obtained by (e) GC_{ME} (DM= 0.94); (f) STAPLE(DM= 0.90); (g) MAP-STAPLE(DM= 0.88); (h) Local MAP STAPLE(DM= 0.87).

2.3 Obtaining the Final Labels

A second order MRF cost function is given by,

$$E(L) = \sum_{s \in P} D(L_s) + \lambda \sum_{(s,t) \in N_s} V(L_s, L_t), \tag{5}$$

where P denotes the set of pixels; N_s is the 8 neighbors of pixel s (or sample x); L_s is the label of s; t is the neighbor of s, and L is the set of labels for all s. $\lambda = 0.02$ determines the relative contribution of penalty cost (D) and smoothness cost (V). We have only 2 labels ($L_s = 1/0$ for object/background), although our method can also be applied to the multi-label scenario. The final labels are obtained by graph cut optimization [13].

The penalty cost for MRFs is normally calculated with respect to a reference model of each class (usually distribution of intensity values). The implicit assumption is that the annotator's labels are correct. However, we aim to determine the actual labels of each pixel and hence do not have access to true class distributions. To overcome this problem we use the consistency scores of experts to determine the penalty costs for a voxel. Each voxel has R labels (after predicting the missing labels). Say for voxel x the label y^r (of the rth expert) is 1, and the corresponding SC score is SC_x^r (Eq. 4). Since SC is higher for better agreement with labels, the corresponding penalty cost for $L_x = 1$ is

$$D(L_x = 1)^r = 1 - SC_x^r, \tag{6}$$

where L_x is the label of voxel x. The penalty cost for label 0 is

$$D(L_x = 0)^r = 1 - D(L_x = 1) = SC_x^r. \tag{7}$$

The final penalty costs for each L_x is the average of costs from each expert,

$$D(L_x = 1) = \frac{1}{R}\sum_{r=1}^{R} D(L_x = 1)^r,$$
$$D(L_x = 0) = \frac{1}{R}\sum_{r=1}^{R} D(L_x = 0)^r. \tag{8}$$

Since iterative approaches may get stuck in local minima, GC optimization is appealing as it gives a global minima for binary labeled problems.

Smoothness Cost (V): V penalizes discontinuities amongst neighboring voxels and is a function of their intensity differences. V is given by

$$V(L_s, L_t) = \begin{cases} e^{-\frac{(I_s - I_t)^2}{2\sigma^2}} \cdot \frac{1}{\|s-t\|}, & L_s \neq L_t, \\ 0 & L_s = L_t. \end{cases} \tag{9}$$

I is the intensity and σ is the intensity variance over N_s (i.e., the 8 neighbors).

3   Experiments and Results

We refer to our method as GC_{ME} (Graph Cut with Multiple Experts) and test it's performance on synthetic images and medical images from patients afflicted with CD. Our results are compared with the fused segmentations obtained using STAPLE [5], MAP-STAPLE [6], and Local MAP-STAPLE [7]. After obtaining the consensus segmentation of all images we adopt a 5 fold cross validation segmentation approach. A fully supervised RF classifier (RF-FSL) is derived from the training set (comprising the final annotations of different methods). RF-FSL calculates probability maps for each test voxel, whose negative log-likelihood is the penalty cost. The segmentation cost function is,

$$E(L) = \sum_{s \in P} -\log\left(Pr(L_s) + \epsilon\right) + \lambda \sum_{(s,t) \in N_s} e^{-\frac{(I_s - I_t)^2}{2\sigma^2}} \cdot \frac{1}{\|s - t\|}, \tag{10}$$

where $Pr(L_s)$ is the probability map of test image obtained by RF-FSL. If the training labels were obtained using GC_{ME} then the RF-FSL segmentation of the test image is compared with the ground truth segmentation from GC_{ME}. Similar tests are performed for all other label fusion methods. Each dataset was part of the test set exactly once. The method giving the most accurate consensus segmentation would result in a RF-FSL that gives the most accurate probability maps, and the corresponding segmentation would have higher agreement with the ground truth consensus segmentations. Thus the relative merit of different label fusion techniques can be judged by the accuracy of consensus segmentations obtained through them. λ was varied from $[0, 1]$ in steps of 0.001 while running our algorithm on 10 patient volumes. The maximum DM was obtained for $\lambda = 0.02$, and was the value used for all our experiments. We have 50 trees in the RF, and the maximal tree depth was fixed at 20.

3.1   Synthetic Image Dataset

Figure 1(c) shows an example synthetic image where the 'diseased' region is within the red square. Pixel intensities are normalized to $[0, 1]$. Intensities within the square have a normal distribution with $\mu \in [0.6 - 0.8]$ and different σ. Background pixels have a lower intensity distribution ($\mu \in [0.1-0.3]$ and different σ). A set of 20 adjacent boundary points are chosen and randomly displaced between $\pm 10 - 20$ pixels to obtain 3 sets of simulated segmentations (colored contours in Fig. 1(d)). The segmentations are fused using different methods to get the final segmentation, which is compared with the reference segmentation (in Fig. 1(c)) using Dice Metric (DM) and Hausdorff Distance (HD).

For GC_{ME} some of the expert annotations are intentionally removed to simulate real world scenarios. Variations of our method are (1) ME_{All} where all annotation information is available; (2) ME_{wSSL}, i.e., GC_{ME} without SSL for predicting missing labels. In this case the penalty costs are determined from SC_i's of available annotations. (3) ME_{wSC}, i.e., GC_{ME} without our SC score. The penalty cost is the $\chi 2$ distance between the reference distribution in the ground truth annotation of Fig. 1(c) and the distribution from the 'expert's' annotation. Note that this condition can be tested only for synthetic images where we know the actual labels of each pixel.

Table 1 summarizes the performance of different methods. ME_{All} gives the highest DM and lowest HD values, followed by GC_{ME}, [5–7], ME_{wSSL} and ME_{wSC}. Since ME_{All} had access to all annotations, it obviously performed best. However GC_{ME}'s performance is very close and a Student t–test with ME_{All} gives $p < 0.042$ indicating very small difference in the two results. Importantly GC_{ME} performs much better than all other methods ($p < 0.01$).

The results show: (1) SSL effectively predicts missing annotation information since GC_{ME} has very close performance to ME_{All} and ME_{wSSL} shows a significant drop in performance from GC_{ME} ($p < 0.01$). (2) Our proposed self consistency score accurately quantifies the consistency level of each expert as is evident from the performance of GC_{ME} and ME_{wSC} ($p < 0.001$). Figure 1(e)–(h) shows the final segmentations obtained using four different methods. The best results are obtained by GC_{ME}, followed by [5–7].

3.2   Real Patient Dataset

3D T1-weighted spoiled gradient echo sequence (SPGE) images were acquired from 45 CD patients (excluding the 10 used to calculate λ) in supine position using a 3-T MR imaging unit (Intera, Philips Healthcare). The spatial resolution of the images was $1.02 \times 1.02 \times 2$ mm, and the acquired volume dimension was $400 \times 400 \times 100$ voxels. 2 experts annotated each slice showing CD activity. All aforementioned label fusion techniques were used to generate consensus segmentations for all patients. A 5-fold cross validation strategy was used for RF-FSL training and subsequent segmentation. The same set of features as described in Sect. 2.1 were used.

Table 1. Quantitative measures for segmentation accuracy on synthetic. DM- Dice Metric in %; HD is Hausdorff distance mm and p is the result of Student $t-$tests with respect to GC_{ME}.

	Synthetic images							Medical images				
	ME All	GC ME	[7]	[6]	[5]	ME $wSSL$	ME wSC	GC ME	[7]	[6]	[5]	ME $wSSL$
DM	92.3	91.2	88.8	87.1	85.3	84.0	83.7	89.5	87.7	85.1	83.8	82.3
HD	6.1	7.4	9.0	10.1	11.9	13.5	13.9	8.2	9.8	12.0	13.9	14.7
p	.042	–	<.01	<.01	<.01	<.01	<.001	–	<.01	<.01	<.01	<.01

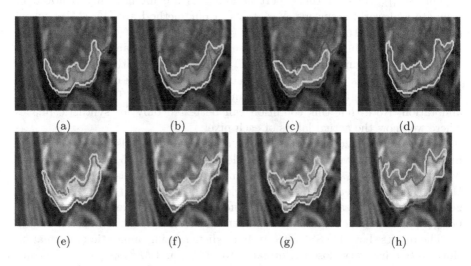

(a)   (b)   (c)   (d)

(e)   (f)   (g)   (h)

Fig. 2. First Row: The predicted ground truth for UCL Patient 23 by different methods: (a) GC_{ME}; (b) [7]; (c) [6]; and (d) [5]. Red and blue contours are expert annotations and yellow is the final annotation obtained by the respective methods **Second Row:** Segmentation results on patient 23 for: (e) GC_{ME}; (f) [7]; (g) [6]; and (h) [5]. Red contour is the ground truth segmentation while yellow contours show the final segmentation obtained by training on annotations obtained by the respective methods.

Table 1 summarizes the performance of different label fusion methods. The relative performance of different methods is similar to those observed for synthetic images. Note that we do not show the results for ME_{All} since all cases do not have annotations from all experts. There is also no way to know the actual labels and hence ME_{wSC} has no relevance for real medical images. Once again the importance of SSL and SC is highlighted. By incorporating these stages we achieve significant improvement in segmentation accuracy, as compared to other methods. Figure 2 the intermediate consensus segmentation (first row) followed by the final segmentations of the respective methods in the second row. As in the case of synthetic images, GC_{ME} gives the best results followed by [5–7].

4 Conclusion

We have proposed a novel framework using SSL, self consistency, and GC to combine labels of multiple experts for obtaining a consensus annotation. Its performance is demonstrated by segmenting CD regions from MR images. RF based SSL classifiers predict labels of missing annotations, and avoid the iterative EM approach of other methods. Self consistency scores quantify the reliability of each expert's labels and serve as penalty costs for a second order MRF cost function. Spatial smoothness constraints are a function of intensity difference of neighboring pixels. Experiments on synthetic and real patient datasets show the importance of our SC measure, and the effectiveness of RF-SSL in predicting missing labels. Our proposed method achieves better segmentation accuracy than competing approaches for combining multiple annotations.

References

1. Vos, F.M., et. al.: Computational modeling for assessment of IBD: to be or not to be? In: Proceedings of IEEE EMBC, pp. 3974–3977 (2012)
2. Mahapatra, D., Schüffler, P., Tielbeek, J., Makanyanga, J., et al.: Automatic detection and segmentation of Crohn's disease tissues from abdominal MRI. IEEE Trans. Med. Imaging **32**, 1232–1248 (2013)
3. Mahapatra, D., Schüffler, P., Tielbeek, J., Vos, F., Buhmann, J.: Semi-supervised and active learning for automatic segmentation of Crohn's disease. In: Proceedings of MICCAI, Part 2, pp. 214–221 (2013)
4. Schüffler, P., Mahapatra, D., Tielbeek, J., Vos, F., et al.: A model development pipeline for crohns disease severity assessment from magnetic resonance images. In: Proceedings of MICCAI-ABD, pp. 1–10 (2013)
5. Warfield, S., Zhou, K., Wells, W.: Simultaneous truth and performance level estimation (STAPLE): an algorithm for the validation of image segmentation. IEEE Trans. Med. Imaging **23**, 903–921 (2004)
6. Commowick, O., Warfield, S.: Incorporating priors on expert performance parameters for segmentation validation and label fusion: a maximum a posteriori STAPLE. In: Proceedings of MICCAI Part III, pp. 25–32 (2010)
7. Commowick, O., Akhondi-Asl, A., Warfield, S.: Estimating a reference standard segmentation with spatially varying performance parameters: local MAP STAPLE. IEEE Trans. Med. Imaging **31**, 1593–1606 (2012)
8. Raykar, V., Yu, S., Zhao, L., Valadez, G., et al.: Learning from crowds. J. Mach. Learn. Res. **11**, 1297–1322 (2010)
9. Chatelain, P., Pauly, O., Peter, L., Ahmadi, A., et al.: Learning from multiple experts with random forests: application to the segmentation of the midbrain in 3D ultrasound. In: Proceedings of MICCAI Part II, pp. 230–237 (2013)
10. Budvytis, I., Badrinarayanan, V., Cipolla, R.: Semi-supervised video segmentation using tree structured graphical models. In: IEEE CVPR, pp. 2257–2264 (2011)
11. Criminisi, A., Shotton, J.: Decision Forests for Computer Vision and Medical Image Analysis. Springer, London (2013)
12. Breiman, L.: Random forests. Mach. Learn. **45**, 5–32 (2001)
13. Boykov, Y., Veksler, O.: Fast approximate energy minimization via graph cuts. IEEE Trans. Pattern Anal. Mach. Intell. **23**, 1222–1239 (2001)

Gastrointestinal Tract - Colonoscopy, Colonography

Automatic Assessment of Image Informativeness in Colonoscopy

Nima Tajbakhsh[1]([✉]), Changching Chi[1], Haripriya Sharma[1], Qing Wu[2], Suryakanth R. Gurudu[3], and Jianming Liang[1]

[1] Department of Biomedical Informatics,
Arizona State University, Phoenix, AZ, USA
{Nima.Tajbakhsh,Changching.Chi,Haripriya.Sharma,Jianming.Liang}@asu.edu
[2] Department of Biostatistics, Mayo Clinic, Scottsdale, AZ, USA
Qing.Wu@mayo.edu
[3] Division of Gastroenterology and Hepatology, Mayo Clinic, Scottsdale, AZ, USA
Gurudu.Suryakanth@mayo.edu

Abstract. Optical colonoscopy is the preferred method for colon cancer screening and prevention. The goal of colonoscopy is to find and remove colonic polyps, precursors to colon cancer. However, colonoscopy is not a perfect procedure. Recent clinical studies report a significant polyp miss due to insufficient quality of colonoscopy. To complicate the problem, the existing guidelines for a "good" colonoscopy, such as maintaining a minimum withdrawal time of 6 min, are not adequate to guarantee the quality of colonoscopy. In response to this problem, this paper presents a method that can objectively measure the quality of an examination by assessing the informativeness of the corresponding colonoscopy images. By assigning a normalized quality score to each colonoscopy frame, our method can detect the onset of a hasty examination and encourage a more diligent procedure. The computed scores can also be averaged and reported as the overall quality of colonoscopy for quality monitoring purposes. Our experiments reveal that the suggested method achieves higher sensitivity and specificity to non-informative frames than the existing image quality assessment methods for colonoscopy videos.

Keywords: Optical colonoscopy · Image information assessment · Discrete cosine transform · Quality monitoring

1 Introduction

Optical colonoscopy is the preferred method for colon cancer screening and prevention, during which a tiny camera is inserted and guided through the colon. The goal of a colonoscopy is to detect and removal colorectal polyps, which are precursors to colorectal cancer. Colonoscopy is an effective screening method and has led to a significant decline of 30 % in the incidence of colorectal cancer [1]. However, colonoscopy is an operator dependent procedure whose efficacy largely depends on human factors such as attentiveness, diligence, and navigational skills. A Canadian study [2] reports a 6 % cancer miss-rate after a negative

© Springer International Publishing Switzerland 2014
H. Yoshida et al. (Eds.): ABDI 2014, LNCS 8676, pp. 151–158, 2014.
DOI: 10.1007/978-3-319-13692-9_14

colonoscopy and attributes this to the polyps that are missed due to insufficient quality of procedures. Other clinical trials have also reported significant levels of polyp miss-rates [3–5].

In response to the increasing concerns for missed polyps and cancers, American Society for Gastrointestinal Endoscopy (ASGE) established a number of guidelines for a quality colonoscopy in 2002. Among the suggested guidelines is maintaining minimum withdrawal time of 6 min, which is designed to discourage colonoscopists from a hasty colon examination. However, such a constraint on raw withdrawal time may not guarantee a quality and thorough inspection. This is because a colonoscopist may spend a large amount of time in one segment of the colon (for removing a polyp or getting a biopsy) but performs a quick examination in the other parts. Therefore, more effective ways are needed to monitor the quality of colonoscopy and encourage diligence during procedures.

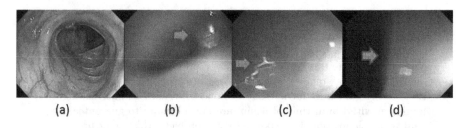

(a)   (b)   (c)   (d)

Fig. 1. Comparison between informative and non-informative frames. (a) An informative frame where the information content is well-spread all over the image. (b–d) Examples of non-informative frames: (b) an out-of-focus image with bubbles inside, (c) an image captured during wall contact with light reflection artifacts, (d) a motion blurred image captured close to wall contact. Two distinguishing characteristics of non-informative frames are blurry edges and appearance of salient features in only a few local regions of the images (e.g., bubbles in (b) and reflection artifacts in (c)).

We propose a system that can monitor the quality of colonoscopy and warn colonoscopists against hasty or poor colon examinations. We base our method on the observation that a poor colon examination shot consists of a large number of non-informative frames including blurry, out-of-focus images, or those captured during wall contact (see Fig. 1). Our method assigns each colonoscopy image a quality or informativeness score. By monitoring the informativeness scores during a procedure, we can detect the onset of a hasty or low quality colon examination upon identifying a number of consecutive non-informative images. In addition to the warning mechanism, the suggested method can report a segmental quality score during a procedure as the average of informativeness scores recorded in a segment of the colon. The overall quality score of a procedure can be computed as the average of the segmental scores, which can be used along with overall withdrawal time for quality monitoring purposes.

We trained and evaluated the suggested system using our collection of 5500 colonoscopy images. Quantitative evaluations demonstrate that our method provides a significantly higher area under the ROC curve, yielding higher sensitivity and specificity to non-informative frames than the existing image quality assessment methods for colonoscopy videos. Qualitative comparisons also show that quality scores computed by our system are more inline with that of human perception.

The rest of this paper is organized as follows: Sect. 2 reviews the existing works for image quality evaluation in colonoscopy. We describe the suggested method in Sect. 3, and present the experimental results in Sect. 4. Section 5 explains the related research aimed at reducing polyp miss-rate, discusses their limitations, and underlines the importance of image informativeness assessment as an effective tool for improving the quality of colonoscopy. Finally, this paper is concluded in Sect. 6.

2   Related Works

There are several methods for automatic image quality assessment in colonoscopy. Filip et al. [6] proposed a simple method based on image variance and contrast to detect blurry and out-of-focus images. Oh et al. [7] suggested a more sophisticated method based on gray level co-occurrence matrix (GLCM) in the Fourier domain. The main idea was to identify frequency patterns associated with non-informative images. Arnold et al. [8] computed the l^2-norm of 2D discrete wavelet transform (DWT) coupled with a Bayesian classification approach for image quality classification. Park et al. [9] trained a hidden Markov model using entropy-related features. Our experiments, however, reveal that these methods fail to achieve high sensitivity and specificity for our diverse set of informative and non-informative images. This motivates our research to develop a more effective image quality assessment for colonoscopy.

3   Proposed Method

We base our methodology for detecting non-informative frames on 2 key observations (see Fig. 1): (1) non-informative frames most often show an unrecognizable scene with few details and blurry edges and thus their information can be locally compressed in a few Discrete Cosine Transform (DCT) coefficients; however, informative images include much more details and their information content cannot be summarized by a small subset of DCT coefficients; (2) information content is spread all over the image in the case of informative frames, whereas in non-informative frames, depending on image artifacts and degradation factors, details may appear in only a few regions. We use the former observation to design our global features and the latter to design our local image features.

Our method begins with dividing an input image to non-overlapping image patches. We then apply 2D DCT transform to each patch and reconstruct the patch using the dominant DCT coefficients. The reconstructed patches are then put together to form the reconstructed image. We create a difference map by taking the absolute difference between the original input image and the reconstructed image. The difference maps are computed in multiple scales, their histograms are constructed, and then concatenated to produce a global feature vector. We also compute a local feature vector to measure how information is spread all over the input image. To do so, we divide each difference map into a 3×3 grid and then in each cell, we compute the energy as the sum of squared intensities. The local feature vector is formed by concatenating all the local energy values computed in multiple scales. We experimentally found out that feature fusion is the best way to combine local and global information, outperforming other alternatives such as score-level and decision-level fusion. Once fused feature vectors are formed, we train a classifier to assign a probabilistic score to each input image with 0 and 1 indicating images with minimal and maximal information content, respectively. We refer to this score as "quality score" or "informativeness score" throughout the paper. We use random forest for classification. Random forest has been successfully applied to a variety of computer vision and medical image analysis applications, and has been shown to outperform other widely-used classifiers such as AdaBoost and support vector machines [10]. The two main ingredients of random forest are bagging of a large number of fully grown decision trees and random feature selection at each node while training the trees, which together achieve high generalization error

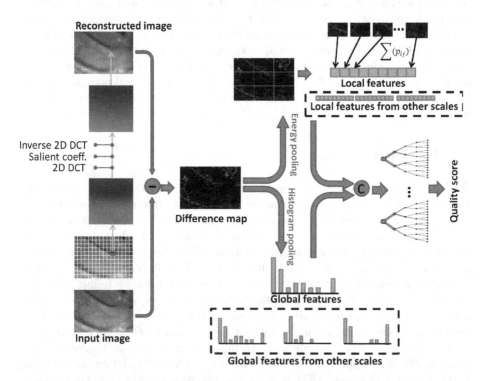

Fig. 2. Overview of the suggested method for image informativeness assessment. Our method is based on global and local image features that are extracted by histogram pooling over the entire image reconstruction error and region-based energy pooling, i.e. l^2-norm of reconstruction error in each of the 9 sub-regions.

and high quality probabilistic outputs. Figure 2 illustrates how the suggested method works. We should note that our method is fundamentally different from JPEG image compression. Unlike JPEG, our method is not meant to compress images, rather, it is designed to generate global and local feature vectors from the image reconstruction error.

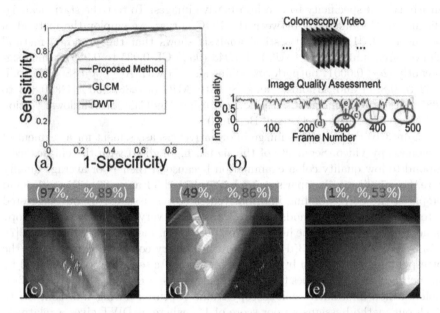

Fig. 3. (a) Comparison between the proposed method, DWT [8], and GLCM [7]. Our method excels in all operating points with a large margin. (b) Image informativeness assessment for a short colonoscopy video. The higher the score, the more informative the frame. Segments of the signal with average low quality scores correspond to hasty or low quality colon examination, in which case our method warns colonoscopists, encouraging a more diligent examination. (c–e) Three colonoscopy frames and their corresponding quality scores (our method in blue, GLCM in green and DWT in red). A seen, the scores assigned by our method are in more agreement with human perception (Color figure online).

4   Results

To evaluate our proposed system, we used 6 entire-length colonoscopy videos each captured from a different patient. We manually labeled the frames and assigned informative frames to the positive and non-informative frames to the negative class. The manual labeling was then reviewed and refined by a gastroenterologist. We collected a balanced dataset of 5500 colonoscopy frames, and used 3000 frames for training, 1000 frames for validation, and 1500 frames for testing. The validation set was used to tune the parameters of the method. We trained a random forest classifier consisting of 100 fully grown decision trees. Randomness was induced by randomly selecting a subset of features at the tree nodes.

We use receiver operating characteristic (ROC) curves to compare the performance of the suggested method with that of Oh et al.'s [7] and Arnold et al.'s [8]. Figure 3(a) shows the resulting ROC curves. As seen, our system outperforms the other two methods in all the operating points, achieving higher sensitivity and specificity to non-informative images. To test the statistical significance of the difference between the ROC curves, we employ the method of DeLong et al. [11]. Our statistical analysis shows that the proposed method achieves area under curve (AUC) of 0.948 (95 % CI, 0.935 to 0.959), which significantly ($p < 0.0001$) outperforms Oh et al.'s [7] with AUC of 0.880 (95 % CI, 0.862 to 0.897) and Arnold et al.'s [8] with AUC of 0.867 (95 % CI, 0.848 to 0.885). Statistical analyses are performed using MedCalc for Windows, version 13.3 (MedCalc Software, Ostend, Belgium).

Figure 3(b) demonstrates image informativeness assessment for a segment of a colonoscopy video. Segments of the signal, highlighted with the ellipses, correspond to low quality colon examination because of their poor average quality score. For qualitative comparison, we have selected 3 frames from this video and compared the corresponding informativeness scores assigned by our suggested system and the other methods. Figure 3(c) shows a very informative colonoscopy frame, which is assigned the high score of 97 % by our method, 62 % by GLCM [7], 89 % by DWT [8]. Figure 3(d) shows a rather blurry colonoscopy frame and the corresponding scores given by the three methods. As seen, the score assigned by our method (49 %) describes the image quality more accurately. Finally, Fig. 3(e) depicts a non-informative colonoscopy frame captured during wall contact, to which our method assigns a poor score of 1 % where as DWT gives a relatively high score of 53 %. In summary, the scores generated by our system are more inline with that of human perception.

On a desktop computer with a 2.4 GHz quad core Intel, our MATLAB implementation runs at 10 frame/s, which outspeeds [7] performing at 6.5 frame/s. Compared with [8] that operates at 65 frame/s, our method is significantly slower; however, for real-time clinical applications, our method requires a speed-up of only 2.5, which is achievable using C++ Multithreaded Programming.

5   Discussion

The concerning issue of polyp miss-rates has been approached from different angles. One can categorize such approaches in three major groups:

- Computer aided diagnosis (CAD) for automatic polyp detection [12–14]. These systems are useful for detecting the polyps that appear in the videos clearly but get overlooked due to operators' eye fatigue or inattentiveness. The major drawbacks with such CAD systems are computational complexity and high false positive rates.

 – Objective measurement of the existing quality guidelines for colonoscopy. Examples include automatic documentation of cecum intubation [15] and automatic measurement of net withdrawal time [16]. While such objective documentations are important for quality monitring, they cannot reflect the actual quality of colon examination in a particular segment of the colon.
 – 3D colon reconstruction for providing feedback on the colon segments that have remained unseen during colonoscopy [17]. This approach offers complimentary values to CAD system for polyp detection. However, practicality of this approach is limited by the complexity of the colon as a non-rigid and constantly deforming object.

In contrast to the above-listed approaches, which are computational expensive and are of limited clinical value, objective assessment of colon examination based on image information content is more indicative of quality and more amenable to the current clinical practice. Such a system can not only warn against hasty examinations but also can be employed as a prepossessing stage for all above mentioned tasks where removal of non-informative frames can significantly improve efficiency. Vicari, in his recent article [18], states that "one lesson for all colonoscopists is simple: just slow down!", which further motivates the need for objective analysis of examination speed. In this paper, we sought to detect hasty examination shots by objective measurement of image information content.

6   Conclusion and Future Work

In this paper, we presented a method for objective assessment of information content in colonoscopy images. The suggested method was designed according to 2 observations: (1) non-informative frames most often contain blurry edges; (2) information content is spread all over an image in the informative frames, whereas in non-informative frames, depending on image artifacts and degradation factors, details may appear in only a few regions. Our experiments based on a collection of 5500 colonoscopy images demonstrated the superiority of the suggested method over the existing works both quantitatively and qualitatively. Our future work will investigate the correlation between the computed quality scores and colonoscopists' adenoma detection rates.

Acknowledgments. This research has been supported by an ASU-Mayo Clinic research grant.

References

1. Siegel, R., DeSantis, C., Jemal, A.: Colorectal cancer statistics. CA: Cancer J. Clin. **64**, 104–117 (2014)
2. Bressler, B., Paszat, L.F., Chen, Z., Rothwell, D.M., Vinden, C., Rabeneck, L.: Rates of new or missed colorectal cancers after colonoscopy and their risk factors: A population-based analysis. Gastroenterology **132**, 96–102 (2007)

3. Van Rijn, J.C., Reitsma, J.B., Stoker, J., Bossuyt, P.M., van Deventer, S.J., Dekker, E.: Polyp miss rate determined by tandem colonoscopy: a systematic review. Am. J. Gastroenterol. **101**, 343–350 (2006)

4. Heresbach, D., Barrioz, T., Lapalus, M.G., Coumaros, D., et al.: Miss rate for colorectal neoplastic polyps: a prospective multicenter study of back-to-back video colonoscopies. Endoscopy **40**, 284–290 (2008)

5. Gelder, R.E.V., Nio, C., Florie, J., Bartelsman, J.F., et al.: Computed tomographic colonography compared with colonoscopy in patients at increased risk for colorectal cancer. Gastroenterology **127**, 41–48 (2004)

6. Filip, D., Gao, X., Angulo-Rodríguez, L., Mintchev, M.P., et al.: Colometer: a real-time quality feedback system for screening colonoscopy. World J. Gastroenterol. WJG **18**, 4270 (2012)

7. Oh, J., Hwang, S., Lee, J., Tavanapong, W., Wong, J., de Groen, P.C.: Informative frame classification for endoscopy video. Med. Image Anal. **11**, 110–127 (2007)

8. Arnold, M., Ghosh, A., Lacey, G., Patchett, S., Mulcahy, H.: Indistinct frame detection in colonoscopy videos. In: 2009 13th International Machine Vision and Image Processing Conference, pp. 47–52 (2009)

9. Park, S.Y., Sargent, D., Spofford, I., Vosburgh, K.: Colonoscopy video quality assessment using hidden markov random fields. In: SPIE Medical Imaging, pp. 79632P–79632P. International Society for Optics and Photonics (2011)

10. Criminisi, A., Shotton, J.: Decision Forests for Computer Vision and Medical Image Analysis. Springer, New York (2013)

11. DeLong, E.R., DeLong, D.M., Clarke-Pearson, D.L.: Comparing the areas under two or more correlated receiver operating characteristic curves: a nonparametric approach. Biometrics **44**(3), 837–845 (1988)

12. Tajbakhsh, N., Gurudu, S.R., Liang, J.: A classification-enhanced vote accumulation scheme for detecting colonic polyps. In: Yoshida, H., Warfield, S., Vannier, M.W. (eds.) Abdominal Imaging 2013. LNCS, vol. 8198, pp. 53–62. Springer, Heidelberg (2013)

13. Tajbakhsh, N., Chi, C., Gurudu, S.R., Liang, J.: Automatic polyp detection from learned boundaries. In: 2014 IEEE 10th International Symposium on Biomedical Imaging (ISBI) (2014)

14. Bernal, J., Sanchez, J., Vilarino, F.: Towards automatic polyp detection with a polyp appearance model. Pattern Recogn. **45**, 3166–3182 (2012)

15. De Groen, P.C., Tavanapong, W., Oh, J., Wong, J.: Computer-aided quality control for colonoscopy: Automatic documentation of cecal intubation. Gastrointest. Endosc. **65**, AB354–AB354 (2007)

16. Oh, J., Hwang, S., Cao, Y., Tavanapong, W., et al.: Measuring objective quality of colonoscopy. IEEE Trans. Biomed. Eng. **56**, 2190–2196 (2009)

17. Hong, D., Tavanapong, W., Wong, J., Oh, J., de Groen, P.C.: 3D reconstruction of virtual colon structures from colonoscopy images. Comput. Med. Imag. Graph. **38**, 22–33 (2014)

18. Vicari, J.: Performing a quality colonoscopy: Just slow down!. Gastrointest. Endosc. **71**, 787–788 (2010)

Information-Preserving Pseudo-Enhancement Correction for Non-Cathartic Low-Dose Dual-Energy CT Colonography

Janne J. Näppi[1]([✉]), Rie Tachibana[1], Daniele Regge[2], and Hiroyuki Yoshida[1]

[1] 3D Imaging Research, Department of Radiology, Massachusetts General Hospital and Harvard Medical School, 25 New Chardon Street, Suite 400C, Boston, MA 02114, USA
{janne.nappi,rtachibana,yoshida.hiro}@mgh.harvard.edu
[2] Institute for Cancer Research and Treatment, Candiolo Str. Prov. 142, 10060 Turin, Italy

Abstract. In CT colonography (CTC), orally administered positive-contrast fecal-tagging agents can cause artificial elevation of the observed radiodensity of adjacent soft tissue. Such pseudo-enhancement makes it challenging to differentiate polyps and folds reliably from tagged materials, and it is also present in dual-energy CTC (DE-CTC). We developed a method that corrects for pseudo-enhancement on DE-CTC images without distorting the dual-energy information contained in the data. A pilot study was performed to evaluate the effect of the method visually and quantitatively by use of clinical non-cathartic low-dose DE-CTC data from 10 patients including 13 polyps covered partially or completely by iodine-based fecal tagging. The results indicate that the proposed method can be used to reduce the pseudo-enhancement distortion of DE-CTC images without losing material-specific dual-energy information. The method has potential application in improving the accuracy of automated image-processing applications, such as computer-aided detection and virtual bowel cleansing in CTC.

Keywords: CT colonography · Pseudo-enhancement · Dual-energy CT · Virtual colonoscopy

1 Introduction

Computed tomographic colonography (CTC) uses orally administered positive-contrast fecal-tagging agents for opacifying residual fluid and feces on CTC images. The expectation is that, because fecal-tagged fluid and feces should have high CT values of >100 Hounsfield units (HU) on CTC images, they can be differentiated reliably from the CT values of soft-tissue lesions (approximately 0 – 100 HU). However, if the fecal-tagging agent has high radiodensity (>300 HU), it tends to cause artificial local elevation of the CT values of adjacent soft-tissue lesions and haustral folds. This makes reliable visualization and

© Springer International Publishing Switzerland 2014
H. Yoshida et al. (Eds.): ABDI 2014, LNCS 8676, pp. 159–168, 2014.
DOI: 10.1007/978-3-319-13692-9_15

automated detection of lesions challenging, because CT values of >100 HU may now indicate both lesions and tagged fecal materials [1].

Previously, an automated image-based pseudo-enhancement correction (PEC) method was developed for single-energy CTC [1]. Studies have shown that the application of PEC can improve the performance of automated polyp detection [2] and electronic cleansing [3]. Later approaches have included a scale-based scatter correction method [4] and a non-linear correction method [5].

Recently, dual-energy CTC (DE-CTC) has been used to improve the accuracy of image-processing applications over conventional single-energy CTC, because it can provide quantitative material-specific measurements for differentiating fecal tagging and partial-volume artifacts from soft-tissue lesions more precisely than does single-energy CTC which only provides intensity information [6,7]. However, pseudo-enhancement is still present on dual-energy CTC (DE-CTC) images, which are typically acquired at 140 kVp and 80 kVp energy levels. This can degrade the ability of DE-CTC to differentiate reliably between materials.

The PEC methods of single-energy CTC cannot be applied directly to DE-CTC images, because this would distort the dual-energy information (Fig. 1). Therefore, in this study, we developed an information-preserving method for performing PEC on DE-CTC images. A preliminary evaluation of the method was performed by use of clinical non-cathartic low-dose DE-CTC cases.

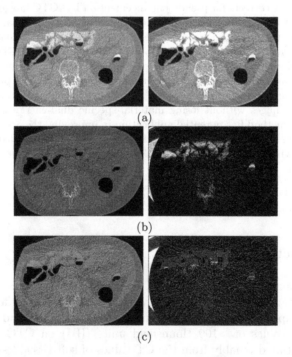

Fig. 1. (a) An example of a 140 kVp and 80 kVp energy image pair. (b) The corresponding water-iodine basis material decomposition. (c) After performing a single-energy pseudo-enhancement correction independently on each energy image, the subsequent basis material decomposition indicates the presence of iodine incorrectly.

2 Materials and Methods

2.1 Materials

Ten patients were prepared for a non-cathartic CTC examination by oral inges-
tion of 50 ml of iodinated contrast agent (Gastrografin, Therapex, Canada) on
the day before and two hours prior to CT acquisitions by a dual-energy CT
scanner (SOMATOM Definition Flash, Siemens Healthcare, Germany). The CT
acquisitions were performed in supine and prone positions at 15 mA for the
140 kVp scan and at 40 mA for the 80 kVp scan. The average CT dose index
by volume was 0.95 mGy and the effective dose was 0.75 mSv per CT scan volume. The dual-energy images were constructed by use of a sinogram-affirmed
iterative image reconstruction (SAFIRE) algorithm [8,9] at 0.6 – 1.0 mm reconstruction intervals. The locations of 13 clinically significant polyps ($\geq$6 mm in
largest diameter) that were confirmed by same-day colonoscopy were correlated
with the CTC images by a radiologist with extensive experience on interpreting
CT colonography (>1000 cases read).

2.2 Pseudo-Enhancement Correction (PEC1) for Single-Energy CTC

Because the dual-energy PEC method is based in part upon a single-energy PEC
method, we will briefly discuss the basic idea of the latter. In the remainder of
this text, we will denote this single-energy method as PEC1 and its dual-energy
version as PEC2.

In the PEC1-method [1], pseudo-enhancement is modeled as a process of iterative enhancement that radiates three-dimensionally from voxels with high CT
value into their surrounding voxels, thereby causing increment in the observed
CT values of the surrounding voxels. More precisely, if v_p denotes the correct
CT value at voxel p, and $\tilde{v}_p$ denotes the observed pseudo-enhanced CT value,
the observed CT value is modeled as

$$\tilde{v}_p = v_p + \delta_p, \qquad (1)$$

where δ_p denotes the effect of pseudo-enhancement at p. The value of δ_p is
estimated by use of an iterative algorithm. First, we assume that each voxel with
a high CT value distributes some amount of initial pseudo-enhancement energy
to its adjacent voxels. At a voxel q, the initial pseudo-enhancement energy is
approximated as $e_q = \max\{0, \tilde{v}_q - \tau_q\}$, where τ_q is a parameter threshold for the
smallest CT value that is considered to cause pseudo-enhancement.

At the first iteration, e_q is distributed to the surrounding voxels according
to a 3-D Gaussian field function. Each affected voxel receives some pseudo-
enhancement energy from its surrounding voxels. Let $r^0(p)$ denote the total
pseudo-enhancement energy received by voxel p at the first iteration.

At subsequent iterations, the pseudo-enhancement energy that was received
by voxel p at the previous iteration is redistributed to the surrounding voxels (Fig. 2(a)). Simultaneously, the total pseudo-enhancement energy that has

been received by p is being accumulated at p. Let $r^i(p)$ denote the pseudo-enhancement energy that was received by p at ith iteration.

The iterations continue, until the distributable pseudo-enhancement energy becomes negligible, i.e. when the effect of the largest pseudo-enhancement energy received by a voxel drops to less than 1 HU. The iterations converge, because the total distributed pseudo-enhancement energy is reduced at each iteration. From Eq. (1), the pseudo-enhancement correction for a voxel p is calculated as

$$v_p = \tilde{v}_p - \delta_p = \tilde{v}_p - \sum_{i=0}^{m} r^i(p), \qquad (2)$$

where m is the number of completed iterations. After the application of Eq. (2), pseudo-enhanced soft-tissue lesions can be seen in a soft-tissue display window (Fig. 2(b)).

The method was calibrated by use of an anthropomorphic phantom that was filled partially with three radio-densities of diluted iodine corresponding to observed CT values of 300 HU, 600 HU, and 900 HU. The CT acquisitions were performed at 140 kVp tube voltage and 50 mA current with an eight-channel CT scanner (LightSpeed Plus, GE Medical Systems, Milwaukee, WI, USA) using a 2.5-mm collimation and 1.8-mm reconstruction interval. The calibration involved the optimization of two parameter functions that provide the radius of the Gaussian distribution field as a function of e_q and r^i, respectively. The objective function was the observed difference of CT values in the three partially filled phantoms in comparison with an empty phantom [1].

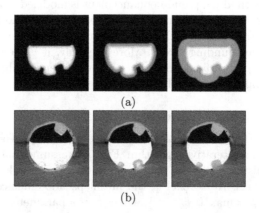

(a)

(b)

Fig. 2. Illustration of the calculation of pseudo-enhancement correction. (a) A 2-D cut-plane view of the pseudo-enhancement correction field after 1, 10, and 20 iterations. (b) The corresponding corrected image shows how the CT values of two pseudo-enhanced polyps covered by tagged fluid are gradually corrected by the method.

2.3   Information-Preserving Pseudo-Enhancement Correction (PEC2) for DE-CTC

To perform dual-energy PEC, first we use the PEC1 method of Sect. 2.2 to correct the 140 kVp image of the dual-energy image pair independently from the 80 kVp image. Next, we correct the 80 kVp image according to

$$v_{80} = \frac{v_{140}}{\tilde{v}_{140}} \tilde{v}_{80} \,, \tag{3}$$

where v_{80} is the corrected CT value, v_{140} and $\tilde{v}_{140}$ are the PEC1-corrected and uncorrected CT values of the 140 kVp image, respectively, and $\tilde{v}_{80}$ is the uncorrected CT value of the 80 kVp image.

It is easy to see that Eq. (3) preserves the dual-energy image information. For the dual-energy ratio (DER) feature, from Eq. (3) we have

$$\mathrm{DER} = \frac{v_{140}}{v_{80}} = \frac{v_{140}\tilde{v}_{140}}{v_{140}\tilde{v}_{80}} = \frac{\tilde{v}_{140}}{\tilde{v}_{80}} \,. \tag{4}$$

The dual-energy index (DEI) feature is calculated as [10]

$$\mathrm{DEI} = \frac{v_{80} - v_{140}}{v_{80} + v_{140} + 2000} \,. \tag{5}$$

From Eq. (3), we have

$$\mathrm{DEI} = \frac{\tilde{v}_{140}(v_{140}\tilde{v}_{80} - v_{140}\tilde{v}_{140})}{v_{140}\tilde{v}_{80} + v_{140}\tilde{v}_{140} + \tilde{v}_{140}2000} = \frac{\tilde{v}_{80} - \tilde{v}_{140}}{\tilde{v}_{80} + \tilde{v}_{140} + \frac{\tilde{v}_{140}}{v_{140}}2000} \,. \tag{6}$$

Thus, to preserve the value of DEI after the correction, it would be necessary to adjust the constant 2000 in the denominator relative to the correction of the 140 kVp image at each point.

2.4   Evaluation Methods

For a pilot study, we evaluated the PEC2-method both visually and quantitatively by use of the 20 DE-CTC scan pairs (see Sect. 2.1). For visual evaluation, we calculated water-iodine basis decomposition images and virtual monochromatic images (VMIs) [11] from uncorrected and PEC2-corrected 140 kVp and 80 kVp energy images. For quantitative evaluation, we calculated the mean CT values of polyps covered partially or completely by fecal tagging in 100 keV and 120 keV VMIs without and with the application of PEC2. The CT values of each polyp were sampled from the center voxel and its 6-neighborhood voxels.

To calculate VMIs, we solved the material fractions from [11]

$$\begin{pmatrix} \mu_1 \\ \mu_2 \end{pmatrix} = \begin{pmatrix} M_1 \\ M_2 \end{pmatrix} \times \begin{pmatrix} \frac{\mu}{\rho_1}(E) \times \rho_1 \\ \frac{\mu}{\rho_2}(E) \times \rho_2 \end{pmatrix} \,, \tag{7}$$

where μ_1 and μ_2 are the observed linear attenuation coefficient values, M_1 and M_2 are the material fractions, ρ_1 and ρ_2 are the material densities, and $\frac{\mu}{\rho_1}$ and $\frac{\mu}{\rho_2}$ are the mass attenuation coefficients at an average energy E. After solving of the material fractions, the VMI is calculated by reapplication of Eq. (7) at the desired monochromatic energy E.

3   Results

Figures 3(a) and (b) show an example of the water-iodine basis image decomposition with pseudo-enhancement correction by the PEC2 method for the same region as that of Fig. 1. The presence of iodine (tagging agent) is now indicated correctly by the iodine image (Fig. 3(b)). Figure 3(c) shows the corresponding VMI calculated at 120 keV.

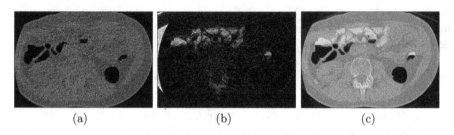

(a)   (b)   (c)

Fig. 3. (a) Water and (b) iodine basis decomposition images calculated from the PEC2-corrected 140 kVp and 80 kVp input images. (c) VMI of the region at 120 keV.

Figure 4 demonstrates the effect of the adjustment term $\frac{\tilde{v}_{140}}{v_{140}}$ of Eq. (6). The use of original DEI of Eq. (5) yields differences between DEI images calculated from the uncorrected and PEC2-corrected dual-energy images (Fig. 4(a)), whereas the use of adjusted DEI of Eq. (6) yields identical values (Fig. 4(b)).

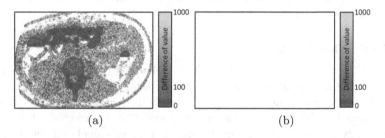

(a)   (b)

Fig. 4. Difference images of the DEI-feature calculated from the uncorrected and PEC2-corrected dual-energy images. White color indicates identical value, i.e., no difference. (a) Original DEI (Eq. (5)) indicates some differences. (b) Adjusted DEI (Eq. (6)) yields identical values (white color) with the original data.

Figure 5 shows a comparison of the CT values within polyps sampled from VMIs calculated at 100 keV and 120 keV energies from the uncorrected and PEC2-corrected dual-energy images. Each point represents the CT value of a voxel within a polyp. The measurements indicate that the PEC2 method is able to reduce pseudo-enhancement of the CT values of polyps without affecting the CT values of polyps that are not pseudo-enhanced.

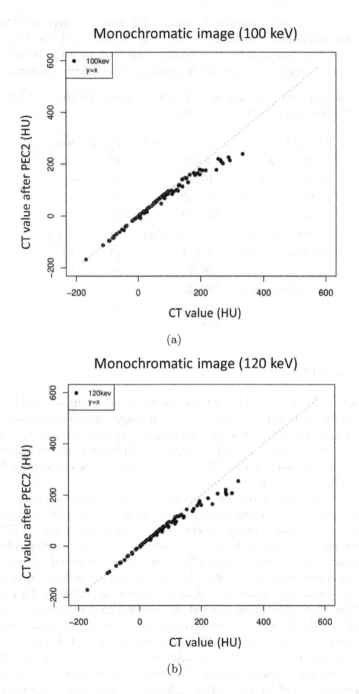

Fig. 5. Comparison of the CT values of VMIs calculated from uncorrected (x-axis) and PEC2-corrected (y-axis) dual-energy images, respectively, (a) at 100 keV and (b) at 120 keV.

Table 1 shows measurements of the average CT value of polyps in VMIs before and after the application of the PEC2 method. As expected, the correction is largest for small polyps and for those covered by fecal tagging. Because of the small number of samples (n), we did not estimate statistical significance.

Table 1. Measurements of the average CT values of polyps (in HU) on VMIs without and with the application of the PEC2 method.

E = 120 keV	n	Uncorrected	PEC2	Change
Small (6 – 9 mm)	3	72	47	−25
Large (≥10 mm)	10	70	62	−8
Partially covered	3	27	24	−3
Submerged	6	93	76	−17
E = 100 keV	n	Uncorrected	PEC2	Change
Small (6 – 9 mm)	3	57	33	−24
Large (≥10 mm)	10	76	68	−8
Partially covered	3	20	16	−4
Submerged	6	103	86	−17

4 Discussion

Pseudo-enhancement is considered to originate largely from the combined effect of x-ray scattering, beam hardening, and their inappropriate correction by commercial CT scanners [12]. Although the proprietary algorithms of CT scanners are probably attempting to correct for conventional beam-hardening effects, they have not been designed to correct for the variable presence of fecal-tagging contrast agents in CTC [1,13].

Previously, the use of retrospective image-based pseudo-enhancement correction methods was shown to reduce pseudo-enhancement and to improve the performance of automated image-processing methods in single-energy CTC. The preliminary results of this study indicate potentially similar benefits in DE-CTC by the application of the proposed PEC2 method. The method was shown to preserve material-specific information in terms of two key features that are used commonly in image-based material-specific analyses: the DER and DEI features.

On VMIs that were reconstructed by use of PEC2-corrected images, the results indicate similar trends than those observed previously in the correction of single-energy CTC images. The PEC does not affect the CT values of polyps that were not affected by pseudo-enhancement, but it does reduce the observed CT values of pseudo-enhanced polyps. The correction becomes larger as the effect of pseudo-enhancement increases (Fig. 5). The quantitative measurement results showed that the correction is largest for polyps submerged in fecal tagging and for small polyps, and that after the correction the average CT values of polyps are within the expected soft-tissue range (Table 1).

Recent efforts to reduce the theoretical risks of medical radiation have resulted in efforts to minimize radiation dose in CTC examinations [14]. The iterative SAFIRE algorithm that we used in this study enables the use of low effective CT dose without compromising diagnostic image quality. However, the algorithm does not completely compensate for pseudo-enhancement which can be seen especially at the 80 kVp energy CT images. The proposed PEC2-method can be used to reduce such artifacts.

The DE-CTC data of this study were acquired by use of a non-cathartic CTC protocol. Bowel preparation has been identified as one of the major obstacles to colorectal screening. The use of non-cathartic or completely laxative-free [15–17] bowel preparation could provide substantial increment in patient adherence to colorectal screening guidelines [18].

This study had several limitations. First, the PEC2-method is based on a single-energy PEC1-method that was optimized for a different CT scanner by a different manufacturer than that used in our study. Previous studies have shown great variability when CT data are compared between different brands and models of scanners [19,20]. Therefore, a more accurate pseudo-enhancement correction can be expected if the method was optimized for the particular CT scanner and acquisition parameters used in a study. Second, the number of samples was small. Third, we did not perform a phantom study, where the exact CT values of target materials would be known. Nevertheless, the quantitative experiments indicate that the proposed PEC2 method can indeed be used to restore the expected soft-tissue CT values of pseudo-enhanced polyps on DE-CTC images without distorting the dual-energy information.

5   Conclusion

We developed a pseudo-enhancement correction method for dual-energy CT colonography. Preliminary evaluation indicates that the method is able to reduce pseudo-enhancement in dual-energy data while preserving the material-specific information of dual-energy images. The method has potential to improve the accuracy of material-specific analysis and automated image processing of dual-energy CTC images.

Acknowledgments. This study was supported in part by the grants of CA095279, CA131781, CA166816, and CA182107.

References

1. Näppi, J., Yoshida, H.: Adaptive correction of the pseudo-enhancement of CT attenuation for fecal-tagging CT colonography. Med. Image Anal. **12**, 413–426 (2008)
2. Näppi, J., Yoshida, H.: Fully automated three-dimensional detection of polyps in fecal-tagging CT colonography. Acad. Radiol. **25**, 287–300 (2007)

3. Zhang, H., Li, L., Zhu, H., Han, H., Song, B., Liang, Z.: Integration of 3D scale-based pseudo-enhancement correction and partial volume image segmentation for improving electronic colon cleansing in CT colonography. J. Xray Sci. Techol. **22**, 271–283 (2014)

4. Liu, J., Yao, J., Summers, R.: Scale-based scatter correction for computer-aided polyp detection in CT colonography. Med. Phys. **35**, 5664–5671 (2008)

5. Tsagaan, B., Näppi, J., Yoshida, H.: Nonlinear regression-based method for pseudoenhancement correction in CT colonography. Med. Phys. **36**, 3596–3606 (2009)

6. Näppi, J., Kim, S., Yoshida, H.: Automated detection of colorectal lesions with dual-energy CT colonography. In: van Ginneken, B., Novak, C. (eds.) SPIE Medical Imaging 2012: Computed-Aided Diagnosis, vol. 8315, pp. 83150Y1–83150Y6 (2012)

7. Näppi, J., Kim, S., Yoshida, H.: Volumetric detection of colorectal lesions for noncathartic dual-energy computed tomographic colonography. In: Conference Proceedings of IEEE Engineering in Medicine and Biology Society, pp. 3740–3743 (2012)

8. Kalra, M., Woisetschläger, M., Dahlström, N., Singh, S., Linblom, M., et al.: Radiation dose reduction with sinogram affirmed iterative reconstruction technique for abdominal computed tomography. J. Comput. Assist. Tomogr. **36**, 339–346 (2012)

9. Grant, K., Raupach, R.: SAFIRE: sinogram affirmed iterative reconstruction. Technical report, Siemens (2012)

10. Zachrisson, H., Engström, E., Engvall, J., Wigström, L., Smedby, O., Persson, A.: Soft tissue discrimination ex vivo by dual energy computed tomography. Eur. J. Radiol. **75**, e124–e128 (2010)

11. Yu, L., Leng, S., McCollough, C.: Dual-energy CT-based monochromatic imaging. Am. J. Roentgenol. **199**, S9–S15 (2012)

12. Maki, D., Birnbaum, B., Chakraborty, D., Jacobs, J., Carvalho, B., Herman, G.: Renal cyst pseudoenhancement: beam-hardening effects on CT numbers. Radiology **213**, 468–472 (1999)

13. Boas, F., Fleischmann, D.: CT artifacts: causes and reduction techniques. Imaging Med. **4**, 229–240 (2012)

14. Chang, K., Yee, J.: Dose reduction methods for CT colonography. Abdom. Imaging **38**, 224–232 (2013)

15. Zalis, M., Blake, M., Cai, W., Hahn, P., et al.: Diagnostic accuracy of laxative-free computed tomographic colonography for detection of adenomatous polyps in asymptomatic adults: a prospective evaluation. Ann. Intern. Med. **156**, 692–702 (2012)

16. Lefere, P., Gryspeerdt, S., Baekelandt, M., Van Holsbeeck, B.: Laxative-free CT colonography. Am. J. Roentgenol. **183**, 945–948 (2004)

17. Johnson, C., Manduca, A., Fletcher, J., MacCarty, R., et al.: Noncathartic CT colonography with stool tagging: performance with and without electronic stool subtraction. Am. J. Roentgenol. **190**, 361–366 (2008)

18. Beebe, T., Johnson, C., Stoner, S., Anderson, K., Limburg, P.: Assessing attitudes toward laxative preparation in colorectal cancer screening and effects on future testing: potential receptivity to computed tomographic colonography. Mayo. Clinic. Proc. **82**, 666–671 (2007)

19. Grosjean, R., Daudon, M., Chammas Jr., M., Claudon, M., et al.: Pitfalls in urinary stone identification using CT attenuation values: are we getting the same information on different scanner models? Eur. J. Radiol. **82**, 1201–1206 (2013)

20. McCullough, E.: Factors affecting the use of quantitative information from a CT scanner. Radiology **124**, 99–107 (1977)

Application of Pseudo-enhancement Correction to Virtual Monochromatic CT Colonography

Rie Tachibana$^{(\boxtimes)}$, Janne J. Näppi, and Hiroyuki Yoshida

3D Imaging Research, Department of Radiology, Harvard Medical School
and Massachusetts General Hospital, 25 New Chardon Street, Suite 400C,
Boston, MA 02114, USA
{rtachibana,janne.nappi,yoshida.hiro}@mgh.harvard.edu

Abstract. In CT colonography, orally administered positive-contrast fecal-tagging agents are used for differentiating residual fluid and feces from true lesions. However, the presence of high-density tagging agent in the colon can introduce erroneous artifacts, such as local pseudo-enhancement and beam-hardening, on the reconstructed CT images, thereby complicating reliable detection of soft-tissue lesions. In dual-energy CT colonography, such image artifacts can be reduced by the calculation of virtual monochromatic CT images, which provide more accurate quantitative attenuation measurements than conventional single-energy CT colonography. In practice, however, virtual monochromatic images may still contain some pseudo-enhancement artifacts, and efforts to minimize radiation dose may enhance such artifacts. In this study, we evaluated the effect of image-based pseudo-enhancement post-correction on virtual monochromatic images in standard-dose and low-dose dual-energy CT colonography. The mean CT values of the virtual monochromatic standard-dose CT images of 51 polyps and those of the virtual monochromatic low-dose CT images of 20 polyps were measured without and with the pseudo-enhancement correction. Statistically significant differences were observed between uncorrected and pseudo-enhancement-corrected images of polyps covered by fecal tagging in standard-dose CT ($p < 0.001$) and in low-dose CT ($p < 0.05$). The results indicate that image-based pseudo-enhancement post-correction can be useful for optimizing the performance of image-processing applications in virtual monochromatic CT colonography.

Keywords: Dual-energy CT · Virtual monochromatic imaging · Pseudo-enhancement correction · CT colonography

1 Introduction

CT colonography (also known as virtual colonoscopy) has been recommended by the American Cancer Society as a screening option for colon cancer [1]. When performed well and interpreted by experienced radiologists, CT colonography provides a safe and accurate method for examining the complete region of the colon. However, poor bowel preparation, suboptimal CT acquisition, and/or the presence of retained fluid and stool, may obscure or imitate polyps, thereby reducing the accuracy of CT colonography [2].

© Springer International Publishing Switzerland 2014
H. Yoshida et al. (Eds.): ABDI 2014, LNCS 8676, pp. 169–178, 2014.
DOI: 10.1007/978-3-319-13692-9_16

For confident detection of polyps, orally administered positive-contrast fecal-tagging agents are used in CT colonography for opacifying retained fluid and feces on the CT colonography images [3]. However, the presence of high-density fecal-tagging agent in the colon can also cause local pseudo-enhancement distortion of the CT values of adjacent soft-tissue structures on the reconstructed CT images [4]. The resulting uncertainty between the higher-than-expected CT values of pseudo-enhanced polyps and the lower-than-expected CT values of unclearly tagged fluid or feces presents significant challenges to automated image-processing algorithms, such as computer-aided detection (CAD) of polyps [2, 4, 5] and electronic cleansing of fecal-tagged materials [6]. Therefore, image-based post-correction algorithms have been developed for pseudo-enhancement correction of CT colonography images. The application of pseudo-enhancement correction has been shown to improve the detection performance of CAD and the accuracy of electronic cleansing in CT colonography [4, 6].

Dual-energy CT (DECT) [7] provides an alternative method for correcting pseudo-enhancement artifacts by the calculation of virtual monochromatic (VM) images. In principle, the VM images should be free from pseudo-enhancement and beam-hardening artifacts, and they can also provide quantitatively more accurate attenuation measurements than does single-energy CT [8, 9]. However, empirical studies have shown that VM images can still contain some pseudo-enhancement artifacts [8].

In this study, we investigated the potential benefit of the application of image-based pseudo-enhancement correction to VM images in standard-dose and low-dose DECT colonography. To perform low-dose DECT colonography without producing excessive noise on the low-energy images, the low-dose DECT images were reconstructed by use of iterative reconstruction (IRT).

2   Methods

2.1   Virtual Monochromatic (VM) CT Colonography

In DECT colonography, two CT colonography scans are acquired per scan position simultaneously at 140 kVp and 80 kVp energy levels. Given two basis materials, such as water and iodine, the CT values can be expressed as a linear combination of water and iodine as [9]

$$x_1 = a + f_1 \times c,$$
$$x_2 = a + f_2 \times c, \tag{1}$$

where x_1 and x_2 are the observed low-energy (80 kVp) and high-energy (140 kVp) CT values, a is the water density, c is iodine concentration, and f_1 and f_2 are calibration measurements with iodine. The unknown parameters a and c can be calculated by solving of the equations based on the CT values acquired at the different energy levels.

The basis material images can be used to calculate VM images (Fig. 1). A CT value x_E of a VM image can be calculated by

$$x_E = a + c \times g(E), \tag{2}$$

where $g(E)$ is the mass attenuation coefficient derived from tabulated data at the desired VM energy E [10].

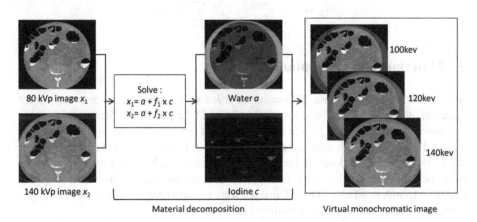

Fig. 1. Calculation of virtual monochromatic images [9].

2.2 Image-Based Pseudo-enhancement Correction

Pseudo-enhancement correction can be performed retrospectively on reconstructed CT images by use of an image-based method [4]. In this method, the effect of pseudo-enhancement on a voxel p of an observed CT image is modeled as

$$v_p = \widehat{v}_p + v_p^{PEH}, \tag{3}$$

where $\widehat{v}_p$ is the true radio-density of the underlying material and v_p^{PEH} is the effect of pseudo-enhancement at p. To estimate v_p^{PEH}, we assume that the adjacent voxels of p are distributing some amount of pseudo-enhancement on p. The initial pseudo-enhancement energy emitted by nearby voxels q (and possibly by p itself to its surrounding voxels) is estimated as

$$r^0(p) = \sum_q \frac{C}{\sqrt{2\pi}\sigma_1(v_p)} \exp\left(-\frac{1}{2}\left(\frac{D(p,q)}{\sigma_1(v_q)}\right)^2\right), \tag{4}$$

where $\sigma_1(v_q)$ is a parameter function, $D(p,q)$ is the distance between voxels q and p, and C is a scaling constant. The CT value of p is updated according to $v_p^1 = v_p - r^0(p)$, and the process is repeated by estimation of the total distributed energy at iteration n as

$$r^n(p) = \sum_q \frac{r^{n-1}(q)}{\sqrt{2\pi}\sigma_2(r^{n-1}(q))} \exp\left(-\frac{1}{2}\left(\frac{D(p,q)}{\sigma_2(r^{n-1}(q))}\right)^2\right), \tag{5}$$

where $\sigma_2(r^{n-1}(q))$ is a second parameter function. The iteration over Eq. (5) ends when the distributed energy becomes negligible. Therefore, the final corrected value of p is calculated as

$$\widehat{v}_p = v_p - v_p^{\text{PEH}} \approx v_p - \sum_{i=0}^{n} r^n(p). \tag{6}$$

3 Materials and Evaluation

Standard-dose and low-dose CT scans of 19 and 12 patients, respectively, were acquired by use of a DECT scanner (SOMATOM Definition Flash, Siemens) in supine and prone positions. The CT slice thickness varied between 0.6 mm and 0.7 mm. For standard-dose DECT, the tube current was 82–159 mA at 140 kVp and 379–549 mA at 80 kVp. The standard-dose CT images were reconstructed by use of the filtered back-projection method. For low-dose DECT, the tube current was 25–36 mA at 140 kVp and 61–115 mA at 80 kVp. The CT images were reconstructed by use of the sinogram-affirmed iterative reconstruction method [11].

In total, there were 71 colonoscopy-confirmed polyps measuring 5–20 mm in their largest diameter, where the locations and sizes of the polyps on CT colonography images had been established by an expert radiologist. There were 51 polyps on the standard-dose DECT cases and 20 polyps on the low-dose DECT cases. The polyps were separated into two groups based on the presence of fecal tagging on their site: group "None" included polyps that were not affected by fecal tagging, and group "Covered" included polyps that were covered by fecal tagging. Figure 2 shows examples of polyps in the two groups.

To evaluate the effect of image-based pseudo-enhancement correction on VM images of pseudo-enhanced polyps, we calculated the VM images of standard-dose and low-dose DECT colonography data at 100 keV, 120 keV and 140 keV VM energies. A region-of-interest (ROI) was defined on each polyp as a 3-mm diameter sphere that was placed at the center of the polyp on the CT colonography images. Next, we measured the difference of the mean CT values within the ROI between the original VM images and pseudo-enhancement-corrected VM (VM-PEC) images. The statistical significance of the differences in CT values was compared by use of the paired t-test.

4 Results

Table 1 shows the differences of CT values between polyps in VM images and VM-PEC images. In low-dose DECT images, the means and standard deviations of the 15 polyps in group "Covered" at 100 keV, 120 keV, and 140 keV were 93.2 ± 95.9 HU, 82.0 ± 78.1 HU, and 69.6 ± 61.9 HU on VM images, respectively. On VM-PEC images, the means and standard deviations were 64.3 ± 56.6 HU, 59.8 ± 49.0 HU, and 52.1 ± 43.1 HU, respectively. The corresponding means and standard deviations of the 32 polyps in group "Covered" on standard-dose DECT images were 82.4 ± 90.3 HU,

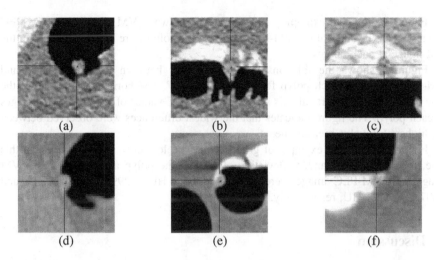

(a)   (b)   (c)

(d)   (e)   (f)

Fig. 2. Examples of polyps in the two fecal-tagging groups. (a) A polyp in group "None" on low-dose DECT (140 kVp). (b), (c) Polyps in group "Covered" on low-dose DECT. (d) A polyp in group "None" on standard-dose DECT (140 kVp). (e), (f) Polyps in group "Covered" on standard-dose DECT images.

Table 1. Paired *t*-test results of the difference between VM images and VM-PEC images.

	Tagging group	Cases	keV	Paired differences					
						95 % Confidence interval of the difference			
				Mean	SD	Lower	Upper	t	p-value
Low-dose DECT	None	5	100	18.9	−3.7	−3.1	41.0	2.4	0.0757
			120	14.0	−1.2	1.6	26.3	3.1	0.0348
			140	12.0	2.0	5.6	18.4	5.2	<0.01
	Covered	15	100	28.9	39.3	4.6	53.1	2.6	0.0229
			120	22.2	29.2	3.9	40.4	2.6	0.0211
			140	17.5	18.8	4.9	30.1	3.0	<0.01
Standard-dose DECT	None	19	100	0.9	0.9	0.1	1.7	2.3	0.0324
			120	0.7	0.7	0.0	1.3	2.2	0.0418
			140	0.6	0.6	0.0	1.1	2.2	0.0411
	Covered	32	100	25.8	19.3	14.7	36.8	4.8	<0.001
			120	20.1	14.4	11.3	28.8	4.7	<0.001
			140	14.9	10.5	8.1	21.6	4.5	<0.001

72.0 ± 81.3 HU, and 60.5 ± 74.1 HU, respectively, and those on the VM-PEC images were 56.6 ± 71.0 HU, 52.0 ± 66.9 HU, and 45.7 ± 63.6 HU, respectively.

In both standard-dose and low-dose DECT images, significant differences were observed between VM images and VM-PEC images at all energy levels for group "Covered" in both standard-dose DECT (p < 0.001) and low-dose DECT (p < 0.05) images.

Figure 3 shows an example of the difference between VM images and VM-PEC images. The CT values of the VM-PEC image of the polyp were lower than those of the VM image at each energy.

Figure 4 shows the relationship of CT values between the VM images and VM-PEC images of each polyp for group "Covered". The horizontal axis shows the case number and the vertical axis shows the mean CT values of VM/VM-PEC images of each polyp. The figure indicates that the widest differences were observed between the highest CT-value measurements.

Figure 5 shows the example of group "None" in low-dose DECT images. In this case, the means and standard deviation of ROI in the polyp at original image, VM image, and VM-PEC image were -299.1 ± 404.2 HU, -299.2 ± 404.2 HU, and -307.6 ± 395.4 HU, respectively.

5 Discussion

At present, clinical CT colonography examinations are performed largely with conventional single-energy CT scanners. However, studies have indicated that the performance of automated image-processing applications, such as CAD and electronic cleansing, could be improved substantially by use of DECT colonography [12, 13].

Recently, there have been concerns about the theoretical risk of radiation-induced cancers by CT examinations [14]. In this study, we used low-dose DECT cases that have less than 1 mSv effective radiation dose per scan position. To compensate for the potential increment in image noise at low-dose scans, we used an IRT method for reconstruction of the CT colonography images. The results indicate that the application of IRT yields a feasible approach for performing low-dose DECT colonography.

Figure 4 shows how the effect of pseudo-enhancement correction is increased on the VM-PEC images as the pseudo-enhanced CT values increase to values of over 50 HU on VM images. The largest corrections were observed for polyps in the tagging group "Covered" on low-dose and standard-dose DECT images (Table 1) that are clearly pseudo-enhanced in the VM images. On the other hand, in standard-dose DECT, there is no difference in the CT values of polyps between the VM and VM-PEC images in group "None".

However, for low-dose DECT images that were reconstructed by use of an IRT algorithm, the CT values of polyps in group "None" were slightly different before and after the pseudo-enhancement correction, even though pseudo-enhancement correction is not expected when tagging is not present. Figure 5 shows an example of such a case. In this example, the local pseudo-enhancement correction is performed on a polyp, because some of the CT values within the polyp are higher than 100 HU on the CT image. In principle, the soft-tissue material of polyps should have CT values of less than 100 HU. The unusually high CT values of the polyp might reflect the use of the IRT algorithm over conventional reconstruction by filtered back-projection. This suggests that, for quantitative imaging, image-processing methods such as pseudo-enhancement correction may need to be optimized specifically for low-dose DECT which is likely to be used more often in clinical practice than standard-dose DECT.

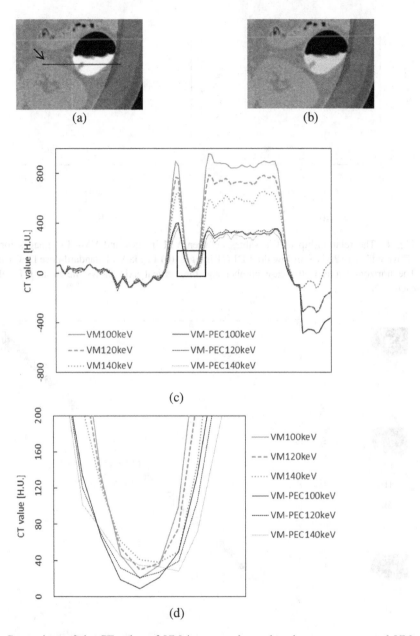

Fig. 3. Comparison of the CT value of VM images and pseudo-enhancement-corrected VM images. (a) Example of a VM image at 120 keV. The arrow indicates the location of the line samples shown in (c). (b) Example of a pseudo-enhancement-corrected image of (a). (c) The line samples of each image. (d) The enlarged image of a box shown in (c).

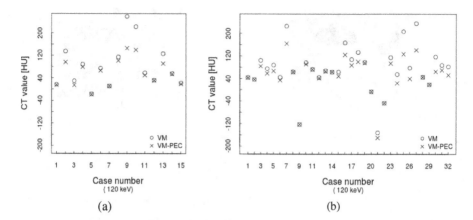

Fig. 4. The relationship of CT values between VM images and VM-PEC images for group "Covered". (a) 120 keV of low-dose DECT images. (b) 120 keV of standard-dose DECT images. The horizontal axis is the case number and the vertical axis shows the mean CT values of each ROI.

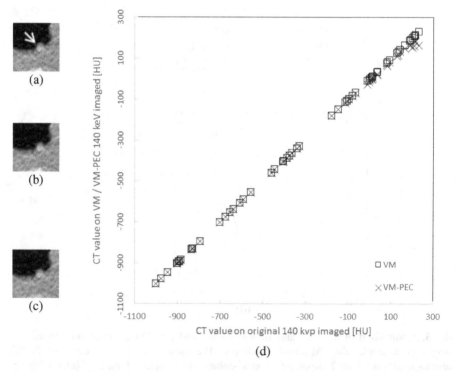

Fig. 5. Comparison of the CT values of original 140 kVp image and the corresponding 140 keV VM /VM-PEC images in low-dose CT colonography. (a) Original image acquisition at 140 kVp. The arrow indicates the location of polyp. (b) the 140 keV VM image of (a). (c) Pseudo-enhancement-corrected 140 keV image of (b). (d) The relationship of the CT values between images (a) and (b)/(c). Each point represents a CT value sampled from the polyp.

This study had several limitations. One of the limitations was that the pseudo-enhancement correction algorithm was developed originally for single-energy CT colonography examinations performed at 140 kVp and calibrated for a different CT scanner than that used in this study. For optimal results, the method should be recalibrated for the same CT scanner and energy levels that are used for measurements. Another limitation of this study was that we used clinical CT colonography cases with the expectation that true CT values of soft-tissue polyps should range approximately between 0 and 100 HU. Ideally, we should perform the experiments on a phantom where the undistorted CT values of colonic structures are known precisely.

The results of this study suggest that the application of pseudo-enhancement correction can be useful for optimizing the performance of CAD and electronic cleansing in virtual monochromatic DECT colonography. Thus, further studies that demonstrate the effectiveness of these methods are warranted.

Acknowledgments. This work was supported in part by grant CA095279, CA131781, and CA166816 from the National Cancer Institute at the National Institutes of Health.

References

1. Levin, B., Lieberman, D.A., McFarland, B., et al.: American cancer society colorectal cancer advisory group, US multi-society task force, american college of radiology colon cancer committee: screening and surveillance for the early detection of colorectal cancer and adenomatous polyps, 2008: a joint guideline from the american cancer society, the US multi-society task force on colorectal cancer, and the american college of radiology. Gastroenterology **134**, 1570–1595 (2008)
2. Mang, T., Gryspeerdt, S., Schima, W., Lefere, P.: Evaluation of colonic lesions and pitfalls in CT colonography: a systematic approach based on morphology. Attenuation and mobility. Eur. J. Radiol. **82**, 1177–1186 (2013)
3. Neri, E., Lefere, P., Gryspeerdt, S., et al.: Bowel preparation for CT colonography. Eur. J. Radiol. **82**, 1137–1143 (2013)
4. Näppi, J., Yoshida, H.: Adaptive correction of the pseudo-enhancement of CT attenuation for fecal-tagging CT colonography. Med. Image Anal. **12**, 413–426 (2008)
5. Regge, D., Halligan, S.: CAD: how it works, how to use it, performance. Eur. J. Radiol. **82** (8), 1171–1176 (2013)
6. Zhang, H., Li, L., Zhu, H., et al.: Integration of 3D scale-based pseudo-enhancement correction and partial volume image segmentation for improving electronic colon cleansing in CT colonography. J. Xray Sci. Technol. **22**, 271–283 (2014)
7. Johnson, T., Fink, C., Schönberg, S.O., Reiser, M.F.: Dual Energy CT in Clinical Practice. Springer, Heidelberg (2011)
8. Yu, L., Leng, S., McCollough, C.H.: Dual-energy CT-based monochromatic imaging. AJR Am. J. Roentgenol. **199**, S9–S15 (2012)
9. Heismann, B.J., Schmidt, B.T., Flohr, T.G.: Spectral computed tomography. SPIE Press Book, Bellingham (2012)
10. Berger, M.J., Hubbell, J.H., Seltzer, S.M., et al.: NIST Standard Reference Database. http://www.nist.gov/pml/data/xcom/index.cfm
11. Kalra, M.K., Woisetschläger, M., Dahlström, N., et al.: Radiation dose reduction with sinogram affirmed iterative reconstruction technique for abdominal computed tomography. J. Comput. Assist. Tomogr. **36**, 339–346 (2012)

12. Cai, W., Zhang, D., Shirai, Y., et al.: Dual-energy index value of luminal air in fecal-tagging CT colonography: findings and impact on electronic cleansing. J. Comput. Assist. Tomogr. **37**(2), 183–194 (2013)

13. Eliahou, R., Azraq, Y., Carmi, R., et al.: Dual-energy based spectral electronic cleansing in non-cathartic computed tomography colonography: an emerging novel technique. Semin. Ultrasound CT MRI **31**, 309–314 (2010)

14. Brenner, D.J., Hall, E.J.: Computed tomography–an increasing source of radiation exposure. N. Engl. J. Med. **357**, 2277–2284 (2007)

A Novel Minimal Surface Overlay Model for the Whole Colon Wall Segmentation

Huafeng Wang[1,2(✉)], Wenfeng Song[1], Katherine Wei[3], Yuan Cao[4],
Haixia Pan[1], Ming Ma[2], Jiang Huang[1], Guangming Mao[1],
and Zhengrong Liang[2]

[1] School of Software, Beihang University of Beijing, Beijing 10083, China
wanghuafengbuaa@gmail.com
[2] Department of Radiology, Stony Brook University, Stony Brook, NY 11794, USA
[3] Stuyvesant High School, New York, NY 10282, USA
[4] Civil Aviation Medicine Institute, Civil Aviation Medicine Center
(Civil Aviation General Hospital), Beijing 10000, China

Abstract. To segment the boundary of both inner and outer colon wall is of much significance for colonic polyps detection in computed tomographic colonography (CTC). However, the low contrast of CT attenuation values between colon wall and the surrounding tissues limits many traditional algorithms to achieve this task. Moreover, when sticking presents between two colon walls, the task turns to be much more complicated and the threshold level set segmentation method may fail in this situation. In view of this, we present a minimum surface overlay model to extract the inner wall in this paper. Combined with the superposition model, we are able to depict the outer wall of colon in a natural way. We validated the proposed algorithm based on 60 CTC datasets. Compared with the golden standard (the manual drawing by experts), the new presented method achieved with more than 95 % overlapping coverage rate (OCR).

Keywords: Colonic wall · Computed tomography colonography (CTC) · Levelset · Minimum surface overlay model

1 Introduction

According to the recent statistics from American Cancer Society (ACS) [1], colorectal cancer ranks the third most common occurrence of both cancer deaths and new cancer cases for both men and women in the United States. With the help of the computer assisted detection (CADe) and the computer assisted diagnosis (CADx)the colorectal cancer diagnosis process shall be facilitated. As shown in Fig. 1, segmenting the inner and outer wall from the CT volume will help in determining potential polyps, muscular hypertrophy and diverticulitis of the colon [1]. And the accuracy of the segmentation also has effect on the sensitivity and specificity of the performance of CADe. There are many colon inner wall segmentation algorithms presented in literature during the past decades,

© Springer International Publishing Switzerland 2014
H. Yoshida et al. (Eds.): ABDI 2014, LNCS 8676, pp. 179–187, 2014.
DOI: 10.1007/978-3-319-13692-9_17

such as MAP-EM [2], levelset [3,4], etc. With respect to the outer wall segmentation of colon, [5] proposed to exploit a single thresholding levelset (STL) to achieve the target. However, the STL method may fail when the wall sticking happened and the method dramatically relies on how good the inner wall is extracted.

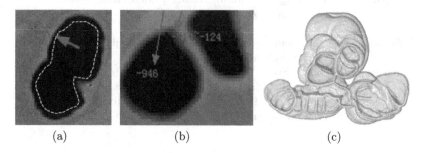

(a)   (b)   (c)

Fig. 1. The illustration of the colon wall: (a) green curve indicates the outer wall; yellow curve indicates the inner wall; (b) one slice of colon wall, where the corresponding CT attenuation has been shown; (c) 3D rendering of colon wall (Color figure online).

In literature, there exist two main approaches to segment the outer colon wall: (1) R. Van Uitert et al. proposed to exploit a two steps method based on the geodesic active contour (GAC) model [6]. The GAC model is good at keeping the shape, but it will deform when encounter the screwy point or the voxel with high curvature. As a result, some fractures on the point will happen when the contrast changes; (2) M. E. Zalis et al. suggested to apply a morphological model for calculation of outer colon wall [7], which is based on morphological structural elements. However, due to the fixation of the shape of the structural elements, it may cause merging phenomenon between the adjacent boundaries. And a mixed tissue distribution or partial-volume effects (PVE) existing in CT images impose challenges for accurately segmentation of outer colon wall [5,8]. In view of this, we presented a new 3D model in this paper. The remainder of this paper is organized as follows. The introduction of the new model is presented in Sect. 2; In order to validate the model, the implementation and experiment results are reported in Sect. 3. In Sect. 4, discussion and conclusions about the new algorithms are given.

2 Methods

The outer colon wall is known as the outer layer of colon wall, same as that the inner wall is actually the inner layer of colon. Regions between the outer wall and the inner wall are filled with mucous membrane and muscles. The segmentation of the outer wall needs to take fully consideration of the lumen, the inner wall of colon, and the synechiae outside the inner wall due to the spatial relationships among them. Figure 2 shows a flowchart of the proposed colon wall segmentation pipeline. The whole pipeline uses the following operations: (1) Electronic colon cleansing (ECC), (2) get the inner colon wall, (3) Extraction of outer colon wall. Figure 3 shows the outputs for each step.

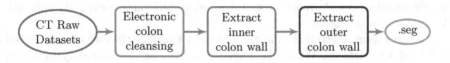

Fig. 2. The pipeline for the proposed colon wall segmentation method.

The ECC process (as opposed to physical cleansing of the bowels) allows removal of tagged intraluminal remains. In this paper, we applied the MAP-EM [9] algorithm for achieving ECC.

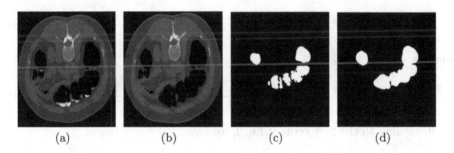

Fig. 3. (a) One slice of the original CT image; (b) The corresponding slice after ECC; (c) The extracted inner colon wall; (d) The outer colon wall mask.

2.1 Minimal Surface Overlay Level Set Model for Extracting the Inner Wall

In order to eliminate the artifacts brought by PVE and noise, we introduced 3D minimal surface overlay model (MSOM) and more details are given below. Given a CT abdomen volume Ω, we define an edge indicator g [7].

$$g \triangleq 1/(1 + |\nabla G_\sigma * I|^2) \tag{1}$$

where G_σ is a Gaussian kernel with a standard deviation. The convolution is used to smooth the image to reduce the noise. The function g usually takes smaller values at object boundaries than at other locations.

Then, we have ϕ in $R_3 \to \Re$, and,

$$
\begin{aligned}
E(\phi) &= \mu R_p(\phi) + \alpha A_g(\phi) + \beta \nu_g(\phi) \\
&= \frac{1}{2}\mu \iint_\Omega (|\nabla\phi| - 1)^2 \mathrm{d}s + \alpha \iint_\Omega g\delta_\varepsilon(\phi)|\nabla\phi|\mathrm{d}s + \beta \iint_\Omega gH_\varepsilon(-\phi)\mathrm{d}s
\end{aligned}
\tag{2}
$$

where $E(\phi)$ is an energy functional, ϕ is an initialized area, μ is distance term which controls the diffusing speed and μ equals to 0.2/timespan in this paper. $R_p(\phi)$ is a distance term, $A_g(\phi)$ is an area term, $\nu_g(\phi)$ is a volume term, α is a constant and $\alpha > 0, \alpha \in R$; δ_ε is the Dirac function and H_ε is the Heaviside function [7]; β is used to control evolution direction: When $\beta > 0$, the initialized surface shrinks inward; When $\beta < 0$, the initialized surface expands outward; When $\beta = 0$, it will stop.

The area term $A_g(\phi)$ is the integral of level set surface after we parameterized zero level set surfaces. When the level set arrives at the boundary of target surface, the area term is with a smallest value. The term of $\nu_g(\phi)$ is the volume term of energy function and we need to compute the weighted volume of the region $\Omega_\phi \triangleq \{(x, y, z) : \phi(x, y, z) < 0\}$. When g equals to one, the energy term is exactly the volume of the region Ω_ϕ. In order to accelerate the evolution of zero level set, its necessary to use the volume term $\nu_g(\phi)$ when the distance between the initialized surface and the target surface is a bit far. Generally, given a potential function p, we have,

$$p(s) \triangleq \frac{1}{2}(s(x, y, z) - 1)^2 \tag{3}$$

where $s = |\nabla\phi|$, thus,

$$p'(s) \triangleq \frac{\partial p(s)}{\partial x} + \frac{\partial p(s)}{\partial y} + \frac{\partial p(s)}{\partial z}, \text{and } d_p(s) \triangleq \frac{p'(s)}{s} \tag{4}$$

Regarding to the first term of Eq. 2, we have,

$$\frac{\partial R_p}{\partial \phi} = -div(d_p(\nabla\phi(x, y, z))\nabla\phi(x, y, z)) \tag{5}$$

Then, by solving its Euler equation we can obtain its gradient descent flow.

$$\frac{\partial \phi}{\partial t} = \mu div(d_p(|\nabla\phi|\nabla\phi)) + \lambda\delta_\varepsilon(\phi)div(g\frac{\nabla\phi}{|\nabla\phi|}) + kg\delta_\varepsilon(\phi) \tag{6}$$

where ϕ is an initialized area. The bigger the time step is, the faster the surface evolves. However, if time step is too big, it might result in errors presented on contour surface. In order to guarantee its stability, we usually use $\Delta t < 0.25$ for most images, $|.|$ means module of vector, δ_ε is a dirac function, g is an edge indicator, and μ, λ, k are coefficient factors.

In implementing the traditional level set methods, it is numerically necessary to keep the evolving level set function close to a signed distance function [3]. Previously, most of the level set methods are fraught with their own problems, such as when and how to re-initialize the level set function to a signed distance function [3]. Fortunately, the variational level set formulation proposed in this paper can be easily implemented by taking a distance item, without the need of re-initialization. Since to minimize the distance item will keep the surface evolving around the target, our proposed model turns to be more efficient.

2.2 An Adaptive Model for the Segmentation of the Outer Colon Wall

Intuitively, the boundaries among the different tissues all have impacts on the determination of the evolution directions and amplifications. And as we know, the first term of the Eq. 6 above is a diffusion equation. Since the diffusion equation in physics also meets well with superposition principle, we applied this theory to the task of outer colon wall segmentation.

By the diffusion equation, the segmentation process will terminate in accordance with the shape of the colon outer wall. As shown in Fig. 4, the force between the adjacent outer wall data is opposite, providing the repulsion for other particles adjacent to them.

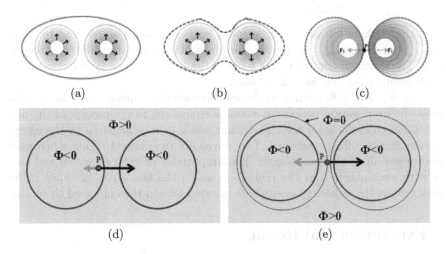

Fig. 4. The diffusion model and evolution analysis: (a) The initial status of the iteration: green circle and blue circle stand for actual boundaries of two adjacent objects, and the red eclipse is the initial levelset; (b) The red dotted circle stands for the outputted boundaries given by the traditional levelset algorithm; (c) The red dotted circles illustrated the results achieved by our proposed algorithm; (d) An illustration of the force unbalanced; and (e) An illustration of that the forces have achieved balance and P is the voxel in the zero levelset (Color figure online).

As shown in Fig. 4(c), when we come to the force analysis of an arbitrary given particle P on the left part, it suffers from the repulsion from the blue region with the magnitude F_2, and is opposite to the expansion force F_1 as shown in Fig. 4(c). In view of the forces from the two contrary directions, we build a new energy functional according to Eq. 2 as shown in the following form,

$$E(\phi, I_1, I_2) = \mu \iint_\Omega (|\nabla\phi| - 1)^2 ds + \alpha_1 A_{g_1(I_1)}(\phi) + \beta_1 \nu_{g_1(I_1)}(\phi)$$
$$+ \alpha_2 A_{g_2(I_2)}(\phi) + \beta_2 \nu_{g_2(I_2)}(\phi) \tag{7}$$

where ϕ is initialized with the inner wall of the colon, I_1 is the inputting target volume, and I_2 is the constructed neighbor regions which contains undetermined voxel. The rest symbols have the same meanings as described above.

When the energy functional comes to the maximum value, the evolution will generate the stable boundaries. According to the superposition principle of PDE and Eq. 6, we have the equation below for calculating its gradient descent flow,

$$\frac{\partial\phi(I_1, I_2)}{\partial t} = 2\mu div(d_p(|\nabla\phi|)\nabla\phi) + \overbrace{\lambda_1\delta_\varepsilon(\phi)div(g_1(I_1) \cdot \frac{\nabla\phi}{|\nabla\phi|}) + k_1g_1(I_1) \cdot \delta_\varepsilon(\phi)}^{F_{outerward}}$$

$$\underbrace{+ \lambda_2\delta_\varepsilon(\phi)div(g_2(I_2) \cdot \frac{\nabla\phi}{|\nabla\phi|}) + k_2g_2(I_2) \cdot \delta_\varepsilon(\phi)}_{F_{innerward}} \tag{8}$$

where the explanation of the signs could be found above as referred to Eq. 6. $F_{innerward}$ and $F_{outerward}$ stand for the forces with contrary directions respectively. The diffusion control factor $k : k_1 < 0$ means the force goes outward and $k_2 > 0$ means the force goes inner ward.

As shown in Fig. 6, similar to the interference phenomenon with interaction forces, the propagation process of waves is equivalent to the process of the outward diffusion of the inner wall. The propagation process is driven by the energy function and it diffuses outward. The waves are in subdued region when their distance is half of the wavelength. The amplitudes of the two waves will subdue with each other. And the regions in which the two waves distance is one wavelength is the enhanced one, which always stays in the enhanced situation.

3   Experiment and Result

We selected a CTC database of 30 patients with 60 CT scans from both supine and prone positions from the Wisconsin hospital. All the selected datasets are in the DICOM formats, and most of their number of slice is between 480 and 700. Because the overall performance of the ECC technique of colon inner wall has been discussed in our recently work [9], in this paper, we focus on validating the segmentation of both inner and outer colon wall. Since the parameters applied to the experiment are of much significance on the evaluation of the proposed algorithm, we listed the suggested values of parameters as shown in Table 1. All the listed parameters are determined according to the experimental comparison.

Table 1. The parameter selection for the experiment.

	λ	μ	k	Iteration times
Inner wall extraction	5.0	0.1	−3	10
Outer wall extraction	5.0	0.15	−10	40

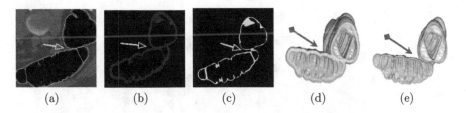

Fig. 5. Comparison of the GAC method and the proposed adaptive MSOM method: (a) the original CT slice where yellow arrow shows the region of interest of merging, and the green color indicates the out layer of colon wall drawn by MD; (b) the segmented result by the GAC method; (c) the segmented result given by adaptive MSOM; (d) the corresponding local 3D visualization of colon wall produced by GAC; (e) the corresponding local 3D visualization of colon wall generated by the adaptive MSOM (Color figure online).

With respect to the challenges currently faced by many previous methods for the colon outer wall segmentation, we will discuss the related topics in the following sections. As discussed in the introduction section, the new method should be robust to the noise, PVE and the merging effects (ME). The evaluation on the sensitivity to noise and PVE shall be conducted by comparison between the results given by the experts' manually drawing and the proposed automatic method. In order to give a quantitative measure, Receiver Operating Characteristics (ROC) graph is exploited for visualizing their performance. For the convenience, we call the proposed MSOM plus superposition model as MSOM for simplification.

Comparing with the GAC method, MSOM is capable of preserving the natural shape of the colon wall as indicated by red arrows in Fig. 5(e). Meantime, as indicated by the green arrow in Fig. 6, the merging happened when we applied the GAC method as indicated by the green arrow; whereas for the MSOM method, it is capable of extracting a clear outer colon wall.

As discussed in [10], without giving any restriction on the g values, as well as possible gaps in the boundary, the propagating curve is not guaranteed to stop. This makes the GAC model inappropriate for the detection of boundaries with unknown high variations of the gradients. While for the MSOM, the two directional forces can direct the propagating surface into the valley of the g function. As a result, the directional forces lead the propagating surface into the boundary and eventually force it to converge.

To address the performance of our proposed algorithm, we made a comparison between the manually drawing by experts and the automatic one. We defined the overlapping voxels between the manually drawing and the automatic method as true positive (TP). And the variance between the number of the total voxels given by the automatic method and the overlapping number is regarded as false positive (FP). The same parameters were also applied to the GAC method for a comparison. The ROC curve is shown in the Fig. 7. The new proposed MSOM have demonstrated a better performance.

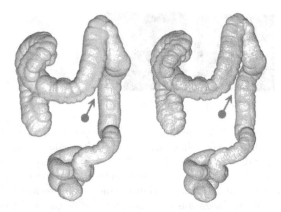

Fig. 6. Comparison of 3D visualization of outer colon wall by the GAC method (left) and the proposed adaptive MSOM method (right).

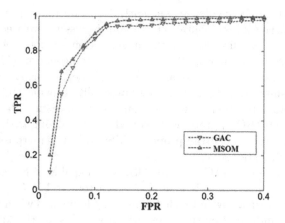

Fig. 7. The ROC curve for GAC and MSOM.

4   Discussion and Conclusion

Experimental results demonstrated that the new proposed MSOM is able to segment the inner and outer colon wall with a better performance than that of GAC model. As stated in previous work [10]: in cases in which there are different gradient values along the edge, as often happens in real images, the GAC model will work inappropriate for the detection of boundaries with high variations of the gradients. As a result, the GAC model will result in an exceptional stop in the Concave data set as shown in Fig. 8.

On the other hand, the proposed MSOM model aims at minimizing a surface in 3D. As stated above, the first term in Eq. 2 will keep the ϕ close to the boundaries and the second term will give a force to pull the ϕ inward or outward during the evolution. Based on the experiment results of the ROC curve, we draw a conclusion that the concave will be better fitted by using the MSOM after iterations. In future, we will work on the whole wall for extracting any effective 3D features [11] to identify the polyps.

Fig. 8. The evolution process demonstration of GAC: object need to be segmented (left) and the GAC process (right): The red rectangle shows the concave area where GAC model often fails; the black is the result generated by GAC model.

Acknowledgments. This work was partially supported by the NIH/NCI under Grant #CA143111, #CA082402, and the PSC-CUNY award #65230-00 43.

References

1. ACS: Cancer facts & figures. American Cancer Society (2013)
2. Wang, H., Li, L., Song, B., Han, F., Liang, Z.: A shape constrained map-em algorithm for colorectal segmentation. In: SPIE Medical Imaging, p. 86702F. International Society for Optics and Photonics (2013)
3. Fedkiw, S.O.R.: Level Set Methods and Dynamic Implicit Surfaces. Springer, New York (2003)
4. Li, C., Xu, C., Gui, C., Fox, M.D.: Distance regularized level set evolution and its application to image segmentation. IEEE Trans. Image Process. **19**, 3243–3254 (2010)
5. Van Uitert, R.L., Summers, R.M.: Colonic wall thickness using level sets for CT virtual colonoscopy visual assessment and polyp detection. In: Medical Imaging, p. 65110S. International Society for Optics and Photonics (2007)
6. Van Uitert, R., Bitter, I., Summers, R.: Detection of colon wall outer boundary and segmentation of the colon wall based on level set methods. In: 28th Annual International Conference of the IEEE Engineering in Medicine and Biology Society, EMBS'06, pp. 3017–3020. IEEE (2006)
7. Zalis, M.E., Perumpillichira, J., Hahn, P.F.: Digital subtraction bowel cleansing for CT colonography using morphological and linear filtration methods. IEEE Trans. Med. Imaging **23**, 1335–1343 (2004)
8. Soret, M., Bacharach, S.L., Buvat, I.: Partial-volume effect in PET tumor imaging. J. Nucl. Med. **48**, 932–945 (2007)
9. Zhang, H., Li, L., Zhu, H., Han, H., Song, B., Liang, Z.: Integration of 3D scale-based pseudo-enhancement correction and partial volume image segmentation for improving electronic colon cleansing in CT colonograpy. J. X-ray Sci. Technol. **22**, 271–283 (2014)
10. Sapiro, G.: Geometric Partial Differential Equations and Image Analysis. Cambridge University Press, Cambridge (2006)
11. Yoshida, H., Nappi, J.: Three-dimensional computer-aided diagnosis scheme for detection of colonic polyps. IEEE Trans. Med. Imaging **20**, 1261–1274 (2001)

A Unified Framework for Automated Colon Segmentation

Marwa Ismail[1(✉)], Aly Farag[1], Salwa Elshzaly[1,2], Robert Curtin[1,2], and Robert Falk[3]

[1] Computer Vision and Image Processing Laboratory,
University of Louisville, Louisville, KY, USA
marwa.tawfik@k-space.org
[2] Kentucky Imaging Technologies, Louisville, KY, USA
[3] 3DR, Inc., Louisville, KY, USA

Abstract. This paper proposes a complete framework for 3D colon segmentation, including detection of its outer walls. Outer wall detection is a challenging problem due to its poor contrast with other structures appearing in the abdominal scans, especially small bowels and other fatty structures. Missing outer walls could severely affect detection of polyps; indicators of colon cancer. A completely automated framework was developed based on level sets as an initial phase of segmentation to extract the lumen. This phase is followed by discarding non-colonic structures. Outer walls of the colon are then detected, and finally the 3d convex active contour model is used to combine the results of both lumen and outer walls. The technique was tested on 30 colon computed tomography (CT) scans and proved effective in both outer walls and polyp detection. The accuracy of the proposed framework is up to 98.94 %.

Keywords: Colonoscopy · Lumen · Colon walls · Convex active contour model · Polyps · Shape index · Curvedness · Haustral folds

1 Introduction

Colon cancer has become one of the leading causes of death in the world and it has been shown by studies that early detection increases the chances of its cure. Virtual Colonoscopy (VC) has emerged as a successful screening method that provides many advantages. Being non-invasive, it prevents complications provided by optical colonoscopy [1]. VC is the current gold standard for screening polyps; the primary cause of cancer [2].

Colon segmentation greatly affects subsequent steps. There are many potential problems that impair accurate colon segmentation, Fig. 1. In practice, contrast agents are injected into patients in order to tag the colon for aiding physicians to visualize hidden parts of its surface [3]. The contrast agent (CA) usually resides into the colon's lower concave parts, disconnecting it into fluid and air parts, and an air-fluid boundary (AFB) region is formed. CA also leaks to small bowels that have similar tomographic appearance to that of colon, which hardens colon extraction [4–6]. Insufflation by the CA might result in under-distended colon, collapsing it into multiple segments.

© Springer International Publishing Switzerland 2014
H. Yoshida et al. (Eds.): ABDI 2014, LNCS 8676, pp. 188–198, 2014.
DOI: 10.1007/978-3-319-13692-9_18

Previous problems appear within the colon inner surface, also known as the lumen. Anatomically, there is also an outer surface that is known as the tissue-serosa boundary. The colonic wall lies between these two surfaces, Fig. 1. The colon's outer surface is hard to detect due to its low contrast with the surrounding fatty structures in CT scans. In addition to its significance in determining some diseases such as Diverticulosis [7], polyps attaching to outer wall will be missed later if the outer wall is not detected.

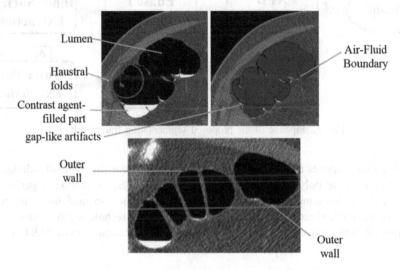

Fig. 1. Colon segments that show: the lumen with leakage of the contrast agent into its lower part, the winding structure caused by haustral folds (HF), air-fluid boundary (AFB) that disconnects colon segments (shown in blue), gap-like artifacts. Finally, colon outer wall which has poor contrast with the surroundings is shown (Color figure online).

2 Review of Colon Segmentation Techniques

There has been extensive work on the literature for lumen segmentation. Earlier techniques for incorporated region growing with morphological operations and anatomical information [8–10]. This approach fails to handle the local intensity changes of colon and leads to broken segments. Other approaches have employed deformable models, such as in [11]. These methods have their own parameters that should handle the variations of local intensity of colon and thus fail to achieve expected results. These same problems exist with level-set based techniques which are very sensitive to initialization [12]. Reference [13] presents a centerline-based method. The method uses a computed centerline for all anatomic structures in CT along with anatomical information in order to discard non-colonic structures. However, this is very sensitive to centerline computation.

There has not been much work on the detection of colon outer surface, which is necessary for outer surface extraction. Reference [14] introduced a CAD system in an effort to reduce false positives of detected polyps on colon walls. The system developed a global curvature term to detect walls. The authors of [15, 16], extracted the outer surface using a 3D geodesic active contour model. This work was adopted in [17] to generate a geodesic distance map for the lumen. The ball filter technique then removed the fused areas of the walls.

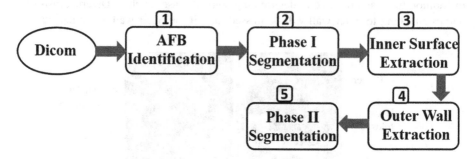

Fig. 2. Pipeline of the proposed segmentation framework.

This paper proposes an automated segmentation technique that will aid radiologists to accurately locate polyps and diagnose other diseases. Segmentation is performed using a hybrid technique for extracting both the lumen surface and the outer wall. The proposed method reduces false positives compared to techniques that extract only the lumen. Results prove the segmentation to be highly accurate (up to 98.94 %).

3   Methods

The proposed colon segmentation method is multi-staged. The five main stages of it are: (1) detection of air-fluid boundary (AFB) that disconnects colon segments; (2) phase I segmentation using adaptive level sets to extract all air segments; (3) use of geometric and anatomic information to segment colon lumen; (4) detection of outer wall that is initialized from lumen surface; and, (5) phase II segmentation using convex formulation of the active contour model to combine both the lumen and outer wall seamlessly (Fig. 2).

3.1   AFB Detection

The framework starts with detection of air-fluid boundary (AFB). AFB is detected based on the information that it is anatomically located between air-filled and fluid-filled colon parts, Fig. 1, with a thickness that does not exceed 2 voxels [18]. Based on these 2 criteria, we locate the air-filled parts and the fluid-filled parts, then search for AFB based on the thickness and location between the two parts. Unfortunately, this operation is not satisfactory due to the appearance of gap-like artifacts between fluid-filled and air-filled parts, Figs. 1, 3(b). Hence a sphere is generated with its center at each detected AFB point, so that the gaps are guaranteed to be closed.

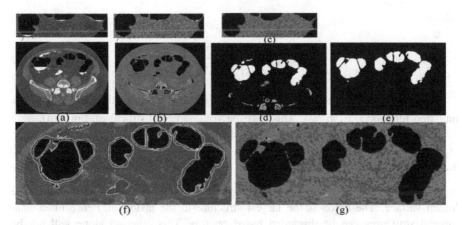

Fig. 3. Illustration of the pipeline of the proposed segmentation framework. (a) A typical CT slice of the abdomen. (b) Result of cleansing from (Sect. 3.1), where AFB is partially detected and fluid-filled parts are set to air intensity. (c) Applying spherical detectors for better AFB detection. (d) Result of level-set segmentation from (Sect. 3.2), where all air-filled structures are detected (colon in white, small bowels in green, and bony areas in pink). (e) Result from (Sect. 3.3), where non-colonic structures are discarded using geometrical and anatomical features. (f) Initializing search for outer wall. HF points (areas in orange) are not involved. All other edge points are involved. The few arrows here are just for illustrating the idea. (g) Result of applying convex formulation of active contour model, where outer wall points are combined with lumen surface. Zoomed in area of colon segments after the final phase of segmentation is shown.

The detected AFB, colon fluid-filled parts, the small bowels with contrast leakage, the lungs, and bony areas in the volume (ribs, spine) are then set to air intensity in order to get consistent colon segments. Figure 3(c) shows results of a typical cleansing process.

3.2 Phase I Segmentation

3D adaptive level sets technique is used to extract all bright structures in the volume [12]. The technique uses bimodal model (for background and foreground structures) with Gaussian distribution. The level set equation is:

$$\Phi(t + \Delta t) = \Phi(t) - F\Delta t |\nabla\Phi|, \tag{1}$$

where $|\nabla\Phi|$ is the norm of the gradient of the curve Φ, and $F = \pm 1 - \varepsilon k$ is the speed function, where K stands for curvature, and ε is the parameter controlling the bending of the curve.

For each class i, whether it is background or foreground, the classification at each voxel is based on the Bayesian criteria:

$$i^*(x) = \arg(max_{i=1,2}(\pi_i P_i(I(x)))), \tag{2}$$

where

$$\pi_i = \frac{\int H_\alpha(\Phi_i)dx}{\sum_{i=1}^{2}\int H_\alpha(\Phi_i)dx},$$ (3)

And H_α is the Heaviside step function as a smoothed differentiable version of the unit step function $\sum_{i=1}^{2}\pi_i = 1$. This gets the volume bright structures, Fig. 3(d).

3.3 Lumen Surface Extraction

Anatomic and geometric features are incorporated in this stage in order to extract the lumen surface. The colon is the largest structure in the abdomen, hence other anatomical structures can be discarded based on this. This criterion alone will not be helpful; however, in case of poorly distended colon. Geometric features are thus added to assure that non-colonic structures are discarded efficiently. The sacculations (also known as haustral folds) that the colon forms due to contraction of taeniae coli, are characteristic features that distinguish it from all other abdominal structures. Haustral folds are deep cervices, Fig. 1, that has some distinctive geometric measures such as its mean curvature which is high compared to other surface points [18]. Lumen surface is extracted based on size and curvature. Figure 3(e) shows results from this stage.

3.4 Outer Wall Initial Detection

The system starts detection of the outer wall from the lumen surface in order to reduce false positives. The outer wall is initially detected by calculating the normal vectors to each colon lumen point. Those initialized vectors continue propagation until an abrupt change in contrast occurs. Propagating normal vectors from all lumen points leads to erroneous results, as it eventually will close the gaps naturally caused by haustral folds, Fig. 4, which distorts the anatomic structure of the colon. Thus haustral folds must not participate in outer wall detection. This requires accurate identification of all folds

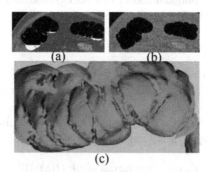

Fig. 4. (a) 2 colon segments. (b) Initializing normal vectors from all surface points drastically changes the anatomy of the colon. Most of the deep cervices of haustral folds are closed. (c) 3D reconstruction of the left segment in (b), where surface appears jittery and HF are distorted.

points. This was not needed in Sect. 3.3, as it was then used just to prove whether a segment was part of a colon or not based on the curved nature of the segment.

3.4.1   Haustral Fold Identification

Geometric measures are initially used to extract haustral folds (HF) candidates. In [19], shape index (SI) was used with a value of 0.7 for initially determining HF points. This criterion is not robust, Fig. 5(a), due to collecting many outliers, thus getting false positives in detection. Combining SI and the curvedness measure (CV) greatly reduces such false positives. This however does not guarantee getting all HF points and might get some false candidates as well. Typical values for HF points are 0.7 and 0.35 for SI and CV respectively [20]. To reduce the chances of false positives, the search starts with higher values; 0.85 and 0.45 respectively. Points satisfying this condition (strong HF candidates) are clustered based on connected component algorithm, and a bounding box centered at each cluster centroid is initiated as shown in Fig. 5(b). The dimensions of this box are the width and the length of a typical fold. From our experiments on 20 colonic data sets, the fold length spans no more than 15 pixels and its width spans no more than 8 pixels. Each point within this box is tested and accepted as HF point if SI > 0.7, and CV > 0.35. This search strategy greatly reduces false positives and correctly locates HF candidate points, Fig. 5(c).

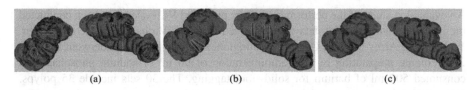

Fig. 5. (a) Using SI >= 0.7 for excluding folds points gets many outliers as the ones highlighted. (b) Using SI > 0.8 and CV > 0.45 to get strong candidates for initializing the search for HF points from. The search is within the experimental values of the fold dimensions. Minimum value for SI is 0.7 and is 0.35 for CV. (c) Final HF points candidates.

3.5   Phase II Segmentation

In order to obtain smooth and seamless surface, both the lumen and the outer wall need to be detected robustly [21]. The detected fold points are not involved in the search for outer wall, Fig. 3(f). In this phase, the convex formulation of the active contour model is employed for segmentation. This model is particularly of interest here because it proved to be efficient for detecting boundaries based on large image gradients, as it provides the link between the active contour without edges model (ACWE) and geodesic active contour model (GAC) with an edge indicator function [21]. It is also very sensitive to poor contrast changes [21]. The input to this phase is the CT slices with the cleansed colon, Fig. 3(c), where the fold points of the lumen are now well-known. These fold candidates are marked with an intensity value that is far from the range of that of lumen and outer wall in order to be excluded from the process. In this paper, the proposed technique in [21] is extended to the 3D case for the final phase of segmentation, where lumen surface is combined with the outer wall seamlessly as shown, Fig. 3(g).

The following energy function is optimized in 3D:

$$E_1(u, c_1, c_2, \lambda) = TV_g(u) + \lambda \int r_1(x, c_1, c_2)u\,dx \tag{4}$$

$$r_1(x, c_1, c_2) = ((c_1 - f(x))^2 - (c_1 - f(x))^2) \tag{5}$$

f is the given image, λ is a positive parameter controlling the tradeoff between regularization process and fidelity of solution with respect to f and $c_1, c_2 \in R$. $TV_g(u)$ is the weighted total variation that convexifies the energy function [21]. Since c_1, c_2 can take any values at the interval $[0, 1]$ due to the convex nature of the problem, this helped combining both the lumen and the outer wall seamlessly through an exhaustive search for the best values. Any false attachments with surrounding fatty structures were then discarded using the fact that the outer wall thickness is 4–6 mm from the lumen surface. The algorithm converges at 200 iterations, and best results are at $\lambda = 0.001$.

4 Experimental Results

An evaluation study of the performance of the proposed VC system has been conducted on 30 colon data sets. The data were received from the Virtual Colonoscopy Center, Walter Reed Army Medical Center, Washington, DC. The patients underwent standard 24-h colonic preparation by oral administration of 90 ml of sodium phosphate and consumed 500 ml of barium for solid-stool tagging. The 30 sets include 35 polyps. Ground truth was constructed for all sets with the aid of two gastroenterologists. The proposed segmentation framework is first compared to [12], where colon is extracted using adaptive level sets, ignoring the outer wall. This is to emphasize the importance of outer wall detection and subsequently polyp detection. Quantitative validation was carried out based on the measures of accuracy, sensitivity, and specificity of each technique with respect to ground truth.

Table 1 shows the improvement in measures after detecting the outer wall points and adding them to get the entire colon surface.

Table 1. Comparison results of the two segmentation techniques in terms of soft tissue preservation

Technique / Measure	Lumen-only Segmentation	Proposed Framework
Accuracy	92%	98.94%
Sensitivity	93.7%	98.7%
Specificity	90.0%	96.5%

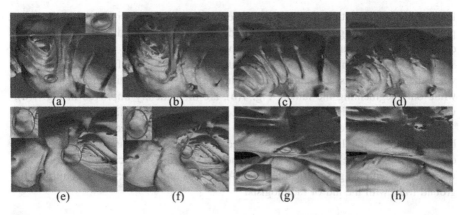

Fig. 6. Results of the proposed framework (a, c, e, g) vs. the lumen-only segmentation (b, d, f, h) where the walls are better constructed and the broken parts are remedied. 2 flat polyps in (a), (g) are detected and a false positive (f) was correctly identified as a thick fold in (e). HF are far better preserved with the proposed technique. This is because lumen-only segmentation neglected many surface points at the cleansing stage in Sect. 3.1 when they failed to achieve the intensity criterion for inversion form fluid-filled parts to air-filled parts, leading to incomplete surfaces as shown.

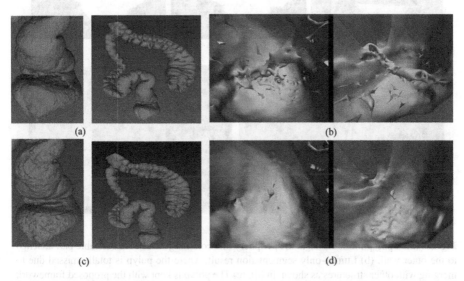

Fig. 7. (a) 3D model result of the segmented colon in [12]. The proposed framework provides better results as shown in (c), where more details are visible on the surface at the zoomed in area. (b) shows the internal structure from the lumen-only segmentation where some parts are severely broken. Adding wall points enhanced the construction of the colon as shown in (d).

Figure 6(b, d, f, h) show results of the segmentation framework where the colon walls are better constructed than extracting the lumen only as in Fig. 6(a, c, e, g). Two flat polyps were missed when the lumen only was segmented, but survived with the proposed framework, Fig. 6(a, g). Also Fig. 6(e) shows a case where the lumen-only segmentation resulted in a false positive that was eliminated by the proposed framework, Fig. 6(f), and identified as a thickened fold. All findings were confirmed by an experienced radiologist from ground truth.

Figure 7 shows an example of the significant improvement of colon segmentation when the outer wall is combined with the lumen. The broken parts that were notable while only segmenting the lumen, Fig. 7(b), are dramatically improved in Fig. 7(d), where the outer wall is effectively combined with the lumen surface.

Figure 8 shows a case, where the polyp shown in the CT slice was merged with a haustral fold in the lumen-only segmented set. The polyp was totally lost in the detection process. The proposed technique helped keep the spherical structure of it, and was detected with the geometrical features. All polyps findings were to be confirmed by ground truth with the aid of radiologists.

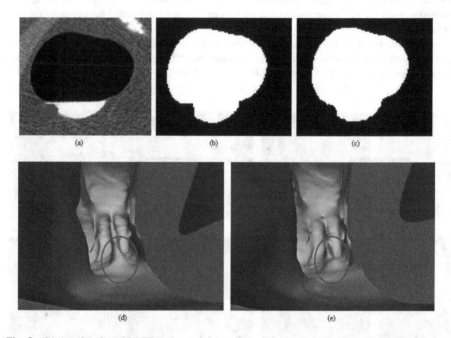

Fig. 8. (a) A polyp found in CT at the periphery of a colon segment, with a notable part attached to the outer wall. (b) Lumen-only segmentation result, where the polyp is totally missed due to merging with other structures as shown in (d). (c) The polyp is kept with the proposed framework as shown in (e).

5   Conclusions and Future Work

This paper proposes a fully automated system for colon segmentation that aims at aiding physicians in accurately screening polyps; colon cancer indicators. The proposed segmentation method combines both the lumen and outer wall segmentation with an accuracy that is up to 98.94 %. Having an accurate knowledge of the colon thickness is important for certain diseases, and this emphasizes the importance of outer wall detection. Future work aims at comparing the proposed outer wall detection technique to other techniques proposed in literature and to validate it on some clinically related cases such as detection of diverticulosis disease.

References

1. Nappi, J., Yoshida, H.: Feature-guided analysis for reduction of false positives in CAD of polyps for computed tomographic colonography. Med. Phys. **30**(7), 1592–1601 (2003)
2. Abbruzzese, J., Pollock, R.: Gastrointestinal Cancer. Springer, Heidelberg (2004)
3. Pineau, B., et al.: Virtual colonoscopy using oral contrast compared with colonoscopy for the detection of patients with colorectal polyps. Gastroenterology **125**(2), 304–310 (2003)
4. Li, H., Santago, P.: Automatic colon segmentation with dual scan CT colonography. J. Dig. Imag. **18**, 42–54 (2005)
5. Li, X., Liang, Z., Zhang, P., Kutcher, G.: An accurate colon residue detection algorithm with partial volume segmentation. In: SPIE, pp. 1419–1426 (2004)
6. Chen, D., Liang, Z., Wax, M., Li, L., Li, B., Kaufman, A.: A Novel approach to extract colon lumen from CT images for virtual colonoscopy. IEEE Trans. Med. Imag. **19**(12), 1220–1226 (2000)
7. http://www.fascrs.org/patients/conditions/diverticular_disease/
8. Wyatt, C.L., Ge, Y., Vining, D.J.: Automatic segmentation of the colon for virtual colonoscopy. Comput. Med. Imag. Graph. **24**(1), 1–9 (2000)
9. Masutani, Y., Yoshida, H., MacEneaney, P.M., Dachman, A.H.: Automated segmentation of colonic walls for computerized detection of polyps in CT colonography. J. Comp. Ass. Tomogr. **25**(4), 629–638 (2001)
10. Zalis, M.E., Perumpillichira, J., Hahn, P.F.: Digital subtraction bowel cleansing for CT colonography using morphological and linear filtration methods. IEEE Trans. Med. Imag. **23**(11), 1335–1343 (2004)
11. Wyatt, C.L., Ge, Y., Vinning, D.J.: Segmentation in virtual colonoscopy using a geometric deformable model. Comput. Med. Imag. Graph. **30**(1), 17–30 (2006)
12. Chen, D., Fahmi, R., Farag, A., Falk, R., Dryden, G.: Accurate and fast 3D colon segmentation in CT colonography. In: ISBI, pp. 490–493 (2009)
13. Nappi, J., Yoshida, H.: Fully automated three-dimensional detection of polyps in fecal-tagging CT colonography. Acad. Radiol. **14**(3), 287–300 (2007)
14. Wang, Z., Liang, A., Li, L., Li, X., Li, B., Anderson, J., Harrington, D.: Reduction of false positives by internal features for polyp detection in CT-based virtual colonoscopy. Med. Phys. **32**(12), 3602–3615 (2005)
15. Uitert, R.L., Summers, R.M.: Automatic correction of level set based subvoxel precise centerlines for virtual colonoscopy using the colon outer wall. IEEE Trans. Med. Imag. **26**(8), 1069–1078 (2007)
16. Uitert, R., Bitter, I., Summers, R.: Detection of colon wall outer boundary and segmentation of the colon wall based on level set methods. In: Engineering in Medicine and Biology Society, EMBS '06 (2006)
17. Lu, L., Chen, K., Zhao, J.: Virtual colon flattening based on colonic outer surface. In: International Conference of IEEE EMBS, vol. 35, pp. 2316–2319 (2013)
18. Ismail, M. Elhabian, S., Farag, A., Dryden, G., Seow, A. : Fully automated 3D colon segmentation for early detection of colorectal cancer based on convex formulation of the active contour model. In: CVPR MCV Workshop, pp. 58–63 (2012)

19. Zhu, H., Barish, M., Pickhardt, P., Liang, Z.: Haustral fold segmentation with curvature-guided level set evolution. IEEE Trans. Biomed. Eng. **60**(2), 321–331 (2013)
20. Ismail, M., Elhabian, S., Farag, A., Dryden, G., Seow, A.: 3D automated colon segmentation for efficient polyp detection. In: Cairo International Biomedical Engineering Conference (CIBEC), pp. 48–51 (2012)
21. Bresson, X., Esedoglu, S., Vandergheynst, P., Thiran, J., Osher, S.: Fast global minimization of the active contour/snake model. J. Math. Imag. Vis. **28**(2), 151–167 (2007)

A Novel Visualization Technique for Virtual Colonoscopy Using One-Sided Transparency

Robert Curtin[1,2(✉)], Aly Farag[1], Salwa Elshzaly[2], Marwa Ismail[1],
Charles Sites[1], and Robert Falk[3]

[1] Computer Vision and Image Processing Laboratory, University of Louisville,
Louisville, KY, USA
recurt02@louisville.edu
[2] Kentucky Imaging Technologies, Louisville, KY, USA
[3] 3DR, Inc, Louisville, KY, USA

Abstract. This paper proposes a new visualization technique for tubular shape visualization called one-sided transparency (OST). The technique effectively removes the exterior face of a surface, making it transparent, while keeping the interior opaque for viewing. OST is particularly useful in virtual colonoscopy, giving superior visibility coverage with reduced data memory requirements compared to state-of-the-art techniques. The technique achieved surface visibility coverage of up to $99.5 \pm 0.2\,\%$ when applied on 5 clinical sets using a fly-over (FO) approach. OST also lends improvements to other VC approaches that depend on centerline extraction of the colon volume.

Keywords: Mesh · Orientability · Transparency · Colonoscopy · Fly-through · Fly-over · Polyps · Normal · Centerline

1 Introduction

Visualization is an established field in computational geometry, and is often applied to medical imaging (e.g., [2, 4, 6]). In representing a surface using computational geometry, data points are often grouped as triangular faces, then effectively glued together as 3D triangular meshes. A triangular mesh has many topological properties, including orientability. A mesh is orientable if its interior and the exterior parts are well differentiable.

One-sided transparency (OST) of orientable surfaces removes the faces of the exterior part of the surface, thus making the exterior transparent while keeping the surface interior opaque (Fig. 1). By exploiting this capability, OST allows accurate visualization of the inside volume with excellent visibility coverage using a virtual camera. Therefore, OST has potential applications to a wide variety of tubular objects, with particular benefits to biomedical applications in virtual colonoscopy, thoracoscopic and laborscopic image-guided interventions and in dentistry.

For example, Fig. 1 (lower) shows a visualization of the inside of a tooth that could be used in procedures such as a root canal. This paper will examine mesh representation of orientable surfaces and will introduce a novel application of one-sided transparency (OST) in Virtual Colonoscopy. OST will be shown to possess strong

H. Yoshida et al. (Eds.): ABDI 2014, LNCS 8676, pp. 199–208, 2014.
DOI: 10.1007/978-3-319-13692-9_19

characteristics in its own, and will lend benefits for other VC techniques that depend on centerline, such as Fly-Through [2] and Fly-Over [8], and other colon transformations; e.g., cylindrical [12].

Virtual Colonoscopy (VC) is increasingly used for the detection of colon cancer. Its main goal is early detection of polyps, which are the primary indicator of cancer [1], but this requires effective visualization. In addition to the complex structure of the colon itself, a major hurdle is the accurate representation of early-stage polyps. These polyps can be flat and barely detectable. VC is a follow-up step after volume segmentation and 3D reconstruction of the colon. In many cases, the mesh representation of the 3D reconstructed colon is the starting point of VC. There also exist methods that use volume rendering, but those methods will not be discussed here. Applying OST on

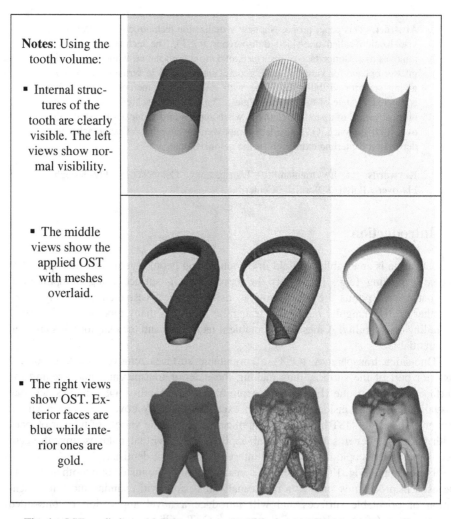

Notes: Using the tooth volume:

- Internal structures of the tooth are clearly visible. The left views show normal visibility.

- The middle views show the applied OST with meshes overlaid.

- The right views show OST. Exterior faces are blue while interior ones are gold.

Fig. 1. OST applied on: (a) Tube (upper), (b) Klein bottle (middle); (c) Tooth (lower)

colon surfaces in VC achieves excellent visibility coverage (up to $99.5 \pm 0.2\%$) with high sensitivity of polyp detection, even for polyps at challenging positions. Moreover, other state-of-the-art VC techniques require significantly more memory and computational requirements than OST.

In virtual colonoscopy (VC), early attempts for VC included the fly-through (FT) technique [2], which suffers from poor visibility coverage and long examination time. Several flattening and panoramic techniques developed for colon visualization [3–7] have proved problematic. In general, flattening creates geometric distortion, while panoramic techniques can overlook polyps. [8] proposed a technique called fly-over (FO) for colon visualization, and claimed that FO enhanced visibility over FT and was more robust than other 2D visualizations such as flattening. FO suffers from the need to make multiple cuts though, which may affect polyps at haustral folds with high curvatures. The OST approach presented here can be used in a standalone mode or with any other VC approach, such as cylinder mapping and fly-over.

For example, [4, 5] initially transform the colon into a cylinder-like shape (cylinder mapping) to reduce its overall tortuosity, before mapping the straightened colon onto a single image (flattening). Applying OST to the cylindrical colon created prior to flattening would result in a simple linear navigation of the colon, which could either supplement or replace the flattening. In this paper, however, we focus on OST's application to FO, and leave incorporating it with cylinder mapping techniques for future work.

Originally, FO cut the colon model into exactly two halves and assigned a camera to each half for navigation, Fig. 2(a). This technique covered up to 20 % more surface than FT. Additionally, FO only required two traversals of the colon compared to four with FT. However, splitting the colon runs the risk of obscuring polyps located exactly at the severance line. Also, the data computation required for this splitting is memory-intensive, which slows navigation time. Speed and accuracy are both crucial issues for physicians, who need quick and reliable visualization techniques for polyp detection. This is what OST delivers.

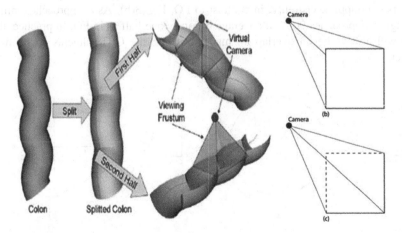

Fig. 2. (a) Original FO cutting method [8]. (b) Normal view of an object (c) One-sided transparency (OST) view of an object. OST sees through the exterior faces.

By simplifying computations, OST speeds up the whole navigation process and significantly reduces memory requirements. It also provides visibility coverage comparable to FO, as illustrated in the next section.

2　Materials and Methods

The concept of OST is closely related to back-face culling, a computer graphics method used to optimize rendering. In back-face culling, polygon faces that are currently facing away from the camera are removed from rendering, as they are occluded by the opposite faces facing the camera [9]. OST uses front-face culling, where, the faces exterior to an object are removed from rendering, leaving the interior faces opaque as shown in Fig. 2(b) and (c).

Two cameras are set for OST, one for the interior and one for the exterior. Although FO also uses two cameras, one for each half of the colon, OST still provides better capabilities. This comes in terms of visibility coverage, ease of navigation, and polyp detection.

2.1　OST Camera Setup

Figure 3 shows the wider visibility coverage of OST versus that of FO. Consider a tomographic slice of the colon volume, represented by the circle in Fig. 3(a). VC visibility starts at the point where the line from the camera to the colon is tangent.

From Fig. 3(a), the angle of transparency α is computed from the following formula:

$$\alpha = cos^{-1}(\frac{r}{d+r}) \tag{1}$$

For example, at a distance $d = r$, 240° of the colon are visible. Each of the two OST cameras thus covers two-thirds of the entire colon. Figure 3(a) shows how OST delivers overlapping visibility, in contrast to FO, Fig. 3(b). As d approaches infinity, the angle α approaches 90° and coverage becomes one-half as in FO. In practice, then, there will always be an overlap no matter how far the OST cameras are from the subject.

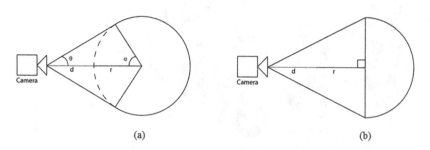

(a)　　　　　　　　　　　　　　(b)

Fig. 3. Visibility using (a) OST versus (b) FO.

Camera orientation is crucial to any visualization method. The camera must be located perpendicular to the centerline in order to create a top-down view. During movement, the views must remain consistent. A camera that spins wildly around the centerline or shakes erratically is of little use.

In order to locate the camera perpendicular to the centerline in OST, we calculate the normal at each point of the centerline. The first normal is determined by finding the vector between the first two points p_1 and p_2:

$$v_{\Delta 1} = p_2 - p_1 \tag{2}$$

If this vector is not along the Z axis, then an arbitrary normal can be determined by:

$$v_{N_1}(x, y, z) = (v_{\Delta 1}(y), -v_{\Delta 1}(x), 0) \tag{3}$$

If it is along the Z axis, then there is a normal vector v_{N_1} at:

$$v_{N_1}(x, y, z) = (1, 0, 0) \tag{4}$$

The first camera point p_{cam_1} is then:

$$p_{cam_1} = p_1 + v_{N_1} \tag{5}$$

There must be a second camera located opposite from the first camera in order to ensure coverage. We position this camera at the reverse camera point $p_{cam_1\_R}$:

$$p_{cam_1\_R} = p_1 - v_{N_1} \tag{6}$$

In order to maintain continuity between camera views while moving, we developed a method that relates each normal to the previous normal. Figure 4 depicts the method for determining each normal vector. First, we use the previous normal vector and the vector from the previous point p_{k-1} to the current point p_k to determine O_i, the offset we need to move the point with:

$$v_{\Delta k} = p_k - p_{k-1} \tag{7}$$

$$O_i = v_{\Delta k} \cdot (p_k - p_{cam_{k-1}}) \tag{8}$$

Next, we use this distance to find the new camera point p_{cam_k} by offsetting the previous camera point $p_{cam_{k-1}}$:

$$p_{cam_k} = p_{cam_{k-1}} + O_k \widehat{v}_{\Delta k} \tag{9}$$

With this new camera point we can now find the new normal as well as the reverse fly-over point:

$$v_{N_k} = p_{cam_k} - p_k \tag{10}$$

$$p_{cam_{k\_R}} = p_k - v_{N_k} \qquad (11)$$

So the camera position is set at p_{cam_k} and its focus is p_k. Finally, the camera must maintain a constant rotation. We achieve this through our selection of view up vectors. To align each vector to the centerline, we choose a vector that is normal to the centerline. The view up vector for point p_{i-1} is shown as V_{up} in Fig. 4. The vector permits the camera to rotate easily in a perfect circle around the centerline. It also keeps a consistent left-to-right traversal of the colon, which provides a stable frame of reference for the viewer. The view up vector v_{up} for point p_k is determined by

$$v_{\Delta k+1} = p_{k+1} - p_k \qquad (12)$$

$$v_{up} = v_{N_k} \times v_{\Delta k+1} \qquad (13)$$

In short, the calculation of the navigation path and all associated computations is far more efficient in OST than in FO [7].

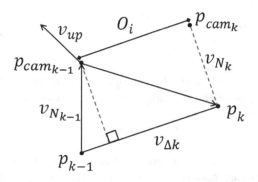

Fig. 4. Normal and view up vector calculation

3   Results

OST was applied on 5 computed tomography (CT) colonography sets that were received from the Virtual Colonoscopy Center, Walter Reed Army Medical Center, Washington, DC. The patients underwent standard 24-hour colonic preparation by oral administration of 90 ml of sodium phosphate and 10 mg of bisacodyl; they consumed 500 ml of barium for solid-stool tagging and 120 ml of Gastrografin to opacify luminal fluid. The CT protocol included 1.25 to 2.5 mm collimation, and 100 mAs and 120 kVp scanner settings. Each dataset contained 400 to 500 slices, and the spatial resolution was $1.0 \times 1.0 \times 1.0$ mm^3. The data include 9 real and synthetic polyps. Synthetic polyps were situated with the aid of physicians.

3.1   Data Processing

Proper visualization requires accurate segmentation of the colon scans. Segmentation is a crucial stage in VC, as improper colon segmentation results in broken constructed surfaces, thus obscuring polyps. We used the proposed technique in [10] to segment the colon and some pre-processing operations to remedy partial volume and contrast agent leakage problems. This was followed by 3D segmentation using the convex formulation of the active contour model. Finally, some anatomical and geometrical features were employed to extract the colon.

3.2 Quantitative and Qualitative Assessment

Qualitative assessment was conducted by a radiologist who reviewed the datasets in a blinded manner using both OST and FO. Any suspected polyps were to be confirmed by ground truth. The radiologist observed several distinctive features of OST: navigation was easier and one can see both sides of a fold while flying over it. Also, because OST obviates most of the FO's extensive initial computation, the physician can pull up the visualization significantly faster. OST greatly reduces the memory requirements. It is also worth mentioning that the FO program takes $\sim$ 5 minutes to start, whereas OST takes $\sim$ 20 s. One downside of the OST method occurs when the camera moves inside of another segment of colon than the one it's looking at, such as at a bend in the colon. In this case, the intended view will be occluded by the inside of the colon segment that the camera is located in.

In order to quantitatively validate the proposed method, surface visibility coverage of OST was computed using the Z-buffer test outlined in [8] and compared to that of FO. The visibility provided by OST was up to $99.5 \pm 0.2\%$ by navigating in only one

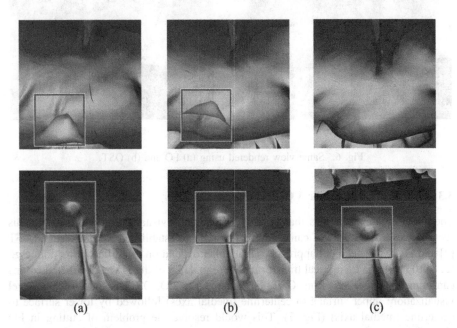

Fig. 5. (a) The polyp is visible in both views. (b) The polyp begins to disappear in one view. (c) The polyp has fully disappeared in one view, and is now clearly visible in the other view.

direction. FO would get comparable results only if navigation was conducted in both antegrade and retrograde directions. FO risks overlooking polyps on the boundary, as will be demonstrated. The authors of [11] proposed making multiple VC cuts, thus catching the boundary polyps in other views. This is plausible, but too costly computationally. It might seem that OST could resolve this issue by rotating about the centerline, but such maneuvers are not even needed. As Fig. 5 demonstrates, no boundary issue exists with OST. This is because a polyp is not transparent until its edges become aligned with a camera, and this occurs only when the polyp is well within view of the opposing camera. Therefore two cameras provide a sufficient visualization.

Figure 6 also highlights how FO's boundary issue is resolved using OST. With FO, polyps on the boundary would be cut off and might not be recognizable as a polyp; see Fig. 6(a). With OST, as in Fig. 6(b), not only is the polyp straddling the boundary clear, but we also see the third polyp just beyond it. It is clear that OST outperforms FO in terms of polyp detection rate. For the 10 known polyps in the datasets, the polyp detection rate was 100 % with OST compared to 80 % for FO, with polyps missed on boundaries.

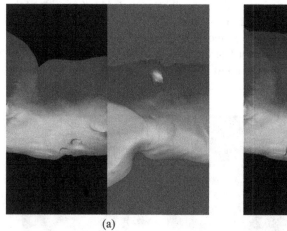 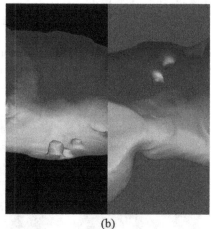

(a)   (b)

Fig. 6. Same view rendered using (a) FO and (b) OST.

3.3 Application to Other VC Techniques

The above treatment shows that OST is a standalone visualization approach. In this section, we show how OST can lend great benefits to established methods, such as FT [2] and FO [8]. Indeed, all approaches that either depend on centerline extraction (e.g., [2, 8, 10, 11]) or a cylindrical transformation (e.g., [12]) of the 3D reconstructed colons can immediately benefit from OST. For example, in FO, OST can perform two-level visualization: upper surface to centerline (medial axes) followed by lower surface to centerline (medial axis) (Fig. 7). This would resolve the problem of cutting in FO altogether.

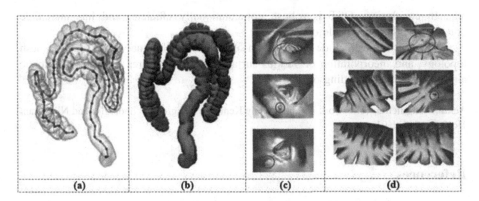

Fig. 7. Fly-Through (FT) and Fly-Over Visualization (FO), starting from the centerline of a 3D reconstructed colon. (a) Centerline extraction, (b) upper and lower colon surfaces, (c) Sample FT and (d) corresponding sample FO. OST can conduct two-stage visualization on the surface in (b), thus eliminating the cutting problems in FO.

Finally, we refer to two immediate extensions of FO and cylindrical representation based on OST visualization: (a) the cutting approach in FO generates rings on which cutting is performed, then a combination of split rings provide the two halves for visualization; and (b) texture analysis of the rings using OST.

From a geometric representation point of view, the rings can be realigned to expand the colon into a cylinder, keeping an exact correspondence (no distortion) between the original 2D CT slices, the 3D reconstructed colon, and the cylindrical representation. Visualization of a cylindrical object is the easiest, hence, OST will be deployed in reading the colon in either a "scroll-like" form, or in a two-stage visualization as stated above.

Another benefit for OST, in the context of automatic polyp detection and computed aided diagnosis (CAD) in VC, is that its mesh representation allows geometric measurements of the surface (i.e., its thickness), hence, polyps can identified in terms of spatial support as well as height map.

4 Discussion and Conclusion

This paper proposes a novel visualization technique in virtual colonoscopy based on one-sided transparency. OST offers powerful advantages in surface visibility and polyp detection as well as computational efficiencies. OST opens new realms of possibilities for many types of visualization besides VC, and within VC it represents a major leap forward. As time is important to a physician, any method that will speed up processes while improving accuracy is surely welcome.

Future work will include further validation of OST within VC and incorporation of OST with other existing VC visualization techniques, such as cylinder mapping. As applying OST to VC has numerous benefits for physicians, it has strong commercial opportunity. It will also see integration of OST into other medical applications outside

VC. In conclusion, OST is robust, computationally efficient, and has incredible potential inside and outside of VC.

Current activities include optimization of the OST technique with respect to mesh topology, and incorporation of various surface texture measures to enable automatic allocation and color-coding of polyps.

Acknowledgments. This work is supported by Kentucky Imaging Technologies and NIH Grant 1R43CA179911-01.

References

1. Abbruzzese, J., Pollock, R.: Gastrointestinal Cancer. Springer, Heidelberg (2004)
2. Bouix, S., Siddiqi, K., Tannenbaum, A.: Flux driven fly throughs. In: Proceedings of IEEE CVPR '03, pp. 449–454 (2003)
3. Hong, W., Gu, X., Qiu, F., Jin, M., Kaufman, A.: Conformal virtual colon flattening. In: Proceedings of ACM Symposium on SPM '06, pp. 85–93 (2006)
4. Bartroli, A.V., Wegenkittl, R., Konig, A., Groller, E.: Nonlinear virtual colon unfolding. In: Proceedings of VIS Visualization'01, pp. 411–420 (2001)
5. Bartrolí, A.V., Wegenkittl, R., König, A., Gröller, E., Sorantin, E.: Virtual colon flattening. Data Visualization, pp. 127–136 (2001)
6. Beaulieu, C., Jeffrey, R.B., Karadi, C., Paik, D., Napel, S.: Display modes for CT colonography part ii: Blinded comparison of axial CT and virtual endoscopic and panoramic endoscopic volume-rendered studies. Radiology **212**, 203–212 (1999)
7. Lee, S.S., Park, S.H., Kim, J.K., Kim, N., Lee, J., Park, B.J., Kim, Y.J., Kim, A.Y., Ha, H. K.: Panoramic endoluminal display with minimal image distortion using circumferential radial Ray-Casting for primary three-dimensional interpretation of CT Colonography. Eur. Radiol. **19**, 1951–1959 (2009)
8. Hassouna, M.S., Farag, A.A., Falk, R.: Virtual fly-over: A new visualization technique for virtual colonoscopy. Med. Image Comput. Comput. Assist. Interv. **9**(Pt. 1), 381–388 (2006)
9. Laurila, P.: Geometry culling in 3D engines. Graphics Programming and Theory (2000)
10. Ismail, M., Elhabian, S., Farag, A., Dryden, G., Seow, A.: Fully automated 3D colon segmentation for early detection of colorectal cancer based on convex formulation of the active contour model. In: Proceedings of IEEE CVPRW'12, pp. 58–63 (2012)
11. Ismail, M., Farag, A.A., Hassouna, M.S., Dryden, G., Falk, R.: Improved colon navigation for efficient polyp detection in virtual colonoscopy. In: 5th MICCAI Workshop on Abdominal Imaging: Computational and Clinical Application, Japan (2013)
12. Roth, H.R., McClelland, J.R., Boone, D.J., Modat, M., Cardoso, M.J., Hampshire, T.E., Hu, M., Punwani, S., Ourselin, S., Slabaugh, G.G., Halligan, S., Hawkes, D.J.: Registration of the endoluminal surfaces of the colon derived from prone and supine CT colonography. Med. Phys. **38**(6), 3077–3089 (2011)

Abdominal Operation Planning - Registration, Segmentation

Total Variation Regularization of Displacements in Parametric Image Registration

Valeriy Vishnevskiy[(✉)], Tobias Gass, Gábor Székely, and Orcun Goksel

Computer Vision Laboratory, ETH Zurich, Zürich, Switzerland
valery.vishnevskiy@inf.ethz.ch
{gass,szekely,ogoksel}@vision.ee.ethz.ch

Abstract. Spatial regularization is indispensable in image registration to avoid both physically implausible displacement fields and potential local minima in optimization methods. Typical ℓ_2-regularization is incapable of correctly recovering non-smooth displacement fields, such as at sliding organ boundaries during time-series of breathing motion. In this paper, Total Variation (TV) regularization is used to allow for accurate registration near such boundaries. We propose a novel formulation of TV-regularization for *parametric* displacement fields and introduce an efficient and general numerical solution scheme using the Alternating Directions Method of Multipliers (ADMM). Our method has been evaluated on two public datasets of 4D CT lung images as well as a dataset of 4D MR liver images, demonstrating accurate registrations both inside and outside moving organs. The target registration error of our method is 2.56 mm on average in the liver dataset, which indicates an improvement of over 24 % in comparison to other published methods.

Keywords: Medical image registration · Total variation · 4D CT · ADMM

1 Introduction

Image registration is an essential part of several applications in modern medical imaging, such as atlas-based segmentation, volumetric reconstruction from slices, tissue parameter estimation and motion tracking. All these applications rely on correctly estimating spatial anatomical correspondences between images. The existence of such correspondences and an underlying bijective mapping cannot be guaranteed in some registration contexts, such as inter-patient or 2D registration. However, in other contexts where the anatomy changes minimally, for example, in intra-patient registration of time-series 3D (4D) volumes, one-to-one correspondences do exist between images when the image margins that may move inside/outside the field-of-view are neglected. Such 4D motion, however, often involves sliding between different parts of anatomy, such as the liver or the lungs over their surrounding (cf. Fig. 1). The resulting non-smooth motion fields are difficult to represent and estimate using typical ℓ_2-regularized registration techniques.

© Springer International Publishing Switzerland 2014
H. Yoshida et al. (Eds.): ABDI 2014, LNCS 8676, pp. 211–220, 2014.
DOI: 10.1007/978-3-319-13692-9_20

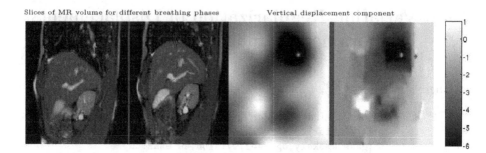

Fig. 1. Sliding motion example from a 4D MRI liver sequence during breathing. Left: Displacements for landmarks inside (green) and outside (red) the rib cage are visualized. Right: Inferior-superior component of displacement fields estimated by the smooth ℓ_2-regularized (left) and our TV-regularized (right) registration techniques. Note that the sliding organ boundaries are captured better by our TV-regularized method (Colour figure online).

A simple way to accommodate for discontinuities near sliding boundaries is to use binary masks for objects to be registered, such that deformations (or image similarity) outside object's masks can be ignored. For motion estimation inside the lungs, masks were identified in [1] using automatic lung segmentation from 4D CT. To guarantee physically possible motions along the mask surface, in [2] two separate displacement fields were estimated simultaneously with additional constraints. Nevertheless, motion masking has several disadvantages: They require an initial segmentation stage that is cumbersome when done manually and error-prone when automatic. Furthermore, sliding can *only* be recovered at the *mask interface*, making registration efficacy dependent on the hard decision made at the prior masking stage. This problem was addressed by Kiriyanthan and Cattin in [3], where they have proposed to estimate a motion mask automatically *during* the registration process using the segmentation model of Chan et al. [4].

Another way to allow for sliding motion is to model motion trajectories in the time domain using intermediate images between breathing phases [5]. This approach necessitates simultaneous processing of several image pairs, which imposes severe time and memory limitations. Also, heuristic techniques exists that allow for sliding motion, such as the modified demons method [6,7] or the anisotropic demons [8], in which the Gaussian smoothing step is replaced with anisotropic filtering. However, such methods do not have an explicit definition of regularization and hence lack a formal cost definition. Therefore, they do not allow for a coherent optimization scheme. Total Variation (TV), in contrast, can be defined as a penalty and hence the registration can be solved in a well-defined optimization framework as shown in this work.

Constraining spatial Total Variation penalizes spatial incoherence, but does not restrict the displacement field to be smooth. This property of the TV norm as a regularizer received much attention in the computer vision literature for correctly estimating optical flow between scenes with independent motion of overlapping objects [9]. A major difficulty with TV is the involvement of ℓ_1-norm, which is non-differentiable at zero leading to numerical instabilities for gradient-based methods. In [9], the use of its smooth seminorm approximations, i.e. $\|x\|_1 \approx \varphi_\varepsilon(x) = \sqrt{x^2 + \varepsilon}$, was proposed. However, for small ε, common optimization algorithms easily become unstable. It is possible to employ discrete optimization methods, formulating the registration problem on Markov random fields [10]. This approach was applied for breathing motion estimation in [11], however commonly-used message passing and graph-cut based algorithms are inefficient for registering 3D volumes on fine grid resolutions. Fine displacement estimation requires a dense discretization of the displacement search space, which is extremely memory consuming for 3D data.

A recent approach for solving ℓ_1-norm problems is based on duality, which was applied to *non-parametric* medical image registration in [12] using the sum of square differences (SSD) metric. A census cost function was also used as image residual yielding improved results for 4D CT lung images with breathing motion [13]. However, such non-parametric pixel-level approaches easily lead to physically implausible motion fields, for which the authors proposed a combined median and Gaussian filtering of the displacement fields following each method iteration. Such heuristic regularization may lead to unstable or suboptimal solution schemes as mentioned above. Furthermore, non-parametric registration methods are highly susceptible to local-minima and not robust during optimization. As a remedy, a complex image metric based on local image statistics was proposed in [13], leading to time-ineffective implementations with still no theoretical guarantees on the validity of the solution. Due to these and other difficulties, most registration techniques use parametric deformation models such as B-splines, which offer physically plausible displacements in robust schemes with large displacement capture ranges. In this work, we present a *parametric* image registration approach formulated as a minimization problem with TV-regularization, to recover anatomical non-smooth (sliding) motion in a coherent optimization framework. To accommodate the ℓ_1-norm cost of TV, we introduce an efficient solution scheme using the *alternating directions method of multipliers* (ADMM).

1.1   Image Registration as Energy Minimization

Estimating the D-dimensional local transformation field $\mathbf{t} : \Omega \to \mathbb{R}^D$, that maps image $I_\mathrm{m} : \Omega \to \mathbb{R}$ to image $I_\mathrm{f} : \Omega \to \mathbb{R}$, is commonly formulated as the following optimization problem:

$$\min_{\mathbf{t}} \; E_\mathrm{D}(\mathbf{t}; I_\mathrm{f}, I_\mathrm{m}) + \lambda E_\mathrm{R}(\mathbf{t}), \tag{1}$$

where Ω is the image domain, E_D is an image dissimilarity metric and E_R is a regularization term while λ controls the amount of regularization. Typically, E_D is a smooth metric such as the SSD, which allows for easy differentiation. For regularization, a popular choice is to component-wise penalize the ℓ_2-norm of displacement field derivatives, which leads to differentiable functionals [14].

Penalizing the ℓ_2-norm of the first derivative leads to the well-known *smoothness* regularization: $E_R^{\text{smooth}}(\mathbf{t}) = \sum_{d=1}^{D} \sum_{\mathbf{x}\in\Omega} \|\nabla t_d(\mathbf{x})\|_2^2 \delta\mathbf{x}$. Any gradient-based solver can then be used for minimizing (1) by computing the derivatives of the smooth metric E_D and smooth regularizer E_R with respect to the transformation parameters.

1.2   TV-Regularization

Anisotropic TV-regularization can be written as the ℓ_1-norm of the finite differences of displacement field components as follows:

$$E_R^{\text{TV}}(\mathbf{t}) = \sum_{d=1}^{D} \sum_{\mathbf{x}\in\Omega} \|\nabla t_d(\mathbf{x})\|_1 \, \delta\mathbf{x}, \tag{2}$$

where ∇ is a linear operator for finite differences, and $\delta\mathbf{x}$ is the volume of a voxel. This functional is convex but no longer smooth, i.e. it is non-differentiable with respect to $\mathbf{x}$ at $\|\nabla t(\mathbf{x})\|_1 = 0$. This leads to poor performance when using standard gradient-based optimization methods. This is addressed in our work by employing ADMM optimization [15,16], described later below. First, we introduce our displacement parametrization approach which allows us to impose TV regularization on the displacement field simply and efficiently.

1.3   Parameterizing Displacement Fields

Parameterizing a displacement field greatly reduces the dimensionality of the registration optimization problem. This constrains the size of parameter search space, while discarding many physically meaningless transformations. This allows for robust numerical methods that are more resilient to suboptimal local minima.

We parametrize the displacement field $\mathbf{t}$ using trilinear interpolation (1st order B-splines) with displacements $\mathbf{k}$ on control points that are placed with N-pixel spacing, i.e. $\mathbf{t} = \mathbf{t}(\mathbf{k})$, where $\mathbf{k}$ and $\mathbf{t}$ are displacements stacked into column vectors. Unlike higher order B-splines, linear interpolation guarantees that the interpolated displacement values at grid knots are equal to the corresponding B-spline coefficients. We then impose regularization on the displacement control grid points $\mathbf{k}$ instead of the displacement field $\mathbf{t}$ itself. Such approximation is commonly used in smooth registration methods, where it was reported in [17] to be practically equivalent to imposing constraints directly on the displacement field itself.

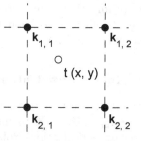

Fig. 2. Control grid points.

Parametric Upper Bound for TV. For linear interpolation in the 1D case, it is obvious that the TV of both the control grid and the underlying displacement field are exactly the same, i.e. $E_R^{TV}(\mathbf{t}(\mathbf{k}))=E_R^{TV}(\mathbf{k})$. For 2D and 3D cases this equality does not necessarily hold. However, an upper bound on such displacement field TV given the TV on the control grid can be computed which we show as given below.

For simplicity, we consider the TV of a single component of a 2D displacement field within a single patch shown in Fig. 2. The TV of the patch control points $\mathbf{k}$ and the field $\mathbf{t}$ are then, respectively:

$$E_R^{TV}(\mathbf{k}) = (|k(1,2) - k(1,1)| + |k(2,2) - k(2,1)|)\, N, \tag{3}$$

$$E_R^{TV}(\mathbf{t}) = \sum_{i=0}^{N-1} \sum_{j=0}^{N-1} \Big(\left| t\left(\tfrac{i+1}{N}, \tfrac{j}{N}\right) - t\left(\tfrac{i}{N}, \tfrac{j}{N}\right) \right| \tag{4}$$
$$+ \left| t\left(\tfrac{i}{N}, \tfrac{j+1}{N}\right) - t\left(\tfrac{i}{N}, \tfrac{j}{N}\right) \right| \Big).$$

Using the fact that t is linearly interpolated from $\mathbf{k}$ and employing the triangle inequality, we can infer that:

$$E_R^{TV}(\mathbf{t}(\mathbf{k})) - E_R^{TV}(\mathbf{k}) \leq N \max(|\nabla \mathbf{k}|) . \tag{5}$$

In other words, the TV approximated on the control grid is an upper bound for TV on $\mathbf{t}$, and such approximation error decreases linearly as the parametrization grid is refined. Accordingly, we start with a coarse grid and refine it gradually by initializing the optimization at each step from upsampled lower-resolution grid.

1.4   Numerical Scheme: ADMM

As was mentioned in the introduction, accurate and robust minimization of the parametrized TV-regularized energy (1) is difficult because the gradient required to *simultaneously* minimize both the data term E_D and the regularization term E_R^{TV} does not always exist. To overcome this challenge, we utilize the alternate direction method of multipliers (ADMM), which allows us to iteratively minimize each of the two terms separately, while constraining their solutions to be similar.

To this end, we introduce a redundant variable $\mathbf{z}$ to (1), which leads to the following equivalent problem:

$$\min_{\mathbf{k},\mathbf{z}}\ E_D(\mathbf{t}(\mathbf{k}); I_f, I_m) + \lambda \|\mathbf{z}\|_1 , \qquad \text{s.t.}\quad \nabla \mathbf{k} = \mathbf{z}. \tag{6}$$

Writing the augmented scaled Lagrangian for the problem above and performing the dual descent method [15] results in the following iterative ADMM scheme, where the optimization of E_D and ℓ_1-norm terms are decoupled into two separate subproblems.

$$\mathbf{k}^{j+1} = \arg\min_{\mathbf{k}}\ E_D(\mathbf{t}(\mathbf{k}); I_f, I_m) + \frac{\rho}{2}\|\nabla \mathbf{k} - \mathbf{z}^j + \mathbf{u}^j\|_2^2, \tag{7a}$$

$$\mathbf{z}_d^{j+1} = \arg\min_{\mathbf{z}_d}\ \frac{\lambda}{\rho}\|\mathbf{z}_d\|_1 + \frac{1}{2}\|\nabla \mathbf{k}_d^{j+1} + \mathbf{u}_d^j - \mathbf{z}_d\|_2^2, \quad d = 1,\dots,D, \tag{7b}$$

$$\mathbf{u}^{j+1} = \mathbf{u}^j + \mathbf{k}^{j+1} - \mathbf{z}^{j+1}. \tag{7c}$$

The **k**-update step (7a) finds control grid displacements that optimize the image similarity metric. It is a smooth optimization problem that can be solved using any gradient-based optimization technique by adding $\rho\nabla^\top(\nabla\mathbf{k} - \mathbf{z}^j + \mathbf{u}^j)$ to the gradient of the similarity metric. The penalty parameter ρ is usually set to 1 and can be updated heuristically to accelerate convergence [15]. **u** is a scaled dual variable. The **z**-update step (7b) is called the proximity operator of the ℓ_1 norm and can be solved by element-wise shrinkage:

$$\mathbf{z}_d^{j+1} = \max\{\mathbf{u}^j + \mathbf{k}^{j+1} - \lambda/\rho, 0\} - \max\{-\mathbf{u}^j - \mathbf{k}^{j+1} - \lambda/\rho, 0\}. \qquad (8)$$

Implementation. Input image intensities are first scaled to the [0, 1] interval. Gaussian pyramids are used by starting the registration with both downsampled images and a coarse control grid. Registration at each consecutive image level is then initialized by interpolating from the previous level's control grid displacements. When the finest level of the image pyramid is reached, we start to subdivide the control grid, effectively decreasing the pixel span of each control patch and hence refining the estimated displacement resolution. We use SSD for CT images and normalized cross correlation for MRI as similarity metrics.

The method was implemented in `Matlab` with parallelized `mex`-functions for warping images and calculating E_D gradient. The **k**-update step in (7a) is solved with the limited-memory BFGS method of the `minFunc`[1] package with the maximum number of iterations set to 10. Variables **x**, **z**, **u** were initialized with zeros. The algorithm was executed on a 6-core Intel Xeon 2.4 GHz processor.

2 Results and Discussion

We evaluated our *parametric TV* registration (pTV) method on the following three abdominal time-series datasets that involve breathing motion:

4D-CT POPI Dataset. The public POPI[2] dataset [18] consists of: 10 3D CT images of different phases of one breathing cycle; 41 corresponding landmarks for each of the images; a binary lung mask; and the deformation fields estimated by the POPI organizers using both the standard demons algorithm and the free-form deformation method (FFD). We resampled all images to an isotropic $2 \times 2 \times 2\,\text{mm}^3$ pixel resolution, resulting in $235 \times 176 \times 141$ voxels/image. We then registered the first image (phase) to all other 9 images as in [18], resulting in 9 individual registrations. The regularization parameter λ was set to 0.001. The average run-time of our registration method was 30 seconds per image pair.

Table 1 shows the target registration error (TRE) of our pTV algorithm in comparison to Demons and FFD results reported in [18]. It can be observed that our method achieves an improved registration accuracy overall. One source of such improvement is the replacement of ℓ_2-regularization of FFDs, which is unable to capture sliding motion near the lung wall. This is is demonstrated in

---

[1] http://www.di.ens.fr/~mschmidt/Software/minFunc.html.

[2] http://www.creatis.insa-lyon.fr/rio/popi-model.

Table 1. Mean TRE [mm] over 41 landmarks for the 9 POPI registrations.

Method	TRE for each image pair									Average
	#1	#2	#3	#4	#5	#6	#7	#8	#9	TRE
Demons	1.28	1.38	1.39	1.22	1.24	1.25	1.29	1.12	1.11	1.25
FFD	0.79	0.80	1.13	1.11	**1.10**	1.20	1.20	0.88	0.92	1.01
pTV	**0.72**	**0.71**	**1.12**	**1.01**	1.11	**1.03**	**1.06**	**0.84**	**0.81**	**0.93**

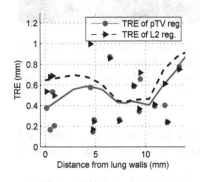 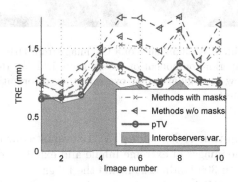

Fig. 3. Registration spatial accuracy with respect to target distance from the lung wall. Local regression curves are also presented for illustration purposes.

Fig. 4. Our proposed method pTV compared to the top 6 out of 20 results, published and reported on DIR website.

Table 2. Mean (snap-to-pixel) TRE on DIR data set, where cTV is the non-parametric TV method [13] with ℓ_1-norm census cost function and cTVmask is the same method with motion masks provided.

Method	TRE for each 4D sequence										Mean
	#1	#2	#3	#4	#5	#6	#7	#8	#9	#10	
cTVmask [13]	0.78	0.78	0.93	**1.24**	**1.22**	0.94	1.01	**1.11**	0.98	0.94	0.99
cTV [13]	0.79	0.80	1.02	1.23	1.27	1.09	1.87	3.01	1.11	1.17	1.37
pTV	**0.76**	**0.78**	**0.82**	1.31	1.25	1.11	**0.97**	1.28	1.04	0.99	1.03

Fig. 3 on one image pair for targets within 15 mm of the lung wall. Our method pTV is seen to have significantly lower TRE for targets closer to the lung wall.

4D-CT DIR Dataset. The public DIR dataset[3] contains 10 4D CT sequences from different individuals, each sequence with 10 images/breathing-phases with an average resolution of $1 \times 1 \times 2.5 \, mm^3$ and sizes varying between $256 \times 256 \times 94$ and $512 \times 512 \times 136$ voxels (see Fig. 5). On this dataset, we empirically set λ to 0.001 and the finest control grid spacing to 3 voxels. This led to an average

---

[3] http://www.dir-lab.com.

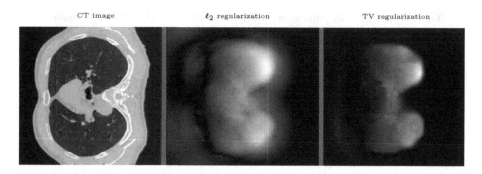

Fig. 5. An axial slice of a CT image from DIR dataset and the corresponding inferior-superior component of deformation fields for different regularization techniques. Note how ℓ_2 regularization oversmoothes deformations near lung borders at the sliding interface.

run-time of 3 min for pTV. To evaluate our method, from each sequence we used the images of extreme inhale and exhale breathing phases, which are annotated with 300 landmarks inside the lungs.

DIR is an ongoing benchmark, where TRE is computed by the organizers from submitted participant registration results (using a snap-to-voxel fashion for consistency with annotations). Those results are published online, allowing for a relative assessment of the performance of our pTV algorithm. Figure 4 shows the average TRE for each sequence, comparing pTV to the top 6 published methods (out of 20 in total at the time of evaluation) from DIR. Note that most DIR submissions are customized particularly for lung (pulmonary CT) registration, and several of them use lung masks to recover motion *only* inside the lungs. This is depicted in Fig. 4 by representing methods using masks with different markers. Despite not using any customization particular for the lungs, our general image registration method pTV yields comparable results to the other techniques. Furthermore, pTV outperforms all other methods that do not utilize a lung mask, despite the relatively small margin for consistent improvement over the reported inter-observer variability. A slice of the estimated displacement field is seen in Fig. 5 to better capture sliding motion.

We also compare pTV with the non-parametric TV-regularized registration method of [13] that uses a *census* cost function. Two results with and without using lung masks are reported in [13], namely *cTV* and *cTVmask*, with which we compare our pTV results in Table 2. A 24 % reduction in TRE can be observed when comparing pTV to the cTV version without mask.

4D-MRI liver sequences. Since the above lung datasets have landmarks only inside the lungs, we also evaluated our method on the dataset from [8]. Therein, landmarks are provided on both sides of the sliding liver interface, allowing for improved assessment of sliding-motion registration algorithms. 32 and 20 landmarks were provided inside and outside the liver, respectively, in the extreme breathing phases of 8 4D-MR sequences, where two sequences each were recorded

Table 3. Average mean TRE [mm] for the liver dataset. For e_i^j being the TRE for landmark i in sequence j, each cell reports: $\text{mean}_j\{\text{mean}_i\, e_i^j\}$ $(\text{mean}_j\{\text{max}_i\, e_i^j\})$. The proposed method pTV (with $\lambda = 0.0005$) is compared to regular and anisotropic demons registrations.

Method	Inside the liver	Outside the liver	Overall
Demons	3.57 (12.87)	4.25 (14.38)	3.83 (15.77)
Aniso. Demons [8]	3.00 (11.86)	4.05 (13.15)	3.40 (14.03)
pTV	**2.42** (11.0)	**2.64** (7.52)	**2.56** (9.78)

from 4 volunteers. The images have $1.37 \times 1.37 \times 4\,\text{mm}^3$ resolution and an average size of $164 \times 189 \times 23$ voxels, for which pTV required an average run-time of 50 s. Table 3 shows substantial improvement of pTV (19 % inside and 35 % outside the liver) in comparison to the results reported in [8].

3 Conclusions

In this paper we have presented a parametric approach for image registration with total variation regularization. We have evaluated our method on datasets of different imaging modalities and anatomies. Our method was shown to accurately estimate anatomical displacements near breathing-induced sliding boundaries. For thoracic 4D CT images, the registration accuracy of the proposed algorithm was shown to be comparable to the best methods from the DIR dataset, which rely on lung segmentation masks, and to outperform the best *mask-free* methods published to date. For 4D breathing motion estimation, our method was also shown to outperform both the non-parametric TV-regularized registration method of [13] and the anisotropic smoothing method of [8]; with an overall reduction of the TRE by 24 %. Furthermore, our proposed approach allows for using any registration method based on energy minimization for solving the **k** update step in the ADMM solver. This can facilitate adapting the algorithm to specific image modalities or existing workflows in clinical practice, which is an interesting direction for further research.

References

1. Hu, S., Hoffman, E.A., Reinhardt, J.M.: Automatic lung segmentation for accurate quantitation of volumetric X-ray CT images. IEEE Trans. Med. Imaging **20**, 490–498 (2001)
2. Delmon, V., Rit, S., Pinho, R., Sarrut, D.: Registration of sliding objects using direction dependent B-splines decomposition. Phys. Med. Biol. **58**, 1303–1314 (2013)
3. Kiriyanthan, S., Fundana, K., Cattin, P.C.: Discontinuity preserving registration of abdominal MR images with apparent sliding organ motion. In: Yoshida, H., Sakas, G., Linguraru, M.G. (eds.) Abdominal Imaging. LNCS, vol. 7029, pp. 231–239. Springer, Heidelberg (2012)

4. Chan, T.F., Esedoglu, S., Nikolova, M.: Algorithms for finding global minimizers of image segmentation and denoising models. SIAM J. Appl. Math. **66**, 1632–1648 (2006)
5. Castillo, E., Castillo, R., Martinez, J., Shenoy, M., Guerrero, T.: Four-dimensional deformable image registration using trajectory modeling. Phys. Med. Biol. **55**, 305–327 (2010)
6. Risser, L., Vialard, F.X., Baluwala, H.Y., Schnabel, J.A.: Piecewise-diffeomorphic image registration: Application to the motion estimation between 3D CT lung images with sliding conditions. Med. Image Anal. **17**, 182–193 (2013)
7. Papież, B.W., Heinrich, M.P., Risser, L., Schnabel, J.A.: Complex lung motion estimation via adaptive bilateral filtering of the deformation field. In: Mori, K., Sakuma, I., Sato, Y., Barillot, C., Navab, N. (eds.) MICCAI 2013, Part III. LNCS, vol. 8151, pp. 25–32. Springer, Heidelberg (2013)
8. Tanner, C., Samei, G., Székely, G.: Investigating anisotropic diffusion for the registration of abdominal MR images. In: IEEE International Symposium on Biomedical Imaging (ISBI), pp. 484–7 (2013)
9. Sun, D., Roth, S., Black, M.J.: Secrets of optical flow estimation and their principles. In: IEEE Conference on Computer Vision and Pattern Recognition (CVPR), pp. 2432–2439 (2010)
10. Glocker, B., Komodakis, N., Tziritas, G., Navab, N., Paragios, N.: Dense image registration through MRFs and efficient linear programming. Med. Image Anal. **12**, 731–741 (2008)
11. Heinrich, H., Jenkinson, M., Brady, M., Schnabel, J.A.: MRF-based deformable registration and ventilation estimation of lung CT. IEEE Trans. Med. Imaging **32**, 1239–1248 (2013)
12. Pock, T., Urschler, M., Zach, C., Beichel, R.R., Bischof, H.: A duality based algorithm for TV-L^1-optical-flow image registration. In: Ayache, N., Ourselin, S., Maeder, A. (eds.) MICCAI 2007, Part II. LNCS, vol. 4792, pp. 511–518. Springer, Heidelberg (2007)
13. Hermann, S., Werner, R.: TV-L_1-based 3D medical image registration with the census cost function. In: Klette, R., Rivera, M., Satoh, S. (eds.) PSIVT 2013. LNCS, vol. 8333, pp. 149–161. Springer, Heidelberg (2014)
14. Rueckert, D., Sonoda, L.I., Hayes, C., Hill, D.L., Leach, M.O., Hawkes, D.J.: Non-rigid registration using free-form deformations: application to breast MR images. IEEE Trans. Med. Imaging **18**, 712–721 (1999)
15. Boyd, S., Parikh, N., Chu, E., Peleato, B., Eckstein, J.: Distributed optimization and statistical learning via the alternating direction method of multipliers. Found. Trends Mach. Learn. **3**, 1–122 (2011)
16. Figueiredo, M.A., Bioucas-Dias, J.M.: Algorithms for imaging inverse problems under sparsity regularization. In: IEEE Int Workshop on Cognitive Information Processing (CIP), pp. 1–6 (2012)
17. Schwarz, L.A.: Non-rigid registration using free-form deformations. Ph.D. thesis, Technische Universität München, Germany (2007)
18. Vandemeulebroucke, J., Sarrut, D., Clarysse, P., et al.: The POPI-model, a point-validated pixel-based breathing thorax model. In: International Conference on Computers in Radiation Therapy (ICCR), pp. 195–9 (2007)

A Bilinear Model for Temporally Coherent Respiratory Motion

Frank Preiswerk[(✉)] and Philippe C. Cattin

Medical Image Analysis Center, University of Basel, Basel, Switzerland
{frank.preiswerk,philippe.cattin}@unibas.ch

Abstract. We propose a bilinear model of respiratory organ motion. The advantages of classical statistical shape modelling are combined with a preconditioned trajectory basis for separately modelling the shape and motion components of the data. The separation of a linear basis into bilinear form leads to a more compact representation of the underlying physical process and the resulting model respects the temporal regularity within the training data, which is an important property for modelling quasi-periodic data. Bilinear modelling is combined with a Bayesian reconstruction algorithm for sparse data under observation noise. By applying the model to liver motion data, we show that our bilinear formulation of respiratory motion is significantly more parsimonious and can even outperform linear PCA-based models.

Keywords: Respiratory motion · Bilinear model · Liver motion

1 Introduction

Modelling respiratory organ motion is an active field of research. Having an accurate model of respiratory motion is desirable for many practical applications including motion segmentation, registration, tracking and reconstruction as well as tumour tracking in a clinical scenario. A comprehensive overview of the field is available in [1]. Such models can serve different purposes, two of which are worth mentioning here. First, respiratory motion models are used to *estimate* the organ position for a given point in time, *e.g.* based on sparse measurements. Second, they are used to *predict* the future position based on current and/or past values. Respiratory motion is approximately repetitive, thus it is reasonable to take the repetitive nature into account when designing a model. While respiratory motion is very similar from cycle-to-cycle, there are variations that must be taken into account. On the other hand, we wish the model not to be able to describe arbitrary motion patterns. This trade-off between generalisation and specificity is typically encountered in model selection. Recently, statistical motion models which are learned from data, typically by employing Principal Component Analysis (PCA) techniques, have been proposed in various studies [2–7]. In [4], a kernel-PCA is learned to model the relationship between fiducial movement and lung surface motion. In [7] PCA, is computed

© Springer International Publishing Switzerland 2014
H. Yoshida et al. (Eds.): ABDI 2014, LNCS 8676, pp. 221–228, 2014.
DOI: 10.1007/978-3-319-13692-9_21

on dense motion fields extracted from 4DMRI of the liver through non-rigid registration. In [2], the coefficients of a PCA model are further restricted by a single governing parameter as prior which models the distribution of the observed data's PCA coefficients. Although all mentioned approaches provide a compact, low-dimensional parameterisation of valid shapes within a breathing cycle, they do not take into account the temporal regularity of respiratory motion. In [8], a bilinear factorisation of the model coefficients of each sample is proposed to compute a statistical model for reconstruction of the heart at discrete points in the cardiac cycle, inspired by the work on separating *style* and *content* [9]. Recently, a bilinear spatiotemporal model was proposed for facial animation [10]. This model factorises the *basis* of a dataset into separate shape and trajectory bases, as compared to the bilinear factorisation of the model *coefficients* in [8,9].

In this paper, we propose a general approach to model respiratory organ motion based on a bilinear model. We augment the bilinear model with a Bayesian algorithm for reconstruction from sparse and noisy data, leading to a variety of interesting possible applications.

2   Bilinear Motion Model

Let the vector $\mathbf{x} = (x_1, y_1, \ldots, x_n, y_n)^T \in \mathbb{R}^p$ be an instance of a 2d shape (w.l.o.g for higher dimensions) and the matrix

$$\mathbf{X} = [\mathbf{x}_1, \mathbf{x}_2, \ldots, \mathbf{x}_t], \tag{1}$$

a sequence of t shapes. In a linear model of shape, each instance is represented by a linear combination of base shapes

$$\mathbf{x}_j = \sum_i \mathbf{b}_i c_{i,j} \tag{2}$$

and the complete sequence can thus be represented as

$$\mathbf{X} = \mathbf{B}_s \mathbf{C}_s, \tag{3}$$

where $\mathbf{B}_s \in \mathbb{R}^{p \times k_s}$ consists of k_s basis vectors $\mathbf{b}_i \in \mathbb{R}^p$ that span the model space and $\mathbf{C}_s \in \mathbb{R}^{k_s \times t}$ is a matrix of t coefficient vectors that define linear combinations of shape basis vectors. Conversely, a linear model of motion can be built where the rows (not the columns) of $\mathbf{X}$ are modeled as a linear combination of motion trajectories,

$$\mathbf{x}^i = \sum_j c_{i,j} \mathbf{b}_j, \tag{4}$$

and the data matrix is represented as

$$\mathbf{X} = \mathbf{C}_m \mathbf{B}_m^T, \tag{5}$$

where $\mathbf{B}_m = [\mathbf{b}_1, \mathbf{b}_2, \ldots, \mathbf{b}_{k_m}] \in \mathbb{R}^{t \times k_m}$ and $\mathbf{C}_m \in \mathbb{R}^{p \times k_m}$ are k_m motion basis and p coefficient vectors, respectively [10]. In practice, the dimensionality of a linear model is often reduced using some type of dimensionality reduction approach, *e.g.* principal component analysis (PCA). However, in a linear representation, the temporal regularity of trajectories is ignored. As an illustrative example, consider an ordered sequence of shape vectors $[\mathbf{x}_1, \mathbf{x}_2, \ldots, \mathbf{x}_t]$. Any permutation $[\mathbf{x}_{p(1)}, \mathbf{x}_{p(2)}, \ldots, \mathbf{x}_{p(t)}]$ of the columns in $\mathbf{X}$ only results in a permutation of the coefficients in $\mathbf{C}_s$ but does not affect the shape basis $\mathbf{B}_s$. The same also applies for shuffling rows of $\mathbf{X}$, affecting only rows in $\mathbf{C}_m$. In this sense, a linear model is an overparameterisation because it fails to exploit the underlying spatiotemporal structure. For modelling respiratory motion, we would like to respect temporal regularities in the data.

A similar problem has been studied in [10], where it is shown that a factorisation

$$\mathbf{X} = \mathbf{B}_s \mathbf{C} \mathbf{B}_m^T \tag{6}$$

exists that links together shape and motion bases in a single model. In this bilinear model, the matrix $\mathbf{C} \in \mathbb{R}^{k_s \times k_m}$ defines weights for the outer products of the i-th shape vector $\mathbf{b}_s^i$ and the j-th trajectory vector $\mathbf{b}_m^j$. Intuitively, it describes how the points of the shape modes $\mathbf{b}_s^i$ vary over time. Figure 1 shows how the coefficients c_{ij} in $\mathbf{C}$ are related to the outer product of shape and trajectory basis vectors $\mathbf{b}_s^i$ and $\mathbf{b}_m^j$.

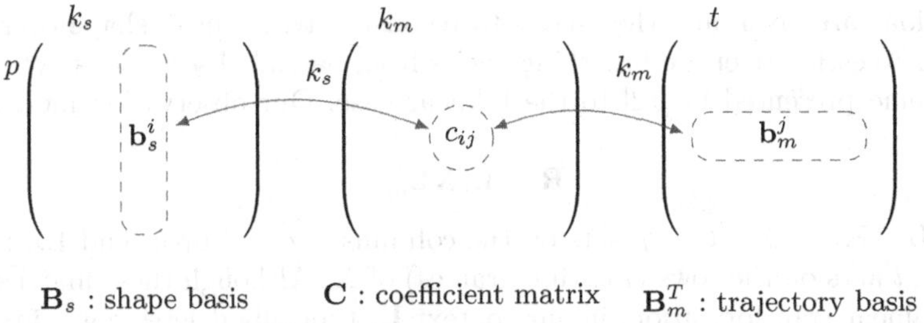

$\mathbf{B}_s$: shape basis $\mathbf{C}$: coefficient matrix $\mathbf{B}_m^T$: trajectory basis

Fig. 1. Illustration of bilinear multiplication. The coefficients c_{ij} define a weighting of each outer product between shape basis vectors $\mathbf{b}_s^i$ and trajectory basis vectors $\mathbf{b}_m^j$.

In general, both bases and the coefficient matrix must be estimated from data using tensor decomposition methods. However, in [10] the problem is considerably simplified by using a conditioned motion basis. It has been shown that the discrete cosine transform (DCT) basis converges to the optimal PCA basis if the data is generated from a stationary first-order Markov process [11]. Moreover, for respiratory motion, we are interested in low-frequency cyclic patterns, which makes the DCT basis a suitable choice for compression. The use of an analytical basis like DCT is also useful for adapting the bilinear model to varying cycle lengths. Since the shape and motion bases factor out separately and as a result, only $\mathbf{B}_m$ depends on t, the motion basis can be adjusted to appropriate size by changing the length of the basis vectors $\mathbf{b}_m^j$ while leaving the shape basis unchanged. This is not possible with a linear model because shape and motion information are intermingled.

Given a conditioned motion basis $\mathbf{B}_m$ and a series of respiratory cycle data $\mathbf{X}_1, \ldots, \mathbf{X}_N$, we can solve for a shape basis that minimises the squared reconstruction error. It is given by the row-space computed through singular value decomposition (SVD) of the matrix

$$\Pi = [\hat{\mathbf{X}}_1^T, \hat{\mathbf{X}}_2^T, \ldots, \hat{\mathbf{X}}_N^T]^T, \tag{7}$$

where $\hat{\mathbf{X}}_i = \mathbf{X}_i \mathbf{B}_m \mathbf{B}_m^+$ denotes the reconstruction of $\mathbf{X}$ from its trajectory projection and $^+$ denotes the Moore-Penrose pseudoinverse. This way, the shape basis $\mathbf{B}_s$ can be computed directly from the data in closed form. It defines a space where variations along the individual dimensions are uncorrelated. In order to simplify the calculations in the next section, we assume that coefficients are scaled to unit variance in each of the two subspaces, i.e. $\mathbf{C} = \Sigma_s^{-1} \mathbf{B}_s^T \mathbf{X} \mathbf{B}_m \Sigma_m^{-1}$.

3   Reconstruction from Sparse Data

Applications for the bilinear motion model are manifold. A natural application is to use it as a prior for motion segmentation and registration. Here, we focus on another scenario, which is the reconstruction from only a small set of observations, e.g. when measurements from implanted electromagnetic beacons or 2d projections are given and the goal is to reconstruct the entire shape over time. In order to estimate entire breathing cycles from partial observations, we extend the scheme presented in [12] to the bilinear case. Our observation model is as follows,

$$\mathbf{R} = \mathbf{L}_s \mathbf{X} \mathbf{L}_m^T, \tag{8}$$

where $\mathbf{L}_s : \mathbb{R}^p \to \mathbb{R}^{l_p}, l_p < p$ acts on the columns (i.e. features) and $\mathbf{L}_m : \mathbb{R}^t \to \mathbb{R}^{l_t}, l_t < t$ acts on the rows (i.e. time frames) of $\mathbf{X}$. Although these matrices can be any linear transformation, in our context $\mathbf{L}_s$ typically deletes rows (features) over the entire sequence and $\mathbf{L}_m$ deletes all features in a particular frame. In general, both mappings are not injective, thus there is no unique solution of Eq. 8. The least-squares solution is found by optimising the error function

$$E(\mathbf{C}) = \|\mathbf{Q}_s \mathbf{C} \mathbf{Q}_m^+ - \mathbf{R}\|_F, \tag{9}$$

where $\mathbf{Q}_s = \mathbf{L}_s \Sigma_s \mathbf{B}_s$, $\mathbf{Q}_m = \mathbf{L}_m \Sigma_m \mathbf{B}_m^T$ and $\| \cdot \|_F$ denotes the Frobenius norm. This cost function is minimal for

$$\hat{\mathbf{C}} = \mathbf{Q}_s^+ \mathbf{R} \mathbf{Q}_m. \tag{10}$$

However, the result in Eq. 10 only applies for noiseless measurements.

Assuming that measurements are subject to uncorrelated Gaussian noise of variance σ_N^2, the likelihood of observing $\mathbf{R}$ is given by

$$p(\mathbf{R}|\mathbf{C}_m) = \nu \cdot \exp(-\frac{1}{2\sigma_N^2} \|\mathbf{Q}_s \mathbf{C}_m - \mathbf{R}\|_F), \tag{11}$$

where we have defined $\mathbf{C}_m = \mathbf{C}\mathbf{Q}_m^+$ and with normalisation constant $\nu = ((2\pi)^{\frac{l}{2}} \cdot \sqrt{\sigma_N})^{-1}$. Using Bayes' rule to compute the posterior probability and maximising it leads to the following minimisation problem,

$$E(\mathbf{C}_m) = \|\mathbf{Q}_s\mathbf{C}_m - \mathbf{R}\|_F + \eta \cdot \|\mathbf{C}_m\|_F. \tag{12}$$

The regularisation factor $\eta = \sigma_N^2$ allows to find a trade-off between matching quality and prior probability. It can be shown [12] that the global optimum is obtained via SVD of $\mathbf{Q}_s = \mathbf{U}_s\mathbf{W}_s\mathbf{V}_s^T$ according to

$$\hat{\mathbf{C}}_\eta = \mathbf{V}_s\mathrm{diag}(\frac{w_{s,i}}{w_{s,i}^2 + \eta})\mathbf{U}_s^T\mathbf{R}, \tag{13}$$

where $w_{s,i}$ are the diagonal elements of $\mathbf{W}_s$. Note that all matrices in Eq. 13 except $\mathbf{R}$ are constant and can thus be precomputed.

3.1   Model Size and Compression

Any bilinear model can be rewritten in linear form by computing the Kronecker product,

$$\mathbf{B} = \mathbf{B}_m \otimes \mathbf{B}_s \in \mathbb{R}^{p \times t}, \tag{14}$$

i.e. taking all possible products between the elements of the shape and trajectory bases. Note that this result does not imply that linear and bilinear models are equivalent because the opposite operation, i.e. obtaining a bilinear factorisation from a linear basis, is not always possible. Retaining only the k_s basis vectors in $\mathbf{B}_s$ with highest corresponding singular values leads to optimal dimensionality reduction in a least-squares sense. Since respiratory motion can be encoded primarily by lower-frequency components, the model can be further compressed by only retaining the k_m lowest-frequency basis vectors in $\mathbf{B}_m$. For example, setting $k_s = k_t = 5$ in a model of $p = 100$ coordinates and 10 time steps leads to a shape basis of size 100×5 and a motion basis of size 10×5, totalling in 550 values. The corresponding linear model according to Eq. 14 is of size 1000×25 or more than 45 times the number of entries. Formally, the size of the bilinear model grows linearly in the number of model points $\mathcal{O}(p \cdot k_s + t \cdot k_m)$ while the size of the corresponding linear model grows according to $\mathcal{O}(p \cdot t \cdot k_s \cdot k_m)$, which reflects the fact that the bilinear model exploits the structure of the underlying data more efficiently.

4   Experiments

We applied the bilinear model to a sequence of sagittal 2d MRI images of the liver of a male subject under free breathing. A total of 120 respiratory cycles was acquired and split into a training set of 40 cycles and a test set of $n = 80$ cycles. The images were pre-processed as follows. First, they were non-rigidly registered using NiftyReg [13], an open-source medical image registration suite, by deforming a reference exhalation image to all other images. Due to the discontinuities

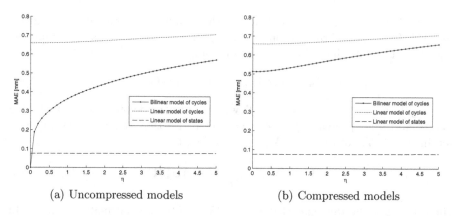

(a) Uncompressed models   (b) Compressed models

Fig. 2. Mean absolute error (MAE) of reconstruction from full testset over different values of the regularisation factor η. In (a), the complete bases were used. In (b), $k_s = 5$ shape and $k_m = 5$ motion basis vectors were used in the bilinear case and 25 basis vectors were used for the linear models.

between the sliding organ and the abdominal wall, the liver was manually masked in the reference image. Additionally, the data was normalised wrt. the number of frames in each cycle, resulting in exactly $t = 10$ states per cycle. The displacement fields were then equidistantly sampled at $n = 85$ locations per frame and a bilinear model was built from these vertices as described above.

4.1   Model Compression

To compare the proposed bilinear model of respiratory cycles, we computed a linear PCA model of cycles (where each of the n test cycles is concatenated into a column vector of size $p \cdot t$) as well as a linear PCA model of states (where the samples consist of $t \cdot n$ column vectors of length p). For the PCA models we use the linear version of the same reconstruction algorithm described above. We reconstructed the full training set without additional noise to see how well the models can describe unseen data. As can be seen in Fig. 2(a), the uncompressed bilinear model has high generalisation capabilities, especially if no regularisation is applied (see $\eta = 0$). When the models are compressed, the bilinear model still outperforms the linear model of cycles for all values of η (Fig. 2(a)). It is not surprising that the linear model of states performs well in both experiments because it fits every observed state individually rather than fitting entire cycles.

4.2   Missing Values

In order to elaborate on the performance of the models in a setting where data is missing and additionally subject to measurement noise, we performed reconstructions on various percentages of randomly removed data. Figure 3(a) shows the error plot for randomly removing an increasing number of model vertices

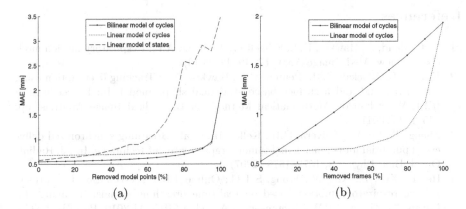

Fig. 3. Mean absolute error (MAE) of reconstruction with Gaussian random noise of $\sigma_N = 1.0$ and fixed regularisation factor $\eta = 1.0$. (a) Model vertices randomly removed over the entire test sequence. (b) Complete time frames randomly removed (linear model of states is not able to reconstruct missing frames).

over the entire test sequence. The bilinear model performs better or equal to its linear counterpart, while the linear model of states clearly performs worse in most cases. Lastly, we randomly removed an increasing number of entire frames from the sequence. Figure 3(b) shows the results. Here, the linear model shows a superior error curve that increases exponentially, while the error of the bilinear model increases linearly. This experiment does not apply for the linear model of states because it cannot produce meaningful reconstructions in case of missing frames.

5   Conclusion

We presented a novel model for modelling respiratory motion that respects the temporal regularity of the underlying data. Shape and motion information is separated into individual bases and a coefficient matrix defines weights of the basis vectors' outer products. This separation leads to significantly more compact models compared to conventional linear models. Furthermore, the model is more flexible because the motion basis can be independently exchanged while leaving the remaining components of the model unchanged in order to generate cycle instances of arbitrary length, although we have restricted our experiments to cycles of the same length for simplicity. We described a Bayesian algorithm for reconstruction from noisy and sparse data in the bilinear case and we could show that the model performs better in most experiments compared to its less compact linear counterparts. All components of the reconstruction algorithm can be precomputed, therefore the algorithm is computationally efficient. The model can potentially be used in registration algorithms as well as for motion compensation in tumour therapy.

References

1. McClelland, J., Hawkes, D.J., Schaeffter, T., King, A.P.: Respiratory motion models: a review. Med. Image Anal. **17**, 19–42 (2013)
2. King, A.P., Blackall, J.M., Penney, G.P., Hawkes, D.J.: Tracking liver motion using 3-D ultrasound and a surface based statistical shape model. In: Proceedings of IEEE Workshop on Mathematical Methods in Biomedical Image Analysis, pp. 145–152 (2001)
3. Zhang, T., Lu, W., Olivera, G.H., Keller, H., et al.: Breathing-synchronized delivery: a potential four-dimensional tomotherapy treatment technique. Int. J. Radiat. Oncol. Biol. Phys. **68**, 1572–1578 (2007)
4. He, T., Xue, Z., Xie, W., Wong, S.T.C.: Online 4-D CT estimation for patient-specific respiratory motion based on real-time breathing signals. In: Jiang, T., Navab, N., Pluim, J.P.W., Viergever, M.A. (eds.) MICCAI 2010, Part III. LNCS, vol. 6363, pp. 392–399. Springer, Heidelberg (2010)
5. Li, R., Lewis, J., Jia, X., Zhao, T., et al.: PCA-based lung motion model. Technical report (2010)
6. Schneider, M.: Model-based respiratory motion compensation for image-guided cardiac interventions. In: Informatiktage. LNI, vol. S-9, pp. 219–222. GI (2010)
7. Preiswerk, F., Arnold, P., Fasel, B., Cattin, P.C.: A bayesian framework for estimating respiratory liver motion from sparse measurements. In: Yoshida, H., Sakas, G., Linguraru, M.G. (eds.) Abdominal Imaging. LNCS, vol. 7029, pp. 207–214. Springer, Heidelberg (2012)
8. Hoogendoorn, C., Sukno, F.M., Ordás, S., Frangi, A.F.: Bilinear models for spatio-temporal point distribution analysis. Int. J. Comput. Vis. **85**, 237–252 (2009)
9. Tenenbaum, J.B., Freeman, W.T.: Separating style and content with bilinear models. Neural Comput. **12**, 1247–1283 (2000)
10. Akhter, I., Simon, T., Khan, S., Matthews, I., Sheikh, Y.: Bilinear spatiotemporal basis models. ACM Trans. Graph. **31**, 17:1–17:12 (2012)
11. Rao, K.R., Yip, P., Rao, K.R.: Discrete Cosine Transform: Algorithms, Advantages, Applications, vol. 226. Academic Press, Boston (1990)
12. Blanz, V., Vetter, T.: Reconstructing the complete 3D shape of faces from partial information. Informationstechnik und Technische Informatik **44**, 295–302 (2002)
13. Modat, M., Ridgway, G.R., Taylor, Z.A., Lehmann, M., et al.: Fast free-form deformation using graphics processing units. Comput. Meth. Prog. Biomed. **98**, 278–284 (2010)

A New Tube Detection Filter for Abdominal Aortic Aneurysms

Erik Smistad[1,2]([✉]), Reidar Brekken[2], and Frank Lindseth[1,2]

[1] Norwegian University of Science and Technology, Trondheim, Norway
[2] SINTEF Medical Technology, Trondheim, Norway
smistad@idi.ntnu.no

Abstract. Tube detection filters (TDFs) are useful for segmentation and centerline extraction of tubular structures such as blood vessels and airways in medical images. Most TDFs assume that the cross-sectional profile of the tubular structure is circular. This assumption is not always correct, for instance in the case of abdominal aortic aneurysms (AAAs). Another problem with several TDFs is that they give a false response at strong edges. In this paper, a new TDF is proposed and compared to other TDFs on synthetic and clinical datasets. The results show that the proposed TDF is able to detect large non-circular tubular structures such as AAAs and avoid false positives.

Keywords: Tube detection · Aortic aneurysm

1 Introduction

Tube detection filters (TDFs) are used to detect tubular structures in 3D images. They perform a shape analysis on each voxel and return a value indicating the likelihood of the voxel belonging to a tubular structure. The likelihood can be used for segmentation and centerline extraction of tubular structures such as abdominal aortic aneurysms from medical images. The segmentation and centerline of these structures are useful for visualization, volume estimation, registration and planning and guidance of vascular interventions.

Many TDFs use second order derivative information to perform the shape analysis like the eigenanalysis of the Hessian matrix. The eigenvalues of this matrix can be used to determine the shape of the local structure and the eigenvectors can be used to find the shape's orientation. To calculate the Hessian matrix at a voxel inside a tubular structure, the gradient information from the edges has to be present. For small tubular structures this is not a problem, but for large ones the gradients have to be propagated from the edges to the center. One way to do this is to compute the Hessian matrix in a Gaussian scale space by convolution with a Gaussian of different standard deviations. The final TDF measure is calculated as the maximum response over all scales. One problem with using Gaussian scale space is that on larger scales objects diffuse into each other and small tubular structures that are close to one another can diffuse

© Springer International Publishing Switzerland 2014
H. Yoshida et al. (Eds.): ABDI 2014, LNCS 8676, pp. 229–238, 2014.
DOI: 10.1007/978-3-319-13692-9_22

together and give the impression that a larger tubular structure is present. Bauer and Bischof [1] suggested to replace the gradient vector field from the Gaussian scale space with an edge-preserving diffusion process called gradient vector flow (GVF), originally introduced by Xu and Prince [2] as an external force field to guide active contours. With the GVF, only one scale is needed and the problem of objects diffusing into each other is avoided.

Frangi et al. [3] introduced a TDF called a vesselness filter. This filter uses the eigenvalues (λ) of the Hessian matrix to determine whether the current voxel x is part of a tubular structure. With the three measures $R_a = |\lambda_2|/|\lambda_3|$, $R_b = |\lambda_1|/\sqrt{|\lambda_2\lambda_3|}$ and $S = \sqrt{\lambda_1^2 + \lambda_2^2 + \lambda_3^2}$ the vesselness filter is defined in (1).

$$T_v(x) = \begin{cases} 0 & \text{if} \quad \lambda_2 > 0 \quad \text{or} \quad \lambda_3 > 0 \\ (1 - e^{-\frac{R_a^2}{2\alpha^2}})e^{-\frac{R_b^2}{2\beta^2}}(1 - e^{-\frac{S^2}{2c^2}}) & \text{else} \end{cases} \tag{1}$$

Frangi et al. used Gaussian scale space methods to do the multi-scale filtering, however Bauer et al. [1,4,5] later used the vesselness TDF successfully with the GVF.

The circle fitting TDF introduced by Krissian et al. [6] uses the eigenvectors of the Hessian matrix to identify the tubes cross-sectional plane. In this plane a circle is fitted to the underlying edge information. The fitting procedure samples N points on a circle with radius r and calculates the average dot product (2) of the edge direction (V) and the circle's inward normal ($-d_i$). The radius is gradually increased and the radius with the highest average is selected. The TDF response is then equal to the average with the select radius r as in (2).

$$T_{cf}(x) = \frac{1}{N} \sum_{i=0}^{N-1} V(x + rd_i) \cdot (-d_i) \tag{2}$$

As a measure of edge direction, Krissian et al. [6] used the gradient calculated at the scale corresponding to the current radius. Bauer et al. [7] used the GVF field instead. Since this TDF assumes that the cross-sectional profile of the tubular structure is circular, it produces a lower response for non-circular tubular structures. Also, the cross-section of a tube is estimated using the eigenvectors of the Hessian matrix which are not accurate, hence even if the tubes are circular the cross-section may often appear as ellipses instead. Furthermore, the circle fitting TDF can give response in voxels where there is not a tubular structure. A semi-circle with a very high contrast can be enough to give a medium response. Pock et al. [8] proposed a symmetry measure to reduce the false response at such edges. This measure reduces the TDF response where the gradient's magnitude, i.e. the contrast, differs along the circle. However, this also reduces the response for tubular structures with a non-circular cross-section. Bauer [9] concluded in his thesis that several TDFs, including the vesselness and circle fitting TDF, have the problem that the response decreases significantly when the cross-section of the tubular structure deviates from a circle, which makes these tubular structures hard to distinguish from noise in the TDF response.

In this paper, a new TDF is proposed that uses GVF and is able to properly detect non-circular irregular tubular structures and reduce the amount of false responses. In addition, it is demonstrated that a multigrid method is necessary for calculating the GVF for large tubular structures such as abdominal aortic aneurysms (AAAs).

2   Methods

Previously, we have developed a framework for extracting airways and blood vessels from different image modalities (e.g. CT, MR and US) using tube detection filters [10]. The framework consists of five main steps that are all executed on the graphic processing unit (GPU) (see Fig. 1). The first step is to crop the volume in order to reduce the total memory usage. The second step involves some pre-processing, such as Gaussian smoothing and gradient vector flow, which are necessary to make the results less sensitive to noise and differences in tube contrast and size. After pre-processing, the TDF is performed. From the TDF result, the centerlines are extracted and finally, a segmentation is performed with a region growing procedure using the centerlines as seeds. The entire implementation is available online[1]. Previously, the circle fitting TDF by Krissian et al. [6] was used in this framework.

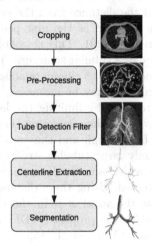

Fig. 1. Block diagram of the implementation

In this paper, a new TDF is proposed as a replacement for this filter to improve detection of large non-circular tubular structures and avoid detection of false tubular structures.

2.1   Large Tubular Structures and Gradient Vector Flow

The most common way to calculate GVF is to use Euler's method as demonstrated by Xu and Prince [2]. However, this method is very slow to converge [11]. And for large tubular structures where the gradients at the edges have to diffuse a long way to the center, this becomes a problem (see Fig. 3). To solve this problem, Han et al. [11] used multigrid methods to calculate GVF and achieved a much better convergence rate. In this paper, a GPU implementation of this multigrid method was used [12].

2.2   A New TDF for Non-circular Tubular Structures

Like the circle fitting TDF, the proposed TDF uses the eigenvectors of the Hessian matrix to identify the orientation of the tubular structures. The two

---

[1] http://github.com/smistad/Tube-Segmentation-Framework/.

eigenvectors associated with the eigenvalues of the largest magnitude e_2 and e_3 span the cross-sectional plane of the tubular structure. In this plane, N line searches are performed from the current voxel x at different angles. For each line search i, a phasor is used to create vectors d_i that define the search direction θ.

$$\theta_i = \frac{2\pi i}{N} \qquad d_i = e_2 \sin \theta_i + e_3 \cos \theta_i \tag{3}$$

Each line search continues until the edge of the tubular structure is encountered and the distance from the center to the edge for line search i is r_i. The edges are detected as the first peak in the vector field's magnitude above the fixed threshold 0.01. This threshold states the minimum gradient magnitude of an edge of a tubular structure. Thus, the value of 0.01 will allow most edges, but it is necessary to eliminate noise. If a dataset has noise with a higher contrast, this threshold may be increased. The problem of detecting false tubular structures is reduced by limiting the length of the line searches with a parameter r_{max}. However, when detecting very large tubular structures, such as AAAs, r_{max} has to be set high and thus might not reduce the number of false positives. Also, if only large tubular structures are to be detected, a parameter, r_{min}, can be set which sets the lower bound for the radius of the tubular structures to be detected. Using these distances, a measure $C(x)$ is created of how likely it is that the voxel x is in the center of the tubular structure (4). This measure enables the proposed TDF to be used for extracting centerlines and was also used by Wink et al. [13].

$$C(r) = \frac{2}{N} \sum_{i=0}^{N/2-1} \frac{\min(r_i, r_{N/2+i})}{\max(r_i, r_{N/2+i})} \tag{4}$$

Finally, the TDF measure T is defined as the product of the center likelihood measure C and a measure M of how well the gradient vectors at the border correspond to the direction of the tubular structure e_1.

$$M(x) = \frac{1}{N} \sum_{i=0}^{N-1} (1 - |V^n(x + r_i d_i) \cdot e_1|) \tag{5}$$

$$T(x) = \begin{cases} 0 & \text{if } \exists i V^n(x + r_i d_i) \cdot (-d_i) < 0 \\ C(r)M(x) & \text{else} \end{cases} \tag{6}$$

Ideally, the gradient vectors V should be perpendicular to the direction of the tubular structure. This can be checked by taking the dot product of the normalized vectors V^n and e_1. The closer the dot product is to zero, the closer the two vectors are to being perpendicular. At the borders of large tubular structures, the data will, locally, resemble more a plate structure than a tubular structure which may lead to an incorrect tube direction e_1. The measure M thus reduces the response in the borders of the tubular structure where the tube direction e_1 may be incorrect. This greatly improves the centerline extraction which uses the tube direction e_1 [10]. Also, if there exist a vector that is more than 90° from the direction to the center $-d_i$, the TDF measure is set to 0. This is done to further reduce the amount of false responses in which the edge gradient has another direction than towards the center and is similar to the circularity measure used by Pock et al. [8].

3 Results

In this section, results of the proposed TDF are presented for both synthetic and clinical data and compared to the vesselness and circle fitting TDF in conjunction with GVF. The parameters used for the GVF are $\mu = 0.1$ with 6 iterations. The vesselness TDF was run with the parameters $\alpha = 0.5$, $\beta = 0.5$ and $c = 100$. And the circle fitting TDF used 32 sample points and the proposed TDF used $N = 12$ line searches.

Synthetic Data: A dataset containing tubular structures with different types of cross-sectional profiles was created. The profiles are displayed in the top of Fig. 2. This dataset contains tubular structures with circular, elliptical, several irregular profiles and one false tubular structure. The vesselness, circle fitting and proposed TDF were performed on this dataset. The responses along a line going through the middle of all of these tubular structures were recorded and are displayed as graphs in Fig. 2. The figure shows that the response of the circle fitting TDF is considerably reduced when performed on tubular structures with a non-circular cross-section, while the proposed TDF detects these almost as

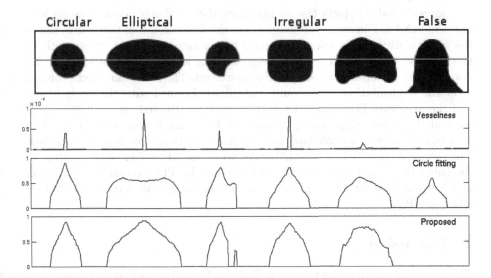

Fig. 2. The top row shows the cross-section of five different tubular structures and one false tubular structure. The three graphs below are the responses from the vesselness, circle fitting and proposed TDFs respectively, measured in a line that goes through the middle of all the cross-sections (the grey line in the top row).

well as the circular structure. The circle fitting TDF also has a high response at the false tubular structure to the far right.

Clinical Data: The TDFs were also executed on clinical CT datasets of abdominal aortic aneurysms (AAAs). Figure 3 illustrates the need for the multigrid method when calculating the GVF on large tubular structures such as an AAA. The figure shows the magnitude of the vector field after running GVF using Euler's method with 1000 iterations (about 6 s) and the multigrid method with 6 iterations (about 1 s). From this figure, it is evident that GVF with Euler's method has problems with diffusing the gradients on the edge of the aneurysm to the center, which is necessary for the TDFs. Over 10 times more iterations would be needed to reach the center with Euler's method which would reduce performance considerably. However, with the multigrid method the gradients are diffused to the center in about 1 s.

Figure 4 shows a maximum intensity projection of the response for each TDF on a CT image of an AAA. The TDFs were all executed on the same GVF vector field thus requiring only one scale. The same window and level were used on the circle fitting and the proposed TDF as both of these TDF have responses from 0 to 1. Also, the minimum radius (r_{min}) and maximum radius (r_{max}) used were 7 and 45 mm. This enables visual comparison of the two TDFs and it is clear that the circle fitting TDF creates a weaker response in the aneurysm than the proposed TDF. Furthermore, the amount of noise, especially from the spine, is higher with the circle fitting TDF. A different level and window were used for the vesselness TDF as its range is exponential. However, the AAA was not detected with this filter.

Figures 5 and 6 depicts the results using three different algorithms on four different AAA CT images. For comparison, the first column in the figures shows the segmentation result using the seeded region growing segmentation method. However, as this method leads to segmentation leakage into the spine on all datasets, the centerline was not possible to extract. The middle and right column show the segmentation surface and centerlines obtained with the circle fitting and the proposed TDF using the framework from [10] and the multigrid GVF method [12]. Here, r_{min} and r_{max} were set to 2 and 45 mm respectively. The vesselness TDF was not able to detect the AAAs and was therefore not included. The datasets consisted of 388–420 slices with size 512 × 512. The runtime of the entire implementation (see Fig. 1) including the TDF, centerline extraction and segmentation for these datasets was 4–10 s using a modern AMD Radeon HD7970 GPU.

4   Discussion

The results shows that the proposed TDF is able to properly detect large non-circular tubular structures such as AAAs in CT images. Figures 5 and 6 show that seeded region growing fails to segment the AAAs due to leakage to the spine and the circle fitting TDF is not able to properly detect some of the AAAs that deviate most from a circular cross-sectional profile.

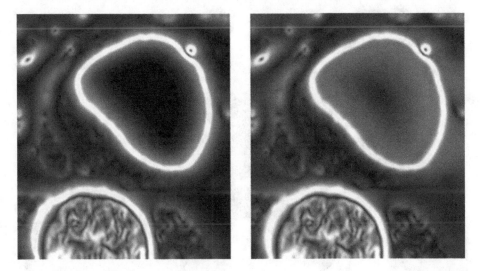

Fig. 3. Magnitude of the vector field after running gradient vector flow (GVF) on a AAA CT dataset. **Left:** Euler's method with 1000 iterations. **Right:** Multigrid method with 6 iterations. The image to the left shows that GVF with Euler's method has problems with diffusing the gradients on the edge of the aneurysm to the center which is necessary for the TDFs.

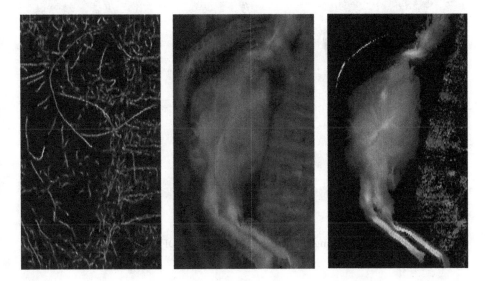

Fig. 4. Maximum intensity projection of TDF responses on a CT image of an abdominal aortic aneurysm (AAA) using the same GVF vector field. **Left:** Vesselness TDF. **Middle:** Circle fitting TDF. **Right:** Proposed TDF. The same level and window were used on the circle fitting and proposed TDF. A different level and window were used for the vesselness TDF as its range is exponential.

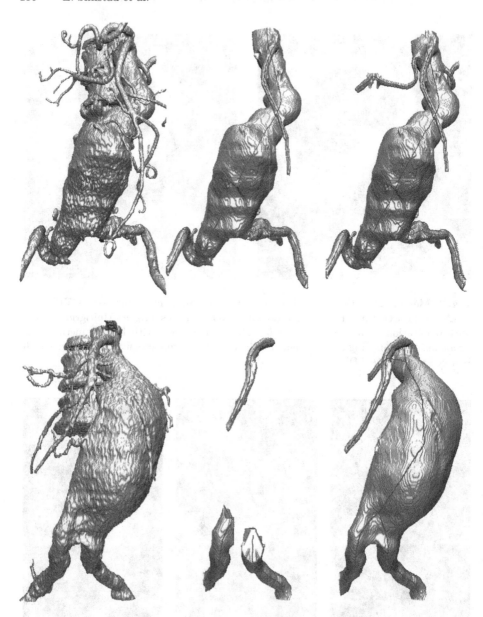

Fig. 5. Left: Region growing. **Middle:** Circle fitting TDF. **Right:** Proposed TDF.

The response of the vesselness and circle fitting TDF is dependent on the contrast due to the use of eigenvalues (Eq. 1) and gradient (Eq. 2). However, the response of the proposed TDF is invariant to the contrast due to the use of the normalized gradient V^n in (5). Nevertheless, Bauer and Bischof [5] proposed a solution to this by adding a parameter F_{max} for the maximum contrast.

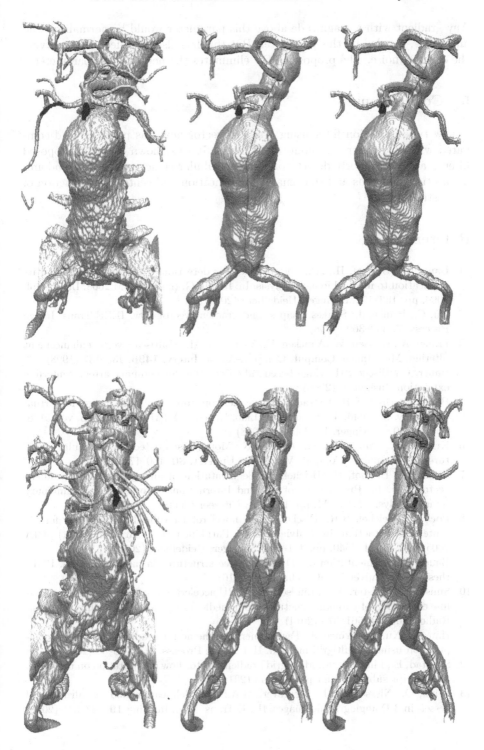

Fig. 6. Left: Region growing. **Middle:** Circle fitting TDF. **Right:** Proposed TDF.

Any gradient with a magnitude above this parameter would be normalized and any below, divided by this parameter. But this has also the effect of amplifying the effect of noise. The proposed TDF eliminates the need for this parameter.

5 Conclusions

A new tube detection filter using gradient vector flow was proposed and compared with two other commonly used filters. It was shown that the proposed filter is able to properly detect non-circular tubular structures such as abdominal aortic aneurysms and thus enable segmentation and centerline extraction of these structures.

References

1. Bauer, C., Bischof, H.: A novel approach for detection of tubular objects and its application to medical image analysis. In: Rigoll, G. (ed.) DAGM 2008. LNCS, vol. 5096, pp. 163–172. Springer, Heidelberg (2008)
2. Xu, C., Prince, J.: Snakes, shapes, and gradient vector flow. IEEE Trans. Image Process. **7**, 359–369 (1998)
3. Frangi, A., Niessen, W., Vincken, K., Viergever, M.: Multiscale vessel enhancement filtering. Med. Image Comput. Comput.-Assist. Interv. **1496**, 130–137 (1998)
4. Bauer, C., Bischof, H.: Edge based tube detection for coronary artery centerline extraction. Insight J. (2008)
5. Bauer, C., Bischof, H.: Extracting curve skeletons from gray value images for virtual endoscopy. In: Dohi, T., Sakuma, I., Liao, H. (eds.) MIAR 2008. LNCS, vol. 5128, pp. 393–402. Springer, Heidelberg (2008)
6. Krissian, K., Malandain, G., Ayache, N.: Model-based detection of tubular structures in 3D images. Comput. Vis. Image Underst. **80**, 130–171 (2000)
7. Bauer, C., Bischof, H., Beichel, R.: Segmentation of airways based on gradient vector flow. In: Proceedings of the 2nd International Workshop on Pulmonary Image Analysis. MICCAI, pp. 191–201. Citeseer (2009)
8. Pock, T., Beichel, R.R., Bischof, H.: A novel robust tube detection filter for 3D centerline extraction. In: Kalviainen, H., Parkkinen, J., Kaarna, A. (eds.) SCIA 2005. LNCS, vol. 3540, pp. 481–490. Springer, Heidelberg (2005)
9. Bauer, C.: Segmentation of 3D tubular tree structures in medical images. Ph.D. thesis, Graz University of Technology (2010)
10. Smistad, E., Elster, A.C., Lindseth, F.: GPU accelerated segmentation and centerline extraction of tubular structures from medical images. Int. J. Comput. Assist. Radiol. Surg. **9**, 561–575 (2014)
11. Han, X., Xu, C., Prince, J.: Fast numerical scheme for gradient vector flow computation using a multigrid method. IET Image Process. **1**(1), 48–55 (2007)
12. Smistad, E., Lindseth, F.: Multigrid gradient vector flow computation on the GPU. Manuscript submitted for publication (2014)
13. Wink, O., Niessen, W.J., Viergever, M.A.: Fast delineation and visualization of vessels in 3-D angiographic images. IEEE Trans. Med. Imaging **19**, 337–346 (2000)

Total Variation Based 3D Reconstruction from Monocular Laparoscopic Sequences

Jan Marek Marcinczak[✉] and Rolf-Rainer Grigat

Vision Systems, TU Hamburg-Harburg, Hamburg, Germany
jan.marcinczak@tu-harburg.de

Abstract. 3D reconstruction from monocular laparoscopic sequences is a significant challenge since illumination changes and specular reflections are present in the majority of the images. In this paper we present a total variation based approach to dense reconstruction from monocular laparoscopic sequences. The method deals with specular reflections and makes use of photometric invariants to gain robustness to illumination changes. The method achieves a median reconstruction accuracy of 0.89 mm in an evaluation of 277 reconstructions of cirrhotic liver phantoms. The nodular structure of the liver is of interest for macroscopic analysis of liver cirrhosis and clinical diagnosis.

Keywords: Monocular laparoscopy · Reconstruction · Total variation · Liver

1 Introduction

In this paper we describe a variational approach to dense multi-view reconstruction of the liver surface from monocular laparoscopic videos. The proposed technique is applied to real laparoscopic sequences of liver cirrhosis to obtain depth maps of the liver surface. Prerequisite for this dense reconstruction is a sparse reconstruction which is obtained by structure from motion (SfM). The presented method is inspired by the algorithm DTAM (Dense Tracking and Mapping) of R. Newcombe et al. [1] where a variational approach is used to perform a dense 3D reconstruction in real-time on the GPU. The advantages of this technique for the dense 3D reconstruction of organ surfaces in laparoscopy are numerous: foremost, this technique is based on a principle which is contrary to many classical approaches; instead of using a set of images with large displacement and perspective change for the 3D reconstruction, a set of images with similar perspectives and short displacements is used. The data term of the method is based on a measure of the pixel intensity. Similar perspectives allow precise measurements of the image intensities and increase the data term accuracy. This argument is even stronger in laparoscopic imaging: the moving light source allows precise tracking only for relatively short displacements. Furthermore, the range of perspectives in the abdomen which can be used for the observation of the liver surface is limited by the incision. In most of the minimal invasive laparoscopies many images are

© Springer International Publishing Switzerland 2014
H. Yoshida et al. (Eds.): ABDI 2014, LNCS 8676, pp. 239–247, 2014.
DOI: 10.1007/978-3-319-13692-9_23

taken from similar perspectives which can be turned into an advantage using this technique. The proposed data term is adjusted to the laparoscopic requirements to consider specular reflections. Additionally, data terms with increased robustness to illumination changes are investigated. For the iterative minimization of the cost function this paper follows the approach described in [2] where the pixel-wise data term and the denoising are alternately solved. Other approaches to 3D reconstruction in laparoscopy have been proposed by Collins et al. [3] using photometric stereo and Stoyanov et al. [4] who used stereo endoscopes for the 3D reconstruction of organ surfaces. Mountney et al. [5] present a detailed survey of existing techniques and the organs under investigation.

To cope with changes in illumination within an image sequence, one usually has two options: the first option is to model the light source and the surface reflectance. The second option is to transform the data into an illumination invariant representation. The first approach has been used by Collins et al. [6] in a Shape from Shading based 3D reconstruction. Our approach follows the second option: it prohibits the evaluation of the data term for specular reflections and transforms the image data to a representation which is less affected by illumination change. It might be argued that specular reflections contain important information about the normal of the surface which is removed by this technique. However, in practice this assumption is often misleading: due to the limited dynamic range, clipping occurs in most specular reflections. For these regions the sensor is saturated and no valid signal (image intensities) can be recovered. Excluding these areas from data term computation avoids the false hypothesis that the image intensity in this region is constant – this would directly affect the estimated normal based on the reflectance model. Therefore, clipping deteriorates the results of approaches which attempt to model these areas with classical illumination models. Additionally, most illumination and reflectance models are high parametric; nonetheless, most of them still do not suffice to model the laparoscopic environment realistically. Inter-surface scattering which occurs regularly in laparoscopy – e.g. the appearance of a liver surrounded by fatty yellow tissue – deteriorates the accuracy of the reflectance model. The appearance of a surface depends on the reflectance spectra which cannot be recovered from RGB triples. Hence, the albedo, sometimes even constant albedo, has been used for reflectance modeling in the literature [6] which is a very simple model for the reflectance of organ surfaces. In [7] Debevec et al. construct a complex light stage, to recover the reflectance field of the human face. Every surface point is recorded under 2000 different lighting directions to obtain the reflectivity. This demonstrates the effort that is necessary to obtain precise reflectance models of the human skin. In laparoscopy, inter-surface scattering and the high variance of the liver appearance would make it even more challenging to obtain a sufficient model. The presented approach avoids the estimation of a high parametric illumination model by transforming the data to a representation which is less affected by illumination change.

The main contribution of this paper is to include the specular reflection segmentation and illumination-robust data terms into a total variation energy formulation similar to [1]. The proposed approach is evaluated on 15 endoscopic sequences of three liver phantoms with nodular surface structure. As the surface of the phantoms is known, ground truth depth maps were computed measuring the relative pose between the phantom and the camera with an optical tracking system. From these sequences, 277 reconstructions based on different reference frames were computed to obtain the distribution of the reconstruction error in millimeter for RGB and spherical data terms.

1.1 Preliminaries

In the following section we use the same notation as in [1]: $\mathbf{u} \in \Omega := (u, v)^{\mathrm{T}}$, with $\Omega \subset \mathbb{R}^2$, denotes an image coordinate, $\mathbf{I} \colon \Omega \to \mathbb{R}^3$ is an RGB image and the dot notation $\dot{\mathbf{u}} := (u, v, 1)^{\mathrm{T}}$ indicates homogeneous variables.

The function $\pi(\mathbf{x}) := (x/z, y/z)^{\mathrm{T}} = \mathbf{u}$ maps the 3D point $\mathbf{x} = (x, y, z)^{\mathrm{T}}$ to the image coordinate $\mathbf{u}$. The inverse mapping which back-projects an image coordinate $\mathbf{u}$ with the given inverse depth $d = \xi(\mathbf{u})$ to the corresponding 3D point $\mathbf{x}$ is defined as $\pi^{-1}(\mathbf{u}, d) = \frac{1}{d}K^{-1}\dot{\mathbf{u}}$, where K is the intrinsic camera matrix and $\xi \colon \Omega \to \mathbb{R}$ is the inverse depth map.

Frames are denoted by v, while v_{ref} is the reference frame. The re-projection from frame v_{ref} into frame v is given by:

$$\Pi_{\{v_{\mathrm{ref}}\}, \{v\}}(\mathbf{u}, d) = \pi\left(K\left(R_{\{v_{\mathrm{ref}}\}, \{v\}}\pi^{-1}(\mathbf{u}, d) + t_{\{v_{\mathrm{ref}}\}, \{v\}}\right)\right). \tag{1}$$

Transformations from a reference frame v_{ref} to another frame v are denoted as

$$\dot{T}_{\{v_{\mathrm{ref}}\}, \{v\}} = \begin{bmatrix} R_{\{v_{\mathrm{ref}}\}, \{v\}} & t_{\{v_{\mathrm{ref}}\}, \{v\}} \\ 0 & 1 \end{bmatrix}, \tag{2}$$

where $R_{\{v_{\mathrm{ref}}\}, \{v\}} \in \mathbb{R}^{3 \times 3}$ is a rotation matrix and $t_{\{v_{\mathrm{ref}}\}, \{v\}} \in \mathbb{R}^{3 \times 1}$ is a translation vector. The set of all frames in a video will be denoted $\mathcal{I}$, while a subset of frames close to the reference frame will be denoted $\mathcal{I}_{v_{\mathrm{ref}}}$. Pixels which are part of specular reflections in the reference frame are given by $\mathbf{u} \in \mathcal{S}_{v_{\mathrm{ref}}, \mathrm{spec}} \subset \Omega$.

2   Total Variation Based Dense Reconstruction

Total Variation based techniques are popular methods in image processing and computer vision, such as optical flow, denoising or 3D reconstruction [1,2,8]. The approach by R. Newcombe et al. [1] minimizes an energy consisting of the data energy $C_{v_{\mathrm{ref}}}(\mathbf{u}, \xi(\mathbf{u}))$ and the regularization term $\|\nabla \xi(\mathbf{u})\|_\epsilon$, where ϵ indicates the Huber norm. A per pixel weight is used which reduces the costs of the regularization term if a high gradient is present in the image. This formulation is based on the assumption that there is a high probability for a depth discontinuity if an edge is present in the image. In laparoscopic sequences the strongest responses to edge detection filters are commonly caused by specular reflections. Therefore, we propose a different energy formulation which deals with specular reflections in the data term. Let

$$N_{\mathrm{tissue}}(\mathbf{u}, d) = \left|\left\{v \in \mathcal{I}_{v_{\mathrm{ref}}} \mid \Pi_{\{v_{\mathrm{ref}}\}, \{v\}}(\mathbf{u}, d) \notin \mathcal{S}_{v, \mathrm{spec}}\right\}\right| \tag{3}$$

be the count of re-projections $\Pi_{\{v_{ref}\},\{v\}}(\mathbf{u}, d)$ which are not located in specular reflections. The energy

$$\mathbf{E}_\xi = \int\limits_\Omega \left\{ \|\nabla\xi(\mathbf{u})\|_1 + \lambda_{\text{data}} C_{v_{ref}}(\mathbf{u}, \xi(\mathbf{u})) \right\} d\mathbf{u} \tag{4}$$

with

$$C_{v_{ref}}(\mathbf{u}, d) = \begin{cases} w(\mathbf{u}, d) \sum_{v \in \mathcal{I}_{v_{ref}}} \|\rho(\mathbf{I}_v, \mathbf{u}, d)\|_1, & N_{\text{tissue}}(\mathbf{u}, d) > 0 \\ \rho_{\max}, & N_{\text{tissue}}(\mathbf{u}, d) = 0 \end{cases} \tag{5}$$

is proposed to account for specular reflections in the data term $C_{v_{ref}}(\mathbf{u}, d)$. The data term is computed by a voxel volume [1] which is illustrated in Fig. 1. The weighting function $w(\mathbf{u}, \xi(\mathbf{u}))$ accounts for specular reflections $\mathcal{S}_{v,\text{spec}}$ which are segmented by the closed contour segmentation algorithm given in [9]. The last case of (5) considers that for some depth values there might be no good re-projections for any $v \in \mathcal{I}_{v_{ref}}$. These depth values are penalized by $\rho_{\max}$. To omit re-projections which fall into specular reflections, the normalization needs to be dependent on d:

$$w(\mathbf{u}, d) = \begin{cases} 0, & \mathbf{u} \in \mathcal{S}_{v_{ref},\text{spec}} \\ N_{\text{tissue}}^{-1}(\mathbf{u}, d), & \mathbf{u} \in \Omega \setminus \mathcal{S}_{v_{ref},\text{spec}} \end{cases}. \tag{6}$$

The first case sets the data costs to zero for pixels in the reference frame which are part of specular reflections $\mathbf{u} \in \mathcal{S}_{v_{ref},\text{spec}}$. The second case normalizes the data costs by the number of re-projections which do not fall into specular reflections.

2.1 Data Cost Computation

The photometric cost function $\rho(\mathbf{I}_v, \mathbf{u}, d)$ states the similarity of a point $\mathbf{u}$ in the reference frame with its re-projections in frame v, where d is the inverse depth. To ensure that no data costs are computed based on specular reflections, the cost function is given by:

$$\rho(\mathbf{I}_v, \mathbf{u}, d) = \begin{cases} 0, & \Pi_{\{v_{ref}\},\{v\}}(\mathbf{u}, d) \in \mathcal{S}_{v,\text{spec}} \\ \mathbf{I}_{v_{ref}}(\mathbf{u}) - \mathbf{I}_v\left(\Pi_{\{v_{ref}\},\{v\}}(\mathbf{u}, d)\right), & \Pi_{\{v_{ref}\},\{v\}}(\mathbf{u}, d) \in \Omega \setminus \mathcal{S}_{v,\text{spec}} \end{cases}. \tag{7}$$

Furthermore, we investigate the performance of the spherical transform of the RGB color space [10] to cope with illumination changes. The spherical transform of the RGB color space was shown to perform better than all other invariants for optical flow estimation under varying illumination [10]:

$$(R(\mathbf{u}), G(\mathbf{u}), B(\mathbf{u})) \rightarrow \begin{cases} r_s(\mathbf{u}) = \sqrt{R(\mathbf{u})^2 + G(\mathbf{u})^2 + B(\mathbf{u})^2} \\ \theta_s(\mathbf{u}) = \arctan\left(\frac{G(\mathbf{u})}{R(\mathbf{u})}\right) \\ \phi_s(\mathbf{u}) = \arcsin\left(\frac{\sqrt{R(\mathbf{u})^2 + G(\mathbf{u})^2}}{\sqrt{R(\mathbf{u})^2 + G(\mathbf{u})^2 + B(\mathbf{u})^2}}\right) \end{cases} \tag{8}$$

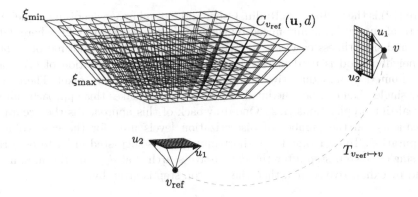

Fig. 1. The data cost volume is shown for $N_d = 3$ different depth values. To obtain the costs $C_{v_{\text{ref}}}(\mathbf{u}, d)$ for a certain depth d of a pixel $\mathbf{u}$, the corresponding voxel is projected into all frames $v \in \mathcal{I}_{\text{ref}}$ and the discrepancy function $\rho(\mathbf{I}_v, \mathbf{u}, d)$ is computed.

Using the Dichromatic Reflectance Model [11] and the white light assumption (equal energy spectrum) one can verify that the $\theta_s(\mathbf{u})$ and $\phi_s(\mathbf{u})$ channels are photometric invariants [12]. Instead of using the RGB differences between the re-projections the $\theta_s(\mathbf{u})$ and $\phi_s(\mathbf{u})$ channels are used to obtain a robust data term.

2.2 Energy Minimization

To minimize (4), we follow the approach of [1,2] and rewrite the energy as

$$\min_{\xi} \int_{\Omega} \left\{ \|\nabla \xi(\mathbf{u})\|_1 + \lambda_{\text{data}} C_{v_{\text{ref}}}(\mathbf{u}, \alpha(\mathbf{u})) \right\} d\mathbf{u} \tag{9}$$

$$\text{subject to} \quad \alpha(\mathbf{u}) = \xi(\mathbf{u}) .$$

The constraint can be embedded into the functional using quadratic relaxation [13] resulting in the following optimization task:

$$\min_{\xi, \alpha} \int_{\Omega} \left\{ \|\nabla \xi(\mathbf{u})\|_1 + \frac{1}{\theta}(\alpha(\mathbf{u}) - \xi(\mathbf{u}))^2 + \lambda_{\text{data}} C_{v_{\text{ref}}}(\mathbf{u}, \alpha(\mathbf{u})) \right\} d\mathbf{u} . \tag{10}$$

As mentioned in [2], this is a strictly convex approximation of (4). The solution is given by iteratively solving

$$\min_{\alpha} E_{\alpha,\text{data}} = \min_{\alpha} \int_{\Omega} \underbrace{\left\{ \frac{1}{\theta}(\alpha(\mathbf{u}) - \xi(\mathbf{u}))^2 + \lambda_{\text{data}} C_{v_{\text{ref}}}(\mathbf{u}, \alpha(\mathbf{u})) \right\}}_{E_{\text{aux}}(\mathbf{u}, \alpha(\mathbf{u}), \xi(\mathbf{u}))} d\mathbf{u} \tag{11}$$

and

$$\min_{\xi} E_{\xi,\text{noise}} = \min_{\xi} \int_{\Omega} \left\{ \|\nabla \xi(\mathbf{u})\|_1 + \frac{1}{\theta}(\alpha(\mathbf{u}) - \xi(\mathbf{u}))^2 \right\} d\mathbf{u} , \tag{12}$$

where (12) is the well-known Rudin, Osher and Fatemi image denoising model [8]. The total energy (4) is minimized by the algorithm described in [2], where data costs and smoothness costs are iteratively minimized. As no information about the neighborhood is used in the data term, the minimal solution of (11) can be computed by an exhaustive 1-dimensional search for every pixel. Therefore, every single pixel can be scheduled in parallel which makes this approach suited for real-time applications [1,2]. One drawback of this approach is the accuracy dependency on the number of discretization levels used for the cost volume computation. To overcome these shortcomings, it is suggested in [1] to perform one single Newton step after the exhaustive search. Let $d_{\min}$ be the minimum found by exhaustive search, then the Newton step is given by:

$$\hat{\alpha}_{\mathbf{u},\mathrm{nt}} = \hat{\alpha}_{\mathbf{u},\min} - h_{\mathrm{nt}} \frac{\left.\frac{\partial E_{\mathrm{aux}}\left(\mathbf{u},\hat{\alpha}_{\mathbf{u}},\hat{\xi}_{\mathbf{u}}\right)}{\partial \hat{\alpha}_{\mathbf{u}}}\right|_{\hat{\alpha}_{\mathbf{u}}=\hat{\alpha}_{\mathbf{u},\min}}}{\left.\frac{\partial^2 E_{\mathrm{aux}}\left(\mathbf{u},\hat{\alpha}_{\mathbf{u}},\hat{\xi}_{\mathbf{u}}\right)}{\partial \hat{\alpha}_{\mathbf{u}}^2}\right|_{\hat{\alpha}_{\mathbf{u}}=\hat{\alpha}_{\mathbf{u},\min}}}. \tag{13}$$

Using this refinement step the exhaustive search can be carried out on a coarse scale using as few as 32 or even 16 depth samples.

3   Results

The proposed approach was evaluated on 15 endoscopic sequences of three liver phantoms with nodular surface structure. As the surfaces of the phantoms are known, ground truth depth maps were computed measuring the relative pose between the phantoms and the camera with an optical tracking system. From these sequences, 277 reconstructions based on different reference frames were computed to obtain the distribution of the reconstruction error in millimeter for RGB and spherical data terms. During recording, the endoscope was moved by hand and the scene was solely illuminated by the light source of the endoscope. For comparison, the same frames were used to compute both data terms. Figure 2 shows the results for one of the 277 images. The improved reconstruction accuracy for the spherical coordinates is evident and confirmed by the results shown in Table 1. The median reconstruction error for the spherical data term is 0.89 mm while the median error using the RGB data term is 2.17 mm.

Figure 3 illustrates the results on real laparoscopic sequences. The videos were recorded with thin laparoscopes (1.9 mm) during real interventions for diagnosis of liver cirrhosis. On the liver surface one can verify that the depth values are consistent with the visual perception of depth in the reference frame. The initial depth map is constructed from a sparse point cloud by nearest neighbor interpolation and smoothing. Commonly, the abdomen wall will not be reconstructed correctly from monocular laparoscopic videos. The main reason is the non-rigid deformation by the breathing cycle which prohibits correct re-projections. In the case of liver cirrhosis, the liver stiffness increases and the breathing cycle will move but not deform the liver.

The quality of the depth maps is mostly dependent on the data term but also a corrupted initialization by the sparse reconstruction can prohibit convergence

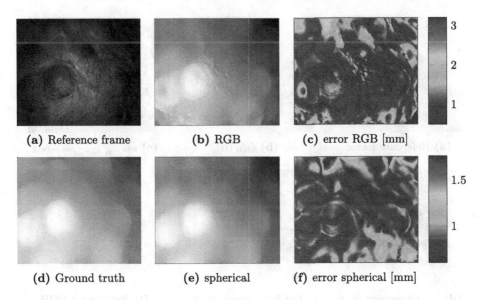

(a) Reference frame   (b) RGB   (c) error RGB [mm]

(d) Ground truth   (e) spherical   (f) error spherical [mm]

Fig. 2. Inverse depth maps estimated with the proposed method using RGB and spherical data terms. The same frames were used for the RGB and spherical data term computation. (a) Reference frame that was used for the construction of the depth volume. (b) Inverse depth map obtained using the RGB data term (c) Reconstruction error in mm for the RGB data term. (d) Ground truth inverse depth. (e) Inverse depth map obtained using the spherical data term. (f) Reconstruction error in mm for the spherical data term.

even if the quality of the data term is high. The accuracy of the data term can be improved by increasing the number of frames used for its computation. Figure 3 shows the resulting inverse depth map in the presence of specular reflections in the reference frame. Therefore, no data term can be computed for these locations and $\xi_{init}(\mathbf{u})$ is used in the first iteration (see (11)). During minimization the depth of these regions is driven by the regularization term.

Table 1. Reconstruction error in millimeters of the dense reconstruction for RGB and spherical data terms. p_{25}, p_{50}, p_{75}, p_{90}, p_{95} and p_{99} are the percentiles of the reconstruction error.

Data Term	p_{25}	p_{50}	p_{75}	p_{90}	p_{95}	p_{99}	[mm]
Spherical	0.38	0.89	1.86	3.44	4.81	8.16	
RGB	0.97	2.17	4.13	6.88	9.15	15.99	

4   Discussion and Outlook

The results demonstrate the accuracy of the proposed reconstruction method in presence of specular reflections and illumination change. The nodules caused

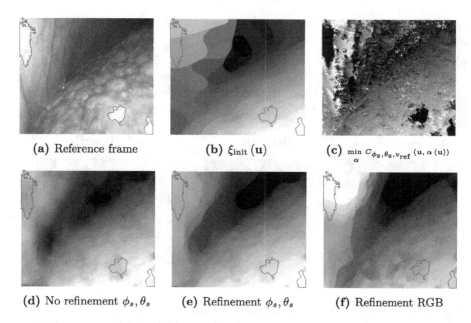

(a) Reference frame   (b) $\xi_{\text{init}}(\mathbf{u})$ (c) $\min\limits_{\alpha} C_{\phi_s,\theta_s,v_{\text{ref}}}(\mathbf{u},\alpha(\mathbf{u}))$

(d) No refinement ϕ_s,θ_s (e) Refinement ϕ_s,θ_s (f) Refinement RGB

Fig. 3. Resulting depth maps with segmented specular reflections. These regions are removed from the data term (c) and instead $\xi_{\text{init}}(\mathbf{u})$ is used in the first iteration (see (11)). During minimization the depth of these regions is driven by the regularization term.

by liver cirrhosis are commonly classified as micronodular (<3 mm), nodular (3–7 mm) and macronodular (>7 mm). With a median accuracy of 0.9 mm most of the nodular and macronodular structures are visible in the reconstruction. For clinical validation, evaluation on real clinical data will be necessary. However, as a CT scan is not part of the standard laparoscopic intervention, no reference surface of the liver is available.

References

1. Newcombe, R., Lovegrove, S., Davison, A.: DTAM: dense tracking and mapping in real-time. In: IEEE International Conference Computer Vision (ICCV), pp. 2320–2327 (2011)
2. Wedel, A., Cremers, D.: Stereo Scene Flow for 3D Motion Analysis. Springer, Heidelberg (2011)
3. Collins, T., Bartoli, A.: 3D reconstruction in laparoscopy with close-range photometric stereo. In: Ayache, N., Delingette, H., Golland, P., Mori, K. (eds.) MICCAI 2012, Part II. LNCS, vol. 7511, pp. 634–642. Springer, Heidelberg (2012)
4. Stoyanov, D., Darzi, A., Yang, G.: Practical approach towards accurate dense 3D depth recovery for robotic laparoscopic surgery. Comput. Aided Surg. **10**, 199–208 (2005)
5. Mountney, P., Stoyanov, D., Yang, G.Z.: Three-dimensional tissue deformation recovery and tracking. Signal Process. Mag. **27**, 14–24 (2010)

6. Collins, T., Bartoli, A.: Towards live monocular 3D laparoscopy using shading and specularity information. In: Abolmaesumi, P., Joskowicz, L., Navab, N., Jannin, P. (eds.) IPCAI 2012. LNCS, vol. 7330, pp. 11–21. Springer, Heidelberg (2012)
7. Debevec, P., Hawkins, T., Tchou, C., Duiker, H., Sarokin, W., Sagar, M.: Acquiring the reflectance field of a human face. In: Proceedings of the 27th Annual Conference on Computer Graphics and Interactive Techniques, pp. 145–156 (2000)
8. Rudin, L., Osher, S., Fatemi, E.: Nonlinear total variation based noise removal algorithms. Phys. D: Nonlinear Phenom. **160**, 259–2680 (1992)
9. Marcinczak, J., Grigat, R.R.: Closed contour specular reflection segmentation in laparoscopic images. Int. J. Biomed. Imaging **2013**, 6 (2013)
10. Mileva, Y., Bruhn, A., Weickert, J.: Illumination-robust variational optical flow with photometric invariants. In: Hamprecht, F.A., Schnörr, C., Jähne, B. (eds.) DAGM 2007. LNCS, vol. 4713, pp. 152–162. Springer, Heidelberg (2007)
11. Shafer, S.: Using color to separate reflection components. Color Res. Appl. **10**, 210–218 (1985)
12. Gevers, T., Smeulders, A.: Color-based object recognition. Pattern Recogn. **32**, 453–464 (1999)
13. Chambolle, A., Caselles, V., Cremers, D., Novaga, M., Pock, T.: An Introduction to Total Variation for Image Analysis Theoretical Foundations and Numerical Methods for Sparse Recovery. De Gruyter, Berlin (2010)

MRI-Based Thickness Analysis of Bladder Cancer: A Pilot Study

Xi Zhang, Yang Liu, Dan Xiao, Guopeng Zhang, Qimei Liao,
and Hongbing Lu(✉)

The Department of Biomedical Engineering/Computer Application,
Fourth Military Medical University, Xi'an 710032, Shaanxi,
People's Republic of China
luhb@fmmu.edu.cn

Abstract. To find an effective way to quantitatively analyze the thickness variation of human bladder wall under different states, in this paper, we proposed a novel pipeline for thickness measurement, analysis, and mapping of bladder wall based on T2-weighted MRI images. The pipeline includes major steps of data acquisition, automatic segmentation of bladder wall, 3D thickness calculation, thickness normalization, and standardized bladder shape mapping. Based on the proposed pipeline, 20 datasets including 10 patients and 10 volunteers were used to explore the distribution pattern of wall thickness and find the difference between cancerous tissue and normal bladder wall. The results demonstrated the potential of wall thickness as a good indicator of bladder abnormalities, indicating its possible use in lesion detection on the bladder wall.

Keywords: Bladder cancer · T2-weighted MRI · Bladder wall 3D thickness

1 Introduction

Bladder cancer, the fourth most common cancer, has become the seventh leading cause of cancer-related deaths in the United States in 2013 [1]. Half of all patients with bladder cancer were diagnosed while the tumor was in situ, for which the 5-year survival rate is 96 % [1]. As the tumor infiltrates deeply, the 5-year survival rate has declined greatly. Therefore, early detection of bladder cancer is crucial to prevent the disease and reduce the death rate. In addition, bladder cancer is difficult to manage because of its high recurrence rate after resection (as high as 70 % for patients with cancerous tissue confined to the mucosa layer in 5 years [2]). An appropriate follow-up procedure is also crucial to prevent the recurrence. Currently, optical cystoscopy (OCy) is the most common diagnostic tool for bladder cancer, with a sensitivity of approximately 87 % and specificity of around 95 %. However, it is invasive, time-consuming with some blind regions, and uncomfortable, with a risk of 5–10 % rate of urinary tract infection following the invasive procedure [3, 4]. Due to the difficulty of OCys, as well as the high cost of patient follow-up management by OCy every three to six months after tumor resection, it is essential to find a noninvasive and convenient way for early detection and follow-up management of tumor recurrence.

© Springer International Publishing Switzerland 2014
H. Yoshida et al. (Eds.): ABDI 2014, LNCS 8676, pp. 248–256, 2014.
DOI: 10.1007/978-3-319-13692-9_24

As reported [2], bladder carcinoma invades gradually from the mucosa into the wall muscles, inducing morphological changes of inner and outer bladder wall. Recent studies indicate that bladder wall thickness tends to be a good indicator of the occurrence of bladder abnormalities [5–8]. However, since bladder shapes change complicatedly due to the volume change of urine inside the bladder and vary diversely variation among the populations, it is quite difficult to make a quantitatively comparison of bladder thickness of the same subject at different filling stages or among different subjects.

To solve this problem, in this study we establish an entire pipeline for thickness measurement, analysis, and mapping of bladder wall based on magnetic resonance imaging (MRI). It includes major steps of image acquisition, automatic segmentation of inner and outer borders of bladder wall, 3D thickness calculation, thickness normalization, and standardized shape mapping for quantitative analysis of bladder wall. Based on the proposed pipeline, statistical analysis on bladder thickness between patients with bladder cancer and volunteers is performed.

The rest of the paper is organized as follows. In Sect. 2 we present an overview of the proposed pipeline, followed by more detailed descriptions of the major steps. In Sect. 3, experimental results on thickness difference are presented using the proposed approach. Finally, in Sect. 4 we conclude the paper and discuss future work.

2 The Pipeline Established for Thickness Analysis of Bladder Wall

2.1 Overview of the Proposed Pipeline

A block diagram of the proposed pipeline for thickness analysis of the bladder wall was shown in Fig. 1. The first step, MRI data acquisition aimed to find a relatively optimal imaging sequence to get better contrast between the bladder wall and its surroundings without the use of exogenetic contrast agent. Then the inner and outer borders of the bladder wall were extracted automatically from MRI bladder images for further thickness calculation and analysis. The Laplacian-based method was used to estimate 3D thickness from bladder wall contours extracted. Considering the variation in thickness of the same bladder at different filling states or in different individuals, thickness normalization was applied to enable quantitative comparison between different states or individuals. Finally, a standardization step that map the bladder wall onto an ellipsoid model was performed to eliminate the influence of shape differences.

2.2 MRI Data Acquisitions

Considering the structural, functional and pathological information it provides for diagnosing bladder tumor, MRI turns out to be a better choice for bladder evaluation. The urine can be used as endogenous contrast medium to enhance the image contrast between bladder lumen and wall, making it a non-invasive procedure with good sensitivity to tissues. To find an optimal imaging protocol for better contrast between the

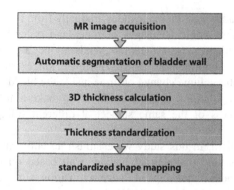

Fig. 1. Block diagram of the proposed pipeline for thickness analysis.

bladder wall and its surroundings, several sequences for abdominal imaging has been tested and a 3D T2-weighted sequence with CUBE technique was chosen, considering its tissue contrast and short acquisition time. All image data were acquired in DICOM format by a whole-body scanner (GE Discovery MR750 3.0T) with a phased-array body coil. Table 1 gives protocol parameters used for the sequence. Prior to the examination, each subject (patient or volunteer) was asked to drink enough mineral water and then waited for an adequate time period so that they felt the bladder was distended sufficiently. To avoid the artifacts caused by respiratory movement and/or intestinal tract movement, all subjects were bound by a bellyband during scan and all patients had their intestinal tracts cleaned before the day of scanning. 20 male subjects including 10 patients and 10 volunteers were recruited in this study. All the patients were confirmed of having urothelial carcinoma by postoperative pathological biopsy. There was no statistical difference in age between two groups. Figure 2 gives 3D T2-weighted MR images acquired from a patient and from a volunteer.

Table 1. Parameters used for image acquisition.

Parameter name	Parameter value
Series description	Ax Cube T2
Acquisition time(ms)	160456
RT(ms)	2500
ET(ms)	131.3310
Slice thickness(mm)	1
Flip angle	90

2.3 Bladder Wall Segmentation

Accurate extraction of the inner and outer borders of the bladder wall is crucial for thickness analysis. However, automatic segmentation of the bladder wall from MRI images is quite challenging due to artifacts inside the bladder lumen, weak boundaries in the apex and base areas and complicated intensity distribution outside. To deal with these difficulties, a coupled directional level set model (CDLS) has been proposed by

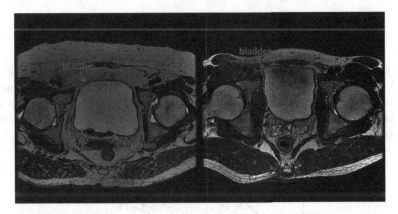

Fig. 2. MR bladder images acquired from a patient and a volunteer, respectively.

our group recently [9]. It utilizes the directional gradient, region information and minimal thickness of the bladder wall as a priori and segments the outer and inner boundaries simultaneously. Figure 3 shows the workflow of the proposed CDLS method with the red and yellow contours representing the inner and outer boundaries of bladder wall, respectively. The method can be roughly divided into two stages: initialization and segmentation. In the first stage, the inner level set function (ILSF) and the outer level set function (OLSF) are initialized one after another using directional gradient-based model. In the second stage, the directional gradient, variance energy and minimum thickness are integrated together to segment the inner and outer boundaries simultaneously. A preliminary test on 3D T2-weighted bladder images confirmed its performance and accuracy [9].

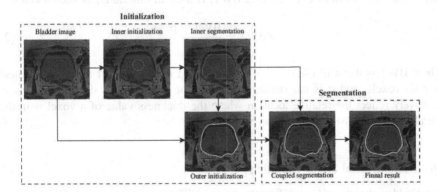

Fig. 3. The workflow of the CDLS method for bladder wall segmentation (Colour figure online).

2.4 Thickness Calculation of Bladder Wall

Based on the segmented bladder inner and outer borders, the Laplacian method is utilized to define and estimate 3D thickness of the bladder wall [10]. The Laplace's equation, a second order PDE, can be expressed by

$$\nabla^2 \psi = \frac{\partial^2 \psi}{\partial x^2} + \frac{\partial^2 \psi}{\partial y^2} + \frac{\partial^2 \psi}{\partial z^2} = 0 \tag{1}$$

As shown in Fig. 4, the potential of voxels on inner and outer boundary was set to 0 and 1 V, respectively. After solving the Laplace's equation inside the wall volume, the streamline length (marked with arrowed lines), as the bladder wall thickness of each voxel inside the bladder wall, can be estimated as the sum of the unit tangent field of each voxel.

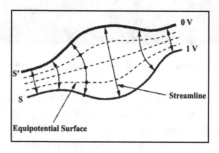

Fig. 4. A two-dimensional (2D) example of Laplacian method.

2.5   The Thickness Normalization

With the calculated wall thickness, we found its absolute value varies significantly at different states or for different individuals. This makes it difficult to compare and analyze the difference quantitatively. To normalize the wall thickness distribution, Z-score of the thickness of each voxel, ZBWT, is used in this study, as shown below:

$$ZBWT = \frac{BWT - \mu}{\sigma} \tag{2}$$

Where BWT is the wall thickness of each voxel, μ is the mean of the wall thickness over all voxels, and σ is the standard deviation of the thickness distribution. It can effectively reflect the relative location where the thickness value of a voxel is in the overall thickness distribution of the bladder wall.

2.6   Standardized Shape Mapping

The bladder shapes vary significantly among different subjects, even for the same subject, it varies at different filling states. Figure 5(a) and (b) show bladder images from two different subjects, and Fig. 5(c) and (d) show bladder images at different filling stages from the same subject. It is essential to find a way to map the bladder wall onto a standard model for possible quantitative comparison of thickness changes.

For shape mapping, a global parametric mapping model has been proposed by our group recently, which can effectively adapt to a bladder with arbitrary shape via the

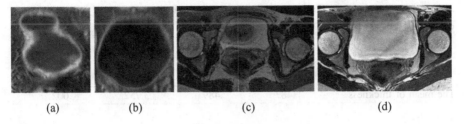

(a)   (b)   (c)   (d)

Fig. 5. Examples of different bladder shapes.

free-form deformation (FFD) [11]. As shown in Fig. 6, an ellipsoid model is first initialized based on scattered points on the bladder wall and then deforms to fit the bladder surface iteratively using FFD. After that, all scattered points are projected onto the surface model for closest point searching and then the mapping relationship between the initialized ellipsoid model and the surface model is established. The proposed method provides a unified way to map the bladder shape onto a unit standard model like a sphere, as well as wall features such as thickness, for quantitative evaluation of the entire bladder.

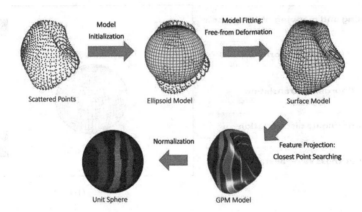

Fig. 6. The basic scheme for the proposed parametric mapping model.

3   Experimental Result

3.1   Difference Analysis of Bladder Wall 3D Thickness

In order to find whether there is difference of bladder wall 3D thickness between patients and volunteers, Based on the proposed pipeline, mean value of bladder wall thickness of both patient group and volunteer group was obtained. Then, the bilateral t test for the mean value of thickness of each subject from two groups was performed in SPSS 19.0, with the test level $\alpha = 0.05$. According to the result of t test listed in Table 2, $p = 0.002 < 0.05$. In other words, there is significant difference of the bladder wall thickness between the patient group and volunteer group.

Table 2. The result of bilateral t test.

Statistic name	Levene's test for homogeneity of variance		Bilateral t test	
	F	.Sig	t	P
The mean of thickness	.487	.489	3.752	.002

3.2 Establishment of the Thickness Template for Normal Bladder Wall

Based on the proposed pipeline and MRI bladder datasets of 10 volunteers, a standard thickness template of normal bladder wall was established, as shown in Fig. 7(a) To build up the template, thickness distributions of all 10 datasets were first calculated and then mapped to an ellipsoid model. After the scale transform, coordinate translation, all thickness values of each voxel from ten datasets were averaged to get the template value of the corresponding voxel. The template, which reflects the approximate thickness distribution of a health bladder, as shown in Fig. 7(b), can be used as a standard template for abnormal thickness analysis.

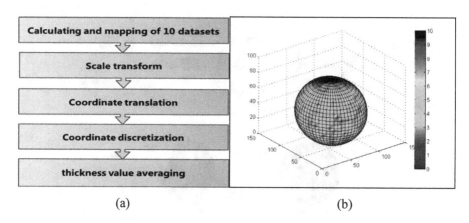

(a)   (b)

Fig. 7. (a) Block diagram for the proposed thickness template overview. (b) 3D visualization effect of the template.

3.3 The Combination of Thickness Normalization and Standardized Shape Mapping in Bladder Wall Thickness Variation Analysis

In order to find the difference of thickness varying between bladder wall tissue and cancerous tissue, standardize the patients' bladder shape via the parametric mapping model, and compare the bladder wall thickness distribution between patients' bladder and the thickness template using Z-score method mentioned above. We wanted to find the optimal Z-score threshold for reflecting the difference between wall tissue and cancerous tissue. Regions where the ZBWT was below the threshold would be considered as normal wall tissue; regions above the threshold would not be considered as wall tissue. The selecting ratio is a ratio of the voxel number of auto selecting by using a certain ZBWT as the threshold over the voxel number of manual drawing by radiologist. Generally, the samples, whose difference to the average μ is in the range of 2σ, is considered coming from the same population. So we choose ZBWT = 2 and ZBWT = 2.5 as the threshold respectively, to select the voxel which have a ZBWT value larger than the threshold. Calculate the selecting ratio of 10 cases of patient dataset and list the result in Table 3. It is obvious that a better threshold may lays in the range of [2, 2.5].

Table 3. The selecting ratio using ZBWT = 2 and ZBWT = 2.5 respectively.

Dataset	Voxel number of manual drawing	ZBWT > 2		ZBWT > 2.5	
		Voxel number	Ratio	Voxel number	Ratio
1	1083	1339	>1	1128	>1
2	1494	1295	**0.87**	983	0.67
3	1503	1623	>1	1250	**0.83**
4	1281	1292	>1	928	0.72
5	1495	1691	>1	1300	**0.87**
6	1337	1470	>1	831	0.62
7	1254	1304	>1	662	0.53
8	1103	1276	>1	771	0.70
9	1348	1286	**0.95**	1193	**0.89**
10	1005	1136	>1	924	**0.92**

4 Conclusion

In this paper, we present an entire pipeline for thickness measurement, analysis, and mapping of bladder wall based on MRI. The pipeline includes main steps described as follow. First of all, 3D T2-weighted MR image sequence with CUBE technique is used for images acquisition of bladder. Then coupled directional level set method is used for automatic segmentation of inner and outer borders of bladder wall. After that, 3D thickness of bladder wall is calculated by the Laplacian-method. Then thickness normalization and standardized shape mapping for quantitative analysis of bladder wall will be done by Z-score and parametric mapping model via FFD, respectively. The establishment of the pipeline makes it possible for quantitative comparison and analysis about bladder wall thickness. Based on the proposed pipeline, statistical analysis on bladder thickness between patients with bladder cancer and volunteers is performed. Result shows that there is a significant difference of bladder wall thickness between patient group and volunteer group. By using the thickness template of normal bladder wall we established to find the difference of thickness varying between bladder wall tissue and cancerous tissue, we draw a conclusion that the optimal Z-score threshold for reflecting the difference between wall tissue and cancerous tissue may lays in the range of [2, 2.5].

Our future work will make better use of bladder wall thickness, which is a good indicator of occurrence of bladder wall abnormalities, to detect the cancer on the bladder wall and furthermore to confirm the infiltration degree of bladder cancer.

References

1. American Cancer Society: Cancer facts and figures 2013, pp. 4–10. Atlanta, American Cancer Society (2013)
2. National Comprehensive Cancer Network: Bladder cancer V.1.2013, pp. 1–3. National Comprehensive Cancer Network, Fort Washington (2013). (MS)
3. Beer, A., Saar, B., Zantl, N., et al.: MR cystography for bladder tumor detection. Eur. Radiol. **14**, 2311–2319 (2004)
4. Suleyman, E., Yekeler, E., Dursun, M., et al.: Bladder tumors: virtual MR cystoscopy. Abdom. Imaging **31**(4), 483–489 (2006)
5. Jaume, S., Ferrant, M., Macq, B., Hoyte, L., Fielding, J.R., Schreyer, A., Kikinis, R., Warfield, S.K.: Tumor detection in the bladder wall with a measurement of abnormal thickness in CT scans. IEEE Trans. Biomed. Eng. **50**, 383–390 (2003)
6. Fielding, J.R., Hoyte, L., Okon, S.A., Schreyer, A., Lee, J., Zou, K.H., Warfield, S., Richie, J.P., Loughlin, K.R., O'Leary, M.P., Doyle, C.J., Kikinis, R.: Tumor detection by virtual cystoscopy with color mapping of bladder wall thickness. J. Urol. **167**, 559–562 (2002)
7. Zhu, H., Duan, C., Jiang, R., Li, L., Fan, Y., Yu, X., Zeng, W., Gu, X., Liang, Z.: Computer-aided detection of bladder tumors based on the thickness mapping of bladder wall in MR images. Proc. SPIE Med. Imaging **7623**, 76234H1–76234H8 (2010)
8. Duan, C., Liang, Z., Bao, S., et al.: A coupled level set framework for bladder wall segmentation with application to MR cystography. IEEE Trans. Med. Imaging **29**(3), 903–915 (2010)
9. Qin, X., Liu, Y., Lu, H., Li, X., Yan, P.: Coupled directional level set for MR image segmentation. In: IEEE ICMLA, vol. 39 (2012)
10. Liu, Y., Li, Y.J., Luo, E.P., Lu, H.B., Yin, H.: Cortical thinning in patients with recent onset post-traumatic stress disorder after a single prolonged trauma exposure. PLoS ONE **7**(6), e39025 (2012). doi:10.1371/journal.pone.0039025
11. Zhao, Y., Liu, Y., Feng, J., Lu, H.: Parametric mapping model for bladder using free-form deformation. In: Conference Record of 2013 IEEE NSS/MIC/RTSD, Seoul, Oct 29–Nov 2 (2013)

Three-Dimensional Respiratory Deformation Processing for CT Vessel Images Using Angiographic Images

Shohei Suganuma[1](✉), Yuya Takano[1], Takashi Ohnishi[2],
Hideyuki Kato[3], Yoshihiko Ooka[4], and Hideaki Haneishi[2]

[1] Graduate School of Engineering, Chiba University,
1-33, Yayoi-cho, Inage-ku, Chiba 263-8522, Japan
s_suganuma@chiba-u.jp
[2] Center for Frontier Medical Engineering, Chiba University,
1-33, Yayoi-cho, Inage-ku, Chiba 263-8522, Japan
haneishi@faculty.chiba-u.jp
[3] Department of Radiology, Chiba University Hospital,
1-8-1, Inohana, Chuo-ku, Chiba 260-8677, Japan
[4] Department of Gastroenterology, Chiba University Hospital,
1-8-1, Inohana, Chuo-ku, Chiba 260-8677, Japan

Abstract. In interventional radiology, fluoroscopy is used to determine the position of the catheter inserted into a vessel. However, since vessels cannot be identified in fluoroscopic images, it is difficult to forward a catheter to a target region only with fluoroscopy. Thus, angiography and preoperative computed tomography (CT) images are used for the clinical purpose. CT images are useful for understanding the three-dimensional (3D) structure, but guidance of catheter is still difficult since the relationship between CT images and the fluoroscopic image is unclear. In this study, we developed a method for 3D representation of deformed vessels in CT images using an angiographic image acquired preoperatively under natural respiration and preoperative CT images. We implemented the registration algorithm and applied it to patient data. As a result, we confirmed that the vessels in CT images were correctly deformed, and a position error was two pixels in the median value.

Keywords: Interventional radiology · X-ray · CT · Registration

1 Introduction

Interventional radiology (IVR) is performed especially in the diagnosis and the treatment of liver region. Figure 1(a) shows an appearance of clinical practice where a physician inserts a catheter through a groin and forwards it to a target region. In IVR, fluoroscopy is used to determine the position of the catheter inserted into a blood vessel. However, since soft tissues such as blood vessels cannot be identified in fluoroscopic image, it is difficult to guide a catheter to the target region only with fluoroscopy as shown in Fig. 1(b). Thus, angiography, digital subtraction angiography (DSA) and the preoperative computed tomography (CT) images are used for the

© Springer International Publishing Switzerland 2014
H. Yoshida et al. (Eds.): ABDI 2014, LNCS 8676, pp. 257–266, 2014.
DOI: 10.1007/978-3-319-13692-9_25

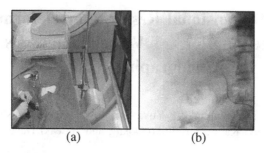

(a)   (b)

Fig. 1. Interventional radiology in clinical practice: (a) An appearance of procedure where physician inserts a catheter through a groin and forwards it to a target region with fluoroscopic images. (b) A fluoroscopic image for the liver region.

clinical purpose. CT images are useful for understanding the three-dimensional (3D) structure. Physician identifies positional relationship between vessel bifurcation and vertebra on way to a target region as preoperative planning. During an operation, physician forwards the catheter to a target region while watching fluoroscopic images with a monitor. The CT images are identified optionally when physician cannot forward correctly the catheter at vessel bifurcation. However, less consideration is given to the translation due to respiratory motion. Because of natural respiration, there is always a discrepancy between the static CT images which shows only one moment within the respiratory cycle, and the continuously moving liver [1]. Therefore the guidance of catheter at a thick vessel is even difficult for inexperienced physicians because the relationship between CT images and the fluoroscopic image is unclear. Hence a correctly deformed CT images are required for inexperienced physicians.

In a previous study, Wein et al. [2] conducted an image registration using CT images and an ultrasound image for the liver region. Ultrasound imaging is also used in IVR and it has no radiation exposure. Nevertheless, fluoroscopy is used primarily in clinical practice. Thus, image registration algorithms for conforming CT images to fluoroscopic images have been developed. A 2D/3D registration using preoperative CT images and a fluoroscopic image has been done [3–5], which is currently an essential technique for the diagnosis and the treatment. In addition, the 2D/3D registration was previously conducted for the rigid object, but non-linear transformation should be also considered. Ohnishi et al. [6] tried to acquire dynamic 3D motion of the human knee joint by employing an image registration with fluoroscopic images and CT images, which could be applied to translation due to respiratory motion. On the other hand, the 2D/3D registration has been already conducted for the liver region [7, 8], but it can be applied only to a DSA image for a single respiratory phase as intraoperative image. It is because breath holding is necessary to match a respiratory phase between images before and after injection of contrast agent in DSA.

In this paper, we conduct a registration using preoperative CT images and continuous angiographic images acquired intraoperative under natural respiration, and show a 3D representation of deformed vessels in CT images in arbitrary respiration phase. We implemented the registration algorithm for liver vessels and applied it to a patient data. We confirmed that the vessels in CT images were correctly deformed.

2   Method

Figure 2(a) shows an outline of processing for 3D representation of deformed vessels in CT images. In this method, the registration is conducted using only vessel regions. As a preprocessing, CT images are acquired preoperatively and only vessel regions are extracted from them by a region growing technique [9]. Here, we call the image of extracted vessels "CT vessel images." Then angiographic images are acquired under natural respiration after deciding a field of view. Our registration method is performed in two steps. In the first step, we conduct a rigid registration as a global position adjustment. Then, in the second step, a non-rigid registration is applied as a local position adjustment. These processes are described in the following sub-sections. After processing angiographic images for all frames, we show a 3D representation of deformed CT vessel images.

2.1   Rigid Registration

We conduct a rigid transformation as a global position adjustment of CT vessel images and an angiographic image by a 2D/3D image registration. Figure 2(b) shows the procedure of the 2D/3D image registration. In computer, the same projection geometry as that of the real single fluoroscopy is virtually constructed. The subject is projected onto virtual detector using this virtual projection system to generate a digitally reconstructed radiograph (DRR) from the 3D data as shown in Fig. 3(a) where the projection is calculated using a ray-summation method [10]. Figure 3(b) shows a DRR of CT vessel images. Gradient correlation (GC) [11] is utilized for the cost function that represents the similarity between a DRR and an angiographic image. To obtain GC, we calculate normalized cross correlation for edge information of each image. The edges in the image are emphasized by applying Sobel filter to the Gaussian-filtered image. Furthermore, we restrict the area to calculate the cost function to a region of interest (ROI) we selected [12].

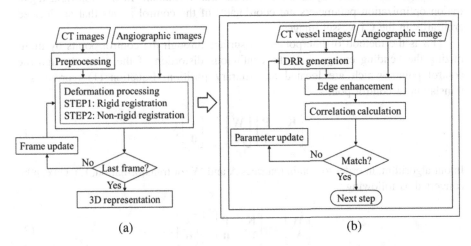

(a)   (b)

Fig. 2. A flowchart of our proposed method: (a) Outline of processing for 3D representation of deformed vessels in CT images. (b) Detailed flow of 2D/3D registration method using an angiographic image and CT vessel images.

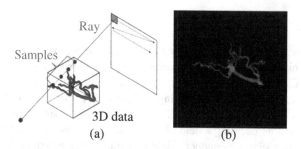

Fig. 3. Generating DRR: (a) Illustration of ray-summation method. (b) An example of DRR in which the red color shows an image projected from 3D data.

The CT vessel images are adjusted by translation and rotation as the cost function is maximized. In this study Powell-Brent method is used to optimize translation and rotation parameters of the CT vessel images [13], and the parameters are initialized manually. It takes so long time to calculate 2D/3D image registration if DRR generation is computed by CPU. Thus we implemented it with Graphics Processing Unit (GPU) and Compute Unified Device Architecture (CUDA) [14].

2.2   Non-rigid Registration

After the rigid registration, we conduct a non-rigid registration as a local position adjustment between CT vessel images and angiographic image. In the non-rigid registration, the CT vessel images are adjusted by non-linear transformation until the cost function becomes a maximum value. Optimization method and cost function used in the non-rigid registration are same as those in the rigid registration. We utilize Thin Plate Spline (TPS) [15, 16] as the non-linear transformation. In the non-rigid registration optimization parameters are coordinates of the control points that are located arbitrarily in the CT vessel images.

TPS is the method of interpolating a surface through the control points by minimizing the bending energy, and the continuous distortion of the plane through the control points which are located an arbitrary position. Equation (1) represents a translation of control points.

$$\begin{bmatrix} \mathbf{K} & \mathbf{P} \\ \mathbf{P}^T & \mathbf{0} \end{bmatrix} \begin{bmatrix} \mathbf{W} \\ \mathbf{A} \end{bmatrix} = \begin{bmatrix} \mathbf{V} \\ \mathbf{0} \end{bmatrix}, \tag{1}$$

In our algorithm, in order to obtain matrices **A** and **W** for transformation, Eq. (1) can be converted as following,

$$\begin{bmatrix} \mathbf{W} \\ \mathbf{A} \end{bmatrix} = \begin{bmatrix} \mathbf{K} & \mathbf{P} \\ \mathbf{P}^T & \mathbf{0} \end{bmatrix}^{-1} \begin{bmatrix} \mathbf{V} \\ \mathbf{0} \end{bmatrix}. \tag{2}$$

The matrices $\mathbf{A}$ and $\mathbf{W}$ are the affine factor [Eq. (3)] and the weighting factor [Eq. (4)], respectively. In calculation of matrices, n indicates the number of control points.

$$\mathbf{A} = \begin{bmatrix} a_{x1} & a_{y1} & a_{z1} \\ a_{x2} & a_{y2} & a_{z2} \\ a_{x3} & a_{y3} & a_{z3} \\ a_{x4} & a_{y4} & a_{z4} \end{bmatrix} \tag{3}$$

$$\mathbf{W} = \begin{bmatrix} w_{x1} & w_{y1} & w_{z1} \\ \vdots & \vdots & \vdots \\ w_{xn} & w_{yn} & w_{zn} \end{bmatrix} \tag{4}$$

$\mathbf{P}$ is a matrix including an initial control point set before moving as elements [Eq. (5)], and $\mathbf{V}$ is a position set matrix after moving the control points defined in Eq. (6). We obtain appropriate matrices $\mathbf{A}$ and $\mathbf{W}$ by optimizing $\mathbf{V}$ until CT vessel images are correctly transformed.

$$\mathbf{P} = \begin{bmatrix} 1 & x_1 & y_1 & z_1 \\ 1 & x_2 & y_2 & z_2 \\ \vdots & \vdots & \vdots & \vdots \\ 1 & x_n & y_n & z_n \end{bmatrix} \tag{5}$$

$$\mathbf{V} = \begin{bmatrix} x'_1 & y'_1 & z'_1 \\ \vdots & \vdots & \vdots \\ x'_n & y'_n & z'_n \end{bmatrix} \tag{6}$$

$\mathbf{K}$ is a matrix which has radial basis functions $U(r)$ as non-diagonal elements and represented as follows,

$$\mathbf{K} = \begin{bmatrix} 0 & U(r_{12}) & \cdots & U(r_{1n}) \\ U(r_{21}) & 0 & \cdots & U(r_{2n}) \\ \vdots & \vdots & \ddots & \vdots \\ U(r_{n1}) & U(r_{n2}) & \cdots & 0 \end{bmatrix} \tag{7}$$

$$U(r) = r^2 \ln r^2 \tag{8}$$

r is pairwise distances of initial control point set and calculated as following,

$$r_{ij} = \sqrt{(x_j - x_i)^2 + (y_j - y_i)^2 + (z_j - z_i)^2} \tag{9}$$

After calculating affine factor matrix **A** and weighting factor matrix **W**, both matrices are applied to translate any points within CT vessel images. The coordinates of translated points are calculated by Eqs. (10), (11) and (12).

$$x' = a_{x1} + a_{x2}x + a_{x3}y + a_{x4}z + \sum_{i=1}^{n} w_{xi}U(r) \qquad (10)$$

$$y' = a_{y1} + a_{y2}x + a_{y3}y + a_{y4}z + \sum_{i=1}^{n} w_{yi}U(r) \qquad (11)$$

$$z' = a_{z1} + a_{z2}x + a_{z3}y + a_{z4}z + \sum_{i=1}^{n} w_{zi}U(r) \qquad (12)$$

3 Validation

We implemented the registration algorithm for liver vessels and applied it to a patient data. INFX-8000C/JV (Toshiba Medical Systems Corp., Otawara, Japan) was used for single angiographic image acquisition. The angiographic image was obtained for 11 frames during a single respiration cycle. We applied preliminarily our method to angiographic images in four frames which include a maximum inspiration and a maximum expiration. The size of an angiographic image was 512×512 pixels, and each pixel had 8 bits. The pixel size was 0.42×0.42 mm^2. On the other hand, CT image size was $512 \times 512 \times 301$ voxels, and the voxel size was $0.65 \times 0.65 \times 0.42$ mm^3. The CT images were obtained with Aquilion One (Toshiba Medical Systems Corp.) for deep inspiration. The ROI for calculating cost function was set to 250×200 pixel rectangle which included whole vessels (Fig. 4). It is located manually for each angiographic image.

We configured the translation and rotation parameters manually before the rigid registration. For the non-rigid registration, we located landmarks as control points of TPS. They were located on branch, end, and characteristic points of the vessels. Figure 5 shows the locations of control points. The red object is the vessels and the yellow points are control points. In this validation, we selected 3 branch points, 3 end points, and 15 characteristic points which located at a curve.

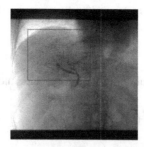

Fig. 4. An ROI selected for calculating cost function which is located in the region with blue rectangle. And it was manually configured for each angiographic image (Color figure online).

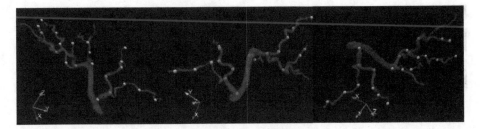

Fig. 5. The locations of landmarks (yellow points). The red object is the vessels and the yellow points are control points (Color figure online).

4   Results

Figure 6 shows the result of each process in the selected ROI. It shows only the angiographic image in the maximum expiration. The gray scale color represents the angiographic image and the red color represents the DRR. Figure 6(a) is the result of the 2D/3D image registration using vertebra instead of the vessels. The vessels in the DRR could not be overlaid onto the vessel pattern of the angiographic image. In other words, it indicates that the deformation processing of CT vessel images is necessity to conform DRR to angiographic image. The deformation processing which considers the respiratory motion is necessary to conform vessels in DRR to that in angiographic images. Figure 6(b) is the result after rigid registration using vessels. Two patterns of vessels are roughly in alignment, but local misalignments are still observed at the green arrows in the image. Figure 6(c) is the result after non-rigid registration. It showed better alignment than rigid registration at the yellow arrows in the image. Although misalignment decreased by non-linear transformation, it remains to some degree. Figure 7 shows a 3D representation of registration results in four frames. The yellow vessel shows the original CT vessel image which is acquired preoperatively. The red and the green vessels are registered CT vessel images in the current frame and the previous frame, respectively. Figure 7(a) is the result for maximum inspiration, Fig. 7 (b, c) are ones for middle phases, and Fig. 7(d) shows the result for maximum

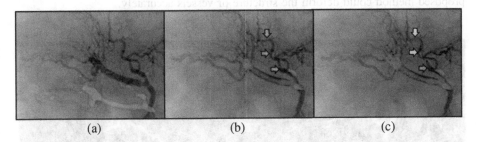

(a)   (b)   (c)

Fig. 6. Comparison of the registration results in each process where the gray scale color shows the angiographic image and the red color shows the DRR. (a) After rigid registration using vertebra instead of the vessels. (b) After rigid registration. (c) After non-rigid registration (Color figure online).

Fig. 7. The 3D representation of registration results in four frames. The yellow vessel shows the original CT vessel image. The red and the green vessels are registered CT vessel images in the current frame and the previous frame, respectively. (a) Maximum inspiration. (b–c) Middle phases. (d) Maximum expiration (Color figure online).

expiration. From the results for each frame, we can see the movement of vessel regions in concert with respiratory motion. Furthermore, the 3D representation of deformed CT vessel images is shown in Fig. 8. It also represents only the angiographic image in the maximum expiration. The red vessel shows the original CT vessel images before non-rigid deformation and the white vessel is the one after non-rigid deformation. We could see detailed and natural deformation by the non-rigid registration on the DRR.

Then, we calculated the position errors between the corresponding points of the vessel in the angiographic image and the DRR. We selected 9 landmarks from 21 control points used in TPS and 9 other landmarks for calculating position errors. We calculated position errors for three cases: using only 9 control points, only 9 other landmarks, and 18 points including both 9 control points and 9 other landmarks. Figure 9 shows a boxplot of position errors for the angiographic images in four frames. The red bar shows the position error for the rigid registration, and the blue bar is the one after the non-rigid registration. In the result of only control points, the position error of non-rigid registration was improved one pixel in the median value compared with that of rigid registration, and the variance also became small. Even in the result of only other landmarks, the median value of non-rigid registration was about one pixel while the variance is bigger than that of only control points. In the result of mixing both control points and other landmarks, the position error of non-rigid registration also could be improved from that of rigid registration. Above results showed that our proposed method could deform the structure of vessels accurately.

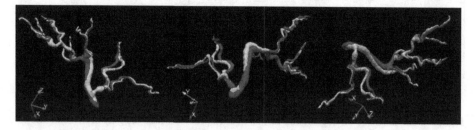

Fig. 8. The 3D representation of deformed CT vessel images. The red vessel shows the CT vessel images before non-rigid deformation and the white vessel is after non-rigid deformation (Color figure online).

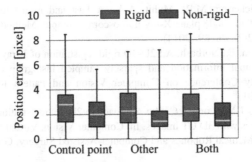

Fig. 9. Evaluation of position errors after registration. The red and blue bars show the position errors in case of the rigid registration and non-rigid registration, respectively. The yellow lines show the median values (Color figure online).

We consider the cause of misalignment as follows. After a review of the position of the landmarks in the non-rigid registration, some positions near the landmarks could not be correctly registered. This is because the number of control points was insufficient around there. Although this problem would be solved by increasing the number of control points, it becomes a trade-off between processing time and accuracy of the registration. In this case, the average processing times in four frames were 170 s for the rigid registration and 22693 s for the non-rigid registration. We have to improve our algorithm in order to reduce the processing time which increases depending on the number of control points. In addition, we will also consider the determination method of the location of control point and the number of control points.

5   Conclusion

In this study, we implemented the registration algorithm for liver vessels and applied it to a patient data. In the results, we confirmed that the CT vessel images were deformed correctly and reasonably, and the median value of position error was one pixel. However, still a portion of deformed image showed less accuracy. As future works, we will improve our proposed method, and apply to other patient data for validating our method. Furthermore, we'd like to present the 3D representation of deformed vessels in CT images synchronously with fluoroscopic image by monitoring respiratory motion.

Acknowledgements. This study was supported by JKA in part.

References

1. Gergel, I., Hering, J., Tetzlaff, R.: An Electromagnetic navigation system for transbronchial interventions with a novel approach to respiratory motion compensation. Med. Phys. **38**(12), 6742–6753 (2011)
2. Wein, W., Brunke, S., Khamene, A.: Automatic CT-ultrasound registration for diagnostic imaging and image-guided intervention. Med. Image Anal. **15**(5), 577–585 (2008)

3. Haque, M.N., Pickering, M.R., Muhit, A.A.: A Fast and robust technique for 3D–2D registration of CT to single plane X-ray fluoroscopy. Comput. Methods Biomech. Biomed. Eng. Imag. Vis. **2**(2), 76–89 (2014)

4. Zollei, L., Grimson, E., Norbash, A.: 2D-3D rigid registration of X-ray fluoroscopy and CT images using mutual information and sparsely sampled histogram estimators. In: IEEE Computer Society Conference on Computer Vision and Pattern Recognition, Hawaii, pp. 696–703 (2001)

5. Weese, J., Buzug, T.M., Lorenz, C.: An Approach to 2D/3D registration of a vertebra in 2D X-ray fluoroscopies with 3D CT images. In: Computer Vision, Virtual Reality and Robotics in Medicine and Medical Robotics and Computer-Assisted Surgery, Grenoble, pp. 119–128 (1997)

6. Ohnishi, T., Suzuki, M., Atsushi, N.: Three-dimensional motion study of femur, tibia, and patella at the knee joint from bi-plane fluoroscopy and CT images. Radiol. Phys. Technol. **3**(2), 151–158 (2010)

7. Groher, M., Jakobs, T.F., Padoy, N.: Planning and intraoperative visualization of liver catheterizations: new CTA protocol and 2D-3D registration method. Academic Radiology **14**(11), 1325–1340 (2007)

8. Groher, M., Zikic, D., Navab, N.: Deformable 2D-3D registration of vascular structures in a one view scenario. IEEE Trans. Med. Imag. **28**(6), 847–860 (2009)

9. Gonzalez, R.C., Woods, R.E.: Digital Image Processing, 2nd edn. Prentice Hall, San Francisco (2002)

10. Lacroute, P., Levoy, M.: Fast volume rendering using a shear-warp factorization of the viewing transformation. In: Proceeding Special Interest Group on Computer Graphics, Orlando, pp. 451–458 (1994)

11. Penney, G.P., Wesse, J., Little, J.A.: A Comparison of similarity measures for use in 2-D-3-D medical image registration. IEEE Trans. Med. Imag. **17**(4), 586–595 (1998)

12. Zhan, X., Miao, S., Du, L.: Robust 2-D/3-D registration of CT volumes with contrast-enhanced X-ray sequences in electrophysiology based on a weighted similarity measure and sequential subspace optimization. In: IEEE International Conference on Acoustics, Speech and Signal Processing, Vancouver, pp. 934–938 (2013)

13. Press, W.H., Teukolsky, S.A., Vetterling, W.T.: Numerical Recipes in C, 2nd edn. Cambridge University Press, Cambridge (1992)

14. Ohnishi, T., Doi, A., Ito, F.: Acceleration of three dimensional information acquisition of a knee joint using CUDA. Inst. Electron. Inf. Commun. Eng. **107**(461), 397–400 (2008)

15. Bookstein, F.L.: Principal Warps: Thin-plate splines and the decomposition of deformations. IEEE Trans. Pattern Anal. Mach. Intell. **11**(6), 567–585 (1989)

16. Sinthanayothin, C., Bholsithi, W.: Image warping based on 3D thin plate spline. In: 4th International Conference on Information Technology in Asia, Kuching, pp. 137–143 (2005)

Special Topics

Reconstruction Method by Using Sparse and Low-Rank Structures for Fast 4D-MRI Acquisition

Yukinojo Kitakami[1(✉)], Takashi Ohnishi[2], Yoshitada Masuda[3],
Koji Matsumoto[3], and Hideaki Haneishi[2]

[1] Graduate School of Engineering, Chiba University, 1-33 Yayoi-cho, Inage-ku,
Chiba 263-8522, Japan
y_kitakami@chiba-u.jp
[2] Center for Frontier Medical Engineering, Chiba University,
1-33 Yayoi-cho, Inage-ku, Chiba 263-8522, Japan
haneishi@faculty.chiba-u.jp
[3] Chiba University Hospital, 1-8-1 Inohana, Chuo-ku, Chiba 260-8677, Japan

Abstract. Previously, we proposed a method for reconstructing 4D-MRI of
thoracoabdominal organs that can visualize and quantify the three-dimensional
dynamics of organs due to respiration. However, the data acquisition time of the
method is long, say, 30 min. In this study, we assume an interleave acquisition
of images with a smaller number of the encoding in the k-space to shorten the
data acquisition time. We also propose to use a reconstruction technique named
k-t SLR that utilizes sparse and low rank structures of the data matrix to avoid
image degradation due to the small number of data acquisition. We performed a
simulation experiment where we regarded 4D-MR images by our previous
method as ideal images, generated down sampled data in k-space, and applied
k-t SLR reconstruction to those data. We evaluated the resultant images from
three viewpoints and confirmed that the combination of fast data collection with
a small number of encoding and the subsequent k-t SLR reconstruction can
produce high quality MR images.

Keywords: 4D-MRI · Compressive sensing · Image reconstruction · Sparseness ·
Low-rank structure · k-t SLR

1 Introduction

We have proposed a reconstruction method named the intersection profile method
[1, 2]. By the method, we can visualize three-dimensional (3D) thoracoabdominal
respiratory movement [1], and quantify the anatomic motion and organ deformation
caused by respiratory motion [2].

The intersection profile method uses a time sequential 2D-MR image in a proper
sagittal plane as a navigator slice (NS) and time sequential 2D-MR images in many
coronal planes as data slice (DS). In our conventional protocol for this method, one
minute continuous data acquisition is performed for each slice. One best respiratory
pattern is chosen from NS and also a best respiratory pattern is determined from each

© Springer International Publishing Switzerland 2014
H. Yoshida et al. (Eds.): ABDI 2014, LNCS 8676, pp. 269–277, 2014.
DOI: 10.1007/978-3-319-13692-9_26

DS by evaluating the similarity with NS respiratory pattern at each intersection where we usually acquire 20–30 slices as DS. As a result, it takes approximately 30 min to collect data for 4D-MRI. This long collection time is one issue for practical use. We use a fast acquisition by reducing the number of encoding in the k-space. We suppress the degradation due to the fact acquisition by using a sparse model based method called k-t SLR reconstruction.

2   Methods

2.1   Data Collection Method

In the current protocol, we assume that a time sequential DS image is continuously acquired for one minute and after that the same data acquisition is repeated at the next DS as shown in Fig. 1(a). We call it frame sequential acquisition, and it takes 150 ms for one frame. By this acquisition technique, it takes two minutes to obtain continuous images at two slice positions.

We want to reduce the number of the encoding in the k-space for fast acquisition. One possibility is schematically illustrated in Fig. 1(b). Here one frame time is a half of 150 ms and data acquisition is alternatively performed in two different coronal planes. As a result, two DS images are obtained in one minute. We call it an interleave acquisition in this paper. If we reduce the frame time to 50 ms and change the data acquisition at three slice positions rapidly, three DS images would be obtained in a minute.

2.2   Image Reconstruction Method

Although fast data collection is enabled by the interleave acquisition, various artifacts become remarkable in time sequential 2D-MR image. A main artifact is the aliasing artifact by reduction of the number of encoding in the k-space. In this study, we employ compressed sensing [3, 4] as a technique to suppress the degradation by the aliasing artifact. Compressed sensing is an approach of reconstructing complete signal with less deterioration from a small number of signals assuming sparse characteristics of the data. There are several studies of the image reconstruction method using compressed

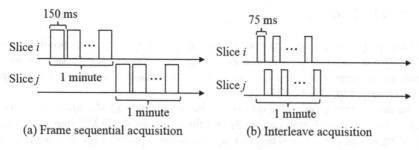

Fig. 1. Timing chart of sequential acquisition. (a) Conventional frame sequential acquisition, (b) interleave acquisition.

sensing in the MRI images [5]. The studies to apply compressed sensing to the time sequential 2D-MR images are also conducted in [6–10].

In this study, we utilize a technique called k-t SLR using low rank structure and sparseness of MR data [10], we assume the interleave acquisition and simulate the image reconstruction. The k-t SLR has been proposed mainly to reconstruct the cardiac MRI. This is the first study to apply the k-t SLR to thoracoabdominal region for 4D-MRI reconstruction. We perform the reconstruction of the time sequential 2D-MR images including the movement of the thoracoabdominal organs in the multi slices. In the following section we explain the k-t SLR [10], which we implemented in our method.

2.3 k-t SLR

We denote the spatio-temporal signal to estimate as $\gamma(\mathbf{x}, t)$, where $\mathbf{x}$ is the position in 2D image space and t denotes time. We define a matrix Γ using $\gamma(\mathbf{x}, t)$ as

$$\Gamma = \begin{bmatrix} \gamma(\mathbf{x}_0, t_0) & \cdots & \gamma(\mathbf{x}_0, t_{n-1}) \\ \vdots & \ddots & \vdots \\ \gamma(\mathbf{x}_{m-1}, t_0) & \cdots & \gamma(\mathbf{x}_{m-1}, t_{n-1}) \end{bmatrix}, \tag{1}$$

where m is the number of pixels in the image for a single frame and n is the number of frames. The columns of Γ represent the images at each time instant t, while the rows of Γ represent the temporal samples at the position $\mathbf{x}$. Because some organs do not move during the sequential image acquisition so much, the matrix Γ has a low rank structure.

In dynamic MRI, data acquisition is performed so as to complete k-t space. Letting $\mathbf{b}$ be the k-t space data observed by MRI, it is expressed as

$$\mathbf{b} = A(\Gamma). \tag{2}$$

Here, $A(\cdot)$ is an operator including the Fourier transformation and under-sampling for reducing the number of encoding.

The reconstructed matrix Γ^* is calculated by solving the minimization problem written as follows

$$\Gamma^* = \arg \min_{\Gamma} \left\{ \|A(\Gamma) - \mathbf{b}\|^2 + \lambda_1 \varphi(\Gamma) + \lambda_2 \psi(\Gamma) \right\}. \tag{3}$$

The first term on the right-hand side is residual between the value of reconstruction and measurement. The second term is spectral penalty using low rank of matrix, and the third term is total variation (TV) penalty using sparse structure of data. λ_1 and λ_2 are weighting factors for penalty terms.

The k-t SLR is an iterative technique. We define a cost function in n-th iteration as

$$\text{cost}_n = \|A(\Gamma_n) - \mathbf{b}\|^2 + \lambda_1 \varphi(\Gamma_n) + \lambda_2 \psi(\Gamma_n). \tag{4}$$

Here, Γ_n is n-th reconstructed matrix. We terminate the iteration when the convergence condition specified by

$$d_n = \left| \frac{\mathrm{cost}_n - \mathrm{cost}_{n-1}}{\mathrm{cost}_n} \right| < 10^{-3} \tag{5}$$

is satisfied.

2.4 Spectral Penalty

Low rank characteristics used in the spectral penalty are represented by the number of singular values obtained from the singular value decomposition of the matrix. Generally, a nuclear norm is used for the reconstruction of low rank matrix. In this study, we use Schatten norm as it improves the result of reconstruction [11].

$$\|\mathbf{\Gamma}\|_p = \left(\sum_{i=1}^{\min\{m,n\}} \sigma_i^p \right)^{1/p}. \tag{6}$$

Here, σ is a singular value, m and n are the numbers of the rows and columns of the matrix, respectively. Schatten norm becomes the same form as a nuclear norm when $p = 1$, and it improves the results of reconstruction when $p < 1$. Practical spectral penalty is given by the Schatten norm to the p-th power as

$$\varphi(\mathbf{\Gamma}) = \sum_{i=1}^{\min\{m,n\}} \sigma_i^p. \tag{7}$$

2.5 TV Penalty

Sparse characteristics used in TV penalty are represented by the number of the nonzero components in sparse domain. In this study, we use a l_1-norm. In addition, we also use Eq. (8) for usage of the multi sparse domains.

$$\varphi(\mathbf{\Gamma}) = \left\| \sqrt{\sum_{i=0}^{q-1} |\mathbf{\Phi}_i^H \mathbf{\Gamma} \mathbf{\Psi}_i|^2} \right\|_{l_1}, \tag{8}$$

where $\mathbf{\Phi}$ is a transformation matrix that sparsifies the 2D spatial domain and $\mathbf{\Psi}$ is an operator that sparsifies the temporal direction. q is the number of the sparse domains. We use three sparse domains: $\mathbf{\Phi}_0 = \mathbf{D}_x, \mathbf{\Psi}_0 = \mathbf{I}$; $\mathbf{\Phi}_1 = \mathbf{D}_y, \mathbf{\Psi}_1 = \mathbf{I}$; $\mathbf{\Phi}_2 = \mathbf{I}, \mathbf{\Psi}_2 = \mathbf{D}_t$; where $\mathbf{I}$ is the identity matrix and $\mathbf{D}_x, \mathbf{D}_y, \mathbf{D}_t$ are difference matrices along x, y, and t. Sparse domain of difference between adjacent values is called TV domain. Because TV represents the gradient of the image, it becomes near to zero in other than the steep gradient such as edges.

2.6 Setting of the Parameters: λ_1, λ_2, p

It is important how we set the weights of the penalty in compressed sensing. Wrong setting of the weights causes inaccurate image reconstruction. The weights of the penalty λ_1 and λ_2 control the balance between residual and other penalties. The parameter p of the Schatten norm affects the reconstruction of the low rank matrix.

3 Experiments

We assumed interleave image acquisition and performed the simulation experiments.

3.1 Simulation

The MR data were acquired by using a whole-body scanner, 1.5T Achieva Nova-Dual (Philips Medical Systems, Best, the Netherlands) with a 16ch SENSE TORSO XL Coil. A 2D Balanced FFE sequence was used. Imaging parameters used were as follows: SENSE factor = 2.2, flip angle = 45 deg, TR = 2.2 ms, TE = 0.9 ms, FOV = 384 mm, in-plane resolution = 192 × 192 pixels and 1.5 × 1.5 mm^2, slice thickness = 7.5 mm, slice gap = 6.0 mm, scan time = 150 ms/frame and 400 frame/slice. The data has 256 × 256 pixels, 400 frames, and total time to obtain is one minute. We perform the simulation for two subjects. Subject A has 25 slices and subject B has 24 slices. In order to determine suitable parameters, we varied parameters and calculated root mean square error (RMSE) in a certain slice. The parameters tested are as follows: $\lambda_1 = \{10^1, 10^2, \ldots, 10^8\}$, $\lambda_2 = \{10^{-6}, 10^{-5}, \ldots, 10^1\}$, and $p = \{0.01, 0.05, 0.1, 0.25, 0.5\}$. The parameters giving the best performance were $\lambda_1 = 10^4$, $\lambda_2 = 10^{-4}$, $p = 0.1$ for subject A and $\lambda_1 = 10^3$, $\lambda_2 = 10^{-3}$, $p = 0.1$ for subject B.

Figure 2 shows the simulation flow. As ideal images we use 2D-MR images at a coronal plane obtained by the conventional frame sequential acquisition. Those images are Fourier transformed and represent the k-t space. Furthermore, in k-t space, we simulate the interleave acquisition by under-sampling. In the simulation, under-sampling is performed in the following way. Because the practically obtained MR image by SENSE method is band limited as shown in Fig. 2, the similar low-pass filtering is performed first. Then, interleave acquisition is performed with radial resampling of k-space. Although the practically obtained MR image is acquired by Cartesian sampling, we approximate each k-space location with nearest neighbor of the radial trajectory. The radial mask is rotated every frame at random and kept randomness in the temporal direction. We use the mask of signal rate 33 % which enables the interleaving of three DS images.

We perform image reconstruction in two ways. One is performed by simple inverse Fourier transformation after zero-filling the non-sampled region of k-space. We call this image zero-filled image. The other is reconstruction by the k-t SLR method [10]. We call this image k-t SLR image. Then we compare the ideal image, zero-filled image and k-t SLR image.

3.2 Evaluation Points

Relative error. We use the average of the relative error for the evaluation of image quality. RMSE divided by the maximum value of the ideal image is calculated for each frame and its average for all frame is used for evaluation.

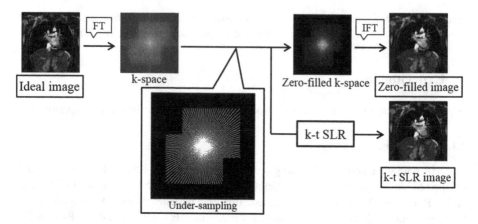

Fig. 2. Simulation flow. We assume k-space encoding of signal rate 33 %, namely, interleave imaging of three slices is simulated.

Evaluation of the time sequential 2D-MR images. We subjectively evaluate the noise and the structure of the images. We compare the images of first frame at 13th slice of ideal images for subject A, the corresponding zero-filled images and k-t SLR images.

Evaluation of the 4D-MRI. Volume rendering of the 4D-MRI data of subject B is performed using medical imaging processing software OsiriX [12]. The structure of the blood vessel of the liver is visually compared.

4   Results

4.1   Relative Error

Figure 3 shows the result of the relative error. The error of k-t SLR is clearly smaller than the zero-filled images in both two subjects.

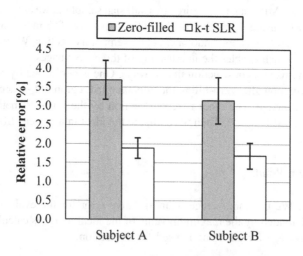

Fig. 3. Relative error. RMSE divided by the maximum value is evaluated.

4.2   Evaluation of the Time Sequential 2D-MR Images

Figure 4 shows the result of the evaluation of the time sequential 2D-MR images. In Fig. 4(b) the aliasing artifact appears over the whole image. In addition, detailed structures such as edges disappeared. In Fig. 4(c), on the other hand, such image noises are suppressed by using k-t SLR.

Figures 4(d)–(f) are magnified versions of the ROI in Figs. 4 (a)–(c). Figure 4(e) illustrates that the blood vessel in the liver becomes obscure by the noise. On the other hand, Fig. 4(f) shows that the structure of the blood vessel in the liver (denoted by the arrow) is still clear as the ideal image in Fig. 4(d).

4.3   Evaluation of the 4D-MRI

Figure 5 shows the volume rendered images of the 4D-MRI. Figure 5(a) is the overview of 4D-MRI in the ideal images and (b)–(d) are closeups of the ROI indicated in Fig. 5(a). The red pattern indicates the structure of the blood vessel in the liver. In the circled region of Fig. 5(c), the structure of the blood vessel is not maintained. On the other hand, Fig. 5(d) illustrates that the structure of the blood vessel in the liver becomes clear as the ideal images in Fig. 5(b). The arrow in Fig. 5(b) shows the bifurcated blood vessel in the liver clearly. On the other hand, in Fig. 5(d), the structure of blood vessel is lost after the k-t SLR reconstruction. This degradation may be improved by setting the optimum parameters for every slice.

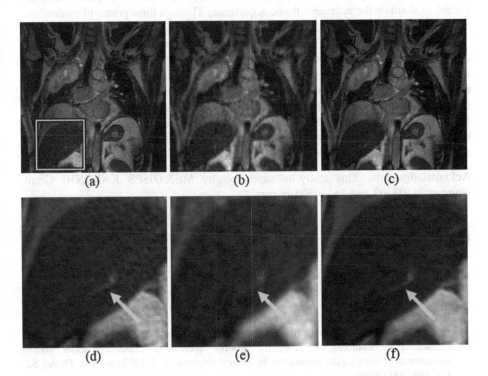

Fig. 4. Evaluation of the time sequential 2D-MR images. (a) Ideal images, (b) zero-filled images, (c) k-t SLR images. (d)–(f) are the magnified images in the ROI in (a).

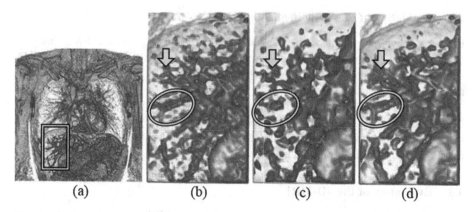

Fig. 5. Evaluation of the 4D-MRI. (a) shows the overview of 4D-MRI. (b)–(d) are enlarged in the ROI that is the liver in (a). (b) Ideal image, (c) zero-filled image, (d) k-t SLR image.

5   Conclusion

We have proposed a combination of fast data acquisition using interleave technique and k-t SLR reconstruction method based on a sparse model for 4D-MRI reconstruction. We performed a simulation experiment where MR images obtained by the conventional frame sequential acquisition were used as ideal images and down sampling was conducted to simulate the interleave frame acquisition. Through three points of evaluation, we confirmed that the k-t SLR reconstruction worked well.

As future work, we will find optimum weights for the penalty to improve image quality further. We will examine the index to evaluate the quality of reconstructed matrix without giving the correct value. One candidate to evaluate the quality of reconstructed low rank matrix is Stein's Unbiased Risk Estimate (SURE) [13]. We will design the reconstruction scheme with optimum weights using SURE. In addition, since the computational burden for k-t SLR reconstruction considerably high, some speed up technique is necessary. Furthermore, we'd like to evaluate clinical difference between zero-filled image and k-t SLR image by the radiological technologist.

Acknowledgments. This study is supported by MEXT/JSPS KAKENHI Grant Number 24103703 and 26120505 in part.

References

1. Masuda, Y., Fujibuchi, T., Haneishi, H.: 4D MR imaging of respiratory organ motion using an intersection profile method. Med. Imag. Tech. **27**(2), 112–122 (2009)
2. Masuda, Y., Nishikawa, T., Wada, H., Yoshida, S., Yoshino, I., Kikawa, T., Ito, H., Haneishi, H.: Construction of a diaphragmatic function map from a 4D magnetic resonance image using the intersection profile method. Med. Imag. Tech. **28**(3), 181–188 (2010)
3. Candès, E.J., Romberg, J., Tao, T.: Robust uncertainty principles: exact signal reconstruction from highly incomplete frequency information. IEEE Trans. Inf. Theory **52** (2), 489–509 (2006)

4. Donoho, D.: Compressed sensing. IEEE Trans. Inf. Theory **52**(4), 1289–1306 (2006)
5. Lustig, M., Donoho, D., Pauly, J.M.: Sparse MRI: the application of compressed sensing for rapid MR imaging. Magn. Reson. Med. **58**(6), 1182–1195 (2007)
6. Jung, H., Ye, J.C., Kim, E.Y.: Improved k-t BLASK and k-t SENSE using FOCUSS. Phys. Med. Biol. **52**(11), 3201–3226 (2007)
7. Jung, H., Sung, K., Nayak, K.S., Kim, E.Y., Ye, J.C.: k-t FOCUSS: a general compressed sensing framework for high resolution dynamic MRI. Magn. Reson. Med. **61**(1), 103–116 (2009)
8. Jung, H., Park, J.S., Yoo, J.H., Ye, J.C.: Radial k-t FOCUSS for high-resolution cardiac cine magnetic resonance imaging. Magn. Reson. Med. **63**(1), 63–68 (2010)
9. Pedersen, H., Kozerke, S., Ringgaard, S., Nehrke, K., Kim, W.Y.: k-t PCA: temporally constrained k-t BLAST reconstruction using principal component analysis. Magn. Reson. Med. **62**(3), 706–716 (2009)
10. Lingala, S.G., Hu, Y., DiBella, E., Jacob, M.: Accelerated dynamic MRI exploiting sparsity and low-rank structure: k-t SLR. Magn. Reson. Med. **30**(5), 1042–1054 (2011)
11. Chartrand, R.: Exact reconstruction of sparse signals via nonconvex minimization. IEEE Signal Process. Lett. **14**(10), 707–710 (2007)
12. OsiriX - DICOM viewer. http://www.osirix-viewer.com/
13. Candès, E.J., Sing-Long, C.A., Trzasko, J.D.: Unbiased risk estimates for singular value thresholding and spectral estimators. IEEE Trans. Signal Process. **61**(19), 4643–4657 (2013)

Combined Homogeneous Region Localization and Automated Evaluation of Radiation Dose Dependent Contrast-to-Noise Ratio in Dual Energy Abdominal CT

Minsoo Chun[1] and Jong-Hyo Kim[1,2,3,4(✉)]

[1] Interdisciplinary Program in Radiation Applied Life Science,
Seoul National University College of Medicine, Seoul, Korea
{msl236,kimjhyo}@snu.ac.kr

[2] Department of Radiology, Seoul National University Hospital, Seoul, Korea

[3] Program in Biomedical Radiation Sciences, Department of Transdisciplinary
Studies, Graduate School of Convergence Science and Technology,
Seoul National University, Suwon, Korea

[4] Advanced Institutes of Convergence Technology, Seoul National University,
Suwon, Korea

Abstract. This study presents a homogeneous region localization technique combined with automated evaluation of radiation dose-dependent contrast-to-noise ratio in dual energy abdominal CT. Patient body size was calculated using region growing segmentation and used to estimate size-specific dose estimate, and contrast-to-noise ratio are automatically evaluated by using proposed technique. Contrast-to-noise ratio turned out to be similar between low and high tube potential for both pre- and post-contrast phases, while radiation dose is remarkably lower at 80 kVp. Low tube potential can be recommended to reduce radiation dose while maintaining contrast-to-noise.

Keywords: Dual energy CT · Homogeneous region localization · CT noise level · Contrast-to-noise ratio · Size-specific dose estimate

1 Introduction

Although computed tomography (CT) has been widely used with the advantages of 3-dimensional imaging of the human anatomy and rapid imaging capability, the main concern, radiation dose, limits its application. Study efforts are widely being made to optimize CT protocols in order to find a combination of kVp and mAs which leads to a lower patient dose and still maintaining diagnostic image quality. In previous studies, image quality assessment has been usually carried out qualitatively in a subjective manner, which makes it difficult to apply to a large number of data set scanned with different scan protocols as well different CT vendors and models that is frequently required for comparison studies.

Often, CT scans producing less noise are preferred, which leads to an adoption of higher kVp settings. However, even though images with low tube voltages are seemingly noisier than those with high tube voltages, recent studies reported that CT

© Springer International Publishing Switzerland 2014
H. Yoshida et al. (Eds.): ABDI 2014, LNCS 8676, pp. 278–286, 2014.
DOI: 10.1007/978-3-319-13692-9_27

scans with lower kVp could produce images without contrast-to-noise ratio (CNR) degradation [1, 2]. Even though radiation dose is known to be much lower with the images at lower kVp, expectation of poor image quality limits the usage of low kVp protocol. Development of a computer assisted technique which allow an objective and efficient image quality assessment could accelerate protocol optimization studies by providing quantitative and reliable evidences.

In this study, we present a homogeneous region localization technique combined with automated evaluation of radiation dose-dependent contrast-to-noise ratio in dual energy abdominal CT. We hope that proposed technique with larger data set allows to find an optimal protocol having a balanced image quality at a lower radiation dose.

2 Materials and Methods

2.1 Materials

An abdominal CT data scanned with dual-energy protocol were downloaded from the picture archiving communication system (PACS) in Seoul National University Hospital. Images were obtained from 128-row multi detector CT (Somatom Definition, Siemens, Erlangen) with scan conditions of dual energy protocols (80 and 140 kVp), and 3 mm slice thickness. Automatic exposure control (AEC) was applied showing 135–184 mAs in 80 kVp scan, and 35–43 mAs in 140 kVp scan, and D30f kernel was used for image reconstruction. A total of 4 volumetric data were obtained over the time of 4 contrast enhancements (pre, early artery, late artery, and portal phase).

2.2 Methods

2.2.1 Overall Procedure

Figure 1 represents a schematic diagram of overall procedure for this study. Body regions were segmented using 3D region growing method, and size-specific dose estimate ($SSDE$) and water-equivalent $SSDE$ ($SSDE_w$) were calculated based on corresponding effective diameter (D_{eff}) and water-equivalent diameter (D_w) with volume CT dose index ($CTDI_{vol}$) from DICOM header [3].

Homogeneous regions of interest (ROI) were automatically selected by using local gradient metric and localized on fat, muscle and contrast-enhanced liver regions, according to the procedure described on Subsect. 2.2.3. CNRs of muscle and contrast-enhanced liver region with respect to fat region were automatically calculated using the selected ROIs. The relationship between CT dose and CNR was then evaluated.

2.2.2 CT Radiation Dose Metrics

In 2011, American Association of Physicists in Medicine (AAPM) task group (TG) 204 developed the conversion factor table which converts $CTDI_{vol}$ to size-specific dose estimates ($SSDE$) [2]. This report asserted that conventional $CTDI_{vol}$ represents the radiation dose of a simplified phantom, rather than presenting the real amount of radiation dose exposed to patients' with different body sizes. According to TG 204,

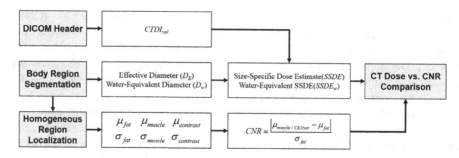

Fig. 1. Schematic diagram of the overall procedure of proposed study.

SSDE is the more accurate radiation dose estimates considering the body size of each patients.

To estimate *SSDE* with effective diameter (D_{eff}), we segmented body regions from axial images using 3D region growing technique (Fig. 2).

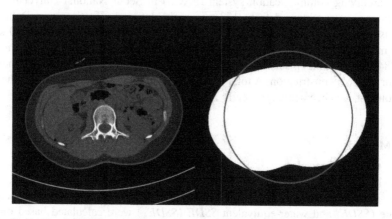

Fig. 2. Example axial CT image (*left*), and its segmented mask. A circle having equal area (in red) was calculated yielding the D_{eff} (*right*) (Color figure online).

D_{eff} was obtained from the body mask, which is defined as the diameter of a circle having the same circle area with that of patient's cross sectional body area. *SSDE* was then yielded by multiplication of the $CTDI_{vol}$ with the conversion factor (f_{size}) as Eq. (1).

$$SSDE = CTDI_{vol} \times f(D_{eff}) \tag{1}$$

Derived from Monte Carlo simulation and 32 cm PMMA phantom experiments, conversion factor (f) happened to be exponentially decreased as a function of patient body diameter. AAPM TG 204 found the best fit between conversion factor and patient body size on different X-ray tube voltage and modeled it as following Eq. (2).

$$f(D) = 4.378 \times e^{-0.143 \times D} \tag{2}$$

For more precise body size estimation, Ikuta et al. suggested the water-equivalent diameter (D_w) as a body size metric, which considers both patient body size and tissue-specific attenuation [4, 5]. SSDE was then calculated as a function of D_w rather than D_{eff}, which we named as water-equivalent SSDE $(SSDE_w)$. $f(D_w)$, D_w and $SSDE_w$ can be defined with Eq. (2–4), as follows:

$$D_w = 2 \times \sqrt{\frac{1}{\pi} \times \sum \left(\frac{HU + 1000}{1000} \right) \times A_\Delta} \tag{3}$$

$$SSDE_w = CTDI_{vol} \times f(D_w) \tag{4}$$

where A_Δ is the unit pixel area.

In our study, $SSDE_w$ was used to investigate the relationship between radiation dose and contrast-to-noise ratio.

2.2.3 Homogeneous Region Localization

Each CT image was Gaussian filtered to reduce the effect of noise on homogeneity assessment. The initial candidate ROIs with circular shape were placed with a criteria where the mean pixel intensities lie within predefined ranges (−200–0 HU for fat region, 0–70 HU for muscle region, and 70–200 HU for contrast-enhanced liver region). We set ROI size to fit on most subcutaneous fat regions showing ROI area 0.65 cm^2, and same ROI size was applied in three different tissue regions. In order to exclude those pixels belonging to transition zones between different tissue structures, the sum of gradient magnitude was calculated at each ROI. Among those candidate ROIs, top 10 homogeneous ROIs were selected for each tissue type by assessing the homogeneity with sum of gradient magnitude within each ROI. Example results of homogeneous ROI localization were shown in Fig. 3.

Images scanned with 80 kVp were shown to be truncated with circular shape because one detector covers the whole field of view (FOV) while the other detector is restricted to a smaller FOV due to space limitations on the gantry [6]. To apply same algorithm on both 80 and 140 kVp image, the truncated body masks obtained with 80 kVp were applied to 140 kVp image.

2.2.4 Noise Level and Contrast-to-Noise Ratio

Mean intensity (μ) and standard deviation (σ) were calculated on localized homogeneous ROIs, and these values were then averaged to give the representative mean ($\bar{\mu}$) and standard deviation ($\bar{\sigma}$) of fat, muscle, and contrast-enhanced liver regions. Standard deviation of each tissue was used to represent the tissue-specific global image noise. Contrast-to-noise ratio (CNR) was calculated with the following Eq. (5) [1, 2].

$$CNR = \frac{\left| \bar{\mu}_{object} - \bar{\mu}_{background} \right|}{\bar{\sigma}_{background}} \tag{5}$$

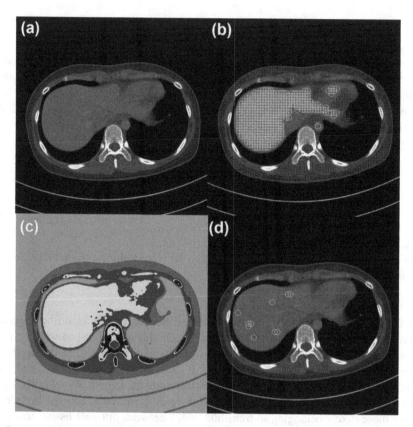

Fig. 3. (*a*) Axial single CT image, (*b*) initial candidate ROIs on predefined ranges: fat, muscle, and liver indicated by red, blue, yellow circle, (*c*) tissue-specific initial mask: Air for −1024−−200 HU (*green*), fat for −200–0 HU (*red*), muscle for 0–70 HU (*blue*), and contrast-enhanced liver region for 70–200 HU (*yellow*), (*d*) selected top 10 homogeneous ROIs of fat with red circle, muscle with blue circle, and liver with yellow circle (*right*) (Color figure online).

CNR of muscle-to-fat and that of contrast-enhanced liver-to-fat region were evaluated on 4 contrast phases for 80 and 140 kVp.

3   Results

Tissue-specific noise levels in pre-contrast phase were compared in Fig. 4. Average noise levels in 140 kVp scan were 12.75 ± 0.78 HU, and 12.85 ± 1.99 HU, and those in 80 kVp scan were 15.43 ± 2.34 HU, and 16.45 ± 1.14 HU on muscle and fat, respectively.

Average CNRs of 140 and 80 kVp scans were shown to be very similar with 11.45 ± 2.35 HU, and 11.26 ± 2.18 HU, respectively. Although images scanned with 80 kVp were seemingly noisier than those with 140 kVp at same display window setting, they were all of much the same in CNR. For pre-contrast phase images, noise

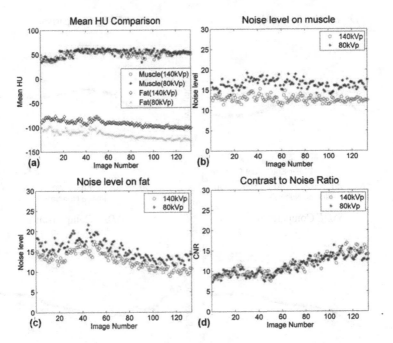

Fig. 4. Noise level and CNR profiles of pre-contrast phase; (a) mean HU of muscle and fat for 140 and 80 kVp, (b) muscle noise level, (c) fat noise level, (d) CNR of muscle-to-fat.

profile of fat showed much fluctuation as compared to that of muscle. Comparison of D_w profile in Fig. 5(a) with that of noise profiles for fat and muscle in Fig. 4(b), (c) reveals that the noise level of fat conforms well to D_w, which indicates the noise level of fat rather than that of muscle better represents the overall image noise. The correlation coefficients between D_w and fat noise level were 0.90 and 0.74 for 140 kVp and 80 kVp, respectively. Among the three radiation dose metrics, $SSDE_w$ correlated best with CNR by showing 0.87 and 0.79 for 140 kVp and 80 kVp, respectively.

CNR on fat and contrast-enhanced liver region and $SSDE_w$ of 4 phases were compared in Fig. 6. CNRs of liver area with 140 kVp and 80 kVp were 8.90 ± 0.99 and 8.96 ± 0.83 for pre-contrast phase, 9.21 ± 0.64 and 9.06 ± 0.68 for early artery phase, 10.09 ± 0.91 and 10.65 ± 1.04 for late artery phase, and 9.22 ± 0.60 and 9.43 ± 0.77 for portal phases. $SSDE_w$ of 140 kVp and 80 kVp were 1.49 ± 0.03, 0.99 ± 0.03 mGy for pre-contrast phase, 1.53 ± 0.03 and 1.01 ± 0.02 mGy for early-artery phase, 1.48 ± 0.05 and 0.98 ± 0.03 mGy for late-artery phase, and 1.50 ± 0.03 and 1.00 ± 0.02 mGy for portal phase, which shows radiation dose exposed to patients remain much the same regardless of contrast enhancement phases. While CNRs of contrast-enhanced region were similar at 80 kVp and 140 kVp, $SSDE_w$ was significantly lower at 80 kVp than at 140 kVp.

4 Discussion and Conclusion

Using our proposed technique including organ segmentation and homogeneous region localization steps, contrast-to-noise ratio and water-equivalent size-specific dose

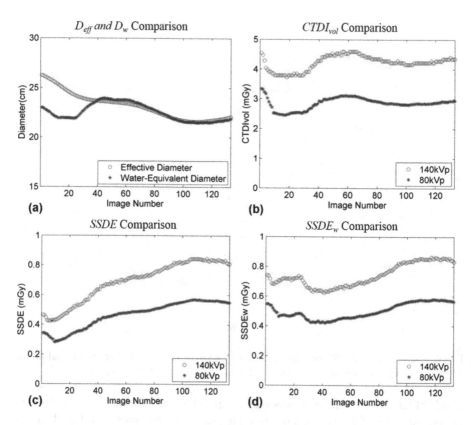

Fig. 5. Profiles of body effective diameter and the derived dose metrics in pre-contrast phase; (*a*) effective diameter (D_{eff}) and water-equivalent diameter (D_w), (*b*) $CTDI_{vol}$, (*c*) $SSDE$, and (*d*) $SSDE_w$ for 140 kVp and 80 kVp, respectively.

estimates could be automatically evaluated. Due to the insufficient amount of photon strike to the detector in low kVp scan, image with low tube potential is noisier than with high tube voltage. Even with noisier image, however, previous studies asserted that the usage of low tube potential can improve the contrast-to-noise ratio while reducing radiation exposure. The results of this study follows this current scan protocol optimization trends. In our preliminary analysis of an abdominal CT scan with multi-phase study, CNRs of 80 kVp and 140 kVp were much the same, while $SSDE_w$ was lower at 80 kVp than at 140 kVp by about 30 %. Our proposed technique has potential to be used as an automated tool in investigating the relationships between CNR and patients' dose, and thereby determining optimal scan parameters for various study applications. In this preliminary study, we applied a simple organ segmentation technique to assess CNR on liver as it was the organ of interest of the particular data set. However, in order to apply to more generalized imaging studies, more sophisticated organ segmentation technique such as atlas-based or probabilistic multi-organ segmentation needs to be incorporated. Also to be an established technique, the proposed technique needs to be tested and validated with larger data set.

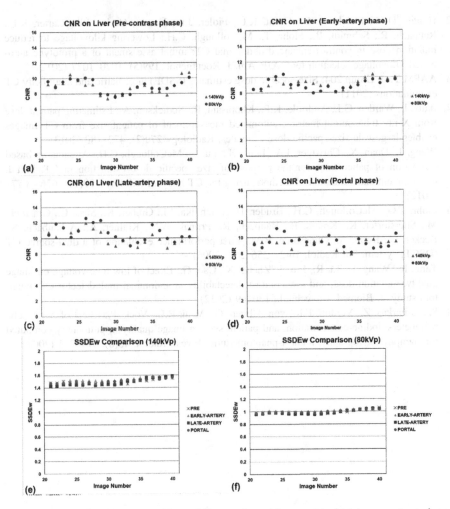

Fig. 6. CNR profiles at contrast-enhanced liver region with respect to fat (*a*) pre-contrast phase, (*b*) early-artery phase, (*c*) late-artery phase, and (*d*) portal phase, and water-equivalent size-specific dose estimates of (*e*) 80 kVp, (*f*) 140 kVp.

Acknowledgments. The research was supported by the Converging Research Center Program through the Ministry of Science, ICT and Future Planning, Korea (2013K000423).

References

1. Razak, H.R.A., Rahmat, S.M.S.S., Md Saad, W.M.: Effects of different tube potentials and iodine concentrations on image enhancement, contrast-to-noise ratio and noise in micro-CT images: a phantom study. Quant. Imaging Med. Surg. **3**(5), 256–261 (2013)

2. Hough, D.M., Fletcher, J.G., Grant, K.L., Fidler, J.L., Yu, L., Geske, J.R., Carter, R.E., Raupach, R., Schmidt, B., Flohr, T., McCollough, C.H.: Lowering kilovoltage to reduce radiation dose in contrast-enhanced abdominal CT: initial assessment of a prototype automated kilovoltage selection tool. AJR Am. J. Roentgenol. **199**(5), 1070–1077 (2012)
3. AAPM Task Group 204: Size-specific dose estimates (SSDE) in pediatric and adult body CT examinations (2011)
4. Ikuta, I., Warden, G.I., Andriole, K.P., Khorasani, R., Sodickson, A.: Estimating patient dose from X-ray tube output metrics: automated measurement of patient size from CT Images enables largescale size-specific dose estimates. Radiology **270**(2), 472–480 (2013)
5. Wang, J., Duan, X., Christner, J.A., Leng, S., Yu, L., McCollough, C.H.: Attenuation-based estimation of patient size for the purpose of size specific dose estimation in CT. Part I. development and validation of methods using the CT image. Med. Phys. **39**(11), 6764–6771 (2012)
6. Flohr, T.G., McCollough, C.H., Bruder, H., Petersilka, M., Gruber, K., Süss, C., Grasruck, M., Stierstorfer, K., Krauss, B., Raupach, R., Primak, A.N., Küttner, A., Achenbach, S., Becker, C., Kopp, A., Ohnesorge, B.M.: First performance evaluation of a dual-source CT (DSCT) system. Eur Radiol. **16**(2), 256–268 (2006)
7. Tang, K., Wang, L., Li, R., Lin, J., Zheng, X., Cao, G.: Effect of low tube voltage on image quality, radiation dose, and low-contrast detectability at abdominal multidetector CT: phantom study. J. Biomed. Biotechnol., 130169 (2012)
8. Szucs-Farkas, Z., Verdun, F.R., von Allmen, G., Mini, R.L., Vock, P.: Effect of X-ray tube parameters, iodine concentration, and patient size on image quality in pulmonary computed tomography angiography: a chest-phantom-study. Invest. Radiol. **43**(6), 374–381 (2008)

Modeling and Analysis of Bioimpedance Measurements

Alexander Danilov[1,2]([✉]), Vasily Kramarenko[2], and Alexandra Yurova[3]

[1] Institute of Numerical Mathematics, Gubkina 8, 119333 Moscow, Russia
a.a.danilov@gmail.com
[2] Moscow Institute of Physics and Technology, Institutsky 9,
141700 Dolgoprudny, Russia
[3] Lomonosov Moscow State University, Leninskie Gory 1, 119991 Moscow, Russia

Abstract. In this work we presented the technology for high-resolution efficient numerical modeling of bioimpedance measurements. This technology includes 3D image segmentation, adaptive unstructured tetrahedral mesh generation, finite-element discretization, and the analysis of simulation data. High resolution anatomically correct model based on Visible Human Project data was created. Sensitivity field distributions for a Kubicek-like scheme, as well as two eight-electrode segmental torso measurement schemes were computed and compared. All presented methods and techniques are well-known and are implemented in several open-source packages.

Keywords: Bioelectrical impedance analysis · Sensitivity analysis · FEM · Unstructured mesh generation

1 Introduction

Measurements of the electrical impedance of biological tissue in response to applied alternating current provide a number of non-invasive, harmless, portable, and relatively low cost techniques for use in medical and biological studies [1–3]. An example is the application of bioelectrical impedance analysis (BIA) for the in vivo human body composition assessment [4,5]. The same measurement and similar methodological principles apply in impedance cardiography (ICG) for the assessment of central hemodynamics and also in impedance plethysmography (IPG) for the evaluation of peripheral vascular function [1]. In contrast to electrical impedance tomography aimed at visualization of the internal body structure (see, e.g., [3,6]), little amount of electrodes is used in BIA, ICG and IPG. But the spectrum of electrode types, their properties and configurations used (local, whole-body, segmental, polysegmental), as well as of the measurement frequencies, is wide. This inspires optimization of bioimpedance measurements for specific purposes. Since a real human body represents complex non-homogeneous and non-isotropic medium with variable cross-section area, the fundamental questions arose about the nature and relative contribution of various organs and

© Springer International Publishing Switzerland 2014
H. Yoshida et al. (Eds.): ABDI 2014, LNCS 8676, pp. 287–294, 2014.
DOI: 10.1007/978-3-319-13692-9_28

tissues to the bioimpedance signal. The latter, as well as the problem of measurement optimization, was studied by means of impedance simulations using computerized models of real human anatomy (see, e.g., [7–9]). Similar approach is also used in radiography, nuclear medicine, radiation protection and other research areas [10,11].

Modeling of sensitivity distributions for various measurement schemes requires solving a number of computational problems using high-resolution anatomically accurate 3D models [12]. Our aim was to describe unstructured mesh generation and computational modeling procedures for bioimpedance measurements, and to illustrate sensitivity field distributions for a several bioimpedance measurement schemes using anatomically accurate 3D model of the human body from Visible Human Project (VHP) [13].

2   Mathematical Model

As described in [2], the electrical fields generated during bioimpedance measurements are governed by the equation

$$\text{div}(\mathbf{C}\nabla U) = 0 \quad \text{in} \quad \Omega \tag{1}$$

with the boundary conditions

$$(\mathbf{J}, \mathbf{n}) = \pm I_0/S_{\pm} \quad \text{on} \quad \Gamma_{\pm} \tag{2}$$

$$(\mathbf{J}, \mathbf{n}) = 0 \quad \text{on} \quad \partial\Omega \backslash \Gamma_{\pm} \tag{3}$$

$$U(x_0, y_0, z_0) = 0 \tag{4}$$

$$\mathbf{J} = \mathbf{C}\nabla U \tag{5}$$

where Ω is the computational domain, $\partial\Omega$ is its boundary, $\Gamma_{\pm}$ are electrode contact surfaces, $\mathbf{n}$ is an external unit normal vector, U is an electric potential, $\mathbf{C}$ is a conductivity tensor, $\mathbf{J}$ is a current density, I_0 is an electric current, $S_{\pm}$ are areas of the electrode contacts. Equation (1) determines the distribution of electric field in the domain with heterogeneous conductivity $\mathbf{C}$. Equation (2) sets a constant current density on the electrode contact surfaces. Equation (3) defines the no-flow condition on the boundary. Uniqueness of the solution is guaranteed by the Eq. (4), where (x_0, y_0, z_0) is some point in the domain Ω.

In our study we use the finite element method for solving of 1–5 with P_1 finite elements on unstructured tetrahedral meshes. We assume that each computational element have a constant conductivity coefficient which corresponds to one of the human tissues. For calculations we use Ani3D package [14].

The convergence study of the presented model was presented in [12]. In summary, our tests demonstrated nearly second order convergence on a simplified geometrical model.

3   Mesh Generation

Our high resolution human body geometrical model was constructed in two steps. First, the geometrical model of the human torso was created for Visible Human man data. The data were clipped and downscaled to an array of $567 \times 305 \times 843$ colored voxels with the resolution $1 \times 1 \times 1$ mm. The initial segmented model of the VHP [13] human torso was kindly provided by the Voxel-Man group [15]. This model has been produced primarily for visualization purposes, contained a significant amount of unclassified tissue and, thus, was not entirely suited for numerical purposes. Therefore, a further processing of the segmented model was needed. It was performed semi-automatically using ITK-SNAP segmentation software program [16]. At the final stage, we used several post-processing algorithms for filling remaining gaps between tissues and final segmented data smoothing. Our segmented model of the human torso contains 26 labels and describes major organs and tissues.

Several meshing techniques were tested for the mesh generation of segmented data. In our work we opted for the Delaunay triangulation algorithm from the CGAL-Mesh library [17]. This algorithm enables defining a specific mesh size for each model material. In order to preserve geometrical features of the segmented model while keeping a feasible number of vertices, we assigned a smaller mesh size to blood vessels and a larger mesh size to fat and muscle tissues. After initial mesh generation we applied mesh cosmetics from Ani3D package. This essential step reduces discretization errors and the condition number of the resulted systems of linear equations. The segmented model and the generated mesh with 413 508 vertices and 2 315 329 tetrahedra are presented in Fig. 1. This mesh retains most anatomical features of the human torso.

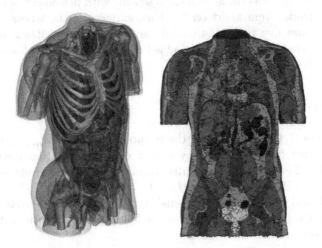

Fig. 1. Geometrical model of (a) the segmented image and (b) unstructured tetrahedral mesh.

The whole body segmented model is based on the torso model. Missing parts were segmented using ITK-SNAP software. The final model is a $575 \times 333 \times 1878$ voxels array with the resolution $1 \times 1 \times 1$ mm segmented in 30 materials.

We used the proposed techniques to construct the computational mesh for the whole body model based on VHP data. The related segmented model and generated mesh containing 574 128 vertices and 3 300 481 tetrahedrons are shown in Fig. 2.

Fig. 2. Segmented whole body model of (a) the Visible Human Man and (b) a part of generated mesh.

After mesh generation, we added a skin layer and multilayered electrodes to the surface of the constructed mesh. Boundary triangulation was used to create a prismatic mesh on the surface, and then each prism was split into three tetrahedrons resulting in a conformal mesh.

In our previous work [18] we analyzed the sensitivity distribution of the Kubicek-like electrode scheme. In this work we compare the obtained results with analysis of eight-electrode segmental scheme with placement of current and potential electrodes 5 cm apart on the back surfaces of the wrists and ankles. In the latter case five pairs of thin bilayer square objects 23×23 mm in size simulating electrode properties were added on the distal parts of arms and legs of the segmented model.

4   Sensitivity Analysis

As described in [2, 19] we introduce the reciprocal lead field $\mathbf{J}'_{\text{reci}}$ which is equal to density vector field generated by a unit current excitation using the two PU electrodes. Field $\mathbf{J}'_{\text{reci}}$ is computed from 1–5, with electrode surfaces $\Gamma_{\pm}$ corresponding to PU electrodes and $I_0 = 1$.

The lead field may be used for sensitivity distribution analysis of the PU electrodes for CC electrodes. We will use the following two equations: the general transfer signal equation

$$u = \int_{\Omega} \rho \, \mathbf{J}_{\text{cc}} \cdot \mathbf{J}'_{\text{reci}} \, dx, \qquad (6)$$

and the general transfer impedance equation:

$$Z_t = \int_\Omega \rho \mathbf{J}'_{cc} \cdot \mathbf{J}'_{reci} \, dx. \tag{7}$$

In these equations u is the measured signal between PU electrodes, ρ is the resistivity, $\mathbf{J}_{cc}$ is computed from 1–5 with electrode surfaces $\Gamma_\pm$ corresponding to the current carrying electrodes, Z_t is the transfer impedance, and $\mathbf{J}'_{cc} = \mathbf{J}_{cc}/I_0$.

The sensitivity analysis is based on the distribution of the sensitivity field, which is computed by

$$S = \mathbf{J}'_{cc} \cdot \mathbf{J}'_{reci}. \tag{8}$$

Using this notation we have the following relations:

$$Z_t = \int_\Omega \rho S \, dx, \quad \Delta Z_t = \int_\Omega \Delta\rho S \, dx. \tag{9}$$

The last relation is applicable only for relatively small changes of ρ and moderate variations of S.

For sensitivity analysis purposes we will split Ω in three parts according to the value of sensitivity field:

$$\Omega^- = \{\mathbf{x}|S(\mathbf{x}) < 0\}, \quad \Omega^+ = \{\mathbf{x}|S(\mathbf{x}) > 0\}, \quad \Omega^0 = \{\mathbf{x}|S(\mathbf{x}) = 0\}. \tag{10}$$

Furthermore, for a specific threshold value $t \in [0, 100]$ we will define W_t^- as a subdomain of Ω^- and W_t^+ as a subdomain of Ω^+ with the following restrictions:

$$\inf_{\mathbf{x}\in\Omega\backslash W_t^-} \rho(\mathbf{x})S(\mathbf{x}) \geqslant \sup_{\mathbf{x}\in W_t^-} \rho(\mathbf{x})S(\mathbf{x}), \quad \int_{W_t^-} \rho S \, dx = \frac{t}{100} \int_{\Omega^-} \rho S \, dx, \tag{11}$$

$$\sup_{\mathbf{x}\in\Omega\backslash W_t^+} \rho(\mathbf{x})S(\mathbf{x}) \leqslant \inf_{\mathbf{x}\in W_t^+} \rho(\mathbf{x})S(\mathbf{x}), \quad \int_{W_t^+} \rho S \, dx = \frac{t}{100} \int_{\Omega^+} \rho S \, dx. \tag{12}$$

In other words, W_t^+ is the region of high positive sensitivity values, which have the transfer impedance contribution equal to t percents of the total transfer impedance. The same applies to W_t^-, which is the region of the most negative sensitivity values.

We will also define in the same way the following subdomains: V_t^+ and V_t^+.

$$\sup_{\mathbf{x}\in\Omega\backslash V_t^\pm} \pm S(\mathbf{x}) \leqslant \inf_{\mathbf{x}\in V_t^\pm} \pm S(\mathbf{x}), \quad \int_{V_t^\pm} S \, dx = \frac{t}{100} \int_{\Omega^\pm} S \, dx. \tag{13}$$

These regions are the most sensitive regions of small local resistivity changes.

In our sensitivity analysis we investigate the shape of the subdomains W_t^+ and V_t^+. These body regions represent the most sensitive parts of the human body in specific measuring scenario. The shape of W_t^+ describes the part of the body in which one measures the transfer impedance. The shape of V_t^+ represents the part which is the most sensitive to local changes of conductivity. This analysis may be applied for validation of an empirically designed electrode schemes.

For visualization purposes we introduce monotone mapping of sensitivity S to $[0, 100]$ range: $S \mapsto \tilde{S}$, such that $\tilde{S}$ may be used as a threshold parameter to represent $V_{\tilde{S}}^+$ subdomain.

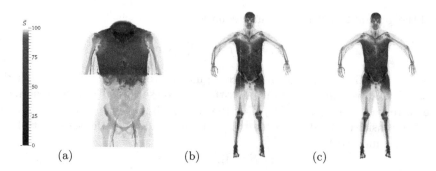

(a)   (b)   (c)

Fig. 3. High sensitivity areas V_{95}^+ for Kubicek-like scheme (a) and torso 8-electrode scheme (b – crossover, c – parallel). Shades of blue correspond to remapped sensitivity field $\tilde{S}$ (Color figure online).

5   Numerical Results

We simulated BIA measurements at the electrical current frequency 50 kHz using our FEM model. Results for Kubicek-like scheme were obtained from [18]. We computed both spatial sensitivity distribution and relative sensitivity distribution of different organs and tissues for Kubicek-like scheme, crossover and parallel eight-electrode schemes. For detailed explanation of electrode positions in 8-electrode scheme refer to Fig. 1 and Table 1 in [20].

Table 1. Relative contribution (%) of organs and tissues to the sensitivity field for Kubicek-like scheme, crossover and parallel eight-electrode schemes.

Organ/tissue	Kubicek	Crossover	Parallel
Muscles	69.44	63.76	63.50
Blood vessels	6.35	2.44	2.49
Left lung	5.49	1.83	1.84
Right lung	5.03	1.29	1.32
Diaphragm	2.39	3.52	3.49
Stomach	2.14	2.60	2.61
Oesophagus	2.00	0.18	0.19
Thyroid gland	1.50	0.00	0.00
Intestine	1.12	20.60	20.66
Heart	1.01	0.46	0.47
Trachea	0.71	0.00	0.00
Visceral fat	0.54	0.73	0.73
Bones	0.51	0.81	0.82
Liver	0.50	0.80	0.80
Other tissues	1.27	0.98	1.08

The high sensitivity areas are presented in Fig. 3. The organs and tissue sensitivity distribution is presented in Table 1.

The Kubicek-like scheme is well-designed for thoracic cavity and barely covers the abdominal cavity. On the other hand, both eight-electrode torso schemes provide the same uniform coverage of ventral body cavity, with emphasis on abdominal cavity.

6   Conclusion

In this work we applied the proposed techniques of bioelectric impedance mathematical modeling to analysis of three electrode schemes. We compared our previous results of Kubicek-like scheme with two eight-electrode schemes for torso measurements. The numerical results demonstrate that the Kubicek-like scheme is more suitable for measuring the impedance changes in blood vessels and heart. The segmental eight-electrode scheme is more suitable for body composition assessment in the abdominal area. These results are the preliminary results. Our future work is concentrated on patient-specific modeling, model verification and some actual clinical applications.

Acknowledgments. This work has been supported in part by RFBR grant 14-01-00830, and by the Russian President grant MK-3675.2013.1.

References

1. Cybulski, G.: Ambulatory Impedance Cardiography. Springer, Heidelberg (2011)
2. Grimnes, S., Martinsen, O.: Bioimpedance and Bioelectricity Basics. Elsevier, Amsterdam (2008)
3. Holder, D.: Electrical Impedance Tomography. Institute of Physics Publishers, Bristol (2005)
4. Kushner, R., Schoeller, D.: Estimation of total body water by bioelectrical impedance analysis. Am. J. Clin. Nutr. **44**, 417–424 (1986)
5. Lukaski, H., Johnson, P., Bolonchuk, W., Lykken, G.: Assessment of fat-free mass using bioelectrical impedance measurements of the human body. Am. J. Clin. Nutr. **41**, 810–817 (1985)
6. Cherepenin, V., Karpov, A., Korjenevsky, A., et al.: Three-dimensional EIT imaging of breast tissues: system design and clinical testing. IEEE Trans. Med. Imaging **21**, 662–667 (2002)
7. Beckmann, L., van Riesen, D., Leonhardt, S.: Optimal electrode placement and frequency range selection for the detection of lung water using bioimpedance spectroscopy. In: Proceedings of the 29th Annual International Conference of the IEEE, pp. 2685–2688 (2007)
8. Kauppinen, P., Hyttinen, J., Malmivuo, J.: Sensitivity distributions of impedance cardiography using band and spot electrodes analyzed by a three-dimensional computer model. Ann. Biomed. Eng. **26**, 694–702 (1998)
9. Yang, F., Patterson, R.: A simulation study on the effect of thoracic conductivity inhomogeneities on sensitivity distributions. Ann. Biomed. Eng. **36**, 762–768 (2008)

10. Caon, M.: Voxel-based computational models of real human anatomy: a review. Radiat. Environ. Biophys. **42**, 229–235 (2004)
11. Xu, X., Eckerman, K.: Handbook of Anatomical Models for Radiation Dosimetry. CRC Press, Boca Raton (2009)
12. Danilov, A., Nikolaev, D., Rudnev, S., Salamatova, V., Vassilevski, Y.: Modelling of bioimpedance measurements: unstructured mesh application to real human anatomy. Russ. J. Numer. Anal. Math. Model. **27**, 431–440 (2012)
13. The Visible Human Project. http://www.nlm.nih.gov/research/visible/
14. 3D generator of anisotropic meshes. http://sourceforge.net/projects/ani3d
15. Höhne, K., Pflesser, B., Pommert, A., et al.: A realistic model of human structure from the Visible Human data. Meth. Inform. Med. **40**, 83–89 (2001)
16. Yushkevich, P., Piven, J., Hazlett, H., et al.: User-guided 3D active contour segmentation of anatomical structures: significantly improved efficiency and reliability. Neuroimage **31**, 1116–1128 (2006)
17. Rineau, L., Yvinec, M.: A generic software design for Delaunay refinement meshing. Comp. Geom. Theory Appl. **38**, 100–110 (2007)
18. Danilov, A., Salamatova, V., Vassilevski, Y.: Mesh generation and computational modeling techniques for bioimpedance measurements: an example using the VHP data. J. Phys. Conf. Ser. **407**, 012004 (2012). doi:10.1088/1742-6596/407/1/012004
19. Geselowitz, D.: An application of electrocardiographic lead theory to impedance plethysmography. IEEE Trans Biomed. Eng. **18**, 38–41 (1971)
20. Danilov, A., Kramarenko, V., Nikolaev, D., Rudnev, S., et al.: Sensitivity field distributions for segmental bioelectrical impedance analysis based on real human anatomy. J. Phys. Conf. Ser. **434**, 012001 (2013). doi:10.1088/1742-6596/434/1/012001

Author Index

Printed in the United States
By Bookmasters

Printed in the United States
By Bookmasters